*Alfred M. Tozzer*

# A MAYA GRAMMAR

### WITH BIBLIOGRAPHY AND APPRAISEMENT
### OF THE WORKS NOTED

DOVER PUBLICATIONS, INC.
NEW YORK

Published in Canada by General Publishing Company, Ltd., 30 Lesmill Road, Don Mills, Toronto, Ontario.

Published in the United Kingdom by Constable and Company, Ltd., 10 Orange Street, London WC2H 7EG.

This Dover edition, first published in 1977, is an unabridged and unaltered republication of the work originally published by the Peabody Museum of American Archaeology and Ethnology, Harvard University, in Cambridge, Mass., 1921, as Vol. IX of the Museum's *Papers*.

*International Standard Book Number: 0-486-23465-7*
*Library of Congress Catalog Card Number: 76-45008*

Manufactured in the United States of America
Dover Publications, Inc.
180 Varick Street
New York, N.Y. 10014

TO THE MEMORY OF

# CHARLES P. BOWDITCH
### 1842–1921
THAT GREATEST OF ALL FRIENDS OF MAYA RESEARCH
THROUGH WHOSE INITIATIVE
AND AID THIS VOLUME HAS BEEN MADE POSSIBLE

# PREFACE

As the first recipient of the Travelling Fellowship in American Archaeology of the Archaeological Institute of America, I spent the winters of the years 1901–1902 to 1904–1905 in Yucatan, Chiapas, and Tabasco, Mexico, and northern Guatemala.[1]

A report on the ethnological work of this Fellowship was published as a special paper of the Archaeological Institute of America, "A Comparative Study of the Mayas and Lacandones," (New York, 1907, xx, 195 p., xxix plates). In that report (p. v) a promise was made that the linguistic part of the work undertaken under the Fellowship would be published later. The long-delayed fulfillment of this promise is the present study of the Maya language. The permission of the Archaeological Institute, through its President, has kindly been given to have this work published by the Peabody Museum.

I can do no better than repeat what I said in 1907 regarding my obligations. "I desire at this time to express my appreciation and thanks to the three original members of the Committee on American Archaeology, Mr. Charles P. Bowditch, Chairman, Professor F. W. Putnam, and Professor Franz Boas. To Mr. Bowditch, through whose initiative and aid the Travelling Fellowship in American Archaeology was founded, and to Professor Putnam,[2] both of whom have given unsparingly of their time in advice and counsel both before and during the four years of the Fellowship, and to Dr. Boas, who has been of great aid in his advice on the linguistic side of the work, I am deeply grateful."

These obligations are quite as heavy today as they were in 1907. Dr. Boas has continued to give me valuable aid and it is owing to the never-ending interest and generosity of Mr. Charles P. Bow-

---

[1] For brief reports of the work of the Fellowship, see *American Journal of Archaeology*, 2d series, supplement, v. 6 (1902), p. 2–4; v. 7 (1903), p. 45–49; v. 8 (1904), p. 54–56; v. 9 (1905), p. 45–47.

[2] Professor Putnam has died since this paragraph was first written. His death took place on August 14, 1915.

ditch that the Peabody Museum has been able to bring this study out as a Paper of the Museum.

I also wish at this time to thank some of my many friends in Yucatan who aided me throughout the time I was there. Mr. and Mrs. Edward H. Thompson and Mr. and Mrs. William James of Merida gave me abundantly of their generous hospitality. I have spoken in another place of my obligations to the late Señor Don Audomaro Molina and to Señor Don Juan Martínez Hernández.

# CONTENTS

## PART II — MAYA TEXTS

## PART III — AN APPRAISEMENT OF WORKS
### RELATING TO THE MAYA LANGUAGE

## PART IV — A BIBLIOGRAPHY OF WORKS RELATING TO THE MAYA LANGUAGE

## APPENDICES

# PART I
# GRAMMAR

# PART I

# GRAMMAR

## INTRODUCTION

MAYA STOCK. *Location.* The Maya linguistic stock stands with
Nahuatl as the two most important languages of Middle America.
With the exception of the Huastecan region, north of Vera Cruz on
the Panuco River, the territory occupied by the Maya speaking
peoples is practically continuous, including the greater part of the
two southernmost states of Mexico, Chiapas and Tabasco, the
peninsula of Yucatan which is composed of the Mexican states of
Yucatan and Campeche, the Mexican territory of Quintana Roo,
and British Honduras, Guatemala, and the northern part of Honduras. The Maya territory in Guatemala is broken up by islands
of Nahuatl speaking people and by a few independent stocks such
as Xinca.

The geographical unity of the Maya speaking peoples is remarkable when one takes into consideration the colonies of Nahuatl
speaking peoples scattered along the Pacific coast of Central America even as far south as the Isthmus of Panama. The Mayas seem
to have been content to remain very much in one place and it is
evident that it was not their general custom to send out colonies
to distant parts of the country. Moreover the wandering of the
Mayas among themselves in the comparatively small territory occupied by them is not shown by investigation to have been great.

Most of the dialects of the Maya seem to have been identified
with certain localities from the time of the earliest Spanish records
down to the present. There does not seem to have been that
shifting of population which one might naturally expect. The
geographical conditions may have had something to do with this
seeming lack of mingling of the people of one dialect with those of
another. The peninsula of Yucatan is comparatively isolated from
the rest of the Maya territory and the dialect spoken there is very

little changed as far as can be made out from the earliest times of which we have records. The various mountain ranges in the south often render communication difficult and a mountain system often separates distinct linguistic differences as regards dialects of the Maya. Geography cannot, however, in all cases explain the freedom of mixture of two dialects occupying neighboring territory.

Spanish speaking people are found in almost all parts of the country occupied by the Mayas and their influence has, of course, been very great in changing the native dialects. The Indians in most cases have picked up enough Spanish to make themselves intelligible in all parts of the country. When intercourse is to be carried on between the people speaking two different dialects of Maya, Spanish is usually the medium. This may explain in part the distinct dialectic areas still to be made out.

The Maya stock has no affiliation as far as can be made out with any other language of Mexico or Central America. Some authorities claim that the Zapotec is nearer akin to Maya than it is to Nahuatl. Maya is morphologically distinct from the latter.

*Dialects.* The Maya stock has a large number of dialects which may be divided according to their structure into a certain number of groups. Stoll's classification (1884) is the most satisfactory one and it has been followed in the main here.[1] The different divisions are as follows:

1. Maya group proper including the Maya of Yucatan, the Itza or Peten, the Lacandone and possibly the Mopan dialects.

2. Tzental or Tzeltal group including the Tzental, Chontal of Tabasco, Tzotzil, Chañabal, and Chol (Cholti and Chorti) dialects.[2]

3. Mam group including the Mam, Ixil, and Aguacateca dialects.[3]

4. Quiche group including the Quiche, Cakchiquel, Tzutuhil, and Uspanteca dialects.

5. Pokom or Pokonchi group including the Kekchi, Pokoman and Pokonchi dialects.

---

[1] For other classifications, see p. 158–160.

[2] Sapper (1897, p. 393) makes a Chol group including Chontal, Chorti, and Chol. Gates (1920, p. 606) also makes a separate group of Cholti and Chorti.

[3] Gates (1920, p. 606) also includes in this group Solomeca, Jacalteca, Chuje, Chicomucelteca, and Motozintleca.

6. Huasteca.[1]

A further classification can be made based on the use of the pronoun. In the Maya, Tzeltal and Mam groups the verbal pronoun is a suffix: in the Quiche and Pokom groups this pronoun is a prefix.[2]

The relative antiquity of the various dialects is a subject which has not received much study. The great length of time necessary for the development of these dialects from a mother-tongue must be taken into consideration not only from a linguistic but also from an archaeological point of view.[3]

MAYA DIALECT. *Location.* The language treated in this paper is the Maya dialect of the Maya linguistic stock.[4] This dialect is spoken by the natives of the entire peninsula of Yucatan, a larger territory than that occupied by any of the other dialects. This idiom is commonly regarded as the purest of all the Maya dialects owing to the isolation of Yucatan.[5] The language may show a certain pureness and stability lacking in other places where the Maya stock is spoken but there is little reason to suppose that the Maya dialect is the most primitive and that it was from a language such as is spoken in Yucatan that all the other Maya dialects have sprung. Investigations have not gone far enough into the comparative morphology of the Maya for us to ascribe with certainty a primordial character to any of the various dialects. It is com-

---

[1] Sapper (1905, p. 9) has the Chicomucelteca of southeastern Chiapas as a dialect of the Huasteca. He also gives here the approximate number speaking the various dialects.

[2] Compare Seler, 1887. The page references throughout this paper to this work of Seler apply to the 2d edition, published in v. 1 of his collected works.

[3] Stoll (1884, p. 157) estimates the period of 2000 years as the shortest time required to explain the difference between Maya and Cakchiquel.

[4] Henceforth when speaking of the Maya, the dialect alone will be understood unless the term Maya stock is employed.

[5] Berendt (1878, p. 7) writes in this connection, "The Maya language proper (**Mayathan**) is spoken through the whole peninsula of Yucatan, the ancient name of which was **Maya**. It is the purest and, at present, the most highly developed of all the languages of the family, and is used not only by the Indians, but also by the greater part of the white and *mestizo* population; in the interior of Yucatan I have met with white families who do not understand one word of Spanish. The Maya language is likewise generally used in writing and in printing books of instruction and devotion."

monly supposed, however, that Huasteca shows evidences of
greatest age with Mam second in point of time.

No attempt will be made in this study to treat the comparative
aspects of the Maya dialect with other dialects of this stock.[1]

*Hieroglyphic Writing.* In the treatment of the Maya language I
shall omit completely any discussion of the phonetic character of
the Maya hieroglyphics. There is reason to suppose that there is a
number of distinct symbols in the hieroglyphic writing of Central
America which denote certain phonetic characters of the Maya
speech.[2] For the purpose of this paper, however, the Maya will be
regarded as a language unrecorded up to the time of the Conquest.

A complete elucidation of the hieroglyphic inscriptions will probably be impossible until an advance has been made in our ac-
quaintance with the phonetic elements in the composition of the
glyphs. Within recent years our knowledge in this respect has not
advanced at all in comparison with the gains made in deciphering
the numerical parts of the hieroglyphic writing. A successful correlation of the Maya language and the Maya hieroglyphs holds
out a prospect of the greatest interest and importance from the
point of view of Maya research.[3]

*Written Maya.* The Spaniards found the natives speaking the
Maya language. Their missionaries throughout New Spain easily
recognized the impossibility of accomplishing any work in christian-
izing the people without first learning the native languages. This
they set about doing in every case and many of the Spanish Padres
became proficient in the languages of the conquered peoples.[4]

---

[1] Seler (1887) has successfully attempted this. See also the works of
Charencey.

[2] See Bowditch, 1910, p. 254–258 for a discussion of this point.

[3] It is needless to comment here on the "Landa Alphabet" and its failure
to produce the results hoped for.

[4] Zavala (1896, p. iv, v) gives the following quotations from the records
of the Third Mexican Council which considered affairs relating to Yucatan.
I give these verbatim as quoted by Zavala although the Latin is incorrect in
several places. "*Clericos in regionibus Indorum beneficia cum onere obtinentes
in materna erumden regionum lingua examinent, Episcopi, et quos repererint
linguæ hujusmodi ignaros, sex mensium spatio prefinito, ad discendam linguam
compellant, admonentes eos, quatemus elapso termino, si linguan hujusmodi non
didiscerint, beneficium quod obtinent, ipso facto, vacabit, et alteri de eo fiet pro-*

One of the first acts was to record the native languages phonetically as nearly as they could with the Spanish characters at their command. It was impossible to write down many of the sounds occurring in the different native dialects with the Spanish letters and, in some cases, arbitrary signs or marks were adopted to designate these sounds as, in the Maya, the inverted c (ɔ) was early used as the sign for a ts sound frequent in the language.

The natives soon learned to write their own languages, which hitherto had been unrecorded, by using the same Spanish characters and the signs adopted by the Spaniards. To their ability in this line we owe many valuable documents connected with the native culture of the country, manuscripts written in the native language but with Spanish characters.[1]

*Early grammars on Latin model.* The Spanish priests did not stop with translations of documents into the native languages but they wrote grammars and collected vocabularies as well. These grammars and dictionaries exist in great numbers. There is hardly a dialect spoken in Mexico or Central America that has not some sort of a grammar dealing with the structure of the language. The difficulty met with in using these grammars written by the Spanish is the same as that found wherever a primitive language has been studied and recorded along the lines and with the corresponding forms found in Spanish, Latin, or some other Indo-European grammar. The Spanish priest thought he had successfully written a grammar of a native language if he had found forms in that lan-

---

*visio. . . . In quo, et in Regula decima octava Cancellariæ Apostólicæ contientiæ Episcoporum onerantur."* (Lib, III, Tit. 1 De doctr. cura, V.)

"*La Regla decimaoctava, dice Arrillaga, es la vigesima que estampa Murillo en el tit. de Institutionibus, num. 82; y en ella se prescribe que la provision de algun beneficio parroquial, hecha en alguna persona que no sepa el idioma de sus feligreses, ni pueda explicarse en él, aun cuando proceda del mismo Papa, sea nula y de ningun valor"* (*Notas al Cons. III mex.*).

"*20. Item voluit, quód si contingat, ipsum (Urbano VIII) alicui personæ de parochiali Ecclesia, vel quovis alio beneficio exercitium curæ animarum parochianorum quomodolibet habente, prouideret, nisi ipsa persona intelligat, & intelligibiliter loqui sciat idioma loci, ubi Ecclesia, vel beneficium huiusmodi consistit, prouisio, seu mandatum, & gratia desuper, quoad parochialem Eccleisam, vel beneficium huiusmodi, nullius sint roboris vel momenti.*"

[1] The Books of Chilam Balam (p. 182) are examples of Maya texts written by the natives phonetically.

guage to correspond to every term in his Spanish grammar. The
desire to find words which fitted the different categories of thought
expressed in his own grammar often outweighed his keenness in
realizing that many grammatical forms used in Spanish could not
be properly expressed in the native language. Parallels were sought
for every form in the Spanish or Latin. The investigators usually
found some native term which seemed to them to conform to the
same expression in their own language. If a native did not seem
able at first to give words for the pluperfect tense in his language,
the more one insisted that there must be such forms the sooner
the native would give something which superficially seemed to be
a pluperfect.

The whole difficulty lies in the fact that it is impossible to build
up a grammar of a primitive language by following a Latin or
Spanish model.[1] This rigid adherence to such a model leads to two
defects. Forms are given the investigator, often after repeated
questioning, which only vaguely express corresponding forms in
Spanish or Latin. These are often unnatural and are compounded
so as to express in a most artificial way the idea desired. The second
defect is the greater as scores of native expressions are entirely
overlooked and are never recorded in the early grammars as there
are no forms corresponding to them in Latin.

The Spanish missionary did not realize that the different categories of a grammar of a primitive language are entirely different

---

[1] Palma y Palma (1901, p. 159) in criticizing Beltran's grammar expresses
the same idea. "*Fray Pedro de Beltran, el mejor autor de gramática maya, hay
que admitir que la carencia de un signo propio en el idioma para la expresión de
los verbos sustantivos es efectiva. Tan hábil en la lengua como diestro en el latín,
se esforzó en calcar su Arte del idioma maya á la gramática de la de Virgilio, sin
tener en cuenta el genio y diversidad de índole de cada una. De aquí sus errores en
esto y en otras cosas de que no me es posible hablar, lo que no desdice en nada su
talento que me es tanto más grato reconocer, cuanto que el P. Beltrán fué yucateco
nato y todo el vigor de su entendimiento claro se desarrolló en las aulas de su suelo
nativo al cual prestó un gran servicio con su obra que da á conocer mejor que
ninguna otra, una de las más ricas lenguas americanas que se acaba y desapare-
cerá quizá pronto.*"

Berendt (1878, p. 5) writes in this connection, "A striking instance of this
method is presented by the Spanish grammarians, who, in treating the aboriginal languages, are particularly bent upon finding similarities or concordances
with the Spanish or Latin grammar, and, if they do not find them, frequently
invent them.

from those of an Indo-European language. The only possible
method of approach to the study of a primitive language is an
analytical one, working out the different thought units and the
methods of expressing these entirely divorced from any model
based on Latin or Spanish lines.[1]

This difference in categories will be seen at many places in the
following pages. Here it is only necessary to point out a few of
these differences. The distinction between the noun and the verb
is vague in many of the Maya stems — many verbs are really
nouns and used with the possessive pronoun as the subject. Time
particles attached to the nominal pronoun are entirely overlooked
in the early grammars. There is no true case in Maya except in
the pronoun where we find only the nominal pronoun used as the
subject and as a possessive and the verbal pronoun used as an object. No gender is expressed except that particles are found denoting the sex of the actor in the "*nomen actoris.*" The inclusive and
exclusive forms for the plural are found in the pronoun.

Maya is a polysynthetic or incorporating language where a pronominal subject of the verb is always expressed. Maya follows, in
general, the same methods of expression as those found in the
greater number of American languages. From the point of view
of lexicography it is distinct from any of the other languages spoken
in Mexico or Central America. It is therefore in its structure alone
that it corresponds to other American languages.

In the analytical treatment of the grammar I desire, as Boas [2]
expresses it, to present the data "as though an intelligent Indian
was going to develop the forms of his own thought by an analysis
of his own form of speech."

*Grammars of Coronel, San Buenaventura, and Beltran.* In spite
of many omissions and forms which are more or less artificial, the
old Spanish grammars are of distinct service in understanding the
language. I have made frequent reference to these grammars in
the footnotes when my forms differ from those given by them.

There are three early grammars of the language which are worthy
of special mention, that of Coronel, published in 1620, that of San

---

[1] For a masterly treatment of this point of view, see Boas, *Handbook of
American Indian Languages*, Bulletin 40, Bureau of Ethnology, Washington,
1911. Introduction, p. 5–83.

[2] *Op. cit.*, p. 81.

Buenaventura in 1684, and that of Beltran de Santa Rosa in 1746.[1]

The first grammar to be written on the Maya language was by Villalpando, one of the first Catholic priests to arrive in Yucatan. He died in 1551 or 1552. His work was never published and the manuscript has disappeared.[2] This grammar, with additions by Landa, was probably the basis of Coronel's work.[3] The latter starts with the pronouns giving nothing on the phonetics which are treated by both San Buenaventura and Beltran.

It is quite evident that San Buenaventura based his work almost entirely on that of Coronel. The examples in Maya given to illustrate the different parts of the grammar are often identical with those given by Coronel. There are, in fact, only a very few cases where San Buenaventura has material not to be found in Coronel. The list of particles (fols. 20–37) given by San Buenaventura contain many not listed by Coronel. Coronel, on the other hand, has many not given by San Buenaventura. Coronel also discusses the optative which is not mentioned by San Buenaventura and he gives a much fuller treatment of the subjunctive than that given by San Buenaventura. The latter's work, written about 1675, was published in 1684, 64 years after that of Coronel. There is no internal evidence that the language had changed during that time.

Beltran called San Buenaventura, "*el Protomaestro del Idioma Yucateco.*" He was not aware of the grammars of Villalpando, Landa, and of Coronel when he wrote his work.[4] Beltran follows San Buenaventura in using the same verbs for his paradigms but he has a large amount of new material in his grammar and often refers to what he considers mistakes in San Buenaventura's work. In every way Beltran's grammar should be considered by far the best of the three printed early treatises on Maya. His qualifica- tions for writing a grammar are many as he himself states.[5] He

---

[1] For full discussion of the different editions of these grammars, see p. 163–165.

[2] For a list of the large number of authorities whose works have been lost see p. 151–153.

[3] Beltran, 1859 ed., p. 242. Hereafter references to Beltran will be to this edition.

[4] See Beltran, p. 242.

[5] § 148. "*Para exponer al público mi dictámen (habiendo de asentar mis conjugaciones diversas de las del R. P. Fr. Gabriel [San Buenaventura]) necesario*

was a native of Yucatan, grew up among the Indians and lived among them practically all his life. San Buenaventura, on the other hand, was a Frenchman and probably lived almost exclusively with Spanish speaking people in Merida.

It has already been pointed out that there are practically no differences between the Coronel and San Buenaventura grammars. Beltran, on the other hand, finds much to differ with in the language as he records it and as given by San Buenaventura.[1] The differences between the present author's version of the grammar and that of Beltran and of the other grammarians will be noted throughout the paper.

There are four possible explanations for these differences:

1. Time.
2. Mistakes of each of the authors in question.
3. Omissions due to following the Latin model.
4. Difference in locality where the data were collected.

Beltran's work, written in 1742, was published in 1746, 62 years after that of San Buenaventura (1684) and 126 years after that of Coronel (1620). It has been pointed out that the grammars of Coronel and San Buenaventura do not differ in substance and yet presumably each recorded the language as spoken at or near the time they were published, 64 years apart. The question may then be asked, did 62 more years cause the differences in the idiom as noted by Beltran from that of the time of San Buenaventura? Again, are the differences noted in the language as spoken today

es dar las razones, que me asisten para esto, que parece cosa nueva. Es, pues, la primera que siendo yo hijo de esta provincia, criado entre estos naturales y habiendo habitado con ellos una montaña yerma, predicándoles, confesándoles, instruyéndoles y con ellos de continuo en su idioma confabulando, de modo que se me llegó á olvidar mucho de los vocablos castellanos; y estando juntamente instruido del Arte gramático latino, me es preciso confesar que entiendo con claridad sus periodos y que conozco con evidencia en que cláusulas no concuerda su modo de hablar con el comun modo; y tambien donde pueden no regir bien las reglas que se pueden dar para instruccion de los que quisieren sin error aprender su idioma."

[1] Beltran, 1859 ed. in his "Prologo al Lector" writes, "Para este fin, queriendo facilitar mas este negocio; leí el Arte del R. P. F. Gabriel de San Buenaventura, de Nacion Frances, Proto-Maestro de este Idioma, y hasta hoy el único, que dió su Arte á la prensa: en donde habiendo yo hallado muchos yerros de imprenta, falta de muchas reglas, y reglas, que ya prescribieron por el contrario uso; me determiné á formar un nuevo Arte, con el designio de proseguir haciendo un vocabulario y otras cosas curiosas, y necesarias."

and that of Beltran's epoch due to the factor of time? Languages, we are told, never stand still and when we take into consideration the steady advance of the Spanish language we do well to pause before stating that time is not a great factor in causing these differences. I consider, however, that time has played a relatively small part. Those differences pointed out by Beltran in his criticism of San Buenaventura's grammar are undoubtedly, due for the most part, to mistakes in the observation of the earlier grammarian.[1] This point will be made clearer in the comments made later on the specific statements of Beltran, San Buenaventura, and Coronel.[2]

The differences I found in the Maya as now spoken in Yucatan from the forms given by Beltran are, with some few exceptions, due, it seems to me, to the rigid adherence to the Latin model observed by Beltran. My points of difference with Beltran are comparatively few when everything is taken into consideration. The additional data presented here are due to the breaking away from the Latin model and carrying on observations from a different angle of approach.[3] It should be clearly understood that I refer here to

---

[1] Beltran states that some of his criticisms of San Buenaventura are due to the changes of time. He writes as follows (§ 49) "*Para conocer á qué conjugacion pertenece cada verbo, se advierta que estas son cuatro, número á que las redujo el R. P. Fr. Gabriel de S. Buenaventura, Religioso nuestro y Frances de nacion, Protomaestro de este Arte, formando el suyo (que á la Imprenta dió) verdaderamente con gran trabajo y elegancia: regraciable por la conocida utilidad que nos dejó su magisterio; pero como no todo lo pudo andar, nos dejó que advertir algo, y porque los tiempos mudan las cosas, será preciso que haga yo algunas notas cuando sean necesarias.*" This statement is flattering to San Buenaventura and was evidently meant to be so. In the specific objections given throughout Beltran's text it is clear that he considers San Buenaventura to have made actual mistakes in recording the language. The fact that he states that he was brought up among the natives (§ 148) and that San Buenaventura was a Frenchman brings out clearly his own idea that he was the better fitted to write a Maya grammar.

[2] The reader will note that I have endeavored to point out in footnotes the main points where I differ from the old grammarians on the one hand and modern writers such as Seler, Palma y Palma, and Lopez, on the other.

[3] Brinton (1882, p. 35, 36) writes on this point, "I must, however, not omit to contradict formally an assertion made by the traveller Waldeck, and often repeated, that the language has undergone such extensive changes that what was written a century ago is unintelligible to a native of today. So far is this from the truth that, except for a few obsolete words, the narrative of the Conquest, written more than three hundred years ago, by the chief Pech, which

grammatical structure and not to vocabulary. In the latter respect the change has been far greater.[1]

There remain to be examined the differences due to the locality where the material was collected. There are no data to identify the place where Coronel did his work on Maya. San Buenaventura was connected with the Convent of San Francisco in Merida.[2] The name of the Indian who gave him most of the facts regarding the language is known but we are not aware, as Beltran points out, whether or not this Indian was a native of Merida.[3]

Beltran was at the Convent of San Pedro y San Pablo at Tiab in the former province of San José. This town, now called Teabo, is in the present District of Tekax, about half way between Tekax and Peto. It is very probable that the material for his grammar was collected in this vicinity.[4] A contrast should be made between a practically pure Maya population in towns such as Teabo and a mixed population such as is found at Merida.

---

I print in this volume, could be read without much difficulty by any educated native."

[1] See in this connection the discussion of the translation of old Maya texts, p. 114.

[2] According to the *Aprobacion del Br. Juan Gomez Brizeño* in San Buenaventura's grammar, the latter was "*Religioso del Orden del Señor S. Francisco, Difinidor habitual Guardian del Convento del Señor S. Francisco de la Ciudad de Merida y Lector en el Idioma Yucatheco.*"

[3] Beltran (§ 50) writes, "*El R. P. fué Autor primero . . . y lo enseñó todo á los Indios de esta Provincia, fué un Indio llamado* **Kinchahau**, *y por otro nombre* **Tzamná**. *Noticia que debemos á dicho R. F. Gabriel, y trae en su Calepino lit. K. Verb.* **Kinchahau**, *fol. 390, vuelt.; mas no dice como adquirió este Indio tal Idioma: y de aquí se infiere que el Idioma de esta Provincia era otro y muy distinto.*"

[4] Brasseur de Bourbourg (1871, p. 23) writes, "*Le père Beltran de Santa-Rosa Maria était natif de Mérida de Yucatan, où il prit, dès sa jeunesse, l'habit de Saint François, Profitant des travaux faits avant lui, et en particulier de ceux du père Gabriel de Saint Bonaventure, il composa sa Grammaire, dans le temps qu'il enseignait la langue maya au monastère principal de San-Benito de sa ville natale, dont les grandes ruines recouvrent aujourd'hui celles de l'antique demeure des pontifes d'Ahchum-Caan.*" There seems little doubt that Brasseur de Bourbourg is mistaken in thinking that Beltran's Grammar was written in Merida. There is published in the grammar the *Censura* of Miguel Leal de Las Alas, *Predicador* of the Province of San José and of Pedro Martin, *Predicador* at Tiab together with the *Licencia* of Juan Esteban Pinelo of the Province of San José. These add weight to the supposition that Beltran wrote his work when he was at the Convent of San Pedro y San Pablo at Tiab, the present Teabo.

Palma y Palma, who collected his material in Merida, writes of the language as spoken in the east, where Beltran lived, as especially given to contractions.[1] The use of contractions marks the main change in the language as recorded here and that used by the Lacandones. It is probable that simple phonetic variations and a difference in the use of the contracted forms alone distinguish the Maya of these two widely separated localities.[2] The changes in the language in the peninsula itself seem to be correspondingly few and consist for the most part, of a favorite use of one or more possible variations in expression. These variations are commonly known by everyone. Slightly different pronunciations of the sounds are to be noted. The language structurally does not seem to differ much in the whole peninsula.

It is possible to sum this question up by saying that, whereas the vocabulary has changed greatly owing to the more extended use of Spanish and the corresponding loss of Maya words, there seem to be comparatively few differences in the fundamental characteristics of the language, the structure remaining practically unchanged as far as can be made out from a comparison of the language as spoken in the early days of the Spanish Conquest and that spoken today in the smaller towns and away from the large centers of population.

*Maya of present time.* As noted in a previous study of the ethnology of the Mayas[3] one very interesting fact comes out in connection with the Maya language of Yucatan, a fact noted by all historians and writers on the inhabitants of the peninsula. The Maya language has withstood with amazing stability the entrance of the Spanish tongue into the country. The language is still an important factor to be taken into consideration when dealing with this people. Maya is the language spoken by the natives in the large cities quite as much as in the thinly populated regions. Even the natives who have a good knowledge of Spanish almost invariably use Maya when conversing with one another and some absolutely

---

[1] Palma y Palma (p. 179), "*Uin y tló, son contracciones más usadas en el Oriente constituyendo uno de los distintivos del lenguaje y estilo en aquella parte del pais donde vivió largos años de misionero y predicador el P. Beltran 'hasta casi olvidar el castellano,' como él mismo pone en el prólogo de su gramática.*"

[2] For further details in this point, see p. 27.

[3] Tozzer, 1907, p. 36.

refuse to speak anything else, clinging to their own tongue with the greatest devotion.[1]

So general is the use of the native tongue in the peninsula that in some places in the small interior towns it is sometimes difficult to find one who can carry on a continued conversation in Spanish although most of the younger generation understand it when spoken. It is curious to note the varying differences in the tenacity of the mother tongue in various parts of Mexico and Central America. In many isolated places throughout the whole region the native languages still continue to be used. But in most cases with close contact the native tongue has given way to Spanish. Contact, however, since the very earliest days of the Conquest has not had this influence on the Maya of Yucatan and this still remains the language of the country.

On many of the large plantations, Maya is spoken exclusively and the *mayordomos* use it invariably in speaking to the natives. The Spanish priests when making their visits through the small towns preach their sermons in Maya.

*Modern Maya Grammars.* I have attempted to give in the Appraisement (Part III) a full discussion of what I consider to be the relative merits of the many writers on the Maya dialect. It is, therefore, only necessary here to say a few words concerning the modern works to which reference is made in the main body of this paper. The grammar of Ruz (1844) is of very slight value. The work of Seler (1887), although based entirely on the early grammars, is the first attempt ever made to explain the structure of the language. The book of Palma y Palma (1901), although following the lines of the older grammarians, contains a great deal of new and valuable material. The grammars of Zavala (1896) and of Pacheco Cruz (1912) should be mentioned here. The best modern grammar is that of Lopez Otero (1914).

---

[1] Compare Brinton (1882, p. 27–28) who writes, "It has been observed that foreigners, coming to Yucatan, ignorant of both Spanish and Maya, acquire a conversational knowledge of the latter more readily than of the former." He quotes García y Garcia (1865, p. lxxv) who writes on this point, "*La lengua castellana es mas difficultosa que la Maya para la gente adulta, que no ha mamado con la leche, como lo ha enseñado la experiencia en los estranjeros de distintas naciones, y en los negros bozales que se han radicado en esta provincia, que mas facilmente han aprendido la Maya que la castellana.*"

The late Señor Don Audomaro Molina of Merida, Yucatan, was probably one of the best Maya scholars of the present time. He partially completed the difficult task of revising for publication the Motul dictionary. Unfortunately he published nothing on the language.

One of his pupils, however, Daniel Lopez Otero, notes in his *Gramatica Maya* [1] that he is under obligations to Señor Molina who taught him the greater part of the rules he uses in his work.

Mention should be made of another Maya scholar, Señor Don Juan Martínez Hernández of Merida, who has worked for many years on the Maya language and, more especially, on the Books of Chilam Balam and on Maya chronology. His valuable writings are listed in the Bibliography. I am under deep obligations to him for encouragement in this work and more especially for his willingness to read the proof and to suggest changes in the text of this paper.

All Maya scholars are very greatly indebted to Mr. William Gates of Point Loma, California, through whose energy and acumen large stores of material in the Maya language have been made available to students. Further mention of this work is made in Part III (p. 148–149).

*Provenance of material discussed.* The greater part of the linguistic material used in this study was obtained from Benito Can, a native of Valladolid, a town in northeastern Yucatan. The Spaniards under Montejo founded this city in 1543 upon the site of the native town of Saki. During the early days of the Spanish occupation the city arose to some prominence. It was and is, even to this

---

[1] Lopez (1914, p. 5) writes in this connection, "*Tampoco he pretendido conquistar honores que no merezco, sino rendir este humilde recuerdo de gratitud y admiración a mi ilustrado y muy querido maestro, don Audomaro Molina Solís (q. d. D. g.) de quien he aprendido la mayor parte de las reglas que, en esta desaliñada obrita, hallará el indulgente lector que se dignare leerla. Si el Maestro viviera, no me ocuparía en escribir nada acerca de este idioma; pero habiendo fallecido sin haber realizado la noble idea, por él acariciada, de dar a luz una gramática y un diccionario de la lengua maya, y observando que ninguno de sus discípulos ha publicado nada hasta la fecha acerca de este idioma, a fin de que tan sabias como útiles enseñanzas no sean relegadas al olvido, he resuelto publicar en forma gramatical las lecciones que de él he recibido, aumentadas con, algunas reglas tomadas del arte . . . de Beltrán de Santa Rosa María, y otras observaciones que personalmente he tenido ocasión de hacer,*" etc.

day, the farthest point eastward of the country brought under complete Spanish control. The vast territory immediately eastward to the coast is occupied by the "*indios sublevados.*" These wandering bands of Indians have never been wholly conquered by the Mexicans. Valladolid has suffered several attacks and destructions at the hands of these wild tribes and the city is now hardly more than an Indian town.

The language spoken at Valladolid is perhaps more free from outside influence than that used in any other portion of the settled part of the peninsula.

At the time of my four successive seasons in Yucatan, Benito Can was an indented servant upon the Hacienda of Chichen Itza belonging to Mr. E. H. Thompson then American Consul at Progreso, Yucatan. It was while accepting the kind hospitality of Mr. and Mrs. Thompson that I did the greater part of my linguistic work.

The investigations into the language were undertaken at several different times covering the whole period of four years. Thus I was able to check up the material often after periods separated by an absence of a year or more.

Benito Can had a strain of Spanish blood in his veins. He had lived all his life, however, in the town of his birth and had had comparatively little contact with the Spanish speaking population. His knowledge of Spanish, however, was adequate for my purpose. He was one of three brothers the other two of whom could not speak a word of Spanish. This man was of rather a higher grade of intelligence than the average Maya. I used several other interpreters to check up the material obtained from Can.

## PHONETICS

GENERAL CHARACTER. The phonetic system of the Maya is generally simple. The occurrence of the velar **k** (**q**) and the glottalized or fortis forms of the **t, p,** and the two dental surds (ɔ and tš) give the language a certain harshness when compared with the Nahuatl of the north with its smooth liquid sounds.[1]

---

[1] Beltran in his "*Prologo al Lector*" writes, "*Es el Yucateco Idioma garboso en sus dicciones, elegante en sus periodos, y en ambas cosas conciso: pues con pocas palabras y breves sílabas explica á veces profundas sentencias. Y como se acertarán a pronunciar ciertas consonantes, que lo hacen acre, sería muy fácil de*

CONSONANTS. The system of consonants includes one velar, two palatals, alveolars, a double set of dentals in both the surd and the fortis, and labials. It is often difficult to distinguish between the sonant **b** and its corresponding surd **p**. It is probable, however, that they are not interchangeable. The following table represents the system of consonants found in the Maya:

| | Sonant | Surd | Fortis | Spirant | Nasal | Lateral |
|---|---|---|---|---|---|---|
| Velar | | q | | | | |
| Palatal | | k | | H | | |
| Alveolar | | t | t' | s | n | l |
| Dental | | ɔ | ɔ' | | | |
| | | tš | tš' | š | | |
| Labial | b | p | p' | | | |

In addition to these sounds, **w, y,** and **h** sounds occur. I have been much perplexed by what I have long thought to be an **r** sound, possibly a sonant of the spirant. No mention of this sound is made in any of the early grammars and its presence is denied by the Mayas themselves. This sound I seem to have heard in several words written by Maya scholars with a doubled vowel:

> **tin bor-t-ik,** or, as usually written, **tin boo-t-ik,**
> **lerti** or **leeti** or **leti.**

I have come to the conclusion to omit this sound from the list.[1]

There may also be fortis forms for the velar and the palatal surd (**q** and **k**). These are difficult to make out. No differentiation seems to be made between the surd and the fortis in the **k** sounds in the greater number of cases. I have been unable to note any difference in the grammatical structure of the language as a consequence of the failure to differentiate between the surd and the fortis in these two cases. The vocabulary ought naturally to make the distinction if it is present but I have not found it.

The velar **k,** written **q,** is formed between the back of the tongue and the soft palate. The palatal **k** is the common English **k.** The

---

*aprender por Arte; por carecer, no solo de muchas letras, sino tambien de libros enteros, de los cuales fastidian á un Gramático. ¿Quién creyera, que un idioma muy lato se habia de practicar con expedicion y sin tropiezo: sin tardanza, y con prefeccion sin el adminículo de ocho consonantes? Este es el Idioma ó Lengua Maya; y tan cierto, que carece de las siguientes: d, f, g, j, q, r, s, ll."*

[1] The **r** sound is well recognized in Cakchiquel and Quiche where it is used in place of the **y** in Maya. Palma y Palma (p. 145) uses the **r** in one case, at least, in modern Maya.

palatal spirant (**H**) is an intensified **h** sound and is found only in one place as far as could be made out. The first dental surd, really a **ts**, is written with an inverted **c** (ɔ). The second dental surd, **tš**, is pronounced like the first ch in church. The fortis forms, called by the early Spanish grammarians " *las letras heridas*," are found in the alveolar, **t'**, the two dentals, **ɔ'** and **tš'** and the labial, **p'**. These are common and are characterized by a forcible expelling of the breath with glottal closure. The dental spirant, **š**, is pronounced like the sh in hush. The lateral (**1**) is thick and rather strongly sonant.[1] Long combinations of consonant sounds do not occur.

VOWELS. The vowel system is very simple. The vowels all have their continental sounds. There is a long **a** (a) and a short **a** (ă), the first pronounced like **a** in father and the second like **a** in hat. There is also some indication of a long **e** (ē) like **a** in fate, long **i** (ī) like **i** in pique and long **u** (u) like **u** in rule in addition to the ordinary **e**, **i**, and **u**. I did not find a long **o**.[2] The only diphthong is **ai**, written by the early authorities as **ay**.

---

[1] For the best discussion of the phonetics of the Maya as given in the older authorities, see Beltran, §§ 1–16. See also Lopez, §§ 1–11 and Gates, 1920, p. 611–613.

[2] Perez (1866–1877) speaks of two forms of the vowel although he does not distinguish these forms in his dictionary. Under each of the vowels he describes the two forms. Under "A," for example, he writes, "*Esta vocal se pronuncia de dos maneras, una suave que puede ser larga ó breve, y otra fuerte en la que como que se contiene el aliento ó sonido repentinamente al mismo tiempo de emitirlo: como en* na, *casa y* na, *madre.*" A question might well be raised here whether he is not speaking of the doubled vowel in each case. It seems from his illustration of na, *casa*, and na, *madre*, that this is not the case. The a in the word for house is short and in that for mother it is long.

Berendt (1869) also gives two forms for each of the vowels but he expressly states that one is long and the other short.

Palma y Palma (p. 137) refers at length to the confusion caused by the different ways of pronouncing the same vowel. He writes (p. 139), "*Aunque de esto hablaré después en lugar más apropiado, bueno es decir siquiera de paso, que las voces monosilábicas mayas, no tienen una cantidad prosódica fija. Unas son extremadamente breves en la emisión, y otras, sin contar con sus diversas inflexiones y acentos que son otros medios de distinción, son más ó menos largas. Por eso no se representan bien siempre doblando las vocales, pues las hay tan largas, que necesitarían tres ó más.*"

In this discussion of long and short vowels, it is significant to observe that the Landa alphabet has three forms for **a**, two for **o** and two for **u**. See in this connection, Palma y Palma, p. 222–239.

*Doubled Vowels.* These are very common in Maya and great care
is sometimes needed in distinguishing them as: [1]

| | |
|---|---|
| **kan,** snake. | **siil,** to give, to offer. |
| **kaan,** sky. | **ton,** male sexual member. |
| **be,** road. | **toon,** we. |
| **bee,** exclamation of pain. | **hun,** one. |
| **sil,** to tuck up the sleeves. | **huun,** paper, letter. |

NOTATION. It is a matter of no little importance to decide how
the various sounds should be written. The table (p. 21), gives the
alphabets as used by the modern authors on Maya as well as the
letters used by the older Spanish authorities either in their grammars or in their vocabularies. There is a considerable mass of
written Maya and material is still being published in Yucatan in
this language. The usual modern method follows more or less
closely that used by the earlier writers, **c** for our **k,** a **k** for the velar
surd (**q**), a barring or doubling of the letters for the " *letras heridas* "
or fortis forms, **ch, th,** and **pp.** The fortis form of one of the dentals is almost always written **ɔ.** The inconsistency from a phonetic standpoint of this method is great but the fact that there is
a large mass of material already written in this way should be
given due consideration before any changes are suggested.

Furthermore, the ease of printing and the necessity for new
type if diacritical marks are used are other considerations which

---

[1] The later Spanish dictionaries often fail to distinguish the difference between a single vowel and the same one doubled. Perez (1866–77), for example,
gives **qiq** or **qiiq** for blood, **kimil** or **kiimil,** to die. The Motul and Ticul dictionaries, on the other hand, give but one form for each of these words. The
early Spanish grammarians make no reference to these double vowels.

Berendt specifically mentions them. In speaking of false diphthongs he
writes (1869, p. 4) " In languages of the Maya family they are often formed by
a repetition of the same vowel and constitute a remarkable distinction; **kan**
is snake and **kaan** is sky in Maya."

Pimentel (1862–1865, v. 2, p. 7; ed. 1874–1875, v. 3, p. 108) writes "*No se
observa cargazon de consonantes en yucateco, y si la repeticion de una misma
vocal en muchas palabras.*"

---

[1] **e** and **z** were omitted, probably by mistake, from the list of sounds given
by Zavala.

[2] Seler in his first paragraphs writes the sounds as indicated here and in his
text he follows the accustomed usage.

[3] **e** and **ch** were omitted by mistake in the 1859 edition of the grammar. They
occur in the 1746 edition.

## ALPHABETS USED BY VARIOUS AUTHORITIES

| Tozzer | Gates MS. | Palma y Palma, 1901 | Zavala, 1896 | Seler, 1887 | Stoll, 1884 | Brinton, 1882 | de Rosny, 1875 | Berendt, 1869 | Perez, 1866–1877 | Brasseur, 1864 | Pimentel, 1862–1865 | San Francisco Dictionary | Motul Dictionary | Beltran, 1746 | San Buenaventura, 1684 | Coronel, 1620 |
|---|---|---|---|---|---|---|---|---|---|---|---|---|---|---|---|---|
| a, ă | a | a | a | a | a | a | a, a | ā, ă | a, a | a | a | a | a | a, a | a | a |
| ai | .. | .. | .. | .. | .. | .. | .. | ei[?] | .. | .. | .. | .. | .. | .. | .. | .. |
| b | b | b | b | b | b | b | b | b | b | b | b | b | b | b | b | b |
| k | c | c | c | c | c | c | c | k | c | c | c | c | c | c | c | c |
|  |  |  |  | k |  |  |  |  |  |  |  |  |  |  |  |  |
|  |  |  |  | ch |  |  |  |  |  |  |  |  |  |  |  |  |
| tš | ch | ch | ch | tš ² | ch | ch | ch | tx | ch | ch | ch | ch | ch | ch ³ | ch | ch |
|  |  |  |  | ch' |  |  |  |  |  |  |  |  |  |  |  |  |
| tš' | ch' | ch | ch | chh | ch' | ch | ch' | ŧx | ch | çh | ch | ch | ch | ch | ch | ch |
| ē, e | e | e | [e] ¹ | e | e | e | e | e | ē, ĕ | e, e | e | e | e | e³ | e | e |
| H | j | .. | .. | .. | .. | .. | .. | h' | .. | .. | .. | .. | .. | .. | ħ | .. |
| h | h | h | h | h | j | h | h | h | h | h | h | h | h | h | h | h |
|  |  |  |  |  |  |  |  |  |  |  |  |  |  |  | j | j |
| ī, i | i | i | i | i | i | i | i | i | ī, i | i, i | i | ı | i | i | i | i |
|  |  |  |  | c' | c' |  |  | k |  |  |  |  |  |  |  |  |
| q | k | k | k | k' | k' | k | k' | ḳ | k | k | k | k | k | k | k | k |
| l | l | l | l | l | l | l | l | l | l | l | l | l | l | l | l | l |
| ɯ | ɯ | m | m̄ | m | m | m | m | m | m | m | m | m | m | m | m | m |
| n | n | n | n | n | n | n | n | n | n | n | n | n | n | n | n | n |
| o | o | ȯ | o | o | o | o | o | o | ō, ŏ | o | o | o | o | o | o | o |
| ꝑ | ꝑ | p | p | p | p | p | p | p | ꝑ | μ | μ | μ / ρ | ꝑ | ꝑ | p | p |
| p' | p' | p | p | pp | pp | pp | p' | p | pp | pp | pp | pp | pp | pp | pp | pp |
|  |  |  |  |  |  |  |  |  |  |  |  |  |  |  | z | z |
| s | s | z | [z] ¹ | s | s | z | z | s | z | z | z | z | ç | z | ç | ç |
|  |  |  |  | x |  |  |  |  |  |  |  |  |  |  |  |  |
| š | x | x | x | š | x | x | x | x | x | x | x | x | x | x | x | x |
| t | t | t | t | t | t | t | t | t | t | t | t | t | t | t | t | t |
| t' | t' | dt | tħ | th | tt | tħ | t' | ŧ | th | th | th | tħ | tħ | tħ | tħ | th |
| ɔ | tz | tz | tz | tz | tz | tz | tz | ts | tz | tz | tz | tz | tz | tz | tz | tz |
| ɔ' | tz' | ɔ | ɔ | ɔ | tz' | ɔ | ɔ | ŧs | ɔ | ɔ | ɔ | ɔ | ɔ | ɔ | ɔ | ɔ |
| ū, u | u | u | u | u | u | u | u | u | ū, ŭ | u, u | u | u | u | u | .. | u |
| .. | v | .. | .. | .. | .. | v | .. | .. | v | .. | .. | .. | .. | .. | v | .. |
| w | .. | .. | .. | .. | .. | .. | .. | .. | .. | .. | .. | .. | .. | .. | .. | .. |
| y | y | y | y | y | y | y | y | y | y | y | y | y | y | y | y | y |

¹ See footnotes 1, 2, and 3 on opposite page.

should be taken into account. If any changes whatsoever are to be made from the older methods it seems to me that these changes should be along well recognized phonetic lines and that they should be consistent.

In adopting what, in some cases, is a new method I have been largely governed by a desire to follow phonetic practices used by other writers on the languages of America, namely, to use a single character for a single sound and to express consistently all sounds made in the same way by a similar notation as, for example, the fortis by an apostrophe after the letter. For purposes of a grammar of the Maya dialect the following changes in notation are used in this paper:[1]

1. The palatal surd is always written **k** rather than **c** as the **c** in Maya is always hard.

2. The velar surd is written **q**, not **k** which is commonly used.

3. The dental spirant is **š**, not **x** or **sh**, as this is a single sound and should be written by a single letter.

4. One of the dental surds is written **tš**, not **ch**, as the sound is really made by a **t** before the dental spirant. **tsh** would be more correct than **ch**.

5. The second dental surd is written **ɔ**, not **tz** or **ts**.

6. The fortis of the alveolar **t**, the dentals **ɔ** and **tš**, and the labial **p** are written with an apostrophe following the letter, **t'**, **ɔ'**, **tš'**, and **p'** respectively rather than **tħ**, **ɔ**, **cħ**, and **pp**.

7. The **s**, written **ç** or **z** by the Spaniards, is, of course, a well justified change.

8. **W** is added to the alphabet. This letter is not found in any of the former Maya writings from the fact, no doubt, that there

---

[1] In proper names, especially the names of towns, and in the terms given to the divisions of Maya time as shown in the hieroglyphic writing no changes have been made.

I am well aware that these changes in notation will meet with adverse criticism. I do not cherish the hope that my method will be followed by other workers in this field. I have retained the same general system of notation as that used in my previous papers on the Maya language. I have felt that, for purposes of a grammar, it is well to make these changes as, with one exception, the method used here corresponds to that employed by most other writers on American languages. The one exception is the use of the inverted c (ɔ) which is used by all the ancient Maya authorities. It is employed here, however, for the dental surd and ɔ' for the corresponding fortis form.

is no **w** in Spanish. The consonant **w** is clearly different from **u,** a vowel, and should be distinguished from it.

It should be noted that in quoting the Maya of any of the earlier authorities I have used, for the purpose of uniformity, the method of representing the sounds as here given rather than that used by the writers themselves.

PHONETIC CHANGES. These do not play an important part in word composition. When the sign expressing past time, **t,** is used with the nominal pronoun of the 1st person plural, **k,** in both the inclusive and exclusive forms, the **k** is lost and the **t** becomes a fortis:

t-k-putš-ah becomes t'-putš-ah.

In much the same way, when two **k** sounds come together they usually combine into the velar:

ɔ'ok-k putš-ah becomes ɔ'oq putš-ah.[1]

*Syncope, Synalephe, and Apocope.*[2] Contraction by syncope, synalephe, and apocope occur very frequently. As in English, so in Maya, both the contracted and uncontracted forms are in good use. When a native is dictating texts, he is much more inclined to use the uncontracted forms; whereas, in everyday speech, he usually employs the contracted forms.

Syncope is noted in the following places:

1. The transitive verb with a pronominal object may lose the

---

[1] This root is more commonly written **putš'**, to pound, to bruise, to grind something: *despachurrar, machucar, moler,* etc.   **Putš'tuntik,** *despachurrar con piedra, matar apedreando con las grandes.*

[2] Beltran (§§ 129–147) gives ten rules for these changes. He writes, "*Porque en este idioma no se habla en todo como se escribe, ni se pronuncian muchas voces conforme lo pulen las reylus (y es lo que causa, que algunos que lo hablan parezcan forasteros ó se juzgue que no pronuncian como deben; siendo así, que hablan segun las reglas del arte) se advierta que es tan necesario el uso de las sinalefas y síncopas, que sin hipérbole se puede afirmar, que todo el ser y hermosura de esta lengua es el uso de ellas y la parte mas principal del arte es su explicacion.*" And again (§ 135), "*La síncopa no es otra cosa, que comerle á algun vocablo alguna sílaba, ó letra vocal ó consonante. Y esta figura agracia tanto al idioma Maya que sin ella parece que sus vocablos se hacen extraños, poco agradables y en su cadencia feos. En tanta manera, que puedo sin temeridad decir que casi la mitad de sus vocablos se sincopan ó son sincopables.*"

**i** of the ending **-ik** in the present and the **a** of the ending **-ah** in the past:

tan-in putš-ik-etš becomes **tin putš-k-etš** [1]
t-in kambe-s-ah-etš becomes **tin kambe-s-h-etš.**

2. The same vowels (**i** and **a**) of the temporal endings of the transitive verb are lost when the reflexive form of the pronoun is used:

tin han-t-ik-im-ba becomes **tin han-t-k-im-ba**
tin han-t-ah-im-ba becomes **tin han-t-h-im-ba**

3. All polysyllabic transitive verbs lose the vowel of the temporal endings before the **-eš** of the 2d person plural and **-ob** of the 3d person plural: [2]

tun yakun-t-ik-eš becomes **tun yakun-t-k-eš.**
tun yakun-t-ik-ob becomes **tun yakun-t-k-ob.**

4. Verbs using the suffixes **-al, -el, -il, -ol, -ul** lose the vowel of the suffix in the present and the future of the intransitive:

nak-al-in-kah becomes **nak-l-in-kah.**
he-in han-al-e becomes **hēn han-l-e.**

The verbs in **-tal,** following a final consonant in the stem, do not follow this rule.

5. In the future of the intransitive with **bin** and the suffix **-ăk,** the **ă** of the suffix is lost: [3]

bin han-ăk-en becomes **bin han-k-en.**

When the stem ends in **k** the whole suffix is lost:

bin nak-ăk-en becomes **bin nak-en.**

6. In words of two syllables containing two similar vowels, the second vowel is lost when:

---

[1] Beltran (§ 140) gives an example of syncope;

**ten kambe-s-ik-etš** beccming **ten kambe-s-etš.**

This seems to me to be incorrect as the contracted form has lost the **k,** the sign of the present. His second example;

teeš kambe-s-ik-on becoming **teeš kambe-s-k-on,**
correct as it retains the **k.**

[2] Compare Lopez, § 166.

[3] Lopez (§ 165) gives the following:
**bin taketš** for **bin talaketš.**

(a) the plural sign is used:

**taman-ob** becomes **tamn-ob.**

(b) the verbal pronoun is used:

**winik-en** becomes **wink-en.**

(c) the demonstrative pronoun is used:

**lē-winik-a** becomes **lē-wink-a.**

7. When a vowel suffix is added to a stem ending in **l**, the vowel of the stem is sometimes lost:

**tel-o** becomes **tl-o.**

Synalephe is much less common than syncope. It is noted in the following places:

1. Time particles of the present, past, and future attached to the nominal pronoun:

Present, **tan-in** becomes **tin.**

**tan-a** becomes **tan,** etc.

Past, **ti-in** becomes **tin.**

**ti-a** becomes **ta,** etc.

**ɔ'ok-in** becomes **ɔ'in.**

**ɔ'ok-a** beccmes **ɔ'a,** etc.

Future, **he-in** becomes **hēn.**

**he-a** becomes **ha,** etc.

2. The negative **ma** and the nominal pronoun:

**ma-in** becomes **min.**

3. **Ti** and some other prepositions and the nominal pronoun: [1]

**ti-in watotš** becomes **tin watotš.**

Apocope. This is not uncommon in everyday speech. Among the places where it may be found, the following are to be noted:

1. The final **-e**, the sign of the future of the transitive with **bin,** is sometimes lost when followed by a noun:

**bin in han-t-e wa** becomes **bin in han-t wa.**

2. The final **-e** of the future is usually lost when the form in **bin** takes a pronominal object:

**bin in yakun-t-e-etš** becomes **bin in yakun-t-etš.**

---

[1] Beltran (§§ 132, 133) makes a distinction in the contraction of **ti** meaning "in" and **ti** meaning "to or for." Compare also Lopez, § 164.

3. The final -e, the sign of the imperative with transitive verbs, is lost when followed by a pronoun or a particle beginning with a vowel:

ɔik-e a-yum becomes ɔik a-yum.

4. The final -1 of the suffix -il is lost when an adverb or negative is used:

ma sak-en-i for ma sak-en-il.

*Vocalic harmony.* This is observed in many different sets of suffixes especially those in -l, the vowel of the suffix agreeing with that of the stem:

han-al, wen-el, tip'-il, top-ol, qutš-ul.

There seems, however, to be a strong tendency to prefer the suffix -al even when the vowel of the stem is not a.

*Avoidance of hiatus.* In certain suffixes beginning with a vowel, when the stem ends in a vowel, the hiatus is sometimes avoided by adding a b sound. This is seen in some cases in the plural suffix -ob in which case there may be a certain harmony between the consonant of the suffix and the consonant added.

An h sound is also sometimes added in order to avoid an hiatus between two vowel sounds:

meya-h-en, I am a workman.

This should not be confused with the hi, the sign of the past:

meya-hi-en, I was a workman.

*Semi-vowels.* These are added both to nominal and verbal stems beginning with a vowel. Whatever the previous history of these sounds may have been they now show a syntactic relation as we find the change of w and y made, not according to the initial vowel, but rather in relation to the person of the verb or of the nominal pronoun.

Root, al, to see.
tin w-al-ik, I see it (contraction of tan-in w-al-ik).
tan w-al-ik, you see it (contraction of tan a-w-al-ik).
tun y-al-ik, he sees it (contracted to t-i-al-ik).
tank al-ik, we see it.
tan wal-ik-eš, you see it.
tun y-al-ik-ob, they see it (contracted to t-i-al-ik-ob).

It will be noted that **w** is added in the first person singular and the second person singular and plural and **y** in the third person singular and plural. No vowel is added in the first person plural.

*Lacandone Dialect.* Certain simple phonetic changes and a less extended use of contraction alone distinguish the dialect spoken by the Lacandones from that used by the Mayas of Yucatan. Final 1 in stems appears as **n** in the Lacandone, **wen-el** changing to **wen-en.** Certain stems with final n in the Maya change to **m** in the dialect of the Lacandone. The great distinguishing mark, however, between the Maya as spoken around Valladolid, Yucatan, and that spoken in Chiapas is the frequent use of contraction among the people in the former territory. Forms which one is unable to analyze among the Mayas appear separated into their component parts in the dialect spoken by the Lacandones. This is especially to be noted in the time particles used with the nominal pronoun. I shall limit myself hereafter entirely to the language used in Yucatan, leaving it to be understood that that spoken by the Lacandones is essentially the same with the exceptions which have just been noted.

CHARACTER OF STEM. Stems are almost entirely monosyllabic and consist normally of consonant, vowel, consonant. Several are made up only of vowel and consonant, and a smaller number of consonant and vowel.

ACCENT. This is not marked. It is in part dependent upon the length of the vowel. Contracted syllables usually seem to have greater stress of voice laid upon them. In spite of some authorities to the contrary, there seem to be few cases where a difference in accent occasions a difference in the meaning of the form.[1]

The accent in all the Lacandone chants is much more noticeable than in the ordinary speech. There is often a definite rhythm and in the slow chants this is very marked.[2] Syllables composed of the

---

[1] I was unable to find the distinction in accent made by Beltran (§ 98) between the infinitive of certain verbs in -l and the past participle;

   **lub-úl,** to fall and **lúb-ul,** a thing fallen.
   **lik-íl,** to raise and **lík-il,** a thing raised.

[2] Tozzer, 1907, p. 131 and Chant no. 17.

vowel **i** or **ki** are often added at the end of words to fill out a certain measure. These added sounds seem to affect the meaning in no way.[1] The rhythm is very irregular and it is impossible to ascertain the general scheme of long and short syllables.

## GRAMMATICAL PROCESSES

ENUMERATION.
1. Word composition.
2. Affixes.
   (a) Prefix.
   (b) Suffix.
3. Reduplication.
4. Word order.

WORD COMPOSITION. An idea is expressed in Maya either by a single stem, usually monosyllabic, to which one or more particles are affixed, or by the juxtaposition of two stems modified and restricted by one or more prefixes, suffixes, or both. In the latter case each stem remains phonetically a unit and each is separated from the other by an hiatus. Grammatically, however, there is a unity existing between the two. The most important case of word composition is that of the transitive verb with its object. So strong is this unity that the action of the verb as related to its specific object is taken as a whole and is considered as intransitive in sense and thus follows the intransitive in form. It is possible to join all transitive verbs with their objects in this way but only those expressing some common and natural act in relation to the object are usually found in the intransitive form as owe-money, chop-wood, etc.

AFFIXES. These are very common in Maya and are used to express practically all the grammatical ideas. Phonetically there is much closer unity between the root and its affixes than between two juxtaposed roots. In the former case certain phonetic changes

---

[1] Compare in this connection Palma y Palma (p. 144) who writes, "*No obstante, las partículas compositivas que no modifican el sentido, son muchísimas, las cuales, efictivamente, sólo contribuyen á la variedad de las formas de la expresión constituyendo así, como el indicado padre Beltran dice, 'partículas adornativas' que facilitan giros de estilo de que resulta un lenguaje elegante y artístico cuando se habla bien el idioma.*"

tend to strengthen this unity. An intimate relation is also brought about in some cases between the suffix and the stem by vocalic harmony. It is often difficult to draw a line between true word composition and prefixing and suffixing. I have placed under Composition all forms made up of words which can stand alone and thus can be considered as true words in contrast to the affixes which cannot appear alone. There are, no doubt, many of the latter which were once words. **Tan,** for example, which is given here as a particle is shown by Perez to be an impersonal verb.

REDUPLICATION. This is not especially common in Maya and is found only in a limited number of cases.

WORD ORDER. This does not play a great part in expressing syntactical relations.

## IDEAS EXPRESSED BY THE GRAMMATICAL PROCESSES

WORD COMPOSITION. This is employed in the following forms:

1. *Habitual action.* When a verb and its object expresses this idea the two form a unit and the form becomes intransitive in the past tense:

šo[t]-tše-n-ah-en, I cut wood.

This is composed of the root, **šot,** to cut, and **tše,** wood. The idea of cutting wood is regarded as a verb in itself.

2. *Agent.* This is sometimes expressed by word composition in addition to the usual sign for the agent, **t.**

tin tak-ok-t-ik, I am bending something with my foot (ok).

3. *Gender.* In names of animals and, in a few cases, in other nouns:

šibal ke, male deer.
tš'upul ke, female deer.

4. *Indefinite time in the future.* This is expressed by the root of the verb **binel,** " to go," in both the intransitive and transitive verb:

bin nak-ăk-en, I am going to climb.
bin a hant wa-e, you are going to eat the tortilla.[1]

---

[1] This also shows a form of word composition as the object is inserted between the root of the verb and the sign of the future, **-e.**

5. *Action just completed.* This is shown by the root ɔ'ok, to finish:

ɔ'a putš-h-en (ɔ'ok-a putš-ah-en), you have just finished hitting me.

6. *Optative.* This is made by the root of the verb qat, to desire.

in qat bin (el), I desire to go, I may go.

THE SUFFIX. This is found to express the following relations and ideas:

1. *Plurality.* In most nouns, the 3d person of the nominal pronoun, and in some adjectives, by -ob:

na, house, na-ob, houses.
u-na, his house, u-na-ob, their house or his houses.

2. *Plurality.* In the 2d person of the nominal pronoun by -eš:

a-na, your house, a-na-eš, your (more than one) house.

3. *Plurality in some adjectives.* By -ăk:

kan-ăk tšupal-al, tall girls.

4. *Plurality in some nouns.* By -al.

tšupal, a girl.
tšupal-al, girls.

5. *Exclusion of the person spoken to.* In nominal pronoun by -on for dual and -on-eš for plural:

k-na-on, our (his and my house).
k-na-on-eš, our (their and my house).

6. *Inclusion of person spoken to.* In plural by -eš:

k-na-eš, our (your and my) house.

7. *Verbal pronoun.* -en, -etš, etc., when used as subject or object of verbs and as the auxiliary, to be:

putš-en, I hit, I am a hitter.
tan putš-ik-en, you are hitting me.
winik-en, I am a man.

8. *Demonstrative pronoun.* -a, -o, and -u with the prefix lē-:

lē winik-a, this man here.
lē winik-o, that man there.
lē winik-e, that man at a distance.

9. *Reflexive pronoun.* By -ba:

tin putš-im-ba (putš-ik-in-ba) I am hitting myself.

10. *Abstract nouns.* By -il:
kohan-il, sickness.

11. *Collective nouns.* By -il:
u-yoooil-il, the poor.

12. *Attributive relationship.* By -il:
u tunitš-il qaq, the stone of the fire.

13. *Gentilitious relationship.* By -il:
Ho-il, a Meridano.

14. *Habituality.* By -tal:
kohan-tal, a sickly man.

15. *Comparative degree.* By -il:
uɔ na, a good house.
uɔ-il na, a better house.

16. *Present time in transitive verb.* By -ik:
tin ɔ'on-ik, 1 am shooting something.

17. *Present time in intransitive verb of motion.* By -kah:
nak-l-in-kah (nak-al-in-kah) 1 am climbing.

18. *Future time in intransitive and transitive verbs.* By -e:
hěn ɔ'on-e, 1 shall shoot.
hěn ɔ'on-ik-e, 1 shall shoot something.

19. *Future time in verbs of Class IV.* By -tšal or -tal:
hěn winik-tšal-e, 1 shall become a man.

20. *Indefinite future in intransitive verbs.* By ăk with stem bin:
bin nak-ăk-en, 1 am going to climb.

21. *Past time in intransitive and transitive verbs of Classes II, III, IV.* By -ah or h:
tin ɔ'on-ah, 1 shot something.
tši-l-ah-en (tši-tal-ah-en) 1 lay down.
ɔ'on-(n) ah-en, I shot.
keel-h-en, 1 was cold.

22. *Distant past in transitive verb.* By ma-ah:
tin putš-m-ah, 1 hit something a long time ago.

23. *Causal verbs (Class I b).* By s:
tin kim-s-ik, 1 kill something, I cause something to die.

24. *Agent* (*Class III b*). By **t**:

tin mis-t-ik, I am sweeping or I do something with a broom.

25. *Effect of action of verb on subject.* In some cases this serves to express a passive relationship. By **-al, -el, -il, -ol, -ul**:

tin lub-ul, I am falling or my being affected by a fall.

26. *Passive relationship, past tense.* By **b** or **n**:

naɔ-s-ah-b-en, I was approached.
ɔ'on-ah-n-en, I was shot.

27. *Imperative.* Intransitive by **-en**, transitive by **-e**:

ɔ'on-en, shoot!
ɔ'on-e, shoot something!

28. *Inchoative or Inceptive verbs and verbs of Class II.* By **-tal** or **-hal**:

tin winik-tal, I am becoming a man.

29. *Reflexive verbs.* By **-pahal**:

tun tšun-pahal, it begins itself.

30. *Adverbs.* When the verbal pronoun is used and the adverb precedes the verb, the verb takes the suffix **-il**:

tšitš šimbal-n-ah-il-en, I walked rapidly.

31. *Manner of action.* When this is expressed by prefix **bē**, thus, the verbal form takes **-il**, and the demonstrative suffixes **-a, -e,** or **-o**:

bē tal-il-en-a, in this way, I came.

32. *Numeral classifiers* (see p. 103).

THE PREFIX. This is found to express the following relations and ideas:

1. *Gender of the " Nomen actoris."* **H-** for male, **š-** for female:

H-men, a shaman, literally, one who knows.
š-men, a female shaman.

2. *Time, attached to the nominal pronoun.* **tan** for present, **t** for past, and **he** for future:

tan-in (tin) ɔ'on-ik, I am shooting something.
t-in ɔ'on-ah, I shot something.
hēn (he-in) ɔ'on-ik-e, I shall shoot something.

3. *Time, used with the intransitive verb in the past.* By **t**:

t-putš-en, I hit or performed the act of hitting.

4. *Nominal pronoun.* When used as subject of the verb or as the possessive:

tin (tan-in) putš-ik, 1 am hitting something.
Juan, u huun, John, his book.

5. *The semi-vowels.* When used with the nominal pronoun with vowel stems. These have a phonetic and syntactical history (p. 26):

6. *Demonstrative.* le- with the suffixes -a, -o, -e:

lē-winik-a, this man here.

7. *Relative relationship.* By lik or likil:

likil in wen-el the object in which 1 sleep, my hammock.

8. *Adverbial relationships.* Such as those indicating repetition with ka, totality with la, and a large number of others:

tin ka-bin, 1 come again.
tin la-wuk-ik, 1 am drinking all of it.

9. *Manner or state.* By bē and the suffix -il with the demonstratives -a, -e, -o:

bē-tal-il-en-o, in that way, 1 came.

10. *Direction of motion.* pai, motion towards, pilis, motion away, etc.:

tin-pai-bala-ok-t-ik, I am rolling something towards me with the foot.

11. *Negative.* By ma:

m-in (ma-in) qati, 1 do not wish to.

12. *Prepositions* (see p. 107).

t-iñ na, in my house.
yoqol lu ña, above my house.

REDUPLICATION. This is syllabic in form. The process seems to have no effect upon the vowel of the stem. It is employed to express the following relations and ideas:

1. *Distant past in the intransitive verb:*

šimbal-n-ah-ah-n-en, 1 ran a long time ago.

2. *Iterative or frequentative verbs:*

tin bi-bi qab, 1 tap with my fingers frequently.

3. *Plural with some adjectives:*

ta-taš be-ob, smooth roads.

**4.** *Plural with some participles:* [1]

tšak, to cut with a blow.
tšak-an, a thing cut.
tšak-an-tšak, things cut.

**5.** *Diminutive with nouns and adjectives:*

| | |
|---|---|
| kah, pueblo. | sa-sak, *medio blanco.* |
| ka-kah, small pueblos. | noh or nohotš, great. |
| sak, white. | no-noh or no-nohotš, *grandecillo.* |

WORD ORDER. In general the word order does not differ greatly from that in English. The Maya, as spoken at the present time, generally follows the word order of Spanish. One exception to this rule is to be noted, namely, the subject of the verb when expressed by a noun follows the verb: [3]

u kim-s-ah Juan Pedro, Peter killed John.

u luum kah-l-ik in yum, good is the land in which my father lives.

## SYNTAX

### THE NOUN

FUNDAMENTAL PLACE IN LANGUAGE. The noun should be considered first as it plays a far greater part in the development of the language than has been supposed in the past. The important place has always been given to the verb.[4] It is not true to say that all verbs were originally nouns but the relation between the verb and the noun is very intimate. There are a far greater number of verbs made directly from nouns than there are nouns from verbs.[5]

---

[1] Compare Seler, p. 111.

[2] Beltran (§ 128) writes, "*Pero se ha de notar tambien, que no siempre esta reduplicacion significa el frecuente ejercicio del verbo ó nombre, porque á veces con ella se minora su significacion, v.g.: tš'uhuk, lo dulce, tš'utš'uhuk, lo que no está dulce, tš'otš', lo salado, tš'otš'otš', lo poco salado: tšokow, lo caliente, tšotšokow, lo poco caliente ó lo tibio. Ay otros vocablos que aunque tienen reduplicacion no son frecuentativos, porque ab origine se pusieron para significar aquella cosa sin frecuencia, v.g.: ɔ'uɔ'uki, lo blando, tšatšak, lo encarnado, sasak, lo blanco &c.*" For other forms using reduplication, see Palma y Palma, p. 150–156.

[3] Compare Seler, p. 89, 120.

[4] Seler writes (p. 66) "*denn der Kern der ganzen Sprache (el blanco de este idioma) liegt, wie der Grammatiker Beltran mit Recht bemerkt, in dem Verbum. Wer das Verbum versteht, versteht die Sprache.*"

[5] Seler (p. 89) explains all transitive verbs with objects as "nominal themes of passive significance."

Stems which seem to occupy this half-way position have been called neutral (Class III):

From **loš**, fist, **tin** (**tan-in**) **loš-ik,** I am hitting something with my fist, literally, present time my fisting it (present time).

The essentially nominal character of the Maya is seen not only in the verbal stems made directly from nouns but also in words denoting action or state and the effect of this action or state on the subject (Class I). This class of verbs are really predicated nouns. The objective pronoun often conveys the verbal idea.

Directly from nouns we have:

From **mis**, a broom; **mis-en,** I am a sweeper, literally a broomer; **mis-n-ah-en,** I was a sweeper, or I swept.
From **ɔ'ib**, writing; **ɔ'ib-en,** I am a writer.

From verbs of action or state,

From **kimi**, death; **tin kim-il,** I am dying, or my being affected by death; **tin kim-s-ik,** I am causing something to die, or my killing something; **kim-en,** I died; **tin kim-s-il,** I am being caused to die, or my being killed.

**Kim-il** is the stem of the intransitive, present, passive relationship, **kim-s-il** of the intransitive, present, passive, and **kim-en,** the past of the intransitive, active, with the verbal pronoun. As will be pointed out later (p. 64), the distinction made in Spanish between the active and passive voices is not found in Maya.

Another feature of the nominal character of Maya is seen in the fact that the nominal pronoun used with predicative verbal expressions is fundamentally a nominal expression showing possessive relationship: [1]

**tin mis-t-ik,** I am sweeping, literally, my brooming something.

INCORPORATION IN VERB. A noun, the object of a transitive verb, may become incorporated in the verb and the unity of the two made so close that the verb passes from the form of the transitive with its object to an intransitive in form. This is found especially in words whose meanings express some habitual action as chop-wood, carry-water, spend-money, etc:

**tin tša-ik ha,** I am carrying water, less common, **tša-ha-in-ka,**
**tin tša-ah ha** or **tša-ha-n-ah-en,** I carried water.
**hēn tša-ik ha-e** or **bin tša-ha-n-ăk-en,** I shall carry water.

---

[1] Compare Seler, p. 66.

The transitive form is usually found in the present and future tenses and the intransitive in the past.[1]

*Incorporation to express the agent.* Another type of incorporation is seen when the noun is used to denote the agent by which the action of the verb is accomplished: [2]

> tin pai-bala-ok-t-ik, I am rolling something towards me with the foot (ok).
> tin wuɔ'-tše-t-ik, I am bending something with a stick (tše).
> tin wop-tunitš-t-ik, I am breaking something with a stone (tunitš).

CLASSIFICATION. There is no classification of nouns with the exception of those used with numerals where there is a broad division of those animate and inanimate together with many minor classes (p. 103).

ABSTRACT NOUNS. These are made by adding the suffix -il to the stem: [3]

> kohan-il, sickness.
> kimako-il, happiness.
> noh-il, greatness.

COLLECTIVE NOUNS. There is a class of collective nouns made from the preceding abstract forms by prefixing the possessive pronoun of the 3d person singular. The root in -l is used when verbs are thus used:

> u-kohan-il, the sick.
> u-y-ooɔil-il, the poor.
> u-kim[i]l-il, the dead.

GENDER. No gender is expressed with one exception. In the *"nomen actoris"* male and female are shown by the prefixes H, for male, and š, for female.[4] The palatal spirant is rather difficult to pronounce correctly. It is a weak breathing and, in many cases,

---

[1] Beltran (§ 58) notes the incorporation of the object in this form and also the fact that the form is made intransitive in the past tense. He finds fault with San Buenaventura who (fol. 6 *ob.*) makes the past in ni (3d person) and not in n-ah.

[2] Compare Palma y Palma (p. 324) who writes, *"Hay verbos que á más del acto, expresan el objecto con que se lleva á cabo"*:

> maš-tun-te, *machácalo con piedra.*
> peɔ'-tun-te, *apésgalo con piedra.*
> peɔ'-qab-te, *apésgalo con la mano.*

[3] Compare Seler, p. 113.

[4] Beltran (§ 23) gives the particles as ah and iš (ix) but he adds that the

passes almost unobserved. It is the only case where this sound is found:

> **H-men,** the shaman, literally, one who knows.
> **š-men,** the female shaman.
> **H-ooqot,** the male dancer.
> **š-ooqot,** the female dancer.

Gender is also shown, especially in the names of animals, by word composition using the words **šibil,** male, and **tš'upul,** female. These forms are also used in some cases with words denoting human beings: [1]

> **šibil-pal,** boy.          **tš'upul-pal,** girl.

NUMBER. The singular and plural alone are found in the noun. The plural ending is usually **-ob** as seen in the third person of the verb:

> **na,** house.          **na-ob,** houses.

When a noun ends in **-al,** plurality is shown by a duplication of the last syllable:

> **tš'upal,** girl.
> **tš'upal-al,** contracted to **tš'upl-al,** girls.

The usual plural ending, **-ob** may be used in these forms in addition to the **-al:** [2]

> **tš'upal-al-ob.**

CASE. There is no case expressed with nouns.[3]

---

more elegant (*mas garbosamente*) forms are **h** and **š** (**x**). San Buenaventura and Coronel do not mention the feminine prefix **š**. Compare Seler, p. 100.

Palma y Palma (p. 221) finds fault with Beltran for calling these particles "*artículos.*" He writes (p. 221) "*No determinan nunca equivaliendo á el, un; de modo que si se les quiere llamar artículos por darles algún nombre como las demás partes de la oración, son artículos sui géneris cuyo oficio apenas se asemeja en algo al de los castellanos.*"

[1] I failed to find the form in **ton** given by Lopez (§ 27) to indicate the masculine sex of animals;

> **ton wakaš,** the bull.          **ton peq,** the dog.

[2] Lopez (§ 23) does not recognize the uncontracted form except when the regular plural ending, **ob,** is used in addition to **-al.**

[3] Beltran (§ 18) states that there is no sign for the nominative and accusative. He gives the genitive of possession as **u** but this is really the possessive pronoun, 3d person. He gives a dative in **ti** or **tial,** a vocative in **é,** or **bee,** and ablatives in **oqlal, men** or **menel, ti,** and **yetel.** These are not true cases as the dative, vocative, and ablative relations are expressed by prepositional particles.

The different relationships such as instrument, location, etc. are expressed by adverbial prepositions. The phonetic connection between these suffixes and the words they modify is weak. They are considered under prepositions (p. 107). The indirect object is sometimes expressed by the particle **t**:

tin wal-ah-t-etš, I told something to you.

ATTRIBUTIVE RELATIONSHIP. This is expressed by means of the suffix **-il**: [1]

u tunitš-il qaq, the stone of the fire, or, the fire, its stone.
u ɔ'on-il ke, the gun for deer.
u na-il winik, the house for the men.
u ha-il ɔ'onot, the water of the cenote.

GENTILITIOUS RELATIONSHIP. This is shown by the suffix **-il**:

Ho-il, a Meridano, a man from Merida (Ho).
Saki-il, Sak-il, a man from Valladolid (Saki).

HABITUALITY. Nouns denoting accustomed condition or state are made from other nouns by means of the suffix **-tal**. There is some reason to believe that this **-tal** is the same suffix as that seen in verbs of Class II and seen again in the inchoative verb:

kohan, a sick man, kohan-tal, a sickly man.
kalan, a drunken man, kalan-tal, a drunkard.

DIMINUTIVES. This idea in nouns and adjectives may be expressed by reduplication:

kah, pueblo.                                   ka-kah, small pueblo.

A more common form of diminutives with nouns is the use of the adjective **tšan,** little; [2]

tšan peq, small dog.

## THE PRONOUN [3]

The pronominal forms are added directly to the root-stem. They do not lose their identity when thus added but they are often

---

[1] Compare Seler (p. 78, 113) where he considers the attributive relationship with adjective forms and also with nouns.

San Buenaventura (fol. 28 *ob.*) mentions this use of -il as follows; "*no propia de persona, sino que por razon de algun oficio se apropia la cosa.*"

[2] Compare Palma y Palma, p. 161-162.

[3] A portion of the material contained in this section was published as "Some notes on the Maya Pronoun" in Boas Anniversary Volume, New York, 1906, p. 85-88.

phonetically changed. The pronouns do not occur as individual words with one exception (p. 42).

FORMS OF THE PRONOUN. There are two forms of the pronoun, the real pronoun called "verbal" and used as a suffix and the possessive pronoun called "nominal" and used as a prefix. These forms are as follows: [1]

| Singular | Verbal Pronoun | Nominal Pronoun |
|---|---|---|
| 1st person, | -en | in- |
| 2d person, | -etš | a- |
| 3d person, | - - -(i) | u- |
| *Dual* | | |
| 1st person, inclusive, | -on | k- |
| exclusive, | -on | k- -on |
| *Plural* | | |
| 1st person, inclusive, | -oneš | k- -eš |
| exclusive, | -oneš | k- -oneš |
| 2d person, | -eš | a- -eš |
| 3d person, | -ob | u- -ob |

DISTINCTIVE FEATURES. The Maya pronoun presents some distinctive features. Among these is the use of two different sets of pronouns for active or transitive verbs and neutral or intransitive

---

[1] Beltran (§§ 32–47) gives the following pronouns:

| 1. *Demonstrative* | | 2. *Demonstrative* | | 3. *Mixed* | |
|---|---|---|---|---|---|
| ten | toon | en | on | in | ka |
| tetš | te- -eš | etš | eš | a | a- -eš |
| lai | lo- -ob | lailo | ob | u | u- -ob |
| 4. *Mixed with vowel stems* | | 5. *Reciprocal* | | | |
| w | ka | inba | kaba | | |
| aw | aw- -eš | aba | aba- -eš | | |
| y | y- -ob | uba | uba- -ob | | |

It will be seen that these five narrow down to the two given here, the two Demonstratives being the verbal pronoun and the verbal pronoun compounded with t, the two Mixed being the nominal pronoun with consonant and vowel stems and the Reciprocal being the nominal compounded with ba. He makes a distinction (§ 61) in the nominal pronoun in the 3d person singular between that used in the present tense where he uses lai and in the preterit and future where he has the usual form, u;

    lai kambesik
     u kambesah
    bin u kambes

I see no reason for this change which he calls "*mi nueva correccion.*"

forms. There is an irregularity of usage of the two sets of pronouns dependent, in many cases, upon tense. Another uncommon feature is the association of forms characterizing different types of verbs.

NUMBER. In both pronouns there is a singular, dual, and plural.[1] In actual conversation the distinction between the dual and plural is very seldom made.

When the verbal pronoun is used as an object there is no form to express the 3d person singular. When this form is used as the subject of an intransitive verb in the past tenses an i is used to express the 3d person.

**kim-en,** I died.                    **kim-i,** he died.

A demonstrative (**leti** or **leeti**) is sometimes used when special emphasis is laid upon the 3d person.[2]

PERSONS EXPRESSED. In the nominal pronoun all three persons are expressed. The inclusive and exclusive forms of the dual and plural of the verbal pronoun are not differentiated whereas in the nominal pronoun there are different forms marking the inclusion or the exclusion of the person addressed: — we, meaning you and I, or we, meaning he and I. As in the case with the dual and plural the distinction between the inclusive and exclusive forms is made very seldom in actual conversation.[3]

It will be noted that in the plural of the nominal pronoun both a prefix and a suffix are used and that the second and third persons plural have the same form prefixed as that of the singular with the

---

[1] Beltran (§§ 225–227) notes the dual and plural forms in only two cases, and he does not fail to mention the difference between the forms of the verbal pronoun in -on and the -oneš as seen in **koon,** come (dual) and **kooneš,** come (plural). There may also be a distinction between the dual and plural of the second person as shown by his forms **koš (cox)** for the dual and **košeš (coxex)** for the plural.

[2] The early Spanish grammars have lai for the demonstrative of the 3d person. Palma y Palma (p. 209, 210) has the form **leti.** He considers this the pronoun of the 3d person which contracts to i in some cases;

    **nak leti** or **nak-i** he ascended.

Lopez (§ 49) has **lai, lei** or **leti, laiob, letiob** or **leobti** for the 3d person, singular and plural.

[3] The Huasteca has the inclusive and exclusive forms for the nominal pronoun. These forms undoubtedly exist in many of the other dialects of the Maya stock.

addition of the suffix, **-eš** for the second person and **-ob** for the third person. The **-eš** is also used alone in the second person plural of the verbal and is found in the first person plural compounded with **-on,** the regular verbal pronoun for the first person, dual and plural.

There is no way to make clear without the use of the demonstrative the distinction in the pronoun between a singular subject with a plural object and a plural subject with a singular object, as "he hit them" and "they hit him."

PRONOUN WITH VOWEL STEMS. When the root or stem begins with a vowel a semi-vowel is infixed between the nominal pronoun and the stem with the exception of the first person plural. This vowel is **w** in the first person singular and the second person singular and plural and **y** in the third person singular and plural. These vowels, when they occur here, may have had a phonetic origin but a syntactic relation is shown at the present time by the fact that the **w** changes to **y** in the third person.[1]

---

[1] Coronel and the other early grammarians give special forms for the pronoun when used with vowel stems. These forms agree in the main with those found at the present time. It should be noted that the form for the first person plural does not differ from the same form used with consonant stems, thus agreeing with Beltran in saying that no semi-vowel is added in the first person plural. The distinction made by them between the first and second person singular by the use of the regular form of the pronoun for the second person and the semi-vowel alone in the first person is probably incorrect as I found the pronoun of the first person singular (**in**) always retained and used with the semi-vowel, **w**. These points are made clear by the following comparison between the early forms and those used at the present time;

| Coronel, etc. | A. M. T. |
|---|---|
| w-atan | in w-atan |
| a w-atan | a w-atan |
| y-atan | u y-atan or y-atan |
| k-atan | k-atan |
| a w-atan-eš | a w-atan-eš |
| y-atan-ob | u y-atan-ob or y-atan-ob |

Zavala (p. 13) gives the two forms for the 1st person singular;
w-atan and in w-atan, w-al, in w-al,
and two for the third person;
y-atan and u-y-atan, y-al, u y-al.

Palma y Palma (p. 147 and p. 213–215) has the same forms as those given here, using the **u**, however, instead of the **w**. He finds fault and quite correctly,

VERBAL PRONOUN. This is found in the following places:

1. Subject of the intransitive verb in the past tense.
2. Object of intransitive verbs.
3. With verbs of Class IV.

It may stand alone only when compounded with **t** or **te** as **t-en, t-etš, t-o(o)n.** These forms are used as a demonstrative pronoun when emphasis is desired and especially in answer to questions;[1]

The verbal pronoun may be compounded with **ka** which, as pointed out by Seler (p. 98, 99), serves as a conjunction, a relative. This **ka** combines with the pronoun into **k-en, k-etš,** etc.:

**ten ken in Nakuk Pech,** I, who am here, I am Nakuk Pech.

---

with the forms of the pronoun given by the early grammarians as used with vowel stems.

Lopez (§ 172) agrees with the forms given here.

San Buenaventura uses the semi-vowel with vowel verbs even when the nominal pronoun follows the verbal stem;

**wokol-in-kah.**

Beltran (§ 45) finds fault with this with good reason.

[1] Beltran (§ 160) uses the same form in answer to a question;

**ma eš hantik wah la,** who is eating the tortilla?
**ten hantik,** I am eating it.

He also (§ 32) makes this form compounded with **t** his first pronoun which he calls Demonstrative. He uses it in his 2d, 3d, and 4th Conjugations as the subject of the verb in the present and imperfect tenses;

**ten kambesik**          **ten ɔikik**          **ten kanantik**

In the Maya as spoken at Valladolid at the present time the nominal pronoun would be used compounded with its time particles for the present and past. As noted above, the forms of the verbal pronoun compounded with **t** have the meaning of a demonstrative;

**ten kambe-s-ik,** I am the one who is showing something.

The fact that Beltran uses the nominal pronoun in the preterit, pluperfect, and his two futures shows that he has no warrant for using the verbal pronoun in the present and imperfect.

San Buenaventura incorrectly uses the forms **ten, tetš,** etc. as the forms of the verb " to be." Beltran (§ 32) does not agree with this.

Seler (p. 73) notes the use of the verbal pronoun with a " supporter " **t** or **te.** He (p. 79) points out the mistake of San Buenaventura in considering the **te** as a verb. He bases his objection on the fact that it does not, as a rule, have tense characters.

Lopez (§§ 48, 49) gives the personal pronoun in the nominative as **ten, tetš,** etc.

Nominal Pronoun. This is found in the following places:
1. Subject of all transitive verbs.
2. Subject of the present and future of intransitive verbs.
3. Possessive pronoun.

Time Particles. These time particles of the pronoun have not been recognized as such in any of the Maya grammars.[1] It is not without ample verification of the data collected in Yucatan and among the Lacandones that I venture to suggest the presence of a full set of time particles for the nominal pronoun. These are prefixed to the forms of the pronoun and are sometimes so closely joined to the pronoun by phonetic changes that it is difficult to separate them from the form of the pronoun. In general, it can be said, that the uncontracted forms are most common among the Mayas as well as among the Lacandones. The uncontracted forms seem to have been earlier than those where contraction has resulted. Among the Mayas near Valladolid the contracted forms were used almost exclusively.

The time particles seen in the 1st person, dual and plural, usually remain unchanged. The contractions of these particles with the pronoun are shown here.

*Contraction of time particles.* Present, **tan**, may contract with the pronoun as follows:

| *Consonant Stems* | *Vowel Stems* |
|---|---|
| **tan-in** into **t-in** | **tan-in w-atan** into **t-in w-atan,** my wife. |
| **tan-a** into **t-an** [2] | **tan-a w-atan** into **t-an w-atan.** |
| **tan-u** into **t-un** | **tan-u y-atan** into **tan y-atan.** |
| **tan-k** remains **tan-k** | **tan-k atan** remains **tan-k atan.** |

**Ki** or **k** contracts with the pronoun as follows:
- ki-in into k-in.
- ki-a into k-a.
- ki-u into k-u.
- ki-k into q.

[1] Lopez (§ 72), speaks of the **ki-** used with the pronoun for the present and **ti-** for the past, giving, respectively, **kin, ka, ku** and **tin, ta, tu.**

[2] Lopez (§ 163) makes this contraction **ta** instead of **tan, tu** instead of **tun,** resulting in the same forms as the contraction seen in the past tense of **t** or **ti** and the pronoun into **ta** and **tu.** In the 1st person, singular, the resulting forms in the present and past agree, **tan-in,** and **t-in** both giving **tin.** In all the other persons the forms in the present and past do not agree.

Past, **t,** forms with the pronoun the following:

**t-in** remains t-in or t'-in.
**t-a** remains t-a or t'-a.
**t-u** remains t-u or t'-u.
**t-k** becomes t'.

**ɔ'ok** may contract with the pronoun as follows:

ɔ'ok-in into ɔ'-in.
ɔ'ok-a into ɔ'-a.
ɔ'ok-u into ɔ'-u.
ɔ'ok-k becomes ɔ'oq.

Future, **he,** may contract with the pronoun as follows:

he-in into hē-n.
he-a into h-a.
he-u into h-u.
he-k remains he-k.

A more detailed consideration of these particles will now be attempted.

*Present time.* This is expressed in the pronoun by the Indians with whom I worked by the particle **tan.**[1] The union of this par-

---

[1] The early Spanish grammars do not recognize these time particles. Beltran, however (§ 262) notes the particle **tan** as expressing present time. He does not speak of the contracted forms. The Motul Dictionary has the following entry under **tan,** " *presencia,* **tin tan, ta tan, tu tan.**" Perez (1866–1877) has the following, "**Tan,** *verbo impersonal: el acto ó capacidad de hacer ó ejecutar.* **Tan u tal,** *está viniendo.*" This would seem to show that the uncontracted forms were employed in early times.

The Ticul dictionary (Perez, 1898) gives the following under **tan,** " *en presencia, con* **tin, ta, tu,** *se usa* **tin tan,** *en mi presencia, ante mi.*"

San Buenaventura (fol. 19) gives the particle **tan** as always prefixed to the active verb in **ik:**

**tan in kambesik,** ] am showing something.

This indicates that the uncontracted form was in good use in his time.

Cruz (1912) frequently uses the uncontracted form of the nominal pronoun with **tan** in his examples of the present tense. He is more inclined, however, to employ it with a negative;

**ma tan a betik,** you are making nothing.

**baaš ten tan u kănik,** why does he not learn?

Palma y Palma (p. 177) uses the forms **tin, tan, tun,** etc., for his transitive verbs in the present tense. These are undoubtedly the contracted forms of **tan-in, tan-a, tan-u** as he specifically mentions (p. 177) these forms compounded with **taan.** His interpretation of **tin,** however, differs from the one given here. He states that it is formed from **ti** " *cuando se dice al por à el.* . . . **Tin** *en el*

ticle with the pronoun is seen above. **Tan** seems to convey the idea of continued action in the present:

> **tin (tan-in) šotik tše,** I am now cutting wood or I am now engaged in the act of cutting wood.
>
> **tan-k han-al,** we are eating, we are engaged in the act of eating.
>
> **tun (tan-u) wen-el,** he is sleeping.

With vowel stems, where **y** is the semi-vowel added only in the 3d person, the form of the pronoun of this person with **tan** shows the dropping of the **u,** the true pronoun, and the **tan** is retained:

> **tan yooqot,** he is dancing.

rather than

> **tun (tan-u) yooqot.**

which might be expected.

The use of **tan** with the pronoun to express present time seems to be less common in many parts of the peninsula than the use of the **ki-** or **k-** compounded with the nominal pronoun.[1] This form is

---

*presente de indicativo tanto se puede considerar síncopa de* **ti in,** *como de* **taan in. Ti in betik.** *Esto vale lo hago.* **Taan in betik.** *Esto vale lo estoy haciendo."*

Lopez (§§ 158, 163), in writing of synalephe, uses as illustrations forms in **tan:**

> **tin bin** for **tan in bin,** I am going.
>
> **tin hanal** for **tan in hanal,** I am eating.

He makes no mention in any other part of his grammar of this use of **tan** in the present tense.

[1] Beltran (§ 161) gives the form **ki** as denoting present time when compounded with the nominal pronoun. He often uses his pronoun **t-en, t-etš,** etc., with this;

> **ten ki-in wal-ik,** contracting to **ten kin walik,** I am saying it.

He repeats the same form (§ 34) in the preterit;

> **ten kin yakunah,** I loved someone.

These sentences should more properly be translated;

> I am the one who is talking.
>
> I am the one who loved someone.

In § 101 he states that the particle **ki** appears as if it were a pronoun but it is merely used for ornament or for greater signification and denotes present time. Here he uses it without the verbal pronoun compounded with **t,** as above, but notes that it combines with the nominal pronoun into **k-in, k-a, k-u,** etc.

Palma y Palma uses the forms in **k-.** He states (p. 171) that it indicates accustomed action;

recognized at Valladolid but is far less common than that with **tan.**

The forms in **k-** or **ki-** seem, in some cases, to express the idea of a potential mood when used with the future stem in **-e:**

> **k-in putš-e,** I may strike it.
> **k-in hant-e,** I may eat it.
> **tuuš k-a bin,** where may you be going, where are you going?

The contrast between the use of **tan** and **k** with the nominal pronoun is seen in the following:

> **le winik k-u tal,** the man is going to come, the man may come.
> **le winik t-un (tan-u) tal,** the man is coming, the man is in the act of coming.

When **k-** or **ki-** is used the idea may in some cases be translated by the Spanish term "*á veces,*" sometimes.

*Future time.* This may be expressed by the nominal pronoun compounded with the particle **he.** The uncontracted forms are found in use among the Mayas as well as among the Lacandones. The contracted forms are shown above. Here, as in the case with the present particle, **tan,** the first person, dual and plural, does not show contraction. I have been unable to find the derivation of this particle. Undoubtedly this **he,** as in the case of the **tan** and **ɔ'ok,** is derived from a former stem.[1]

---

> **t-in be-t-ik,** I am doing it.
> **k-in be-t-ik,** I am accustomed to do it.
> **k-in bin,** I am accustomed to go.

Zavala uses the forms in **k** for the present, both of the transitive and intransitive;

> **k-in naak-al,** I am climbing.
> **k-in kanan-t-ik,** I am guarding it.

Lopez follows Beltran and uses the forms in **k-** or **ki-** with the nominal pronoun. He uses it always in combination with the verbal pronoun with t-; **ten, tetš,** etc.

Martínez thinks that the **k-in** is a contraction of **ka-in.**

[1] This particle for future time may be a late development. Whereas **tan, t,** and **ɔ'ok** are mentioned by the early writers as having some time significance I have found this future time particle, **he,** given only by several of the later authorities.

Cruz (1912) has the following;

> **he in ɔikti,** I shall give it.

Ruz (1844, p. 88) has the following;

| | |
|---|---|
| **ten he in binel,** I shall go. | **k-toon he k binel,** we shall go. |
| **tetš he a binel,** thou wilt go. | **teeš he a binel,** you will go. |
| **letilé he u binel,** he will go. | **leti le-ob he u binel,** they will go. |

hĕn (he-in) bin-[el]-e, 1 shall go.
he-k han-al-e, we shall eat.
hu (he-u) han-t-ik-e (han-t-k-e), he will eat something.

*Past time.* This is expressed in the nominal pronoun with the particle **t.** This **t** unites with the pronoun as we have shown above (p. 44). The resulting form for the first person singular **t-in** is the same as that for the present pronoun with **tan, tan-in** contracting to **t-in.** The history of the two forms is, however, entirely different. It may be possible that the form expressing past time is pronounced with a slightly more explosive character to the initial **t** than is given to the same form expressing present time. In the first person dual and plural there is an unusual change. The pronominal prefix **k** is dropped and the sign of the past (**t**) is changed to the fortis (**t'**). There is necessarily a slight hiatus in this form before the explosive **t** and the initial consonant sound of the verbal stem.[1]

t-in or t'-in putš-ah, 1 hit something.
t' (t-k) han-t-ah, we ate something.

This **t,** expressing a past, is undoubtedly the same as that found used directly with the intransitive verb (p. 72):[2]

t-bin-en, 1 went.                    t-han-en, 1 ate.

The prefix ɔ'ok is used with the nominal pronoun to convey the idea of action just completed.[3] This ɔ'ok is the root of the verb,

---

Lopez (§ 107) writes; " *En vez del futuro imperfecto de indicativo se usa frecuentemente el presente, anteponiéndole la partícula* **he** *seguida de los pronombres* **in, a, u,** *etc. y posponiéndole una* **e:**

he in betike, 1 shall do it.

Martínez has suggested to me that **he** is a contracted form of **helel,** now, to-day. He does not consider the forms in **he** good Maya.

Tho Motul and Ticul dictionaries give **he** as meaning " *el que, la que, lo que.*"

[1] Palma y Palma (p. 212) accepts this time particle compounded with the nominal pronoun. In the 1st person plural, however, he gives **k** or **ka** instead of **t'.**

Lopez (p. 50) has **t** in this place but makes no mention of it being the fortis. Martínez consider this **t** stands for **ten.**

[2] Compare Beltran, § 85. This tense sign, **t,** should not be confounded with **ti** or **t,** meaning " to " and given in the early Spanish grammars as the sign of the dative.

[3] Beltran (§ 85) also uses the verb ɔ'ok for a pretèrit with transitive and in-

" to finish or complete." This is added directly to the forms of the pronoun. Here, again, the Lacandones and many of the Mayas use the uncontracted forms. The contracted forms used by some are seen above. The only unusual contraction is that for the first person dual and plural where ɔ'ok-k becomes ɔ'oq, the two k sounds making a velar k (q). The verb is used in the present stem with ɔ'ok:

ɔ'in (ɔ'ok-in) wen-el, 1 have just been sleeping.

ɔ'oq (ɔ'ok-k) han-t-ik, we have just been eating something, or we have finished eating something.

CASE. It is only in the pronoun that we have any suggestion of case in Maya and even here there are only three; — subjective, objective, and possessive. The oblique cases are all expressed by prepositions.

*Subjective.* The subject of the verb is always expressed by the pronoun even when there is a noun for the subject. This subject, the nominal pronoun, is really a possessive:

winik u putš-ik Pedro, or u putš-ik winik Pedro, the man is hitting Peter, literally, the man, his hitting something, Peter.

*Objective.* The forms of the verbal pronoun are used as the object:

tin putš-ik-etš, 1 am hitting you; literally, present time, 1 am hitting something, present time, you; or, you are the object of my hitting.

In the future the -e, the sign of this tense, is placed at the end of the form:

hu putš-ik-en-e, he will hit me.

---

transitive verbs. He does not mention the contracted forms made with the nominal pronoun;

ɔ'ok u hantik, he ate it, (*ya lo comió*),

ɔ'ok u lubul, he fell (*ya acabó de caer*).

Coronel and San Buenaventura (fol. 17) show the form ɔ'ok in an example which they both give to illustrate the statement that the -ik form is used when an active verb follows a neuter and the latter does not denote action;

ɔ'oki in kanik paialtši, *acabé de aprender á rezar.*

Lopez (§ 106) states that the form in ɔ'ok is used " *con mucha frecuencia* " as a preterit perfect; " *que significa terminar, acabar y ya* ";

han-en, *yo comí.*                    ɔ'ok in han-al *ya comí.*

He has another form with ɔ'ok combined with ili to form the pluperfect. 1 did not find this form.

ɔ'okili in hanal, 1 had eaten.

The indirect object is expressed by the particle t and the verbal pronoun:

tin ɔ'ib-t-ik-t-etš, contracted to tin ɔ'ib-t-etš, I am writing something to you.

POSSESSIVE PRONOUN. The nominal pronoun is really a possessive and is naturally used to express possession. There is little doubt that the possessive idea is uppermost even in the use of this nominal pronoun with a finite verb.[1]

tin (tan-in) šotik tše, I am cutting wood; literally, in present time, my cutting something, in present time, wood.

The forms of the nominal pronoun used to convey the idea of possession are attached to the name of the object possessed rather than to that of the possessor;

u-huun Juan, John, his book.
u peq winik, the man's dog.

With nouns beginning with a vowel the nominal pronoun of the third person (u) is often dropped when the semi-vowel is added. There is no cause for confusion in this as y is only added in the 3d person:

u-y-ototš, becomes y-ototš, his house.

*Natural possession.* There is another form indicating possession made by prefixing the usual form of the nominal pronoun to the name of the object possessed and, at the same time, suffixing the particle -il to the same word. This indicates in most cases, not so much possession, as a natural and often inseparable relationship between the possessor and the thing possessed. The possessor is very often an inanimate object; [2]

---

[1] Lopez (§ 56) seems to fail to recognize the idea of possession when these forms are used as the subject of the verb. He calls this pronoun "mixed" "*porque se usa indistintamente como pronombre personal y como adjectivo posesivo.*

in qat in hant in wah, *quiero comer mi pan,*

*donde tenemos el pronombre* in *empleado, en el primer caso, como personal y en el segundo, como posesivo.*"

[2] Seler (p. 115) writes in this connection, "*Im Maya wird dabei, wenn der betreffende Gegenstand zu einer dritten Person gehört und diese dritte Person ausdrücklich genannt ist, das Possessivpräfix der dritten Person als überflüssig night gesetzt.*"

**u-ha-il tš'en,** the water of the well.
**u-na-il Chichen,** the houses of Chichen, more properly, **u-na-il-ob.**
**u-na-il winik,** the houses for the men.
**u-ɔ'on-il kĕ** the gun for deer.

DEMONSTRATIVE PRONOUN. This is found in three forms. There is no well developed system defining the noun in relation to the speaker, the person addressed, and the person spoken of. The demonstrative roughly corresponds to the Spanish, *este, ese,* and *aquel.* I am inclined to think, however, that this similarity is more apparent than real and that there are distinctions in the three sets of forms which will come out later.

The demonstrative is expressed by the suffixes **-a, -o,** and **-e;** the first denoting " this one here," the second, " that one there," and the third, " that one at a distance." When one of these is found it is always in connection with the prefix **lē,** itself a demonstrative or a sort of definite article. The latter is sometimes used alone:

**lē winik-a,** this man here.
**lē winik-o,** that man there, pointing to the place.
**lē winik-e,** that man at an distance.

The prefix **lē-,** also found in the form **leeti** or **leti,** the demonstrative of the 3d person, is used, in some cases, in place of the personal pronoun with past tenses of the intransitive:

**leeti bini,** he went (usually written **lay ti**).

The same form is used redundantly with transitive verbs and the nominal pronoun:

**leeti tu putš-ob,** he hit them, more correctly, **putš-ah-ob.**
**leeti-ob tu putš-ob,** they hit them.
**maš putše,** who hit him?
**leeti putše,** he hit him.

The demonstrative particles are also used with **tē,** as **tē-la, tē-lo,** and **tē-le** contracted, in some cases, into **t-la, t-lo, t-le.**[1]

REFLEXIVE PRONOUN. This is made by adding the particle **-ba** to the usual forms of the nominal pronoun. This is best seen in

---

[1] The Spanish grammars give only the forms **tē-la** and **tē-lo.** Beltran (§ 145) notes the syncopation of the e into **t-la, t-lo,** and they note that with **le** an e is added to the noun;
**le-peq-e,** that dog.

transitive verbs with the nominal pronoun as subject and the same form repeated as the object;

**tin putš-k-im-ba,** contracted from **putš-ik-in-ba,** 1 am hitting myself.

The n changes for euphony to **m** as Chilam Balam for Chilan Balam. It should be noted that the verbal pronoun is not used as the object as might be expected. In a past tense we have

**tin putš-im-ba,** 1 hit myself.

The normal form does not seem to be used. This would be

**tin putš-ah-in-ba.**

The reflexive is also seen in the form

**tin naɔ'-k-im-ba,** 1 approach, literally, my nearing it, my, myself.

RECIPROCAL PRONOUN. This relation is expressed by the particle **tan-ba** or **ba-tan:** [1]

**u ba-tan-ba-ob,** *entre si mismos.*
**tun putš-k-u-tan-ba-ob,** they are hitting one another.

INTERROGATIVE PRONOUNS. These end in **š** and occur at the beginning of the sentence:

**maš il-etš,** who saw you?
**maš ta-wil-ah,** whom did you see?
**baaš ta-ɔ'ibol-t-ah,** what do you desire?
**tuuš ka-bin,** where are you going?
**maš meya-n-ah-i,** who worked?
**baaš ta-mis-t-ah,** what are you sweeping?

## THE VERB

CLASSIFICATION.

I. Action or state in -al, -el, -il, -ol, -ul.
    (a) Pure action or state.
    (b) Causal, **s.**
        Root in **be.**
II. " Endowed with " in -taI.

---

[1] San Buenaventura states that **tanba** is used as a reciprocal in the 2d and 3d person plural. Beltran (§ 47) correctly adds that it can also be used in the 1st person plural.

Palma y Palma (p. 216) gives the reciprocal pronoun as **tam-ba;**
    **tin qol-tam-ba.**
In explaining this form he writes " *No vale, me golpeo á mí, sino me golpeo con otro ó con otros en pelea.*"

III. Neuter stems.

    (a) Stem alone.

    (b) Agent, **t.**

      Roots in **kin** and **kun.**

      Verbs in **-ankil.**

IV. Auxiliary " to be " (verbal pronoun).

    Root in **yan.**

V. Irregular and defective verbs.

It does not seem necessary to classify the verbs into the four conjugations according to the methods of the early Spanish grammarians.[1] In place of these conjugations it has seemed more wise to make the following divisions: [2]

*Class I.* Verbs in **-al, -el, -il, -ol,** and **ul,** denoting action or state. The ending in **-l** with a vowel corresponding to that of the root denotes the effect of the action or state upon the subject of the verb: [3]

    **tin lub-ul,** I am falling, literally, I am affected by the act of falling, my fall.

    **tin kim-il,** I am dying, literally, I am affected by the act of death, my death.

    **tin kim-s-il,** I am being killed, literally, I am affected by someone causing me to die, my caused death.

    **tin wem-el,** I am descending, literally, I am affected by the descent.

---

[1] The 1st Conjugation of Beltran and of the other early grammarians is the intransitive verb, and their 2d, 3d, and 4th Conjugations are the active or transitive verb. There is a general correspondence between these conjugations and the classes given here. The 1st Conjugation is my Class I *a,* the 2d is Class I *b,* the 3d, composed of monosyllabic stems, is Class III*a,* and the 4th, made up of polysyllabic stems, is Class III *b.*

For a comparison of the forms given by Beltran, San Buenaventura, and Coronel with forms found today, see p. 286–289. These tables have been taken, for the most part, from the paradigms given by the early grammarians in question. A few forms have been added from the text of the grammars. It should be noted that the forms of the subjunctive, infinitive, and optative have been omitted as forms corresponding with these are not generally found among the present Mayas.

[2] This classification has been briefly outlined in Tozzer, 1912.

[3] For skeleton paradigms of the various classes of verbs, see p. 283–285.

Lopez (§§ 70, 76), following the analogy of the three Spanish conjugations in *ar, er* and *ir,* makes five conjugations of the verb in **-l,** corresponding to the five vowels used with it.

These verbs may be further divided into two subclasses:

(a) Pure action or state. The transitive or applicative form is made by dropping the suffix in -l and adding -ik and other time particles directly to the root:

> tin het-el, 1 am performing the act of opening.
> tin het-ik, 1 am opening something.
> tin naɔ'-al, 1 am approaching.
> tin naɔ'-ik, 1 am approaching something.
> tin naɔ'-ah, 1 approached something.

(b) Causal verbs. These make the transitive or applicative form by dropping the suffix in -l and adding the causal s before the time particles of the verbal stem:

> tin ban-al, 1 am tumbling down, my being affected by the tumble.
> tin ban-s-ik, 1 am causing something to tumble down.
> tin kim-il, 1 am dying.
> tin kim-s-ik, 1 am causing something to die, 1 am killing something.

Root in be. There is a subdivision in Class I b. A large number of verbal stems are made by adding be, the root of the verb meaning " to make " before the causal and the transitive endings, -ik, -ah, and -e:[1]

> tin kam-be-s-ik, 1 am teaching scmeone, 1 cause to make learn someone.
> tin kim-be-s-ik, 1 injure someone, 1 cause to make someone die.
> tin yah-be-s-ik, 1 wound someone, 1 cause to make someone wounded.
> tin qin-be-s-ik, 1 sun something, 1 cause to make something sunned, 1 warm something.
> tin qiš-be-s-ik, 1 fill something with thorns, 1 cause to make something thorny.

Some of these verbs more properly belong in Class III as they are also used with the sign of the agent, t:

> tin qin-t-ik, 1 warm something, 1 do something by means of the sun.
> tin qiš-t-ik, 1 make something thorny, 1 do something by means of thorns

---

[1] These causal verbs with be form the 2d Conjugation of the Spanish grammars although they are not recognized as causal. The verb used in the paradigm for this Conjugation is kambesah which is described below.

Seler (p. 92, 93) states that t and s (z) are " employed with passive themes to render transitive expressions." His examples of the use of s in this connection show the causal relationship although this is not mentioned by him. The following sentences with his translation make this clear;

> kim, to die, kim-s-ah, to kill.

> aak, fresh, green, aakesah, aksah, to water, to make fresh.

Lopez (§ 103) has much to say concerning the forms of the neuter verb in -l and the corresponding form of the active verb in -s-ik but no mention is made that this s is a causal.

This same root, **be**, is sometimes used with verbal roots or nouns, the sign of the agent, and the transitive endings to denote an intransitive idea. The root or noun always precedes the nominal pronoun: [1]

**tal tin be-t-ik**, 1 am making it to come, 1 am coming.
**qai tin be-t-ik**, 1 am singing, 1 am making it by means of song.

These forms are exactly equivalent to the forms:

**tal-in-kah** or **tin tal**,                **tin qai.**

A distinguishing feature of Class I verbs is that the past tense of the intransitive is formed by dropping the **-l** of the present stem and adding the verbal pronoun directly to the root:

**naɔ'-en**, 1 approached, literally, 1 am an approacher.
**em-etš**, he went down.
**kim-i**, he died.
**ooq-on**, we entered, literally, we are enterers.

Thus it will be seen that all verbs of Class I may be used either in the intransitive or transitive or applicative according to the ending employed; the first, denoting simply the effect of the action or state on the subject, and the second, expressing the action or state as directed toward an object. In considering the intransitive and transitive by themselves this subject will be discussed more fully later (p. 64).

*Class II.* This class of verbs are those in **-tal** which have the meaning " endowed with." [2] They are intransitive only and form the past in **l-ah** with the verbal pronoun: [3]

---

[1] Palma y Palma (p. 172, 173) gives these forms and comments on the fact that neither Beltran nor San Buenaventura speak of them. Palma y Palma uses the ncminal pronoun compounded with **k** in his form with **be**. He gives three ways of saying, " 1 am going ";

**bin-in-kah**                **tin bin**                **bin kin be-t-ik.**

and he adds " *todas son muy corrientes.*" 1t is quite possible that the form used with **be** shows a late development in the language.

[2] Seler (p. 81) explains these forms as follows; — " *Es liegen hier alte Nomina vor.* **kuš**, *das als solches im heutigen Maya nicht mehr existirt, eigentlich* **k'uš** *zu schreiben, entspricht dem Qu'iché-Cakchiquel* **k'uš** *und heisst ' Herz.'* **kah** *ist 'das Gesetzte, Gergründete, die Ansiedlung, das Dorf.*" He repeats the mistake of limiting the use of these forms with the verbal pronoun. 1n the present and future tenses the nominal pronoun is used.

[3] Coronel and the other grammatists have a rule that verbs in **-tal** which have an l in the root form the past, not in **-lah**, but in **-hi**, as **kul-tal, kul-hi**.

**tin kuš-tal,** I am living; literally, my being endowed with a heart.
**kuš-l-ah-i,** he lived.
**tin kah-tal,** I am dwelling; literally, my being endowed with a pueblo.
**kah-l-ah-en,** I dwelt.
**tin tšui-tal,** I am hanging.

The same suffix, **-tal,** is found with verbs of Class IV and with nouns with the same meaning as above:

**keel-en,** I am cold.
**keel-tal-en,** I am always cold (" endowed with " cold).
**kalan,** a drunken man.
**kalan-tal,** a drunkard.

*Class III.* This class is composed of those verbs formed from stems which are nominal in character and which have been called neutral. These verbs may or may not be monosyllabic and they have no uniform ending in the present of the intransitive as those of the former class. The distinction between this class and Class I is seen in these two examples:

Class I. **tin lub-ul,** I am falling, my being affected by the act of falling, my fall.
Class III. **tin ɔ'on,** I am shooting, literally, my gunning.

Other examples of Class III follow: [1]

From **nai,** a dream, **tin nai,** I am dreaming, my dreaming.
**tub,** saliva, **tin tub,** I am spitting, my saliva.
**qai,** a song, **tin qai,** I am singing, my song.
**baab,** a crab, **tin baab,** I am swimming, my crabbing.

There are a few noun stems which are shortened when used in the transitive with **-ik.** This may be a case of syncope as the **t** is retained: [2]

---

The verb **kul-tal,** to sit, is an early form of **ku-tal.** I found a past in **kul-h-i,** he sat down, but the more common one follows the general rule above and we have **ku-l-ah-i.**

[1] As noted by Beltran (§§ 121, 122), **tšibal,** to bite, to eat meat, from **tši,** mouth, belongs in this conjugation. The past is formed in the regular way but the passive is irregular;

**tši-b-il,** I am being bitten.

Beltran also notes (§ 124) the possibility of confusion in the verb **tukul.** This is not a verb of Class I but a noun meaning " thought, idea " and belongs in this conjugation. The past is

**tukul-n-ah-en,** not **tuk-en.**

[2] Compare Beltran, § 124.

p'ulut, smoke, tin p'ulut, 1 smoke, my smoking.
p'ulut-n-ah-en, 1 smoked.
tin p'ul-t-ik, 1 smoke something, I fumigate, for p'ulut-ik.
mulut, a wish, tin mul-t-ik, 1 am wishing something, for mulut-ik.

The distinguishing feature of the intransitive of these verbs is that the past tense is formed by adding n-ah and the verbal pronoun to the root: [1]

| | |
|---|---|
| nai-n-ah-en, I dreamed. | qai-n-ah-i, he sang. |
| tub-n-ah-etš, you spat. | baab-n-ah-on, we swam. |

As with Class I this class may be subdivided according to the method of making the present and future stems in the transitive or applicative:

(a) Some make the transitive by adding the -ik of the present and the -ah of the past directly to the stem:

tin ɔ'on-ik, 1 am shooting something, my gunning something.
tin loš-ik, 1 am hitting something with my fist, my fisting something.
tin putš-ik, 1 am hitting something with my hand.

(b) Verbs of agent. These add a t before the ending for the transitive: [2]

---

[1] Seler (p. 83) calls the verbs of Class I "the intransitive verbs proper" and those of Class III "derived intransitives." He points out that the "intransitives proper" refer to "bodily activity, position in place, changes in time, etc.," but he fails to note the main distinction between the verbs of these two classes, namely that those of Class I express actions or states and those of Class III are all derived directly from nouns. Both may be used in the transitive and intransitive.

Lopez (§ 88) fails also to make the proper distinction between verbs of Class 1 and Class 1II. He recognizes the past as given here for these verbs and states that all neuter verbs not ending in -1 make the past in n-ah.

[2] These, in general, are the verbs placed by the early grammarians in their 4th Conjugation. Coronel and San Buenaventura (fol. 12) are not consistent in this for they include in their 3d Conjugation some verbs in t-ik. Beltran (§§ 118–120) finds fault with this although he places (§ 298) the monosyllabic stems which form the past in t-ah in the 3d conjugation. He also places here (§ 59) verbs made up of two nouns. These correspond to the verbs of agent with t:

Juan u betš-qab-t-ah u mehen, Juan called with his hand to his son.

He also follows the modern practice by making the intransitive form;

betš-qab-n-ah-i, he called with his hand.

He explains the t (§ 296), not as denoting agent, but as added for euphony (buen sonido).

**tin mis-t-ik,** I am sweeping something, my doing something with a broom.
**tin latš-t-ah,** I scratched it, from **latš,** finger nail.
**tin qaq-t-ik,** I am roasting it, from **qaq,** fire.

I have not been able to find any rule to determine which nouns made into verbs of Class III take the sign of the agent and which do not. It must be confessed that the idea of the agent is implied in verbs of Class III *a* quite as much as in those of III *b*.

Class III *a.* **tin ɔ'on-ik,** I am doing something with a gun.
Class III *b.* **tin mis-t-ik,** I am doing something with a broom.

**Root in kin and kun.** All adjectives and some nouns are made into transitive verbs of Class III by being used with the particle **kin** or **kun,** evidently meaning " to make,"[1] the sign of the agent and the usual tense endings:[2]

---

Seler (p. 92) states that the **t** denotes compulsion;

| | |
|---|---|
| **alkab,** speed. | **tšuuk,** coal, live coals. |
| **in alkab-t-ah,** I made him run. | **in tšuuk-t-ah,** I warmed something. |

These forms are much better explained by considering the **t** as agent;
I made use of speed for something.
I made use of live coals for something.

[1] This root, unlike **be,** is not found in the Spanish dictionaries in this significance. The San Francisco and Perez give the verb **kun, kun-ah** meaning " *conjurar hechizando, encantar.*" Perez gives **kin-il** as meaning " *herida reciente.*"

[2] Beltran (§ 91) has this form made with **kun** or **yenkun** with vowel stems. He does not, however, give the sign of the agent, **t.** He places these verbs in his 4th Conjugation. I could find no present use of the form in **yenkun** for vowel stems. San Buenaventura (fol. 9b, *ob.*) and Coronel have the form in **kun.** San Buenaventura changes the **kun** to **kin** when the vowel of the stem is **o:**
**t'on-tal,** to lower oneself.      **t'on-kin-ah,** to lower something.

Seler (p. 92, 93) explains these forms made with **kun** or **kin** as a means of deriving a transitive idea from nominal themes in the same way as using **ah** which has already been discussed (p. 56). All his examples are in the past tense, using **ah;**

**in yaab-kun-ah,** I multiplied it.      **in kul-kin-ah,** I established it.
If these were to be written in the present we would have;

**in yaab-kun-t-ik**      **in kul-kin-t-ik.**
and they would, therefore, have to be explained quite differently according to Seler.

Lopez (§ 95) has the form in **kun-s-ik** as well as in **kun-t-ik.** The first is, of course, the causal and the second is that of the agent. He gives only one example of the use of the causal form;

**toh-kun-s-ik,** to erect, literally, to cause to make straight.

**tin pim-kun-t-ik,** 1 strengthen something, I make something by means of thickness.

**tin keel-kun-t-ik-etš,** 1 make you cold, 1 make someone by means of cold, you.

**tin mul-kun-t-ik,** ] pile up something.

**tin kal-kun-t-ik,** 1 make him drunk.

**tin kal-kin-t-k-im-ba,** 1 make myself drunk.

Verbs in **-ankil.** There is a class of verbs made from nouns with the suffix **-ankil.**[1]

**qiq,** blood, **tin qiq-il-ankil,** 1 am afraid, 1 am trembling.

**sisit',** leap, **tin sisit'-ankil,** 1 am leaping.

**al,** weight, burden, **tun al-ankil,** she is giving birth.

**sakal,** ant, **tun sakal-ankil,** he is crawling.

**eel,** egg, **tun eel-ankil,** she is laying eggs.

The past of these forms is made by dropping the ending **k-il** and adding the sign of the past and the verbal pronoun.

**qiqil-an-ah-en,** 1 was afraid, 1 trembled.

**sisit'-an-ah-en,** 1 leaped.

A second, but seldom used, form of the past is made by dropping the suffix and following the usual rule for verbs of Class III:[2]

**qiqil-n-ah-en,**                    **sisit'-n-ah-en.**

The future retains the entire suffix:

**hēn qiqil-an-k-il-e,** 1 shall be afraid.

*Class IV.* These verbs are intransitive and express a quality or condition, having the idea of the auxiliary " to be." They use the verbal pronoun.[3]

**keel-en,** 1 am cold.                    **winik-en,** I am a man.

---

[1] Beltran (§ 87) states that these verbs are in **-ankal,** not **-ankil.** He finds fault (§ 84) with San Buenaventura for giving the forms in **-ankil** which is the same as that used today. Seler (p. 84) follows Beltran in using **-ankal.** 1 found both forms with that in **-ankil** more commonly used.

[2] Beltran (§ 87) has these forms and also one where only the **-il** of the suffix is dropped in the preterit;

**qiqil-an-k-ah-i,** he was afraid.

[3] Beltran has the same forms and he points out (§§ 185, 186) the mistake of San Buenaventura in using the verbal pronoun compounded with **t** as

**batab-t-en** for **batab-en.**

There is no doubt that the former is incorrect. San Buenaventura uses the verbal pronoun without **t** when the expression is negative;

**ma en batab** or **men batab.**

The form of the verbal pronoun compounded with **t** may be used pleonastically with the predicative expression with the simple verbal pronoun:

**ten batab-en,** I am the one who is chief.[1]

The past of these verbs is formed by adding an **h** sound before the verbal pronoun:

**keel-h-en,** I was cold.  **kohan-h-etš,** you were ill.

It is interesting to compare these forms with those of verbs in other classes. The past tense of verbs of Class I are identical in form with those of the present tense of Class IV:

**lub-en,** I fell, I am a faller.  **kohan-en,** I am ill.

This **h** or **hi,** the sign of the past, with these verbs may be derived from the same source as the **-ah,** the sign of the past, with the transitive verb of Classes I, and III, and with the intransitive of Class III.

The suffix **-tal,** seen in verbs of Class II, may be used with verbs of this class to denote an habitual condition:

**keel-tal-en,** I am always cold.  **kohan-tal-en,** I am always ill.

The verb **yan** or **yantal** comes in this class.[2] It has the meaning " there is " or " there is present." It forms its present by adding the verbal pronoun directly to the root, its past with **h** or **hi** and the verbal pronoun, and its future by the use of the nominal pronoun, **-tal,** and the sign of the future, **-e:**

**yan-en Ho,** I am in Merida.
**yan-h-en Ho,** or **yan-hi-en,** I was in Merida.
**hĕn yan-tal-e,** I shall be in Merida.

The future may also be made by use of the particle **bin** and the suffix **-ăk** with the verbal pronoun:

**bin yan-ăk-en,** or **bin yan-k-en-ăk.**

---

[1] Compare Seler (p. 74). He would translate this as " I am he, I am chief." San Buenaventura (fol. 37) considers the forms, **ten, tetš,** etc. as the verb " to be." Seler (p. 79) points out this mistake. It is quite clear that the verbal pronoun alone has the verbal idea.

[2] Compare Beltran (§§ 198–200) who gives the form as **yanhal.** This change from **tal** to **hal** is the same as that seen in the inchoative forms (p. 90). Compare also Seler, p. 82.

This verb may also have the meaning to have, to take, to hold. In this case the particle t or **ti** may or may not be used with the verbal pronoun: [1]

    **yan-en** or **yan-t-en kĕ,** 1 have a deer, literally there is, to me, a deer.

When this verb is used with the negative **ma,** there is a contraction in the present. This is not seen commonly in the other tenses:

    **ma-yan** becoming **mi nan,** there is none.
    **ma-yan-h-i,** there was none.[2]

*Class V.* This is composed of the irregular and defective verbs of which there is not a great number. Among them are the following:

**Bin-el,** to go. This verb is usually found without its suffix **-el:**

    **tin bin** or **bin-in-kah** rather than **tin bin-el** or **bin-el-in-kah.**

Here there is no vocalic harmony between the vowel of the root and that of the suffix. All forms are regular, belonging to Class I, except the future stem **šik,** and the imperative **šen:**

    **bin-en,** 1 went.
    **bin šik-en,** or **hēn bin-e,** 1 shall go.

**Tal-el,** to come. This verb is usually found without the suffix **-el.** All forms are regular, belonging to Class I, except the imperative which is **kot-en.** The imperatives

    **kon, kon-eš, koš, koš-eš.**

correspond in meaning to the Spanish "*Vamos.*" These forms show the dual and plural endings.[3]

**Qat,** desire. The verb is really a noun meaning, " a wish." It is only found used with the nominal pronoun with no time suffixes.

---

[1] Both Beltran (§§ 199, 200) and Lopez (§ 111) make a distinction between **yan** meaning " *tener* " and **yan** meaning " *haber.*" With the latter meaning **yan** is defective being used only in the 3d person.

[2] Lopez (§ 113) gives the form for the past as **ma t-an-hi.** 1 do not recognize this form. For the positive form corresponding to this he gives **yan-hi,** which agrees with the one given here.

[3] Compare Beltran (§§ 204–206) for the forms **tal-el** and **bin-el.** Beltran (§ 207) gives the verb **il,** to see, as an irregular verb. 1 fail to find any irregularity in its conjugation. In §§ 225, 226, he discusses the forms **kon, koneš,** etc. Among several verbs given by Beltran as irregular appears the verb **ken,** 1 say, **k-en-h-i,** 1 said. 1 found this verb very little used. In its place the noun **t'an,** speech or word, is used as a verb of Class III with a past in **t'an[n]-ah** and the verbal pronoun.

This stem should not be çonfounded with **qat** meaning " question, to question." This latter is found in all forms as a verb of Class III. The verb with **qat** conveys the idea of an optative mode.

> in qat bin(el), 1 desire to go, my wish to go.
> in qat ɔ'ib, 1 desire to write,
> in qat in wil-e, 1 desire to see it.
> in qat in wuq ha, 1 desire to drink water.

The regular verb **ɔ'ibol** (Class III *b*) is also used as a verb meaning " to desire." In tenses other than the present it is more frequently employed than the verb **qat**:[1]

> tin ɔ'ibol-t-ah ha, 1 desired water.

**P'ek,** dislike. This is used with the nominal pronoun. It seems to be found only in the present tense:[2]

> in p'ek bin(el), 1 dislike to go.

**Tak, taktal,** desire. The verb made from this noun differs from the two preceding forms in the fact that the nominal or possessive pronoun is used with the true verb and also that all tenses can be expressed.[3] The conjugation follows that of verbs in Class IV:

> tak or tak-tal in wen-el, 1 desire to sleep.
> tak-hi in wen-el, 1 desired to sleep.
> bin tal-ăk in wen-el, 1 shall desire to sleep.

There is also a reduplicated form, **tak-i-tak** which expresses the idea of desiring something very much, " *tener gana ó deseo vehemente de hacer algo.*"

**Qabet,** necessary. This is used either with nouns or with verbs. In the first case the verbal pronoun compounded with **t** or **ti** is used:

> qabet t-en wa, 1 need tortillas; literally, necessary to me, tortillas.
> qabet-hi t-en wa,[4] past tense.

---

[1] Compare Lopez, § 126.

[2] As pointed out by Lopez (§ 128), in other tenses the regular verb, **p'ek-t-ik, p'ek-t-ah, p'ek-t-e,** is used.

[3] The Perez dictionary gives the form as **tak-tal.** Beltran (§ 224) has the past in **tal-hi.** Lopez (§ 129) writes " *Apenas se usa más que en presente.*"

[4] Lopez (§ 122) uses the inchoative form in **tšah** for the past. Compare p. 90.

When a verb is used, the form takes the nominal or possessive pronoun as with **tak** and the conjugation follows verbs in Class **IV**. The verbal pronoun with **t** may be omitted:

> qabet in bin(el), I need to go, literally, necessary, my going.
> qabet h-in bin(el), past tense.
> qabet in putš-ik, I need to hit him.

**Suk.** accustom. This has forms similar to the preceding:

> suk t-en in han-t-ik wa, I am accustomed to eat tortillas, literally, customary to me, my eating something, tortillas.

The following irregular verbs are impersonal, using, in most cases, the nominal pronoun of the 3d person before the form introducing the expression. The conjugation generally follows that of Class **IV**:

**Pat, patal,** ability.[1]

> u pat in bin(el), I am able to go, literally, its ability, my going.
> u pat h-in bin(el), I was able to go.
> hu pat in bin-e or,
> bin patăk in bin, I shall be able to go.

The second verb in each case may take the suffix, **-e** when it is intransitive:

> u pat in han-l-e (han-al-e), I am able to eat.
> u pat in qai-y-e, I am able to sing.
> u pat in bin-e, I am able to go.

**Nama,** obligation:[2]

> u nama in bin(el), I ought to go.

**Tuub, tuúbul,** to forget. I found this verb only in one form:[3]

> tuub ten, I forgot.

---

[1] Lopez (§ 123) has this and several of the following forms used in connection with the nominal pronoun compounded with **k**, as **ku**. He gives this form as:

> ku pah-tal.

He agrees with me in the past as he drops the suffix -tal and his stem seems to change from **pah** to **pat**.

He is inclined to use the stem with the suffix in -l in the present. My forms usually omit the suffix.

[2] Perez (1898) gives the form **nah**, *necessario*. Compare a corresponding form, **nakma**, given by Beltran (§ 216).

[3] Lopez (§ 118) gives the following forms for this verb:

The active verb is:

**tuub-s-ik, tuub-s-ah, tuub-s-e.**
**tin tuub-s-ik,** I am forgetting something.

**Qaah, qaahal,** to remember. The verbal pronoun in this and several of the following forms takes **t-** or **ti-**:

**u qaah t-en,** I remember, literally, its memory to me.
**qaah[h]i t-en,** past tense.
**bin qaah-ăk t-en,** future tense.

The active verb is:

**qaah-s-ik, qaah-s-ah, qaah-s-e.**

**Tšik-pahal.** to appear. This is a reflexive verb from the stem **tšikaan,** visible and has the literal meaning, to appear itself:

**u tšik-pahal t-en,** it appears to me.
**tšik-pa-hi t-en,** past tense.
**bin tšik-pah-ăk t-en,** future tense.

**Utšul,** to succeed, to happen:[1]

**u y-utšul t-en,** it happens to me, *me sucede.*
**utš-hi t-en,** past tense.
**bin utš-ăk t-en,** future tense.

VERBS WITH STEMS in **-al, -el, -il, -ol, -ul.** For greater clearness it has seemed best to describe these verbs as a whole although they are taken up under other headings. This ending in **-l** preceded by the vowel similar to that of the root signifies that the subject of the verb is affected by the action of the verb.

These forms in **-l** are found in the following places:

(a) Present of the intransitive in Class I.

**tin lub-ul,** I am falling, I am affected by a fall.

(b) Present of the intransitive in Class III *a,* showing a passive relationship:

**tin ɔ'on-ol,** I am being shot, my being affected by a gun.

---

**ku tuubul ten,** I forget.
**tuub ten,** I forgot.
**bin tuubuc ten,** I shall forget.
Beltran (§ 203) has the form:
**ma in tubul tetš** or **ti tetš,** do not forget me.

[1] For other irregular forms, see Beltran, §§ 201, 202, 207, 211, 212, 229.

The causal **s** preceding the form in **-l** is found in the following place:

(*c*) Present of the intransitive in Class I showing a passive relationship:

> **tin kim-s-il,** I am being killed, my being affected by someone causing me to die.

(*d*) Verbs in Class III *b* which form the transitive by using **t,** the sign of the agent, have the form **-tal** regardless of the vowel of the root to show a passive relationship:

> **tun mis-t-al in na,** my house is being swept, literally, my house is being affected by means of a broom.
>
> **tin yakun-t-al,** I am being loved, my being affected by love.

It will be seen from the foregoing that syntactically the passive relationship for verbs in Class III is exactly similar to the active forms of verbs in Class I.

INTRANSITIVE VERB. The preceding classification, as has been noted, is made up without taking into consideration whether the verb is intransitive or transitive. It is well to consider these forms by themselves and endeavor to show how the intransitive and transitive are built up.

Intransitive verbs are found in all classes of verbs and they are distinguished from the transitive of each respective class by certain differences in the method of conjugation, by different pronouns or different time suffixes.

The simplest form of the intransitive verb is seen in the use of the verbal pronoun with verbs of Class IV, nouns or adjective-like forms:

> **batab-en,** I am a chief.          **batab-h-en,** I was a chief.

In the past of verbs of Classes I–III the stem appears with the true personal pronoun, commonly called the objective, but here spoken of as the verbal pronoun. This is the same in form as that used as the object of the transitive verb:

> 1 *a*.  **ah-en,** I woke up.          111 *a*.  **nai-n-ah-en,** I dreamed.
> 1 *b*.  **kim-en,** I died.          111 *b*.  **mis-n-ah-en,** I swept.
> 11.    **kus-l-ah-en,** I lived.          IV.    **keel-h-en,** I was cold.

TRANSITIVE VERB. This is sharply distinguished from the intransitive. The pronoun used with the transitive is similar to the possessive and has been called the nominal pronoun. The connection between the possessive and its noun and the pronoun used with the transitive is very close:[1]

tin ɔ'on-ik kĕ, 1 am shooting with a gun a deer, literally, my gunning a deer.

Two of the classes of transitive verbs may be roughly classified as regards instrument and cause.

The transitive verb is found in Classes I, III, and IV. Class II is not found in the transitive.

TRANSITIVE TO INTRANSITIVE FORM. Transitive verbs may pass over to the intransitive form when the combined meaning of the verb and its object represents habitual action:

tin šul-ik meya, 1 am finishing work.
tin šul-ah meya (transitive form), 1 finished work.
šul-meya-n-ah-en (intransitive form), 1 finished work.
tan šup-ik taqin, you are spending money.
tan šup-ah taqin (transitive form), you spent money.
šup-taqin-n-ah-etš (intransitive form), you spent money.

Both of these verbs are in Class I as the intransitive forms are respectively:

tin šul-ul, 1 am finishing.
sul-en, 1 finished.
tin šup-ul, I am spending.
šup-en, 1 spent.

---

[1] Seler (p. 76) makes this same distinction. He writes, "*nur die absoluten, eines direkten Objekts entbehrenden Verbalausdrucke durch Prädikatskonstruktion mit dem Personalpronomen* (my verbal pronoun) *gebildet; die transitiven Verba dagegen sind wurzelhafte oder abgeleitete Nomina, die als solche mit dem Possessivpräfix* (my nominal pronoun) *verbunden werden.*" He fails to state, however, that it is only in the past tenses of the intransitive, with the exception of verbs of Class IV, that the "personal pronoun" is used. The "possessive prefix" is used in the present and future tenses of both transitive and intransitive forms:

tin lub-ul, 1 am falling.
lub-en, 1 fell.
tin lub-s-ik, 1 am destroying something.
tin lub-s-ah, 1 destroyed something.

He elaborates (p. 89) his former statement and writes, "*Die Maya-Sprachen besitzen also transitive aktive Verben in unserem Sinne nicht. Sie kennen nur Nomina und absolute Verba, die einen Zustand des Seins, eine Eigenschaft oder eine Thätigkeit bezeichnen, die als Prädikate zu einem Personalpronomen oder einer dritten Person als Subjekt konstruirt werden, aber kein direktes Objekt zu sich nehmen können.*"

When the verbal stem combines with an object so closely that the whole idea is considered as an action in itself and is intransitive, the verb passes into Class III on account of the method of making the past with **n-ah** and the verbal pronoun.[1] This is one of the few cases where a verb belonging to one class passes over into another. The complete unity of the object with the action of the verb is seen in the fact that the object is infixed, coming before the sign of the past and the verbal pronoun. The intransitive form for the present is practically never found:

> **šul-meya-in-kah.**

These compounded forms may remain transitive when an object is expressed. In this case they usually go in Class III *b*, that class using **t** as the sign of the agent:[2]

> **tin betš-qab-t-ik Pedro,** I am calling by means of the hand Peter.
> **tin tšin-pol-t-ik winik** I am reverencing the man, literally, I am inclining (by means of the head) the man.

INTRANSITIVE TO TRANSITIVE FORM. The intransitive verb may pass to the transitive in form but it retains the intransitive meaning by the use of the root, **be** to make, and the sign of the agent:[3]

> **tal tin be-t-ik,** I am coming, I am making it to come.
> **qai tin be-t-ik,** I am singing, I am making it by means of song.

TENSE IN THE VERB. The Spanish grammars have, in addition to the present tense of the Indicative, a *Preterito Imperfecto, Preterito Perfecto, Preterito Pluscuamperfecto, Futuro Imperfecto,* and a *Futuro Perfecto.* The Present, *Preterito Perfecto,* and *Futuro Imperfecto* are the true present, past and future respectively. The *Preterito Imperfecto,* is made from the present by the addition of **kutši (cuchi),**[4] the *Preterito Pluscuamperfecto* from the *Preterito*

---

[1] Beltran (§ 58) has the same form in the past and notes that San Buenaventura makes the past of these forms by the addition of the verbal pronoun to the root compounded with the object:

> **tša-hă-n-en,** I carried water.

The correct form is,

> **tša-hă-n-ah-en.**

Beltran adds that the form given by San Buenaventura may have been correct at the time the latter studied the language.

[2] Compare Lopez, § 92.

[3] Compare p. 54, and Palma y Palma, p. 172, 173.

[4] The form **kutši** is undoubtedly from **ka** and **utšul, utši,** or **utšuk** given by Beltran (§ 222) as an irregular verb meaning "to happen" or "to succeed"

*Perfecto* by the addition of **ili kutši**, and the *Futurc Perfecto* from the *Futuro Imperfecto* by the addition of **ili kotšom**. The forms made by the words **kutši, ili kutši**, and **ili koštom** seem to me to be more or less artificial and are the result, in the main, of the desire to present every tense known to the Spaniard in his own language.[1] I found the form **utši** instead of **kutši** could be used to make a past from the present stem but it was not the common way of expressing this tense.

The tenses in the Maya, as spoken today, are: present, a past, a past denoting action just completed, a past denoting action completed some time ago, a future denoting action just about to take place and a future denoting action to take place some time in the future.[2]

---

(*acaecer, suceder, acontecer*). The form of the past as given in the early grammars use this verb as a sort of auxiliary with the present tense to form the past; **nak-al-in-kah kutši**, I climbed, literally, I am climbing, it happened.

Coronel and San Buenaventura (fol. 15 *ob.*) make a distinction, using **kutši** for distant past time and **katši** for time just past.

[1] Palma y Palma (p. 188, 189) expresses the idea of the artificiality of these forms as follows: — "*Los tiempos que aparecen aquí como ejemplos, son tomados de la gramática de Fray Pedro de Beltran. Observando, sin embargo, el común lenguaje de los mayas, se ve que no todos están en uso. ¿En qué consiste esto? ¿Será que ya no es menester emplearlos? Esto es inadmisible, porque la misma causa que obró para establecerlos subsiste: la necesidad de expresar acciones que forzosamente tienen que corresponder á tiempo presente, pasado, ó venidero. Y los que indican absolutamente estos, subsisten; los que vienen á ser como intermedios, según la expresión de la Academia, los cuales en castellano se forman con verbos auxiliares solamente, son los que no se usan. Pero la razón está en que hay otros medios de expresar los tiempos correspondientes á estas acciones cuando se relacionan con los de otras para significar respecto de ellas pasado ó futuro, como había hecho, habré hecho, etc. Lo había hecho cuando llegaste. Lo habré hecho cuando llegues. La forma del pretérito pluscuamperfecto, por ejemplo, según el P. Beltran, es* **binen ili katši,** *ó* **kutši** *como pone y se usaba antes. Yo me había ido. En vez de esta forma los mayas usan:* "
ɔ'ook ilí in bin ka t qutš-etš-e, *me había ido cuando llegaste.*
" *Si se dijera* ":
ka t qutš-etš-e, binen ilí katši.
" *ningún maya lo entendería.*"

[2] Seler (p. 102) writes, "*Das Maya unterscheidet sich von den verwandten guatemaltekischen Sprachen sehr bestimmt dadurch, dass die Tempuspräfixe in ihm nur eine sehr unbedeutende Rolle spielen. Im Präteritum treten, wie erwähnt, die Präfixe* t *und* c *auf. Das ist wichtig, weil es uns beweist, dass das Maya der*

Tense is expressed by means of suffixes added to the root in addition to a time particle used with the nominal pronoun. The former differ in the transitive and intransitive.

An interesting and unusual feature connected with tense in Maya is the fact that the forms of the pronoun vary in the intransitive according to the tense employed. *Tense in the Intransitive Verb. Present Time.* This is expressed in several ways. The most common is the use of the verbal stem with the nominal pronoun compounded with the pronominal sign of present time, **tan.** This is found in all verbs of Classes I, II, III:

Class I *a,* **tin het-el,** I am performing the act of opening.

*b,* **tin kim-il,** 1 am dying.

Class II, **tin tši-tal,** 1 am lying down.

**tin tšen-tal,** 1 am listening.

Class III, **tin ɔ'on,** 1 am shooting.

**tin siit',** 1 am jumping.

/ **tin ɔ'iib,** I am writing.

With verbs of motion and a few others a second set of forms for the present is found composed of the nominal pronoun and the particle **-kā** or **-kah** suffixed to the stem. These may be called " duratives ": [1]

---

*Mittel, welche in den anderen Sprachen sich Geltung verschafft haben, nicht ganz entbehrt. Aber diese Präfixe treten durchaus nicht bestimmt und regelmässig auf. Und Präfixe, welche es gestatten, die verschiedenen Tempora zu unterscheiden, haben sich nicht herausgebildet. Dieses Sprache ist daher genöthigt, zu anderen Aushülfsmitteln zu greifen, um die nöthige Präzision in der Tempusbezeichnung zu erreichen, und sie findet solche in periphrastischen Konstruktionen."* It seems to me that Seler is quite incorrect in this statement. The Maya has very definite tense signs. Seler fails in several cases to recognize the **ik** and the **ah** of the transitive verb as tense signs. He mentions the prefix t as a sign of the past in the intransitive only in the 1st person with k for the 3d person. The **t** is used in all persons as a sign for the past and the **k** is never found.

[1] These forms are given by Coronel, San Buenaventura, and Beltran in their 1st Conjugation.

Coronel and San Buenaventura in their paradigms and Seler (p. 102), also give the forms in **-kah** for the present of the transitive verb (2d, 3d, and 4th Conjugations):

**kambes-ah-in-kah Pedro,** 1 am teaching Peter.

This form in **in-kah** is not used in the transitive. San Buenaventura (fol. 2 *ob.*) recognizes the proper form in his discussion of the pronoun, **ten:**

**ten yakun-ik** (properly, **yakun-t-ik**), 1 shall love someone.

Both Coronel and San Buenaventura use the form in **-ik** rather than in **in-kah**

Class 1, lubul-in-kah, contracted to lub-l-in-kah, I am falling.
nakal-in-kah, contracted to nak-l-in-kah, I am ascending.
bin[el]-in-kah, I am going.
Class 11, ɔ'on-in-kah, I am shooting.

It should be noted that in these forms the pronoun has no time particle. This -kah is probably the root of a defective verb meaning, " to do." The literal translation of the form lubul-in-kah would probably be, "affected by the act of a fall, my doing." [1]

in asking a question when the pronoun is used as the object of the transitive verb:

maš kambes-ik-etš, who is showing you?

The -ik form is also used by them when one verb follows another, especially is this so (fol. 72) when an active verb follows a neuter and the neuter does not denote an action:

tal-u-kah in boo-t-ik in p'aš, I am on the point of paying my debt.

In the discussion of the pronoun en, etš, etc. (fol. 3) San Buenaventura gives the form in in-kah:

yakun-ah in kah etš, I love you.

But in fol. 16 ob. he states that the form in -ik is used if a noun preceded the verb:

Pedro kambe-s-ik Juan, Peter is showing John.

There is therefore great inconsistency in these statements. Beltran points out (§§ 153–157) at length why San Buenaventura is wrong in giving the form in in-kah as a transitive, thus making no distinction between the transitive and the intransitive. The same criticism also applies to the forms of Coronel and of Seler (p. 102).

The latter (p. 103) writes that he has followed the more ancient authority of San Buenaventura rather than " sein jüngerer Kollege," Beltran, and he accepts the use of the form in in-kah for transitives as well as intransitive verbs. As pointed out above, San Buenaventura, Coronel, and Seler are incorrect here.

[1] Beltran (§ 209) gives -kah as the root of the verb meaning " to do." He points out that it is found only in the present stem, the past being made by the addition of kutši. He finds fault with San Buenaventura for giving kibah and kib for the past and future of the form kah. Buenaventura is inconsistent in his forms for the future as these forms in his 3d Conjugation are made with ib added to the root.

Seler (p. 102) explains the -kah in an entirely different way. He derives it from kah, " a village or settlement " and translates it in the verb as " to be stationary." This is probably incorrect as the form is found especially with verbs of motion.

Lopez (§ 132) seems inclined to accept Beltran's explanation that this kah is a defective verb, meaning " hacer." It is perfectly true, as Lopez points out that the form in -kah may be replaced by be-t-ik (see p. 54), but in the latter form we find the transitive ending, the sign of the agent, and the root of a regular verb.

The present tense in verbs of Class IV from noun or adjective stems is made by the simple addition of the verbal pronoun;[1]

**keel-en,** 1 am cold.
**kohan-etš,** you are ill.
**uɔ-ob,** they are good, or the good ones.
**winik-en,** contracted to **winken,** 1 am a man.

*Future Time.* In the intransitive of verbs in Classes J, II, and III, future time is expressed in much the same way as in the transitive. The forms of the nominal pronoun are compounded with the future time particle, **he,** and a final **-e** is suffixed to the present stem:

Class 1 *a.* **hēn (he-in) nak-al-e,** contracted to **nak-1-e,** I shall climb.
Class 1 *b.* **hēn kim-il-e,** contracted to **kim-1-e,** 1 shall die.
Class 11. **he-k kuš-tal-e,** we shall live.
Class III *a.* **hēn qai-y-e,** 1 shall sing.
 **hēn ɔ'on-e,** 1 shall shoot.
Class 111 *b.* **hēn mis-e,** 1 shall sweep.

Indefinite time in the future is expressed by prefixing the root, **bin,** of the verb " to go." When this is used with verbs of Class I the shortened stem without **-1** is employed and the suffix **-ăk** added before the verbal pronoun:[2]

Class 1 *a.* **bin nak-ăk-en,** contracted to **bin nak-en,**[3] 1 am going to climb.
Class 1 *b.* **bin kim-ăk-en,** contracted to **bin kim-k-en,** 1 am going to die.

---

[1] These are the verbs given by the Spanish grammars which use the auxiliary " to be." Beltran shows the same forms as those given here and he notes (§ 195) that San Buenaventura is incorrect in giving the auxiliary as the verbal pronoun compounded with t as **t-en, t-etš,** etc. Beltran is entirely correct in noting this mistake. San Buenaventura uses the verbal pronoun alone when a negative expression is employed.

[2] This is the form for the *Futuro Imperfecto* given in the old grammars for the 1st Conjugation. The preceding form in **he** is not mentioned. I was not able to find the form of their *Futuro Perfecto* in **ili kutšom.** This seems to me to be an impossible form as the past stem is used with **ili kutšom** to express a future.

Palma y Palma (p. 189–190) does not accept this form. He gives as a substitute;

 **ɔ'ook in bin** or **ɔ'ook ilí in bin wal kaan qutšketše,** *me habré ido cuando llegues.*

He writes, " *Si se diɟera*

 **kaan qutšketšé, binen ilí kotšoom**

*ningún maya lo entendería.*"

[3] Seler (p. 110) has some very significant remarks on the particle **-ak.** He

Class III a. **bin ɔ'on-ăk-en,** contracted to **bin ɔ'on-k-en,** I am going to shoot.

Class III b. **bin mis-ăk-en,** contracted to **bin mis-k-en,** I am going to sweep.

The future of adjective and nominal verbs of Class IV is not made, as one might expect, simply by using the nominal pronoun and the suffix **-e,** but it is expressed by the inchoative form by adding the suffix **-tšal** or **-tal** and the final **-e.** The nominal future pronoun is used with these forms: [1]

**he-k kohan-tšal-e,** we shall be sick, we shall become sick.

**hu (he-u) keel-tšal-e,** he will be cold.

*Past Time.* In verbs of Class I, this is expressed by the stem alone compounded with the verbal pronoun. This form is really a verbal noun: [2]

**lub-en,** I fell, literally, I am a faller.

**bin-etš,** you went.

**tal-i,** he came.

**kim-ob,** they died.

The form of the imperative is similar to the first person singular of the past tense, as **lub-en,** fall, or I fell. To distinguish between

translates this form on the basis of a participial meaning as "it goes (will be) raising itself I, *i.e.* it is in the notion to raise itself, I = I will raise myself."

Compare Beltran (§ 137) for the contraction.

[1] Coronel, followed by San Buenaventura (fol. 7 *ob.*) gives a future in om for neuter verbs. Beltran (§ 96) is entirely correct in pointing out that these forms are not found. By the examples given both by Coronel and San Buenaventura it is clear that they have mistaken the **on** of the 1st person plural, written by them, in this case, as **om** for a sign of the future.

[2] This is given by the Spanish grammars as the *Preterito Perfecto.* Friedrich Müller (1882, v. 2, p. 309) considers this form and others like it as exhibiting "the predicative power of the true verb." Adam (1878a, p. 155) says, "The intransitive preterit **nak-en** may seem morphologically the same as the Aryan *ás-mi;* but here again, **nak** is a verbal noun, as is demonstrated by the plural of the 3d person **nak-ob,** 'the ascenders.' **Nak-en** comes to mean 'ascender [formerly] me.'" Brinton (1882, p. 31), who quotes these authorities, writes, "I am inclined to think that the French critic is right, and that, in fact, there is no true verb in the Maya, but merely verbal nouns, *nomina actionis,* to which the pronouns stand either in the possessive or objective relations, or, more remotely, in the possessive relation to another verbal noun in apposition, as **kah, kutši,** etc. The importance of this point in estimating the structure of the language will be appreciated by those who have paid any attention to the science of linguistics."

the two an initial **t** sound, usually glottalized, may be used before the verbal stem:[1]

**t'-lub-en,** I fell.
**t'-bin-en,** I went.
**t'-tal-en,** I came.

The **t'** is the same form as that used with the nominal pronoun as a time particle for the past. The **t'** is often retained throughout all forms for the past:[2]

**t'-bin-i,** he went.
**t'-tal-on,** we came.

As has been noted, the Spanish grammars all give a *Preterito Imperfecto* using the form of the present followed by **kutši** (**cuchi**). This is really the past of the verb **utšul,** to happen. It is recognized at the present time but is not commonly used. The *Preterito Pluscuamperfecto* in **ili kutši** I was not able to find.[3]

Past time in verbs of Class II is expressed by adding to the stem

---

[1] Beltran (§ 85) gives the two forms for the past, **lub-en** and **t-lub-en.** He states that the latter form is the better. He makes no mention, however, of the fact that this **t** is usually glottalized.

Seler (p. 98, 99) seems to limit the use of the **t** as a sign of the preterite to the 1st person. The **t** is used in all persons as a sign for the past in the intransitive. Beltran (§ 81) gives his examples of the use of **t** in the 3d person.

Palma y Palma (p. 185–187) uses an **h** in place of the **t**:

**h-bin-en,** I went.

He writes, "**Á binen** *se adiciona una ache sin poderse haller una razón manifiesto. Acoso sea contracción de* **hi-binen,** *partícula que se emplea en el modo optativo para significar irío, según el P. Beltron.*" On p. 209 he also uses the form in **t,** as given above. In connection with this he writes, "*Para distinguir el préterito perfecto de indicativo del presente de imperativo* '**nacen**' *sube, se antepore una te al primero como se ha visto antes, y á veces una ache con sonido de jota. Así se dice:*"

**t naken** *ó* **h naken,** *subi.*
**t naketš** *ó* **h naketš,** *subiste.*

[2] Seler (p. 98), as already pointed out, limits the use of **t** as a sign of the past to the 1st person and states that a **k** (**c**) is used for the same purpose in the 3d person. He seems to base this statement on the fact that **kutši,** from **utšul,** begins with a **k.**

[3] Palma y Palma (p. 189) also fails to find this form. He gives as a substitute;

ɔ'ook ilí in bin ka t qutšetše, *me había ido cuando llegaste.*

Lopez (1914) follows Palma y Palma in giving the same forms in ɔ'ook ili (see p. 67).

the sign of the past, **-ah,** as seen also in the past of the intransitive verb, and the verbal pronoun:

**tši-tal-ah-en,** I lay down.
**kuš-tal-ah-en ti Ho,** I lived in Merida.

These forms are usually contracted into:

**tši-l-ah-en.**[1]  **kuš-l-ah-en.**

Past time in verbs of Class III is made by adding to the stem the sign of the past, **ah,** and the verbal pronoun. An **n** is inserted between the stem and the pronoun.[2]

**qai-n-ah-en,** 1 sang.  **ɔ'ib-n-ah-oñ,** we wrote.
**baab-n-ah-etš,** you swam.  **ɔ'on-[n]-ah-ob,** they shot.
**tukul-n-ah-i,** he thought.

Verbs of Class III *b*, forming the present of the transitive in **t-ik,** do not show the sign of the agent (**t**) when used in the intransitive:

**tin ɔ'ib-t-ik,** 1 am writing something.
**ɔ'ib-n-ah-en,** 1 performed the action of writing.

---

[1] Beltran (§ 93) does not give the uncontracted forms. He gives only the forms in **l-ah.** Beltran follows Coronel in stating that verbs in **-tal** which have an **l** in the root form the past by substituting **h** for **l-ah.** From the verb **kul-tal** he would get the past **kul-hi** instead of **kul-lah-i.** The complete uncontracted form would be **kul-tal-lah-i.** According to the present method of speaking this would be contracted into **kul-ah-i,** not **kul-h-i** according to Beltran. There is, therefore, no need to make an exception to verbs in **-tal** with an **l** in the stem as the rules for contraction would attend to this.

Seler (p. 81) explains this form by saying that a **t** is added in the present and an **l** in the preterit and future.

[2] Beltran (§ 83) gives this same form for his verbs of the 2d, 3d, and 4th Conjugations when they are changed to the intransitive. He points out (§ 53) the mistake of San Buenaventura who (fol. 6 *ob*) makes these forms by using **ah-n** with the verbal pronoun instead of **n-ah** as **kambe-s-ah-n-en** for **kambe-s-n-ah-en.** Beltran (§ 85) speaks of the forms in **n-ah** as the " elegant " (*garboso*) way of expressing the past.

Seler (p. 83) states that the suffix **-n** has the meaning "to be engaged in the activity in question," "to exert the activity in question." Later (p. 110) he states that the **-n** is used to derive intransitive verbal themes from nouns. On p. 119 he gives the forms in **n-ah** for the past of the intransitive. He calls this **-ah** (p. 122) the " second **ah.**" He notes that this is the " new formation " as San Buenaventura gives only the **n** for the past. This is the case where San Buenaventura (fol. 6 *ob*) incorporates a noun with the verb as a unit. (See discussion of this, p. 29.) Seler overlooks the fact that in the preceding paragraph San Buenaventura gives the form with **-ah** and **-a,** as noted above, although he states that the past is made with **n.**

This form of the past is the one used when a transitive with its object is turned into the intransitive in form:

**tin šot-ah tše,** I cut wood (transitive form).
**šo[t]-tše-n-ah-en,** I cut wood or I performed the action of cutting wood.

A form of the distant past with verbs of Class III is expressed by the duplication of the **-ah,** the sign of the past:

**šimbal-n-ah-ah-n-en,** I walked a long time ago.

An **n** is added between the final **ah** and the pronoun for euphony. This form is seldom used.

Past time with verbs of Class IV is made by adding an **h** or **hi** between the stem and the verbal pronoun:

**keel-h-en,** I was cold.            **kohan-h-on,** we were ill.
**uɔ-h-i,** he was good.              **tšupal-h-i,** he was a boy.

It is quite probable that the actual time particle for the past with these verbs is **hi,** contracting with the pronoun to **h-en, h-etš,** and **h-i.** The Mam dialect shows **hi** as this tense sign.[1]

There are a few verbs ending in **-mal** and **-pal** which belong in this Class IV although at first sight they would be placed in Class I:[2]

**tepal,** ruler, king.
**tepal-h-en,** I ruled, I was a ruler, (also **tepal-n-ah-en** possible).
**ol mal,** to coagulate, probably from **olom,** blood.
**ol mal-h-i** or **olma-h-i,** past tense, 3d person.
**nol mal,** to blunt.
**nol mal-h-i,** or **nol ma-h-i,** past tense, 3d person.
**mutš mal,** to fade.
**mutš mal-h-i** or **mutš ma-h-i,** past tense, 3d person.

---

[1] Beltran (§ 193) states that the past is formed by adding **hi** which combines with the pronoun into **h-en, h-etš,** and **h-i.** Seler (p. 79) follows San Buenaventura and Beltran in this but he states that the sign of the past and the future really belong with the noun. The verbal character of the pronoun is sufficiently clear to justify the statement that the time particles belong, not with the noun, but with the verb.

[2] Lopez (§ 89) gives **nol-mal** and **mutš-mal** as exceptions to the rule that all verbs in -l make the past by dropping last syllable and adding the verbal pronoun. He recognizes that most verbs in **m-al** form the past in the regular way;

    **ulm-al, ulm-en**        **ɔ'am-al, ɔ'am-en**        **lam-al, lam-en.**

There is a tense representing completed action made with the root of the verb ɔ'ok, to finish. This is found in the transitive as well as the intransitive in all classes of verbs: [1]

ɔ'in (ɔ'ok-in) **hanal,** 1 have finished eating.

*Tense in the Transitive Verb.* In addition to the time particles attached to the nominal pronoun, tense in the transitive verb is expressed by suffixes.

*Present Time.* This is shown by the suffix -ik which represents the object in present time or something directed toward something in present time.[2] When there is a pronominal or nominal object, this object is in apposition to the idea contained in -ik.[3]

Class   1 *a.*   **tin putš-ik,** 1 am hitting something.
**tan tšul-ik,** you are wetting something.

---

[1] 1 failed to find the forms of the pluperfect in ɔ'okili given by Lopez (§ 77); ɔ'okili **in hanal,** 1 had eaten.
It is interesting to note that this form is also given by Palma y Palma (p. 189) in place of the artificial form in **ili katši** of the early grammars.

[2] Compare Beltran, § 235.

[3] Seler (p. 80, 120, 121) regards the -ik as showing a relative or an infinitive idea. It is certainly true that in some cases the relative idea seems to be present as when **ik** is compounded to make a form like **likil** (p. 93). But as **ik** is found only with transitives it seems to denote an objective relation. One of the forms given by Seler, **ten-ɔik-ik,** " 1 obey him or 1 am the one who obeys him," shows the relative idea but this is probably expressed in the **t** or **ti** combined with the verbal pronoun **-en,** making **ten,** and not by the -ik in ɔikik. On page 74 he comments as follows on the form in **ik,** " *die Formen auf -ik sind echte gerundivische Formen, die die su Bedeutung eines ganzen Relativsatzes oder Umstandssatzes haben.*"

Beltran (§ 172) gives the form in -ik but uses the verbal pronoun compounded with **t** or **ti:**
**t-en kambes-ik Pedro,** 1 am teaching Peter.

The forms of the pronoun compounded with **t** or **ti,** giving **ten, tetš, toon, te-eš,** are used in answer to the question, " Who is doing this? " The verbal idea is brought out in the answer as in the sentence above, " 1 am the one who is teaching Peter." A more usual way to express this idea, however, is the use of the verbal pronoun compounded with **t** together with the nominal pronoun compounded with **k:**
**t-en k-in kambes-ik Pedro,** 1 am the one who is teaching Peter or 1 am the one who is about to teach Peter.

Beltran (§ 168) also gives this form.

Class 1 *b*. **tan-k lub-s-ik na,** we are destroying the house; literally, in present time, our causing something, in present time, to fall, the house.

**tun kim-s-ik kĕ,** he is. killing the deer, literally; in present time, his causing something, in present time, to die, the deer.

Class III *a*. **tin ɔ'on-ik kĕ,** he is shooting the deer; literally, in present time, his gunning something, in present time, the deer.

Class III *b*. **tun mis-t-ik na,** he is sweeping the house; literally, in present time, his doing something with a broom, in present time, the house.

When the verbal pronoun is used after the suffix **-ik,** there is an elision of the **i** in **-ik:** [1]

**tun kam-be-s-ik-en** becomes **tun kam-be-s-k-en,** he is showing me something.

*Future Time.* In the transitive this is much the same as the imperative. It is expressed by the present stem in **-ik** with the final **-e** together with the usual forms of the nominal pronoun compounded with the sign of the future, **he-.** The causal **s** and the instrumental **t** are retained in Classes I *b* and III *b* respectively.

Class I *a*. **hēn het-ik-e,** I shall open something.
Class I *b*. **hēn kim-s-ik-e,** I shall kill something.
Class III *a*. **hēn ɔ'on-ik-e,** I shall shoot something.
Class III *b*. **hēn ɔ'ib-t-ik-e,** I shall write something.

The omission of the sign of the present transitive, **-ik,** is often made, or the **i** of the suffix **-ik** is lost by syncope:

**hēn kim-s-e,** or **kim-s-k-e,**
**hēn ɔ'on-e,** or **ɔ'on-k-e,**
**hēn ɔ'ib-t-e,** or **ɔ'ib-t-k-e.**

When there is an object expressed, either by a pronoun or a noun, the final **-e** may be added after the object:

**hu (he-u) putš-ik winik-e,** or **wink-e,** he will hit the man.
**hu putš-ik-en-e,** or **putš-k-en-e,** he will hit me.

Indefinite future is expressed by prefixing the root of the word **bin,** " to go," to the forms of the nominal pronoun and suffixing the final **-e** to the root.[2]

---

[1] Compare Beltran, § 140.
[2] Beltran gives the form in **bin** as the regular future in the transitive;
**bin-in-kambes,** 2d Conjugation.
**bin-in-ɔik-e,** 3d Conjugation.
**bin-in-kanan-t-e,** 4th Conjugation.

It should be noted that the stem in **-ik** is never used with **bin** nor does the pronoun have a time particle:

Class I *a*. **bin in het-e,** I shall open something, I am going to open something.

Class III *a*. **bin in ɔ'on-e,** I am going to shoot something.

Class III *b*. **bin in ɔ'ib-t-e,** I am going to write something.

The final **-e** of the future may be lost by apocope when a noun or pronoun is used as the object. If it is retained it is added at the end of the form:

**bin in yakun-t-etš** or **bin in yakun-t-etš-e,** I am going to love you.

**bin a hant-wa** or **bin a hant-wa-e,** you will eat the tortilla.

In verbs of Class I *b*, using the causal **s**, the future sign **-e** may occur either before or after the **s**. The latter is more common at the present time.[1]

**bin a nak-s-e** or **nak-e-s,** you are going to climb something.

**bin a kim-s-e** or **kim-e-s,** you are going to kill something, you are going to cause death to something.

---

Beltran's forms in the 3d and 4th Conjugations agree with corresponding forms given here, using the final **-e** as the sign of the future. He shows the **-e** before the causal **s** in the 2d Conjugation which corresponds to our rule as the verbs in this conjugation belong to our Class I *b*.

Coronel and San Buenaventura show forms similar to those of Beltran in the 2d and 4th Conjugations. In the 3d all give a form in **b** preceded by a vowel similar to that of the root:

**bin-in-tal-ab,**                                    **bin-in-ɔik-ib.**

I was not able to find this form used at the present time. Beltran (§ 112) notes that the form in **-b** is found but the more common form for the future is that in **-e** for verbs of the 3d Conjugation.

Seler (p. 104, 107) follows San Buenaventura in giving the future in **-b**. He explains the more common future in **-e** as having been derived from **-eb**. I see no justification for this as Beltran distinctly states that the form in **-b** is not common and he limits it to the 3d Conjugation. Seler (p. 109) makes the following literal translation for the future;

**bin-in-kambes,** it goes (it is in the work, it will be) that by me is taught = I shall teach him.

[1] The early Spanish grammars give as the form of the 2d Conjugation **bin in kam-be-s.** This probably corresponds to the alternate forms above. It might possibly be explained as formerly,

**bin in kam-be-š-e,**

the **e** being lost after the **e** of the root **be.**

Palma y Palma (p. 185) gives the form agreeing with the latter:

**bin in kam-be-s-e.**

Lopez (§ 91) recognizes the two forms of the future in these verbs.

These forms in **bin** may be used in the subjunctive sense, showing a future possibility.

I was not able to find the forms in **ili kotšom** given for the *Futuro Perfecto* in the early grammars. I question them as they are made from the past stem in **-ah** and are used to express a future.

*Past Time.* In the transitive this is expressed in several ways according to the degree of the distance in the past when the action took place. The idea of past time is brought out by the particles **t** or **ɔ'ok** attached to the forms of the nominal pronoun or by suffixes on the verbal stem or by both. The usual suffix expressing past time is **-ah** which is added to the stem.[1] This **-ah** for the past takes the place of **-ik** for the present and is the same form as that used for past time in the intransitive for verbs of Classes II–III. With this form in **-ah** the nominal pronoun is usually compounded with **t**:[2]

Class 1 *a.* **t-in šul-ah in-meya,** 1 finished my work; literally, in past time, my finishing something, in past time, my work.

Class 1 *b.* **t-a kim-s-ah in yum,** you killed my father.[3]

Class III *a.* **t-u ɔ'on-ah kě,** he shot the deer.

Class III *b.* **t-a ɔ'ib-t-ah huun,** you wrote the letter.

---

[1] It has already been pointed out (p. 68) that Coronel and San Buenaventura make no distinction in the present between the form of the transitive and that of the intransitive. In the past tense, however, both make the same distinction between the transitive and intransitive as that made here and in Beltran. Coronel changes the **-ah** of the past to **i** when a question is asked; **mak kambesi palalob,** who showed (it to) the boys?

Seler (p. 91, 92) has much to say about this **-ah**. He considers this is used with the original passive nominal roots to express a transitive idea. He fails, it seems to me, to recognize that this **-ah**, as a sign of the past, is exactly equivalent to the **-ik** as the sign of the present with transitive verbs, although later in his paper (p. 118) he recognizes the **-ah** as used " in the preterite of the transitive root conjugation."

[2] In a few cases when the verbal pronoun is used as an object this sign of the past is omitted:
**tu putš-en,** he struck me.
As will be pointed out later (p. 94) the **-ah** is usually omitted in response to questions.

[3] Seler (p. 86) gives this form excepting the time particle of the pronoun and translates it literally, " thy dead one is my father." He writes, " *Immerhin kann man sich der Anschauung nicht verschliessen, dass den transitiven und den passiven Verbalausdrücken dieselben Nominolthemata passiver Bedeutung zu Grunde liegen, die zur Bildung der passiven Ausdrücke nach den Regeln der*

As in the present there is a syncopation of the **a** of the ending
**-ah** when the verbal pronoun beginning with a vowel is used as the
object:

tu kam-be-s-ah-en becomes tu kambe-s-h-en, he showed something to me.

Action just completed is expressed by the nominal pronoun compounded with the root of the verb, ɔ'ok, to finish. The verbal
stem takes the **-ah** for the past:[1]

ɔ'ok-a putš-ah-en, contracted to ɔ'a putš-h-en, you have just finished hitting me.

ɔ'ok-k kim-s-ah kĕ, contracted to ɔ'oq kim-s-ah kĕ, we have just finished
killing the deer.

There is a form of the past in **-ki**. This is used in clauses with
the idea of " since " or " after."[2]

Distant past in the transitive is expressed by the suffix **m** compounded with the usual sign of the past, **-ah**.[3] In most cases the
temporal sign with the pronoun is omitted in these forms:

*prädikativen Aussage mit dem Personalpronomen verbunden werden, zur Bildung
der transitiven Ausdrücke mit dem Possessivpräfixe versehen werden."* 1 readily
admit the passive relationship shown in verbs of Class 1 (p. 63) but this form
is to be explained as follows; — my causing (s) someone in past time (ah) to
die (kim) my (in) father (yum). The use of the causal emphasizes the activity
of the subject.

[1] Beltran (§ 85) gives the form in ɔ'ok. He also uses it with the intransitive
verb.

Ruz (1844) has the form in ɔ'ook for the future perfect, the preterit perfect
and the pluperfect tenses.

Lopez has the form in ɔ'ok uncontracted with pronoun and a form in ɔ'okili
for the pluperfect.

[2] Compare Seler (p. 121, 122). Beltran (§§ 174, 175), notes the statement
of San Buenaventura regarding variations in his 4th Conjugation in using the
-ki and not -ah for the past. Beltran states that the form in -ki may be used
with all verbs but he limits the use to the meaning, " *despues que ó desde que.*"

kim-ki in yume oqomuol, after my father died, 1 was sad.

Coronel uses the -ki form for the past with reservation regarding clauses. He
also has the form iki when the verbal root has two consonants preceding this
ending;

kokint-iki.

The forms of the past made by adding kutši to the forms of the present
which are given in all the Spanish grammars are not commonly employed at the
present time. 1 was unable to find the forms given in the early grammars for
the *Preterito Pluscuamperfecto* in ili kutši.

[3] Ruz (1844, p. 81, 82), in his preterit perfect and pluperfect, has a form
in -ma following the -ah of the past rather than preceding it as above;

**in putš-m-ah-etš,** 1 hit you a long time ago.
**u ɔ'on-m-ah-en,** he shot me a long time ago.
**a kim-s-m-ah,** you killed it a long time ago.
**u het-m-ah-ob,** they opened it a long time ago.
**u yal-m-ah tan-il-ob,** he spoke these words a long time ago (Xiu ms.).

MODES. There is no sharp distinction between the different modes in Maya. The Spanish grammarians in their endeavor to find corresponding forms for everything in the Latin grammar give forms for the different modes which are, in many cases, most artificial.

*Indicative Mode.* There is no occasion to comment on this.

*Subjunctive Mode.* This is really lacking in Maya.[1] The idea of a future possibility is expressed by certain forms of the future and

---

**ten in sah-t-ah-ma,** 1 have feared.
**ten in sah-t-ah-ma katši,** I had feared.

Lopez (§ 98) has the same forms as Ruz, calling them a *pretérito indifinido.* He gives examples for both intransitive and transitive verbs;
**u-hant-ma-ob,** *lo han comido.*
**in-hant-ah-ma-wah,** *yo he comido pan.*

[1] Beltran and his predecessors use the form of the *Futuro Imperfecto* with various modifications for all tenses of the Subjunctive. The **bin** is dropped, as observed in my form, and Beltran gets the following forms;

| | |
|---|---|
| **ten nakaken,** 1st Conjugation. | **ten in ɔike,** 3d Conjugation. |
| **ten in kambes,** 2d Conjugation. | **ten in kanante,** 4th Conjugation. |

It will be observed that he prefixes the verbal pronoun compounded with **t.** This verbal pronoun is quite unnecessary. As the form stands with Beltran the meaning of **ten nakaken** would be, " 1 am the one who may ascend." For the *Preterito Imperfecto* of the Subjunctive Beltran uses **hi** or **hiwil** as a prefix to the forms for the present;
**hi** or **hiwil nakaken.**

These forms for the past of the subjunctive are the same as those given by Coronel and San Buenaventura for the present of this mode, Coronel using **hij** for **hi.** The use of this form in **hi** or **hij** is clearly incorrect as **h** conveys the meaning of past time.

Beltran in his text (§§ 73, 74) states that the better form of the subjunctive of transitive verbs adds a final **-e.** This seems to agree with my statement that the subjunctive is a future. He also gives forms for the subjunctive in **-ina:**
**naka-k-en ina,** or **in nah nakal,** *yo subiéra.*
**in kambes ina,** or **in nah in kambes,** *yo lo enseñára.*

It should be noted that Coronel and San Buenaventura give forms in **ka-ina**

I have regarded these forms as belonging to a potential mode. A conditional statement is usually introduced by the particle **wa,** if. The verb has no special form in the conditional clause. The future is usually employed in the main clause:

> **wa** (or **wai**) **yan taqin, hēn bin-e,** if I had money I should go.

*Potential Mode.* The idea of a future possibility is expressed by certain forms of the future. The most common is the use of the nominal pronoun compounded with **k-** (p. 46). The suffix of the future, **-e,** may or may not be retained in intransitives: [1]

> **k-in putš-e,** I may strike him.
> **k-in qai** or **k-in qai-y-e,** I may sing.
> **k-in ɔ'on** or **k-in ɔ'on-e,** I may shoot.

The defective verb, **utšak,** has the meaning, " it is possible, perhaps " and it is sometimes used in connection with the preceding forms.[2]

The future in **ăk** and the verbal pronoun are also used to express a future possibility. The prefix, **bin,** is usually omitted: [3]

> **lub-n-ăk-en,** I may fall.
> **bin-n-ăk-etš,** you may go.
> **ɔ'on-[n]-ăk-i,** he may shcot.

*Imperative Mode.* In the intransitive this is usually formed by adding the suffix **-en** to the shortened stem or root: [4]

---

for the Optative. I consider all these forms in **hi, hiwil** and **ina** alone or combined with **kutši, ili kutši,** and **ili kotšom** as artificial in their formation.

Coronel and San Buenaventura give only the present and the imperfect of the subjunctive. Beltran has, in addition, the preterit and two futures.

Palma y Palma (p. 190) in criticizing these forms of Beltran writes very truthfully, " *Y así formas del subjuntivo. Yo no sabré decir de una manera fija cual es la causa de esto; pero sospecho que consiste en el afán de calcar las formas verbales de los tiempos mayas á las de los verbos castellanos y latinos empleando para esto partículas del futuro, del pasado ó del futuro y pasado para hacer los tiempos llamados mixtos como habré ido.*"

[1] These forms correspond to those given by Lopez (p. 51) for the subjunctive of active verbs.

[2] Compare Lopez (§ 120).

Coronel and San Buenaventura (fol. 18 *ob.*) give the form **utšak** or **utšuk** with the meaning " to be able " ;

> **utšuk in beeltik, lo,** I am able to do this.
> **utšuk a binel,** you are able to go.

[3] These forms correspond to those given by Lopez (p. 39, etc.) for the subjunctive of neuter verbs.

[4] The Spanish grammars have the imperative in **-en** for verbs of their 1st

Class I.  **nak-en,** climb.
          **lub-en,** fall.
          **ah-en,** wake up.
          **em-en,** come down.

These forms for verbs of Class I are the same as the first person singular of the past tense of the intransitive. It has previously been pointed out (p. 71) that the latter may be preceded by a **t** or **t'** to distinguish it from the imperative. This similarity is not seen in the imperative in verbs of Class III which form their past in **n-ah:**

Class III.  **ɔ'on-en,** shoot.
            **sut-en,** jump.
            **qai-y-en,** sing.
            **mis-en,** sweep, broom.

It should be noted that the causal sign or the sign of the agent is not found in the imperative of the intransitive in Class I *b* and III *b* respectively.

In verbs of Class II in **-tal,** the same rule holds, to add **-en** to the stem. The typical ending for verbs of this class, **-tal,** is contracted to **l:**

Class II.  **tši-tal-en** becomes **tši-l-en,** lie down.
           **kuš-tal-en** becomes **kuš-l-en,** live.[1]

This contraction of the stem in **-tal** suggests the possibility that the imperative of verbs of Class I above was formerly made from the stem in **-l:**

**nak-al-en** becoming **nak-en.**          **ah-al-en** becoming **ah-en.**
**lub-ul-en** becoming **lub-en.**          **em-el-en** becoming **em-en.**

---

conjugation. Beltran gives nothing but the present tense of the imperative. Coronel and San Buenaventura give a future imperative compounded with the root of the verb **qat,** to desire.

Seler (p. 111) in his interpretaion of the imperative in **-en** writes, "*Ich bin also in der That geneigt, auch der zweiten Person des Imperativs der Verba neutro-passiva die ursprüngliche Bedeutung eines Participii Perfecti zuzuweisen, welche imperativische Bedeutung in derselben Weise bekommen hat, wie etwa unser Kavalleriekommando 'Aufgesessen!' — Eine Differenzirung des Imperativs und des Partizipium kommt in einfacher Weise durch den Accent zu Stande, indem der Imperativ in eindringlicher Weise die letzte Silbe betont, das Participium den Ton auf der Stammsilbe behält.*" In this he tries to trace a similarity between the **-en** of the imperative and the **-an** of the past participle.

[1] Seler (p. 106) gives the imperative of this form as **kuš-l-ah-en.**

The imperative in the transitive, as already pointed out, is very similar to the future. It ends in **-e** when no pronominal object is expressed. The sign of the present **-ik** is never found as it is sometimes in the future:[1]

Class I *a*. **putš-e,** hit it.
Class I *b*. **kim-s-e,** kill it, cause something to die.
Class III *a*. **ɔ'on-e,** shoot it.
Class III *b*. **mis-t-e,** sweep it.
**mis-t-e na,** sweep the house.[2]

It should be noted that the **-e** is not attached to the object as in the case of the future tense expressed with the same suffix. This **-e** is lost by syncope when a pronominal object or the sign of the plural is used.[3]

---

[1] This form is similar to those used with the 4th Conjugation of the Spanish grammars and of the 3d of Beltran as well. In the latter conjugation Coronel and San Buenaventura use a vowel corresponding to that of the root explaining this as formed from the future stem in **-ab, -eb, -ib, -ob, -ub** with the loss of the final **b.** Beltran (§ 112) does not accept this form and makes the imperative of his 3d Conjugation as is done here.

Seler (p. 104) follows San Buenaventura and gives the imperative of monosyllabic roots ending in the vowel corresponding to that of the root. He recognizes (p. 104, 105) the imperatives of some verbs as ending in **-e** but incorrectly derives these from a future in **eb.**

In the 2d Conjugation of the early grammars the imperative ends in **es** (**ez**). This conjugation corresponds to Class I *b*, the s being causal. It is probable that the imperative of these verbs formerly followed the rule of the transitive and added an **e.** This e was then elided, as stated before, in connection with the future of these forms;
**kambe-s-e** becoming **kambe-s.**

Seler (p. 106) in his attempts to explain all transitive forms as passives gives the following translation;
**u kambe-s Pedro Juan,** John shall teach Peter or by him taught Peter (namely by) John.

[2] Palma y Palma (p. 179) drops the **e** when an object is used;
**kanan-t-e,** *cúidalo.*
**kanan-t le ɔimno,** *cuida ese caballo.*
He adds " *Nunca se dice.*"
**kanan-t-e le ɔimno.**

[3] Beltran (§§ 114, 144) also notes this and gives the form;
**ɔik-en** for **ɔike-en.**
Seler (p. 87, 109) gives the imperative in **i** after San Buenaventura. He explains the preceding form as follows;
**ɔiki-en** or **ɔik-én,** derived from **ɔiki-b-en,** obey me, or " that one to whom (by thee) obedience shall be, am I."

*Optative.* The idea expressed by the Spanish, *Ojala,* forming an optative, is shown in Maya by the root of the verb **qat,** to desire with the future stem.[1] This form is considered under the irregular verbs (p. 60).

THE PASSIVE. It has already been pointed out (p. 63) that syntactically many of the forms expressing the passive relationship cannot be separated from those expressing the active voice.[2] It has seemed best to consider the passive voice here as as whole however.

*Present Time.* In the sense of action still going on, this is expressed by the suffix in **-al, -el, -il, -ol, -ul** which gives the idea of the subject as being affected by the action of the verb. This suffix in **-l** is found either alone, with the causal **s,** or with the instrumental **t.**

Class I *a* and I *b* both use the causal **s** with the suffix **-l** to express a passive relationship:

> Class I *a*. **tun het-s-el,** it is being opened, literally, its being affected by someone causing it to open.
>
> **tin naɔ'-s-al,** I am being approached, literally, my being affected by someone causing a nearness to me.
>
> **tin ah-s-al,** I am being awakened, literally, my being affected by someone causing me to wake.

---

I cannot agree with him in this as the passive relationship is in no way expressed by the simple root of the verb nor can this form be derived from **ɔiki-b-en.**

Coronel and San Buenaventura give forms for a future imperative with the root of the verb **kat,** possibly from the root **qat,** " to ask ";

> 1st Conjugation, **kat a nak-ăk-etš.**
> 2d Conjugation, **kat a kambes.**
> 3d Conjugation, **kat a ɔik-ib.**
> 4th Conjugation, **kat a kanant-e.**

These forms are similar to the future exchanging the **bin** for **kat.** Seler (p. 106) seems to recognize these forms in **ak** only in the 3d person.

[1] Coronel in his paradigms makes an optative by prefixing **kahi** to the future stem. This is undoubtedly the root of the verb **qat.** In his text he states that the optative is made by prefixing **kaina** to the *Futuro Imperfecto.* San Buenaventura gives the form in **kaina** for the optative in addition to the form in **kahi.** Beltran does not show the optative in his paradigms.

[2] Seler endeavors to make out, as previously shown, that all transitive expressions are passive in construction. I think he is incorrect in making this sweeping statement. He admits (p. 86, 90) there are various features which upset this theory.

Class I *b*, **tun ban-s-al,** it is being thrown down, literally, its being affected by someone causing it to tumble down.

**tin kim-s-il,** I am being killed, literally, my being affected by someone causing me to die.

It is interesting to note that, whereas in the passive both subdivisions of Class I use the causal, in the active, transitive, of verbs of Class I *b* the causal is still retained but in Class I *a* it is not found:

Class I *a*.   **tun het-ik,** he is opening something.
          **tin naɔ'-ik,** I am approaching something.
          **tin ah-ik,** I am awakening someone.
Class I *b*.   **tun ban-s-ik,** he is destroying something.
          **tin kim-s-ik,** I am killing something.

There are some cases in the passive where the vowel of the root does not agree with the vowel of the suffix. There is a tendency to use **-al** as the suffix even where the vowel of the root is not **a**: [1]

Class III. These verbs from neuter stems express the passive relationship by adding **-l** either directly to the stem in Class III *a* or to the stem with the sign of the agent, **t,** in Class III *b*; [2]

Class III *a*.   **tin loš-ol,** I am being hit, literally, my being affected by a fist.
          **tin haɔ'-al,** I am being whipped.
Class III *b*.   **tun mis-t-al,**[3] it is being swept, literally, its being affected by means of a broom.
          **tun han-t-al,** it is being eaten.

When the stem ends in a vowel a **b** is prefixed to the suffix: [4]

**tun ɔa-b-al,** it is being given.
**tan-k tši-b-il,** we are being bitten.
**tin tš'a-b-al,** I am being taken.

---

[1] Beltran (§ 56) makes the passive of verbs of his 1st Conjugation by adding **-sal** or **-tal** to the root. He makes no mention in these verbs of an agreement between the vowel of the root with that of the suffix. The **s** of his suffix **-sal** is undoubtedly the causal and the **t** of the suffix **-tal** is the instrument. Palma y Palma (p. 130) has the same rule.

[2] Beltran (§ 57) gives these same forms for the passive and notes the agreement between the vowel of the stem and that of the suffix. All state that verbs in the passive go in their 1st Conjugation.

[3] The same tendency to use the suffix **-al** even when the vowel of the stem is not **a** is seen here as with verbs of Class I.

[4] Coronel and his followers have this same form. Beltran (§ 57) has the form in **-bal** for the passive for verbs of his 2d and 4th Conjugations;
From **kambesah** he gets the passive, **kambesabal.**
From **kanantah** he gets **kanantabal.**

*Future Time.* In the passive this is expressed by the same stems as in the present with the time particle of the future used with the nominal pronoun and the sign of the future, -e:

Class  I *a.*  hu (he-u) het-s-el-e, it will be opened.
Class  I *b.*  hēn (he-in) kim-s-il-e, I shall be killed, literally, in future time, my being affected by someone causing me to die in future time.
       hēn kam-be-s-al-e, I shall be shown.
Class III *a.*  hēn kat-al-e, I shall be asked.
       hēn wal-al-e, I shall be mentioned.
       hēn ɔ'on-ol-e, I shall be shot, literally, I am affected by a gun
Class III *b.*  hu ɔ'ib-t-il-e, it will be written.
       hu han-t-al-e, it will be eaten.

There is a second form for the future in the passive corresponding to the form in **bin** in the active:

Class  I *a.*  bin man-s-al-ăk-en, contracting to bin man-s-ăk-en, I am going to be passed (on the road).
       bin nak-s-al-ăk-en, contracting to bin nak-s-ăk-en, I am going to be climbed.
Class  I *b.*  bin kim-s-al-ăk-en, contracting to bin kim-s-ăk-en, I am going to be killed, literally, I am going to be affected by someone causing me to die.
Class III *a.*  bin kat-al-ăk-en, I am going to be asked.
       bin al-al-ăk-en, I am going to be awakened.
       bin ɔ'on-ol-ăk-en, I am going to be shot.
Class III *b.*  bin mis-t-al-ak-i, contracted to bin mis-t-ăk-i, it is going to be swept, it will be swept.

It should be noted that verbs in Class III *a*, if contracted in these forms, would have the same forms in the future of the passive as in the intransitive active. There is no chance of confusion in the contracted forms of verbs in the other classes as the causal **s** is not found in the intransitive active in verbs of Classes I *a* and I *b*, and the agent **t** is not found in the corresponding forms in verbs of Class III *b*.

---

I consider the passives of these verbs should be **kambe-s-al** and **kanan-t-al.** The form **kambesabal** is the passive participle.

Beltran (§ 116) objects to some of the forms of San Buenaventura in the passive of verbs of the 3d Conjugation where the latter states that a **b** is added together with a vowel similar to that of the root;

San Buenaventura gives **yey-b-il,** Beltran gives **yey-al.**

San Buenaventura gives **nuk-b-ul,** Beltran gives **nuk-al.**

The forms of Beltran agree with those given here.

*Past Time.* This is expressed in the passive in all verbs which have a passive by adding a **b** to the sign of the past and the verbal pronoun directly to the stem in verbs of Class III *a*, to the stem with the sign of the agent in Class III *b*, and to the stem with the causal **s** in verbs of Class I:

| Class I. | ah-s-ah-b-en, I was awakened. |
|---|---|
| | naɔ'-s-ah-b-en, I was approached. |
| Class III *a*. | natš-ah-b-en, I was bitten. |
| | ɔ'on-ah-b-en, I was shot. |
| Class III *b*. | han-t-ah-b-i, it was eaten. |

It is not clear how these forms have been derived. The usual sign of the past is **ah**. The **b** is seen in the present tense of the passive between two vowels, as already pointed out (p. 85).

The **b** is often exchanged for a **n** and we get other forms expressing the same ideas as above:

natš-ah-n-en, I was bitten.[1]
ɔ'on-ah-n-en, I was shot.
ah-s-ah-n-en, I was awakened.

This form in **n** is seen in the past participle:

natš-an, a thing bitten.
ɔ'on-an, a thing shot.
kim-s-an, a thing killed, literally, a thing caused to die.

There is another form expressing distant past in the passive made by duplicating the sign of the past, **-ah**:

ɔ'on-ah-ah-n-en, I was shot a long time ago.

VERBAL NOUNS. There is a large class of verbal nouns made directly from the stem by the use of the verbal pronoun. This pronoun always carries with it the verbal idea, "the one who does something" or "the one affected by the action of the verb." It is never found in the present tense with verbs. It is used with no sign of the past in verbs of Class I to express past time. These forms are really verbal nouns;

---

[1] It is interesting to compare these forms with the intransitive, active, past tense;

natš-n-ah-en, I performed the action of biting.
natš-ah-n-en, I was bitten.
ɔ'on-[n]-ah-en, I shot, literally, I was a gunner.
ɔ'on ah-n-en, I was shot, literally, I was gunned.

Class I. **lub-en,** I fell, I am a faller, I am one who falls.
**man-en,** I bought, I am a buyer, I am a merchant.
**han-en,** I ate, I am an eater.
**nak-en,** I climbed, I am a climber.
**kim-s-en,** I am a matador, I am one who causes something to die.

With verbs of Class III verbal nouns are made in the same way;

ɔ'on-en, I am a gunner.
qai-y-etš, you are a singer.
ooqot-en, I am a dancer.

It should be noted that, unlike verbs of Class I, these forms in Class III are not the same as those used for the past tense. The past of verbs in Class III is made by infixing **n** and the sign of the past, **-ah,** between the root and the verbal pronoun:

ɔ'on-[n]-ah-en, I shot.
qai-n-ah-etš, you sang.
ooqot-n-ah-en, I danced.

The prefixes of gender, **H** for male, and **š** for female, are used with the verbal nouns:

**H-man-en,** I am a male merchant.
**š-qai-etš,** you are a female singer.

There is a chance for confusion in the 1st person of the verbal pronoun especially with verbs of Class I as the same form is used for the imperative of the intransitive as well as for the past tense. As already pointed out (p. 72), the form for the past usually has an initial **t** or **t'** and the verbal noun has the sign of the gender.

There is a class of nouns made from verbs by means of the suffix **-b** preceded by the vowel corresponding to that of the stem.[1] This suffix denotes the instrument with which the action is performed. This **b** undoubtedly is the same as that found in the past tense of the passive.

**bah-ab,** a hammer, from **bah,** to nail.
**he-eb,** a key, from **he,** to open, the instrument by which something is opened.

*Past Participle.* Verbal nouns having the meaning usually assigned to the past participle end in **-an.**[2] This is added to the root;

---

[1] Compare Seler, p. 107.
[2] Lopez (§ 101) states that this participle is formed in **aan** or **ahan:**
**mentaan** or **mentahan,** *hecho.*
**p'oaan,** *lavado.*

neither causal sign nor that of the agent appear in Classes I *b* and III *b* respectively. In verbs of Class II the **t** of the suffix **-tal** may be retained, giving **-tan**, or the form may be made in **-lan**.[1]

Class I *a*. **nak-an**, a thing fallen.
Class I *b*. **kim-an**, a thing dead.[2]
Class II. **kuš-t-an** or **kuš-l-an**, a thing living.
Class III *a*. **ɔ'on-an**, a thing shot.
Class III *b*. **mis-an**, a thing swept.[3]

The plural of the participle follows the same rule as that for the adjective, adding the suffix, **-tăk** or **-ăk**. This may be used with or without the regular plural ending **-ob**. The latter may also be used alone:

**ɔ'iban-ăk, ɔ'iban-ăk-ob, ɔ'iban-ob**, things written.

*Passive Participle.* The passive idea in verbal nouns is brought out by means of the suffixes **-bal** or **-bil** added to the passive stem.[4] When the stem ends in a consonant an **a** is added for euphony between the consonant of the stem and that of the suffix:[5]

Class I *a*. **nak-s-a-bal**, a thing to be climbed.
Class I *b*. **kim-s-a-bal**, a thing to be killed.
Class III *a*. **ɔ'ɵn-a-bal**, a thing to be shot.
Class III *b*. **mis-t-a-bal**, a thing to be swept.

*Infinitive.* There is no infinitive in Maya.[6] The infinitive construction, used in English, after verbs denoting purpose, desire,

---

[1] Beltran (§ 126) and Lopez (§ 101) give the participle of these verbs as ending in **-lan**. I am rather inclined to agree that this is a better form than the one in **-tan**.

[2] Lopez (§ 101) gives this form as **kim-en**.

[3] Beltran (§ 170) states that the participle of verbs corresponding to those of Class III *b* may have the **t** as well as the **-an**:
**ɔ'ib-t-an** or **ɔ'ib-an**, a written thing.

[4] These forms correspond to the future passive participle of the Spanish grammars;

    **nak-s-a-bal**.               **kam-be-s-bil** or **kam-be-s-bal**.

[5] In verbs of Class I the stem would always end in a consonant as the passive stem takes the causal **s**. In verbs of Class III *b*, it also ends in a consonant as this class takes the sign of the agent, **t**, as a part of the stem in the passive.

[6] Much is made in the early Spanish grammars of the infinitive. In their 1st Conjugation the present of the infinitive is the stem in l (**nakal**). The past infinitive in Beltran (**naki il**) is undoubtedly incorrect as it is inconsistent with the past forms he gives in the other conjugations. Coronel and San Buenaventura have a past in **nakijl** which shows the **h** (j) sound which is the usual

ability, etc. is expressed in Maya by a future and is really in the nature of a clause introduced, in many cases, by the particle **ka** (p. 92).

INCHOATIVE OR INCEPTIVE VERBS. These are made by adding the suffix **-hal** or **-tal** to the verbal stem with the nominal pronoun.[1] It should be noted that these inchoative verbs are probably distinct from verbs of Class II in **-tal** which make their past in **l-ah,** although the suffix **-tal** is common to both forms;

> **tin winik-tal** or **winik-hal,** I am becoming a man.
> **tin kana-tal,** I am increasing in height.
> **tun yek-tal,** it is growing dark.

The future is formed in two ways, by using the time particle of the future with the nominal pronoun and the suffix **-e,** retaining the **-tal,** or changing the sign **ah** of the past in the particle **tš-ah** to **al,** obtaining the form **tš-al:**

---

method of showing past time. In the 2d Conjugation, Coronel and San Buenaventura have forms ending in **-ah.** These are clearly incorrect for the present, as pointed out by Beltran (§ 105), and San Buenaventura seems to recognize this as he gives a second form for the present which corresponds with that of Beltran. In the 4th Conjugation, Coronel and San Buenaventura are probably incorrect as they give the past participle, **kanan,** for the present of the infinitive. Beltran in this conjugation gives for the past infinitive a passive form, **kanantabil.** Martínez says there is an infinitive in **-al, -el, -il, -ol** and **-ul** when "taken in a general sense":

> **u tanlah-il Dios,** el servir a Dios,
> **u han-al pišan,** el comer de los almas.
> **u ɔ'on-ol ke,** el cazar venados.

[1] Beltran (§ 90) uses the term neuter in describing these verbs in **-hal.** He does not mention the corresponding form in **-tal** but gives a form in **-hil.** He states that the past is made in **hi,** the future in **ak.**

Coronel and San Buenaventura (fol. 9b, ob.) have only the forms in **-tal.** This is one of the cases where the two older authorities agree with the modern usage.

Seler (p. 80) states that the forms in **-hal,** used by Beltran, are older than the forms in **-tal.** It is difficult to reconcile this statement with the fact that Coronel and San Buenaventura give the forms in **-tal.** Furthermore Seler endeavors to connect the form in **-tal** with the t or te used as a demonstrative with the verbal pronoun. He correctly points out the limitations of meaning when **-tal** is used as that of an inchoative. He uses the form in **kah** with these verbs;

> **winik-hal-in-kah** or **winik-tal-in-kah.**

I did not find this form in common use. The nominal pronoun with the time particle is used as shown below.

**hēn winik-tal-e** or **winik-tš-al-e**, I shall become a man.
**hek kohan-tš-al-e**, we shall become ill.

The past tense seems to be seldom used with these verbs. When found the suffix **-tal** changes to **tš** and the sign of the past, **ah**, with the verbal pronoun is used:

**winik-tš-ah-etš**, you became a man.
**kana-tš-ah-en**, I increased in height.

There seems little doubt that, originally, both **-tal** or **-hal** and **-tš** were used to express the inchoative idea with no distinction as now observed between the use of **-tal** in the present and **-tš** in the past. This supposition is strengthened by the fact that both **-tal** and **-tšal** are found in the future.[1]

Attention may be called again to the nouns denoting accustomed state or condition in **-tal** (p. 38).

ITERATIVE OR FREQUENTATIVE VERBS. These are made by duplicating the first syllable:[2]

**tin bi-qab**, I tap with the fingers.
**tin bi-bi-qab**, I tap frequently with the fingers.
**tin la-k-etš**, I strike you with the palm.
**tin la-la-k-etš**, I strike you several times with the palm.

REFLEXIVE VERBS. There is a class of verbs used with the particle **-pahal**, which are reflexive:[3]

---

[1] Seler (p. 81) gives both the forms in **-hal** or **-tal** and **-tšahal** for the present; **winik-hal** or **winik-tal** to be a man, to prove himself a man.

**winik-tšah-al**, just now to be a man, to become manly, attain a position. I consider that the **-ah** of his infix **-tšah** is the sign of the past and should not be used in the present tense. The proper form would be;

**tin winik-tš-al.**

Seler (p. 84, 85) has much to say regarding the use of **h** which "added to nouns forms neutral themes with the meaning 'made for this and that,' 'being this and that,' e.g.;

**eeq-ha-al**, to be black, to become black."

This is really the inchoative verb and the more usual form is not **-hal** but **-tal.**

[2] Beltran (§ 127) states that this type of verbs almost always is found in the 4th Conjugation. He adds that the adverb **ɔ'eɔ'etak**, signifying *á menudo ó con frecuencia* is used with verbs of his 1st Conjugation;

**lubul**, to fall.
**ɔ'eɔ'etak lubul**, to fall frequently.

Palma y Palma (p. 163–167) describes these forms very clearly.

[3] See also verbs used with the reflexive pronoun, p. 50.

**tšun,** begin.

**tun tšun-pa-hal,** it begins itself.

**tšun-pa-hi,** it began itself.

**tun tšun-pa-hal qin,** the day is beginning.

**tun lotš-pa-hal,** it bends itself.

RECIPROCAL VERBS. See under Reciprocal Pronoun, p. 51.

CLAUSES. *Final clauses expressing purpose or motive.* These are made by using a future construction. The nominal pronoun takes no time particle but the **-e** of the future is retained: [1]

> **tin bin in bet-e,** I go to make something, literally, in present time, my going, my making something in future time.

The form in **-kah** can also be used to express the same idea;

> **bin-in-kah in bet-e,** contracted to **bin-in-k-in bet-e.** I am going to make it.
>
> **bin-in-kah utial in wil-e,** I go in order to see it.
>
> **bin-in-kah in wil-e,** contracted to **bin-in-k-in wil-e,** I go to see it.

When the object is expressed, the **-e** of the future is usually dropped;

> **bin-in-kah in bet na,** I go to build a house.

*Object clauses expressing ability, knowledge, desire, fear, compulsion, command, etc.* These also take the future construction. In some cases the time particle is omitted with the nominal pronoun;

> **in qat in wil-e,** I desire to see it.
>
> **u pat in ɔ'ib-t-e,** I am able to write it.
>
> **in wohel in be-t-e,** I know how to do it.

As in the preceding examples, when the object is expressed by a noun, the **-e** is usually dropped:

> **in qat in hant wa,** I desire to eat tortillas.
>
> **u pat in ɔ'ib-t huun,** I am able to write a letter.

The particla **ka** often introduces these clauses especially with the form of the indefinite future in **ăk** and the verbal pronoun:

> **in qat ka uɔ-s-ăk-etš,** I desire you to be good.
>
> **leeti u qat qai-n-ăk-en,** he (demonstrative) wishes me to sing.
>
> **in qat tetš ka wal-ik-t-en,** I wish you to tell me.

---

[1] Beltran (§§ 99, 100) notes that the future forms are used in some cases after the verb, to desire, where one would expect the infinitive to be used.

or  **in qat tetš ka wal-t-en.**
**tin al-ik ka alkab-n-ăk-en,** I say that I shall run.
**saken ka kohan-(n)-ăk-en,** I fear I shall be ill.
**tin al-t-etš** or **al-ah-t-etš ka sik-etš,** I told you to go.

*Relative clauses.* There is no special difference between the verb in a relative clause and that in any other place:

**lē winik qai-n-ah-i kim-i,** the man who sang is dead, literally, the man sang, he died.

There is a relative relation introduced by the particle **lik** or **likil** denoting in which, by which, for which, etc: [1]

**likil in wenel,**    (the object) in which I sleep, my hammock.
**likil in meya,**    (the object) with which I work, my pencil.
**likil q kuš-tal,**   (the object) by which we live, maize.
**likil in putš-ik,**   (the object) with which I strike, my stick.

There is a relative idea conveyed in the compound formed of the particle **t** or **ti** and the verbal pronoun:

**maš putš-ah-en,** who hit me?
**t-en putš-etš,** I am the one who hit you.

*Temporal Clauses.* These are usually introduced by the particle **ka**:

**tin wal-ah-t-etš ka kutš-en,** I told it to you when I arrived.
**k-in qai k-en sik-en-e,** I may sing when I arrive.

Sometimes the particle is repeated before the main clause as well as before that of the temporal:

**ka tal-etš-e ka kohan-h-en,** when you came, I was ill.
**le ka ɔ'ok in qai-y-e ka bin-en,** after I had sung, I went.

*Conditional Clauses.* These are usually introduced by the particle **wa,** if, or **keš,** although. The verb in these clauses does not differ from that in the main part of the sentence:

---

[1] Beltran (§§ 94, 95) has the form in **lik** or **likil** and states that it denotes *en que, con que, de que, por donde, porque,* etc., also " *que suele hacerse lo que el verbo significa.*" :

**uɔ yaab qan likil á wenel,** good is the hammock in which you are accustomed to sleep.
**uɔ luum kuš lik in yum,** good is the land in which my father lives.

Beltran (§ 240) has another *mutanza* with intransitive verbs in the past when used in a clause meaning *"en que"* etc. In his example he adds a **k** in the 3d person;

**lai tš'en lub-k-i,** Juan, this is the well into which John fell.

Seler (p. 120, 121) identifies this suffix, **-lik** as a combination of **-ik,** our sign of the present transitive verb, and the suffixes **-al, -el, -il, -ol, -ul.**

wa ka al-ik-t-en k-in bin, if you tell it to me, I shall (may) go.
keš tal-i bin-en, although he came, I went.
keš tun qai sut-on t'-na-i, although he is singing, we returned to our house.

INTERROGATIVE. In general there seems to be no particular form of particle marking the interrogative. The rising voice alone seems to indicate a question. This may be a convention of later times. The particle **wa** is sometimes used as an interrogative with the meaning " by chance " or " perhaps " and comes as the final suffix: [1]

ooqot-n-ah-etš-wa, did you, by chance, dance?
t-a-putš-ah-wa, did you, by chance, strike him?

When the interrogative is used with the transitive verb in the past tense the sign of the past is sometimes omitted both in the question and in the answer. A final -e is found in the 3d person in these forms:

maš putš-en, who struck me?
t-en putš-etš, I was the one who struck you.
maš putš-e, who struck him?
t-en putš-e, I struck him, I am the one who struck him.
maš mis-t-e na, who swept the house?
t-en mis-t-e na, I swept the house.

When the answer to a question is in the negative the suffix -i or -il is usually found with the negative **ma**. The use of this same suffix is noted (p. 104) with the adverbs:

bin-etš, did you go?
ma bin-en-i, no, I did not go.

kohan-ob, are they ill?
ma kohan-ob-i, no, they are not ill.

The interrogative pronouns, **maš, tuš, baš,** etc. are considered under the pronoun (p. 51).

In questions asking permission which are expressed in the future an affirmative answer is given in the imperative:

mis-năk-en, may I sweep?
mis-n-en, yes, sweep.
kul-ăk-en, may I sit down?

kul-en, yes, sit down.
mis-(t-e) na, may I sweep the house?
mis-t-e, yes, sweep it.

When permision is not given and the answer is negative the root alone is used in the transitive with the proper ending and the root alone in the intransitive:

mis-năk-en, may I sweep?
ma, mis, no, do not sweep.

mis-(t-e) na, may I sweep the house?
ma, mis-t-ik, no, do not sweep it.

---

[1] Compare Palma y Palma, p. 178, 179.

## THE ADJECTIVE

There is no real adjective in Maya. Words which have usually been considered as adjectives are really intransitive verbs. The term adjective has however been retained as describing these forms:[1]

**keel,** he is cold, it is cold, or something cold.

**keel winik,** the man is cold or the cold man.

**kohan winik tun tal,** the man is sick, he is coming, or the sick man is coming.

The attributive and predicate relationship are not distinguished;[2]

**le na boš,** this house is black or the black house.

These adjective-like forms have been put into a class by themselves in the treatment of the verb as their past tenses are made in a different way from that used in the regular intransitive forms. This is one of the many places where an arbitrary ruling must be made in regard to the place where forms should be considered which are on the dividing line between two categories.

It has been thought best to retain the heading "adjective" for the sake of clearness and to consider number and comparison here rather than under the verb. The idea of time, however, is taken up under Class IV of the verbs (p. 59).

ORDER. The adjective usually precedes the noun but there are many exceptions to the rule;

    **u lak winik,** the other man.     **u winik šan,** the same man.

NUMBER. The plural ending is usually expressed only in the noun used with the adjective. Some cases, however, occur where both the adjective and the noun have the sign of the plural. Plural in the adjective is not usually shown by the same form, **-ob,** as with nouns, but by the suffixes **-ăk, -tăk,** or **-lăk,** the same as those used for participles:[3]

---

[1] For a good discussion of the adjective, see Palma y Palma (p. 160–162.)

Lopez (§§ 30–33) has two classes of adjectives: — qualifying and determinative.

Martínez insists that there is an adjective and, like the English adjective, it precedes the noun.

[2] Seler (p. 77) makes an attributive expression by means of the suffixes **-al, -el, -il, -ol, -ul:**

    **uɔ-ul winik-ob,** the good men.     **ɔak-il na,** the white house.

[3] Coronel notes the plural in **-tăk** as used for participles.

Seler (p. 114) is inclined to interpret the plural ending **-lak** as related to the

uɔ na, a good house, or the house is good,
uɔ-tăk na-ob, the good houses, or the houses are good.

*Reduplication.* This is sometimes employed to express the plural in adjectives:

taš be, a smooth road.                    ta-taš be-ob, smooth roads.

There are a few adjectives which have different forms for the singular and plural:

nohotš tunitš, a large stone.            nukutš tunitš-ob, large stones.

COMPARISON. *Comparative.* The comparative is made by adding the suffix -il to the adjective form:

uɔ, good, uɔ-il or u-yuɔ-il, better.
natš, far, natš-il, farther.

This may be a case where there was at one time a vocalic harmony between the vowel of the stem and that of the ending in -l.[1]

*Superlative.* This is formed by prefixing the word hătš meaning " much, very, or many " to the comparative:[2]

---

passive or intransitive stem in -al, -el, -il, -ol, -ul, the suffix vowel of which is elided with the collective or plural suffix -ak, -ik. As a matter of fact the -lak suffix for the plural is very uncommon. -ak or -tak are much more common. Seler (p. 122, 123) considers the suffix -ak as identical with -ah as a sign of the past. His authority for this is evidently Perez who gives the forms and translations noted by Seler;

alabil, what is or shall be said.          bahun-ak, how much were they?
alabil-ak, it was said.                    biqin, biqinš, when?
bahun, how much?                           biqinš-ak, when was it?

The Motul dictionary seems to make no distinction between bahun and bahun-ak. It does not give the form biqinš-ak and distinctly states that biqin is used for the present and past. The San Francisco dictionary gives bahun and bahunš using them in both the present and past. It does not give bahun-ak. I am rather inclined to consider the -ak in these forms of Perez as denoting a plural although the Motul gives an example of the use of bahun with a plural noun.

[1] Strength is given to this supposition by the fact that Beltran (§ 27) gives the form yuɔ-ul (yutzul) for better, nohol, greater, qasal, worst, but he also notes that the Indian in talking usually uses the suffix -il.

Lopez (§ 36) does not accept this way of making the comparative at the present time. He writes, "*Antiguamente, según asegura el P. Beltrán, se formaba el comparativo repitiendo la última vocal y añadiéndole una ele . . . pero actualmente no se usa. También, dice que se forma añadiendo al positivo la partícula il; pero a mi modo de ver, mejor se le llamaría superlativo relativo.*" Lopez forms the comparative by using the particles, asab, mas, or masab with the positive.

[2] Lopez (§ 37) also uses sem or semketš, lem or lemketš, het, bahan and kalam to form the superlative degree.

hătš uɔ-il na-ob, the best houses.
hătš natš-il, the farthest.

The form hătš is often used directly with the adjective to form the comparative:

in na hătš uɔ ket a na, my house is better than your house.

*Diminutives or diminution of the idea.* This is expressed by reduplication:

noh or nohotš, great.  sak, white.
no-noh or no-nohotš, *grandecillo.*  sa-sak, *medio blanco.*

A more common way of expressing a diminution or an increase of the idea expressed by the adjective is by the words, hătš, very, and the word qas meaning bad.[1]:

tšitšan, small.
qas tšitšan, rather small, *medio chico.*
hătš tšitšan, very small.

NUMERALS. The numeral system is vigesimal.[2] There is a consistent treatment so that there is practically no number that cannot be expressed in Maya.

*Terms given by the early Spaniards.* These are as follows:

20 units  = 1 qal, 1 × 20 = 20.
20 qal  = 1 baq, 20 × 20 = 400.
20 baq  = 1 pik, 20 × 20 × 20 = 8,000.
20 pik  = 1 kalab, 20 × 20 × 20 × 20 = 160,000.
20 kalab  = 1 qintšil, 20 × 160,000 = 3,200,000.
20 qintšil = 1 alaw, 20 × 3,200,000 = 64,000,000 (?).

*Terms used in the hieroglyphic writing.* It is clear from a study of the hieroglyphic writing that the early Mayas were accustomed to deal with very large number series, numbers running into the millions, especially the long number series in the Dresden Codex.[3]

The system now commonly used in the hieroglyphic writing is as follows:

20 **Kin**  = 1 **Uinal,** 20 days.
18 **Uinal**  = 1 **Tun,** 360 days.
20 **Tun**  = 1 **Katun,** 7200 days.
20 **Katun** = 1 **Cycle,** 144,000 days.
13 or 20 **Cycle** = 1 **Great Cycle,** 1,872,000 or 2,880,000 days.

[1] Compare Palma y Palma, p. 161, 162, and Lopez, § 38.
[2] For a complete discussion of the numerals, see Thomas, 1897–1898. See also Part III, p. 181.
[3] For a discussion of these number series, see Bowditch, 1910, Chapter VI.

It is not certain regarding all the names given by the early
Mayas to the different divisions. The numbers were expressed
very simply in the hieroglyphic writing by a system of super-
imposed bars and dots.

There is a certain unity between the numeral system now used
and that on which the ancient calendarial reckoning was based.
In the latter, however, 18 units of the 2d order made one of the
3d. There is also a question whether in the stone inscriptions 20
of the 5th order made one of the 6th or 13 of the 5th made one of
the 6th. The change in the 2d order from 20 to 18 was probably
due to a desire to bring about some degree of accord between the
actual length of a year and a unit of the 3d order, a **Tun** being
360 days.

*Terms used at present time.* The Mayas of the present time
naturally have little occasion for large numbers although some
are capable of counting up into the thousands. The Lacandones,
on the other hand, seem entirely unable to use numbers higher
than three or four. They point to the fingers and toes when they
desire to signify higher numbers.

Taking into consideration the ancient Maya method of expressing numbers by bars and dots, a bar representing five and a dot
one, we might expect a quinary system with multiples of five up
to twenty. This is not so, however, as the change in nomenclature
is made at ten. There are different words used for the numbers
from 1 through 9. The word for 10, **la hun,** probably means " all
of one count." **La** is the particle denoting totality.[1]

The word for 11, **buluk,** is quite different from the word for one.
It is to be noted that in the face numerals the hieroglyph for 11,
as far as can be made out at present, does not show any of the
characteristics of the number for one.

The words for the numbers 12 to 19 correspond in meaning
with the words for 2 to 9 with the addition of the particle **lah,** signifying " all ":

**lah ka,** all of 2.                               **lah oš,** all of 3, etc.

---

[1] Compare Thomas, 1897–98, p. 891. He points out that Henderson in his
manuscript Maya-English dictionary has as the meaning of **lah,** " whole
hands."

It is suggested, as another possibility, that **la** is to be derived from
**laq** meaning " the other " or " the accompanying," giving the
idea of first counting the fingers up to 10 and then starting with
the toes up to 20. This suggestion would have more value if **la**
was found with the number 11 and not with 10.

NUMERATION

| Tozzer | Beltran |
|---|---|
| 1. hun- | hun- |
| 2. ka- | ka- (ca) |
| 3. oš- | oš- (ox) |
| 4. kǎn- | kan- (can) |
| 5. ho- | ho- |
| 6. wǎk- | wak- (uac) |
| 7. wuk- | wuk- (uuc) |
| 8. wašak- | wašak- (uaxac) |
| 9. bolon- | bolon- |
| 10. la hun- | la hun- |
| 11. buluk- | buluk- (buluc) |
| 12. la ka- | lah ka- (lah cá) |
| 13. la oš- | oš la hun- (ox la hun) |
| 14. la kǎn- | kan la hun- (can la hun) |
| 15. la ho- | hol hun- |
| 16. la wǎk- | wak la hun- (uac la hun) |
| 17. la wuk- | wuk la hun- (uuc la hun) |
| 18. la wašak- | wašak la hun- (uaxac la hun) |
| 19. la bolon- | bolon la hun- |
| 20. hun qal- | hun qal- (hun kal) |
| 21. hun qal yete hun- | hun tu qal- (hun tu kal) |
| 22. hun qal yete ka- | ka tu qal- (ca tu kal) |
| 30. hun qal yete la hun- | la hu ka qal- (la hu ca kal) |
| 31. hun qal yete buluk- | buluk tu qal- (buluc tu kal) |
| 32. hun qal yete la ka- | lah ka tu qal- (lah ca tukal) |
| 40. ka qal- | ka qal- (ca kal) |
| 41. ka qal yete hun- | hun tu yoš qal- (hun tu yox kal) |
| 50. ka qal yete la hun- | la hu yoš qal- (la hu yox kal) |
| 60. oš qal- | oš qal- (ox kal) |
| 70. oš qal yete la hun- | la hu kan qal- (la hu can kal) |
| 80. kǎn qal- | kan qal- (can kal) |
| 90. kǎn qal yete la hun- | la hu yo qal- (la hu yo kal) |
| 100. ho qal- | ho qal- (ho kal) |
| 101. ho qal yete hun- | hun tu wak qal- |
| 110. ho qal yete la hun- | la hu wak qal- |
| 111. ho qal yete la hun yete hun- | buluk tu wak qal- |
| 120. wǎk qal- | wak qal- |

## NUMERATION (continued)

| Tozzer | Beltran |
|---|---|
| 130. wăk qal yete la hun- | la hu wuk qal- |
| 140. wuk qal- | wuk qal- |
| 160. wašak qal- | wašak qal- |
| 180. bolon qal- | bolon qal- |
| 200. la hun qal- | la hun qal- |
| 220. buluk qal- | buluk qal- |
| 240. la ka qal- | lah ka qal- |
| 260. la oš qal- | oš lahu qal- |
| 280. la kăn qal- | kan lahu qal- |
| 300. la ho qal- | hol hu qal- |
| 320. la wăk qal- | wak lahu qal- |
| 340. la wuk qal- | wuk lahu qal- |
| 360. la wašak qal- | wašak lahu qal- |
| 380. la bolon qal- | bolon lahu qal- |
| 400. hun baq- | hun baq- |

*Beltran's numeration.* There is little doubt that the Maya numeration for the higher numbers has fallen into disuse at the present time.[1] It is significant that practically all late grammars give the numeration of Beltran rather than the numbers used at the present time.[2]

The reader is given a chance on p. 99–100, to compare the numbers as given by Beltran with those collected by the writer. I have given the numbers only to 400.[3] I present these with some hesitation.

Beltran has the same form for 12 as that given here but for the numbers 13 to 19 he gives:

oš la hun, 13 (3 and 10).          kan la hun, 14 (4 and 10), etc.

The form for 10 is thus carried through all the numbers from 13 to 19. Attention should be called to the analogy here between these

---

[1] Compare Cruz (1912, p. 110) who writes, "*El sistema de numeración maya puede decirse que ha caído en desuso, ¿será posible volverlo á su primitivo estado hoy que está mezclado con el español? Es de dudarse. Día ha de llegar en que hasta el propio idioma quede sepultado eternamente. Nosotros no auguramos á la lengua maya, que fué gloriosa, ningún porvenir, y sí presentimos que tarde ó temprano caiga en desuso eterno. Pueda que fracasemos en nuestros pronósticos pero lo dudamos.*"

[2] See Lopez § 180. Note, however, the numbers given in Appendix IV, p. 301.

[3] For the numbers above 400, the reader is referred to the list in Beltran, "*Articulo Undecimo,*" Thomas, 1897–1898, p. 861, 890–893, or Lopez, § 180.

forms using 10 as a foundation and the face numerals in the hiero-glyphic inscriptions for the numbers 13 to 19. These latter show, in most cases, a fleshless lower jaw signifying 10 in addition to the glyph for the numbers from 3 to 9.

In the forms given here **yetel,** with, is used with all numbers not multiples of 20:

> **hun qal yete hun,** 21 (one 20 with one).

These correspond to forms given by Perez (1866–1877) and Brinton (1882, p. 39) in **katak.** Both **yetel,** and **katak** have the meaning " and," " with." Brinton uses the form in **katak** as an alternative in numbers above 40:

> **ka kal katak ka,** 42 (2 score and 2).

Perez gives the example:

> **hun qal katak ho,** 25 (one score and 5).

Beltran's numbers for 30 and 35:

> **la hu ka qal**                      **hol hu ka qal.**

and all numbers above 40 use the unit of **qal** *above* rather than *below* the number expressed:

> **hol hu ka qal,** 35, literally, 15, 2 qal or, freely, 15 toward the 2d qal (40).

The numbers from 31 to 34 and 36 to 39, on the other hand, use the unit of **qal** *below* the number expressed:

> **wak la hun tu qal,** 36 (16 on the [one] qal).

All numbers above 40 correspond in form with those for 30 and 35, using the unit of **qal** *above* the number expressed:

> **hun tu yoš qal,** 41 (one on the 3d qal).

It seems clear that there is some mistake here in Beltran's num-eration, although all writers have followed him in giving the same forms. The same particle, **tu,** is used both in those forms for numbers below 40 which add the number to the *preceding* unit of **qal,** and also in the forms for 30, 35 and those above 40, where the number is really added, if we accept the meaning of **tu,** to the *suc-ceeding* unit of **qal:** [1]

> **ka tu qal,** 22 (2 to qal).
> **ka tu yoš qal,** 42 (2 to 3 qal, not 2 to 2 qal).

---

[1] In this connection, Thomas (1897–1898, p. 891) writes, "Perez, as quoted by Dr. Brinton, says, in an unpublished essay in the latter's possession, that Beltran's method of expressing the numbers is erroneous; that 41 should be

Under the same rule, after 380 is reached, Beltran starts with
381 counting towards the next higher unit of **baq,** 400:

**hun tu hun baq,** 381 (1 to [1] **baq**).
**ho tu hun baq,** 385 (5 to [1] **baq**), etc.

A point, not previously mentioned in connection with Beltran's
numeration, is that **tu** is not used with the forms adding 10 and
15 to each **qal** unit, namely, 30 and 35, 50 and 55, 70 and 75, etc.:

**la hu ka qal,** 30.                **la hu yoš qal,** 50.
**hol hu ka qal,** 35.              **hol hu yoš qal,** 55.

This omission of the **tu** is to be noted in the same relative places [1]
until 190 is reached when it is found again:

**la hu tu la hun qal,** 190.        **hol hu tu la hun qal,** 195.

The **tu** is then found in the same relative places until 370 is reached
when it is dropped again:

**la hu bolon la hu qal,** 370.

It is found with the next number when 15 is added to the unit:

**hol hu tu bolon la hu qal,** 375.

and it is dropped again for the next 10 added to the **qal:**

**la hu hun baq,** 390.

and added for the next 15:

**hol hu tu hun baq,** 395

I cannot explain this irregularity in these two places in the numeration. The fact that, with the exception of the even **qal** and

---

**hun-tu-kaqal**; 42, **ka-tu-kaqal**; 83, **oš-tu-kanqal,** etc.  Nevertheless, as Dr.
Brinton has pointed out, the numerals above 40 are given in Perez's Dictionary of the Maya Language according to Beltran's system, which appears from
other evidence to be correct. Léon de Rosny suggests that **hun-tu-yošqal**
should be explained thus: 60 − 20 + 1. However, the correct rendering appears to be 1 on the third score, or third 20. It is possible that an old and a
new reckoning prevailed among the Mayas, as apparently among the Cakchi-
quels. According to Stoll the latter people had an old and a more recent
method of enumerating . . . Perez says that **tu** is an abbreviation of the numeral particle **tul,** but Rosny says, '*Je crois que ce n'est point, comme il* Ban-
croft] *le suppose, la simple conjonction et, mais une phrase des mots* **ti-u,** *dans
son, à lui, sien;* **u** *est un pronom appele par les grammairiens Espanols mixte
et qui forme la copulation, comme en Anglais l's du genitif.'* Dr. Berendt adopts
the same opinion, which is probably correct."

[1] That is, 70 and 75, 90 and 95, 110 and 115, 130 and 135, 150 and 155, 170
and 175.

**baq, tu** is always found except in some of the forms adding 10 and 15 to the units seems to show some definite purpose when it is omitted.[1]

The unit above **qal** is **baq** which is equivalent to 20 × 20, 400. This word has the meaning " to roll up, to tie around." It has already been noted that the **baq** unit comes in first with 381.

Beltran's numbers above 400, except even multiples of this unit, **baq**, are evidently abbreviated. Otherwise they are unintelligible.

ho tu baq, 500 — ho qal tu baq.
la hu tu baq, 600 = la hun qal tu baq.

Above 800, in the same way as before, the next higher unit is used:

ho tu yoš baq, 900 = ho qal tu yoš baq (100 on 3d baq).

The unit of the 3d place (20 × 20 × 20, 8000) is **pik**, meaning " cotton cloth or a kind of petticoat." As pointed out by Thomas (1897–1898, p 893), Henderson gives the significance of **pik** as " a bag made out of a petticoat " which corresponds with the Mexican term for 8000.

Beltran points out (§ 312) that the Mayas in his day used the term **pik** as meaning 1000 rather than 8000.

The unit of the 4th place (20 × 20 × 20 × 20, 160,000) is **kalab** and that for the 5th place (20 × 20 × 20 × 20 × 20, 3,200,000) is **qintšil**, and that for the 6th place is **alaw**.[2]

*Numeral Classifiers.* There is a large number of classificatory suffixes in use with the numerals. The latter can never stand alone. These suffixes qualify the term and show into what class the objects counted fall. At the present time all nouns are broadly classified into two classes, animate and inanimate, by the two suffixes **-tul** and **-p'el**:

oš-tul **winik,** three men,                    oš-p'el **na,** three houses.

Apart from a few other classifiers there is not much attention paid by the Mayas of the present time to the finer distinctions formerly made by these suffixes. Some, however, are always used.

---

[1] There is one exception to this rule. Beltran's form for 171, **buluk bolon qal,** omits the **tu.**

[2] For a discussion of the meaning of these terms, see Thomas, *op. cit.* p. 894.

A list of suffixes used as classifiers for the numeral as given, for the most part, by Beltran (§ 313) and translated by Nuttall (1903) [1] is given in Appendix III, p. 290–292.

## THE ADVERB

POSITION. Adverbs, especially those formed from the intransitive verb-adjective, have two positions in regard to the verb and its subject. They may be placed either at the beginning before the nominal pronoun or between the nominal pronoun and the verb:

seeb tin konil, I sell it easily.  tšambe tin ɔ'ib, I write slowly.
qas tin ɔ'ib, I write badly.  tin tšitš šimbal, I walk fast.

I cannot state any rule for the position of the adverb in these forms. Some seem always to be placed before the pronoun and others after the pronoun.

In verbs where the verbal pronoun rather than the nominal is used the adverb comes at the beginning;

tšambe ɔ'ib-n-ah-en, I wrote slowly.

Forms used with the verbal pronoun may have the particle **-il** or **-ik** inserted between the root and the pronoun:

tšitš šimbal-n-ah-il-en, I walked fast, or tšits šimbal-n-ah-ik-en.
tšitš simbal-n-ah-ah-n-il-en, I walked fast a long time ago.
suk kohan-il-en, I am always ill.
suk keel-il-en, I am always cold.

The adverbial particles are very numerous in Maya...No attempt has been made to exhaust the list.[2] The most important are as follows:

NEGATION. This is shown by the particle **ma** which precedes the nominal pronoun and comes immediately before the verb when the verbal pronoun is used:

---

[1] Mrs. Nuttall makes a very pertinent "suggestion to Maya scholars" as to the identity between the significance of some of these classificatory particles and portions of the hieroglyphic writing appearing with the series of numbers. These number series, worked out up to the present time, all relate to periods of time. There is no reference whatever to objects of various classes being counted. It is especially desired that something may be done in this line of research.

[2] The reader is referred to the lists given in Beltran and in San Buenaventura. See also Lopez, Chapter VIII.

mi-nan, contracting from ma-yan, there is none.
ma-in bin, I am not going.
ma-bin-etš, you did not go.

The particle -il, noted above, may be used with the negative coming, however, after the verbal pronoun:

ma sak-en-il, I was not afraid.

The final l is often lost and we get: [1]

ma sak-en-i.                        ma bin-en-i, I did not go.

It will be noted that the forms of the nominal pronoun are not compounded with a time particle in these examples. The sign of the past, -ah, may also be omitted with the negative. The nominal pronoun usually contracts with the negative and the final -l is lost as noted above: [2]

ma-in into min.
ma-a into ma.
ma-u into mu.
ma-u putš-ah-en-il, becoming m-u putš-en-i, he did not hit me.
ma-in putš-ah-il, becoming m-in putš-i, I did not hit him.

REPETITION. This may be expressed in the action of the verb by the particle -ka:

tin ka-bin or ka bin-in-kah, I am going again.
ka tal-etš, you came again.

TOTALITY. This idea is shown by the particle ia or lah, probably derived from the word tulakal, all:

tin la-uk-ik or tin la wuk-ik, I am drinking all of it.
tan la-hant-ik wa, you are eating all of the tortillas.
tun la-qai-ob, they are all singing.

---

[1] Lopez (§ 172) has this final l with the negative forms;
ma in qati, I do not desire.
ma in qat hanali, I do not desire to eat.

[2] Lopez (§§ 97, 99) makes a negative preterit expression by means of the future form without bin and a negative future expression by means of the present form with tin, ta, tu in place of kin, ka, ku:
ma tal-ak-en, I have not gone.
ma tin han-al, I shall not eat.
I cannot understand these forms.

The **la** seems to modify either the subject or the object of the verb.
I cannot find that there is any differentiation in the forms according to the thing modified.[1]
A repetition of the particle **la** is sometimes noted after the root.
This intensifies the meaning:

> **tin la-hant-la-n-t-ik,** I am eating absolutely everything.

This particle is also used with the idea of totality with adjectives:

> **kohan-ob,** they are ill.
> **kohan-tăk-ob,** many are ill.
> **la-kohan-tăk-ob,** all are ill.
> **tun la-kohan-tal-ob,** they all become ill.
> **tun la-kohan-ob,** they are all ill.

MANNER OR STATE. The particle denoting these ideas is **bē**.
This adverb takes the -il or -ik forms noted above (p. 104).

> **bē tin putš-ah-il-etš** or **bē tin putš-il-etš,** thus, I hit you.
> **bē tal-il-en** or **bē tal-ik-en,** thus I came.

DEMONSTRATIVE. Suffixes similar to the demonstrative pronoun,
**a** and **o,** with the meaning " this or that way " are often used with
the adverb **bē** (usually written **bey**):[2]

> **bē tal-il-en-a,** thus I came this way.
> **be tal-il-en-o,** thus I came that way.

The form in **a** is used when the method of coming is shown by some
action, the form in **o** when the method of coming is described by
words:

> **bē putš-il-en-a,** thus I was hit (showing how).
> **be putš-il-en-o,** thus I was hit (telling how).

When these forms take the nominal pronoun the suffix -il is not
used:

> **bē-in wal-ik-a,** I say it like this.      **bē-in beet-ik-a,** I make it like this.
> **bē-in wal-ik-o,** I say it like that.      **bē-in beet-ik-o,** I make it like that.

---

[1] Seler (p. 81) includes the particle -la with the inchoative foms in -hal,
-tal, and -tša-hal and infers that la is used only with intransitive verbs.

[2] Perez (1866–77) makes much the same distinction between the suffixes -a
and -o in the following examples;

> **he le ɔimn-a,** *aquí esta el caballo.*      **he le ɔimn-o,** *allí esta el caballo.*

## PREPOSITIONS AND POSTPOSITIONS

These are interesting as they are used in place of the oblique cases in Maya. When used with nouns all are prefixed:

**yalan poq,** below the hat.  **yetel winik,** with the man.

A distinction is seen, however, when these forms are used with the pronoun. They are then divided into two classes, those prefixed to the forms of the verbal pronoun and those suffixed to the nominal pronoun. It is not clear how this distinction is governed. To the first class belong:

**yetel,** with, **yetel-en,** with me.
**naɔ',** near, **naɔ'-etš,** near you.
**yoqol,** above, **yoqol-i,** above him.

To the second and larger class belong:

**men** or **menel,** by, **t-in-men,** by me.
**tial,** for, **in-tial,** for me.
**ɔel,** beside, **a-ɔel,** beside you, literally, my side.
**walan,** below, **in-walan,** or **t-in walan,** below me.
**ti, in,** from, and to, **tin bin t-in na,** I am going to my house.[1]
**tin tal t-in na,** I am coming from my house.

It seems clear that the idea of a noun with its possessive pronoun is uppermost here but this does not explain why we have,

**in walan,** below me and **yoqol-en,** above me.

---

[1] The **t** or **ti** corresponds to the forms given in the early grammars as the dative case.

# PART II
# MAYA TEXTS

# PART II
# MAYA TEXTS

## INTRODUCTION

MATERIAL AVAILABLE. The reader will gain some idea of the vast amount of literature in the Maya language from the discussion of the Maya texts available for study (Part III, p. 182). These documents date from the days following the Conquest and continue down to the present time. They vary much in content and in value as faithful transcriptions of the language as spoken at the time when they were written.

GRAMMATICAL STRUCTURE. It is pertinent to ask how much help in translating the early texts is to be derived from a grammar such as the present work. The thesis has been advanced in this paper that it is probable the grammatical structure of the language has not changed appreciably from early to late times. If this is the case, and the ancient as well as the modern texts were written grammatically, there would be little difficulty, as far as the grammar is concerned, in understanding the early examples of written Maya. Observations have led me to believe, however, that the early texts were not written with much regard for grammar, even the Maya grammar built upon a Latin model. It is unusual to find in the early texts examples of the greater part of the expressions given by Beltran and the other early grammarians. Their illustrations are, of course, in most cases grammatical but they are not taken from texts but are isolated sentences made up to illustrate the special points to which references are made.

It seems probable that the early Maya texts are generally lacking in the finer shades of meaning which it is possible to express in Maya and, furthermore, it is not to be expected that forms not recognized by the early grammarians would always find expression in the texts.

The Books of Chilam Balam, that most fertile source of texts in Maya, furnish examples of this lack of precise grammatical structure. As I have written elsewhere (1917, p. 183), "It must be remembered that the manuscripts themselves are, no doubt, copies of earlier works, collected from different individuals and often copied by several different hands. Some of the manuscripts seem to have been the work of those who did not know Maya. Several different spellings of the same word occur and common Maya words are frequently misspelled. On the other hand, some of the pages seem to show a surprising ignorance of Spanish — *Iglesia*, for example, is spelled in one place "*Iglayci*." As for the Latin words occurring sporadically in the text, one is not surprised to find forms difficult to recognize."

It seems safe to say that these famous texts are often illiterate in the sense that they are probably copies of copies and have been garbled in passing from hand to hand to say nothing of the fact that in the beginning they probably did not express precisely in every case all the forms of the spoken Maya. We return then to the question asked at the beginning of the section, how much help is a grammar in the translation of these texts. It seems to me that a grammar renders surprisingly little aid in deciphering the documents.

LEXICOGRAPHY. It is in respect to the vocabulary that the Maya has changed most. Words have become obsolete. New words have been coined and Spanish words have been introduced in greater or lesser numbers.[1] In spite of the tremendous advantage of possessing three early Maya dictionaries it is often not possible to determine accurately the meaning of many of the words in the early texts. Several of the vocabularies give examples of Maya construction. These forms are helpful in many cases in determining homonyms.

Even where there are parallel texts in Spanish and Maya as in the *Doctrinas*, there is often little help in elucidating the Maya as these translations are usually poorly done, not necessarily because of an ignorance of the proper words but from a general lack of forms in Maya to express properly the ideas contained in the "*hipérboles y alegorías*" of ecclesiastical Spanish or Latin.[2]

---

[1] Compare Palma y Palma, p. 145, 146.
[2] Perez (1844) writes very pertinently on this point as follows, "*Si consideramos igualmente que los antiguos escritores de doctrina y pláticas eran unos serviles*

On the other hand, the Xiu Chronicles, the Libro de Calcalchen and other secular texts furnish some excellent examples of parallel accounts in the Maya and Spanish of wills and other legal documents. Martínez Hernández writes substantially as follows in a personal letter concerning the collection of documents in the Libro de Calcalchen, "The Maya is very old and is a splendid specimen of Maya literature. Some expressions are unusual and are to be translated only after very diligent research. As we are familiar to a certain extent with the forms of the *Ordenanzas*, they would help us to translate properly and pave the way for other future translations. I am fully convinced that the Books of Chilam Balam can be translated after translating all these documents. Before this literature came into my hands there were many words in the vocabularies the use of which I did not know."

The later Maya texts are naturally far easier to translate on account of the fewer changes in the vocabulary.

The "particles of adornment" are many in Maya.[1] They add to the pleasure of the spoken Maya but they cause no little confusion in deciphering the written language.

There is a large number of words in Maya with a comparatively large number of onomatopœic words.[2]

ORTHOGRAPHY. The spelling of the Maya words is often far from consistent. This is especially true of words with the glottal-

---

*traductores de las hipérboles y alegorías de la lengua castellana y latina, vendrémos en conocimiento que estos modos de decir no podían generalizarse entre los indios, como ajenos y distintos á los que el genio de su lengua demandaba; así es que la expresion figurada de llamar á este mundo un 'valle de lágrimas,' no es usada entre los indios, y cuando la encuentran traducida literalmente en la Salve, la encuentran pesada y no hacen de ella aplicacion alguna, y si alguno muy ladino quiere aplicar la idea, lo hace como muchas veces lo he oido, con las palabras de ucahal numya (pueblo ó lugar de miserias ó trabajos), que para ellos tienen igual fuerza, es el mismo sentido, y diferentes las voces. Hay algunas figuras castellanas que no pueden traducirse literalmente al idioma sin 'ridiculez."*

[1] Compare Palma y Palma, p. 144 who writes, "*No obstante, las partículas compositivas que no modifican el sentido, son muchísimas, las cuales, efectivamente, sólo contribuyen á la variedad de las formas de la expresión constituyendo así, como el indicado padre Beltran dice, 'partículas adornativas' que facilitan giros de estilo de que resulta un lenguaje elegante y artístico cuando se habla bien el idioma.*"

[2] Compare Palma y Palma, p. 133–134, 258–269, 307.
See discussion of the various dictionaries in Part III (p. 169).

ized consonants and those with doubled vowels. In several cases ç is used for z or s and in these instances the omission of the cedilla with the c is a cause of great annoyance, changing, for example, çiçal (sisal) to cical (kikal). The omission of the bar with the h and p also adds to the confusion. In the early texts there is no proper division into words and sentences. Just as a word may be spelled in several different ways on the same page so a word may be divided in many different ways in succeeding lines.[1] This lack of consistency in writing and spacing the Maya is a cause of great confusion.[2] The Berendt copies of many of the Chilam Balam texts are very useful in this respect.[3] The punctuation as used in the early documents is of no value whatsoever and the very common failure to capitalize proper names is still another cause of difficulties.

CHIROGRAPHY. The handwriting in these early texts is often very difficult to make out. There is usually a complete failure to distinguish between v and b. Several different varieties of handwriting are often seen in the same manuscript.

POSSIBILITY OF TRANSLATION. I have already discussed in another place the possibility of a faithful translation of the ancient Maya texts, especially those of the Chilam Balam Books (Tozzer, 1917). I am still of the opinion that many parts of the early documents will defy translation.[4] These portions are, for the most part,

---

[1] On a single page in the Chumayel manuscript within six lines the following varieties of spelling and spacing are found:

| uhool u poop | u hol pop |
| uhol  u pop | u holpop |
| u hol u poop | |

Compare the different versions of the same prophecy as given in the Tizimin, the Chumayel and the Lizana texts (p. 122).

[2] In the Chumayel version of one of the prophecies (Chilam Balam de Chumayel, p. 106) there is found, for example, the following division of words: ytzam = nakauil for ytzamna kauil. As Ytzamna is a main god of the Mayas, one would think that the copyist would have known how to write this name properly.

[3] Compare Tozzer, 1917, p. 183.

[4] I have submitted this portion of the manuscript, as well as a great part of the remainder, to Señor Juan Martínez Hernández and he agrees with me in all the statements contained in Part II. He writes, "The parts dealing with their ancient mythology and the esoteric language of the Maya priests may

those dealing with Maya ritual and, in a figurative way, with the coming of the new religion and the change to the worship of the true God.[1] Many parts are translatable but only after the most careful study. There is a great opportunity for mistakes and there are many places where more than one rendering of the text is possible. It is in such places that time and patience are needed.

There follow some examples of Maya texts with translations, starting with the modern Maya and going back to the Maya of the Prophecies and of the Books of Chilam Balam.

## 1. THE INDIANS OF CHAN SANTA CRUZ [2]

| Tu | haab-il | 1847 | liqil | u-ka-pul | le-wink-ob | leeti |
|---|---|---|---|---|---|---|
| In | the year | 1847 | arose | for second time | these men (Indians) | this |

| u-haab-il | tal-ob | u-took-ob | Săki | tan | nohotš | kah: |
|---|---|---|---|---|---|---|
| its year | they came | to burn | Valladolid | in the midst of a large | | pueblo: |

| yaab | pal-al | tu-kim-s-ob: [3] | bě-šan | tulakal | kah-ob | tu-took- |
|---|---|---|---|---|---|---|
| many | boys | they killed: | thus also | all | the habitations | they |

| ah-ob | ku [4] | ɔ'ok-ol | ka-bin-ob | Santa Cruz | u-qaba |
|---|---|---|---|---|---|
| burned | when its completion | | again they went (to) | Santa Cruz | its name |

| tak | helae | ti-an-ob [5] | ti | buk-ah | haab | yaab: | yet | wink-il-ob |
|---|---|---|---|---|---|---|---|---|
| until | now | there they are | there | so many | years | many: | and | men |

| ɔ'oki | u-kim-s-ik-ob: | luum | utšuk | man-ob | nohotš: |
|---|---|---|---|---|---|
| they have just finished | killing: | the land | where | they pass | is great: |

| yaab-ob | šan: | helae | u-yum | ɔik | běnil | Mexico |
|---|---|---|---|---|---|---|
| (there are) many (of) | the same ones: | now | their lord, his Honorable | | | Mexico |

| tuu | šup-ik | u-taqin | yetel | u-meq-tan-ob | yoklal | u-ɔ'ok-s-ik |
|---|---|---|---|---|---|---|
| he is spending | his money | and | | his dependents | so that | they cause to end |

prevent or defy translation. . . . It is by the abundance of these examples (Maya constructions given in the vocabularies) that we can find our way in ascertaining so many homonyms of the brief and concise monosyllabic Maya. Compound verbs are difficult to make out. These are often conjugated as simple verbs with additional words completing the same."

[1] Compare in this respect the variation in the Maya of the same text (p. 122) as well as the different possibilities in translating the Maya.

[2] This text was collected by the author in 1900 at Uayma, near Valladolid, Yucatan, from an Indian named Marcelino Tas.

[3] Or tu-kim-s-ah-ob, they caused to die.

[4] Ku, a contraction of ka-u.

[5] This is really a contraction of ti-yan-ob.

**lē-batel-o:** utial **lē-wink-ob-o hu-hum-p'it-il** tun ɔ'ok-ol:
that war: in order that those men one by one may be exterminated:

**tan šan u-boot-k-ob tulakal baaš u-meya-m-ob**
they also are paying (the penalty for) all which they worked

**ti Yucatan:** yan **u-ɔ'ok-ol** tumen ɔ'u-qutš-ul **tu haab-il**
in Yucatan: there is its ending because it has arrived the year

**u-ɔ'ok-ol:** lē-buk-ah **luum yan-il-ob** bin-u-kah **p'atal**
its completion: all that land where they are they are coming to leave

**yalan u-qab** yum **halatš winik tu sēbal:** behelae **yaab**
under his arm the lord great man as quickly: now many

**mak** ɔ'ok **u-kah-al te Santa Cruz:** u-tšikul **tu ɔ'oko[l]**
persons finished (making) their town in Santa Cruz: its sign of its ending

**tumen mi-nan u-ɔ'on** lē-wink-ob **hebiš** lē bin-s-ah
because there are no guns the men like (the ones) they raised

**yoqol-ob leeti utšben** baal: kin sut-in-wal-e **utšben ɔ'on-ob**
above them this (in )former custom: I return to say the former guns

**ma tan u-pat-al-ob** ma bē **utši:** qutš **tu haab-il**
they are not serviceable (it was) not thus formerly: there came the year

**tu yalkab-an-s-ob** ɔ'ul **tumen masēwal ku** ɔ'ok-ol
they caused to run the strangers for the Indians after the completion

**ka-sut-n-ah-i yoqol-ob ma tu met-h-ob mišbal tak behelae:**
when they returned above them they did not do anything until now:

**uɔ** šan **yoqlal u-yan-tal ka-p'el hol-be utial yookol koon-ol**
it is well also because they have two doors in order to enter to sell

**tile wai laqin:** tak behelae **ooɔ-il u-kah-il-ob** utšik
by here the east: until now are the poor the ones of the pueblo formerly

**u-took-(i)k-ob yaab** baal: **utši** qas-ob **tumen tu**
they burn many things: formerly they are bad because they

**qas-kun-t-h-ob** behelae **tune** tun **yil-k-ob baš u-ɔ'ok**
bad things they did now finally they see it what its end

**lobil-il biša wa uɔ-h-oob mišma bin me-t-ik šan**
to the wickedness how if they are good nothing comes to cause the same

**lob-ti-ob:** behelae **mišun noq-ob mišun han-l-ob:** yan **tšen**
evil things: now nothing clothes nothing to eat: there is only

**tu tšun-tše ku wen-l-ob tēi yahal-kab-ti-ob:**
the branches of the tree where they sleep there they wake up in the morning:

**bē-ku-kǎš-t-ob** ha **yuq-ob bē tēi ku-kim-l-oob u-hutš**
thus then they seek water to drink thus there they die in the greater

**yaa-h-il leeti lē-ooɔ-il pal-al ku-kim-l-ob tak** tun **leeti-ob boo-t-ik**
misery these poor children they may die until they these pay

| u-sipil | u-tata-ob | u-han-l-ob | tšen | u-moɔ'-tše | yetel |
|---------|-----------|------------|------|------------|-------|
| their sins | their fathers | they eat | only | the roots of the trees | with |

| yitš-tše | mi-nan | šiim: | utial | u-man-s-ik | u-kuš-tal-ob |
|----------|--------|-------|-------|------------|--------------|
| the fruit of the trees | there is no | maize: | in order | to carry on | their lives |

| yetel | tutši | qaanab | tēi- | ku-kăš-t-ik | u-kuš-tal-ob. |
|-------|-------|--------|------|-------------|---------------|
| and | gifts | of the sea | there | they seek it | their lives. |

## Free Translation

For the second time, in the year 1847, these Indians rose in arms. That is the year in which they came to burn Valladolid, the large city. They killed many people. They also burned all the houses. After they had finished, they returned to the place called Santa Cruz where they are now and where they have been for many years. They have just been killing men of their own race. The land where they live is large. There are many of them there. Now their master is the President of Mexico. He is spending his money and his people also in order to put an end to the war, in order that these men, one by one, may be exterminated. They are paying the penalty for all they did in Yucatan. It has to end because the time for the ending has come. All that land where they are is about to come under the rule of the President. Many persons have already gone to live in Santa Cruz. This is a proof of the ending of the war because those Indians do not now have guns like the ones they formerly carried. I repeat, the old guns are now good for nothing, nothing like the former ones with which they put to flight the Spaniards (strangers). After the Indians had finished the attack, they have done nothing up to the present time. This is also well because they have two avenues to sell their wares here in the east. Even to-day the villagers are poor because they formerly burned many things. Formerly they were bad because they did bad things. Now, finally, they see the result of their wickedness; now, if they are good, nothing comes to cause the same evil things.[1] Now they have neither clothes nor food. They have only the branches of the trees under which to sleep where morning

---

[1] Martínez, who has been good enough to offer many suggestions, has translated this still more freely as follows: — "Formerly they were bad because they had bad examples set before them, now, then, they can discriminate better what is right and what is wrong and will no longer do any harm to them."

awakens them. They seek water to drink. They thus die in the greatest misery, this poor people. They may die until they pay for the sins of their fathers. They eat only the roots of the trees and the fruit of the trees. There is no maize to nourish them. In order to find nourishment they go to the shores of the sea.

## 2. LACANDONE CHANT

Fifty-one chants were collected by the writer in 1902 and 1903 among the Lacandones of Chiapas, Mexico. These people, as already pointed out, speak practically the same dialect of the Maya stock as that of the natives of Yucatan. The language of these chants is generally simple. Syllables are often added at the end of words to preserve a rhythm. The single chant given here has already been published (Tozzer, 1907, p. 171–172). I have given a more literal translation than that previously printed. The reader is referred to the former paper (p. 169–189) for the other chants.

#### When Copal and Posole are Distributed in the Ceremony of Renewing the Incense-Burners

Tan    in kub-ik       in pom     k-etš    tiala      kub-ik
I am    restoring it   my offering of copal   to you   for you   to restore it

t-ik [1]   yum     tiala    nas-ik [2]   t-ik    yum.    Hēn   boo-t-ik-etš
to    the father, for you to raise it   up to   the father.   I will   pay it to you

in     tšula     t-etš     uhel     a     kunya     tiala     kub-t-ik
my   offering of posol   to you   again (for)   your   welfare   for you   to restore it

yum.      Hēn boo-t-ik-etš   in     tšula     t-etš tiala     tī-lili.
to the father.   I will pay it to you my offering of posol to you for you yourself.

Tan in mee-t-ik   in sil t-etš-ki     uhel     a     kunya.   Bin-in-kin [3] pok
I am making it   my gifts to you   again (for) your welfare.   I am about to dry

in sil     t-etš          ma tu buh-ul          ma u lak-al
my gifts to you,   may they not be affected by crumble   may they not separate

u-hol     in   sil   t-etš.   Ma tu     wak-al in   sil   t-etš.
(as to) their heads   my gifts to you.   May they not crack   my gifts to you.

Ma tu     paš-al     in sil t-etš.   Il in     mee-t-ik   in sil   t-etš,
May they not break my gifts to you.   See my   making them my gifts to you,

---

[1] Kub-ik t-ik is equivalent to kub-t-ik.
[2] nas-ik is the same as nak-s-ik.
[3] Literally, I am going to.

yume.     Ma tu lub-ul     tšak-wil-ki. Bin-in-k-in pul-ik   etš
oh father.   May not be affected by a fall    fever.    I am about to place you

     yoko    tumu   lăk.    Il   in    mee-t-ik   in   sil   t-etš   uhel
(the idol) in the    new *brasero*.   See my making them my gifts to you   again

    a kunya.    Il   in   mee-t-ik    in   sil   t-etš   tia     yol
(for) your welfare.   See my making them   my gifts to you   for   the health

in pal-al.    Ma u      năk-tan-t-ik      yah-il,    ma u
my children.   May not trample them under foot   harm,    my not trample

năk-tan-t-ik   keel,      ma u năk-tan-t-ik     tšak-wil.   Ooken
them under foot cold,   may not trample them under foot   fever.    Enter,

ta šimbal   a   wil-ik   in   pal,   a-kun-e in   pal.
walk    you   see   my son,   cure   my son.

## 3. A MAYA WITCH STORY

The original text was collected by Berendt in Peten in 1866.
The manuscript is now in the Berendt Linguistic Collection (Br.
498. 21. M. L. 545). The text and an English translation of Berendt's German translation were published by Brinton (1883 and
1890). A few changes have been made and a literal translation has
been added. The simple tale shows certain features which seem to
be of European origin.

Hun-tul H-šib ɔ'ook-u-bel yetel hun-tul š-tš'up ma   tu-yohel-t-ah   wa
  One    man    married   with    one    woman not did he know her   as

š-wai.   Hun-p'e   qin   tu   yal-ah-ti,   " Hutš'e ka-p'el     mut      taab."
a witch.    One    day   he said to her, " Grind    two    measures of salt."

Tu    hutš'-ah   paibe   ka    tu   qat-ah,    " Baaš    tial    tetš? "
She ground them   first   when   she   asked him, " Why    [do] you [wish it?] "

Hun-p'el aqab    pišaan   H-šib-e   ka    tu   yil-ah   u-hoq-ol    u-yatan.
  One    night   awoke   the man when   he    saw   she goes out   his wife.

Ka   tu-tša-ah   u   maskabe,   ka    tu     mukul   t'ul-bel-ah   tu patš   ti
When   he took   his    axe,    when   he   secretly   followed her   behind   to

qaš.     Ka    qutši-ob    ti   tšitšan tšaqan,   yan   u     sas-il
the wood. When   they arrived   at   a little   pasture, there is   its   brightness

uh.     Ka   tu muk-u-b-ah   H-šib    tu    booy    nohotš   yaš-tše.
a moon. When he hid himself, the man, in the shade   of a great seiba tree.

Ka    tu    pul-ah    u    noq    š-tš'up    tu patš    waan
When   she    threw   her   clothes,   the woman,   behind her   standing

š-ma-buk      tu tan   uh;      ka   tu    ɔ'ip-ah    u-yot'el,
she without covering  in its face the moon; when  she  stripped off  her skin,

ka      kul-hi      tšem-bak:    ka      nak-i    ti   kaan:    ka
when  she remained  mere bones:  when  she arose  to  the sky:  when

em-i      tu-ka-ten,   ka   tu-yal-ah-i:    " Saɔ'aba    šta-kaan? "
she descended   again,   when  he said to her, "stretch yourself to the sky? "

Hemak  ma   utšak   u   nak-al tu-ka-ten tumen tu t'oot'-al taab.
But   not  possible  her ascending again  because he sprinkled salt.

### FREE TRANSLATION

A man (once) married a woman. The man did not know that
his wife was a witch. One day, he said to her, "Grind two measures of salt." She ground them and then she asked him, "Why do
you wish this?" One night he awoke and saw his wife go out.
Taking his axe, he secretly followed her to the wood. They arrived
at a little pasture in the bright moonlight. The man hid himself in
the shadow of a great seiba tree. The woman threw her clothes
behind her, standing naked in the moonlight. When she stripped
off her skin she appeared mere bones. Then she arose into the sky,
returning again (to the earth). Then the man said to her, "Would
you reach the sky?" But she could not ascend a second time as he
sprinkled salt.

### 4. PROPHECY OF CHILAM BALAM

This is one of the Maya prophecies which are discussed in Part
III (p. 192).[1] The text is given of the Chumayel version (Chilam

---

[1] This prophecy is undoubtedly the one referred to by Cogolludo (1688,
p. 199) and also in the *Relación de la Ciudad de Merida*, dated 1579 and signed
by Gaspar Antonio Xiu among others. This *Relación* is reprinted in *Colección
de Documentos Inéditos*, v. 11, p. 37–75. As Martínez Hernández has pointed
out, this statement in the Merida report is so very important that I reprint it
here.

"*Ubo algunas provincias que nunca dieron guerra, sino que rrescibieron a los
españoles de paz, en especial la provincia de Tutulxiu cuya cabeçera era y es el
pueblo de Mani, catorce leguas de esta ciudad al sueste, donde ubo pocos años antes
que los españoles viniesen a conquistar esta tierra un yndio principal, que era
sacerdote, llamado Chilan-balam, que le tenian por gran profeta y adivino, y este
les dixo que dentro de breve tiempo vernia de hazia donde sale el sol una jente blanca
barbada, y que traerian levantada una señal como esta ✠, ala qual no podian*

Balam de Chumayel, p. 105–107), the Tizimin version (Chilam Balam de Tizimin, Gates reproduction, p. 17, 18), and the Lizana version (Lizana, 1633; ed. 1893, p. 38–39). I have added a reading of the Maya text as interpreted by Martínez Hernández. The variations in the four versions should be noted, not only in the spellings but in the words themselves. The Chumayel version has frequent interpolations by the author of the copy. The translation of Lizana which, in general, is that followed by Carrillo y Ancona and many others is given in English together with the Spanish text.[1] I have attempted a new translation, following in the main the Martínez text. In a few cases a rendering of portions of the text into English by Martínez is given.

It will be noted that there are several passages which still remain far from clear in spite of the different authors who have worked upon them. Lizana's translation, which is very good as a free rendering, does not follow the text at all closely in several places. He has left out many words and particles.

This passage is given in order to illustrate some of the difficulties spoken of in the introduction to this section. It should be remembered that these Maya texts are transcribed into the system of writing Maya adopted in this work. The division into syllables is the work of the author.

---

*llegar sus Dioses, y huyan della, y que esta jente avia de señorear la tierra, y que a los que los rrecibiesen de paz no les harian mal nynguno, y a los que les hiziesen guerra los matarian, y que los naturales de la tierra dejarian sus ydolos y adorarian un solo Dios, que ellos adoraban y avian de predicar, y les serian tributarios, e hizo tejer una manta de algodon y les dixo que de aquella suerte avia de ser el tributo que les avian de dar, y mando al señor de Many, que se llamaba Mochanxiu, que ofreciese a los ydolos aquella manta para que estubiese guardada y quedase por memoria, y aquella señal de cruz y otras hizo hazer de piedra labrada y ponerlas en los patios de los templos donde pudiese ser vista de todos, y dixo que aquel era el arbol verde del mundo, e yvan aberla mucha jente por cosa nueba, y parecia que la beneraban desde entonzes, y despues quando vinieron los españoles y supieron que trayan la señal de la santa cruz, que era como la que su profeta chilam balam les avia figurado, tuvieron por cierto lo que les avia dicho, y determinaron de rrecebir a los españoles de paz y no les hazer guerra, sino ser sus amigos, como siempre lo han sido despues que poblaron estas provincias, y les ayudaron con mantenimientos e jente de guerra de servicio para conquistar e pacificar otras provincias."*

[1] For bibliographical notes on editions of this Prophecy, see p. 192–194.

| Tizimin: | u profesia | Chilam Balam | tiš kayom [1] kabal | tšen Man: |
|---|---|---|---|---|
| Chumayel: | u profeciado de | Chilam Balam de | siš koyom ka-wi | tšen Mani: |
| Lizana: | profecias de | Chilan Kalam de | siš kayon ka-wi | tšen Mani: |
| Martínez: | u profecia | Chilam Balam | tiš kayon ka-witš | tš'en Mani: |
| Tozzer: | His prophecy | Chilam Balam | of singer Cawich Chen[2] of Mani | |
| Martínez: | | | Kayom | |

| Tiz.: | ošlahun | Ahau u-heɔ'i-wil | Qatun | walak-wil |
|---|---|---|---|---|
| Chu.: | ošlahun | Ahau u-hihɔ'-wil | Qatun-e | walak-wil |
| Liz.: | ošlahun | Ahau u-heɔ'i-wil | Qatun | walak-wil |
| Mar.: | ošlahun | Ahau u-heɔ'i-wil | Qatun | walak-wil |
| Tozzer: | In 13 | Ahau its established | Katun | at this time |
| Lizana: | At the end of the 13th epoch being in power | | | |
| Martínez: | | | | it may be |

| Tiz.: | Itza | walak-wil | tan-kahe | yum | u-tšikul hunab |
|---|---|---|---|---|---|
| Chu.: | Itza | walak-wil | tan-kah-e | yum-e | u-tšikul hunab |
| Liz.: | Itza | walak-wil | tan-katš-e | yum | u-tšikul hunab |
| Mar.: | Itza | walak-wil | tan-kah-e | yum-e | u-tšikul hunab |
| Tozzer: | the Itzas at this time in Tancah | | | oh Father his sign | the only |
| Lizana: | the Itzas | | (and )Tancah [3] | | the sign of a |
| Martínez: | ye Itzas it may be | | ye citizens [4] | Sirs, | |

| Tiz.: | qu kanal u-lom | | u-aom-tše |
|---|---|---|---|
| Chu.: | qu kanal hu-lom | | u-aom-tše |
| Liz.: | qu kanal hu-lom | | u-alom-tše |
| Mar.: | qu kanal hu-lom | | u-ahom-tše [5] |
| Tozzer: | God on high his cross | | his cross of wood |
| Lizana: | God (who is) on high (will come) the cross | | |
| Martínez: | will come from heaven (to us) | | the cross |

| Tiz.: | etsah-om | ti kah-e | u-tšebal | u-sas-hal | yoqol |
|---|---|---|---|---|---|
| Chu.: | etsah-an | ti bal-kah-e | u-tšebal | u-sas-hal | yoqol |
| Liz.: | etkah-an | ti katš-e | u-tšewal | u-kas-hal | yoqal |
| Mar.: | etsah-an | ti bal-kah-e | u-tšebal | u-sas-hal | yoqol |
| Tozzer: | a demonstration | to the world | with which | day breaks | above |
| Lizana: | will show itself | to the world | with which | was lighted | |
| Martínez: | will be shown | to the world | so that | be enlightened the | |

---

[1] The verb, to sing, is **qai**. The text is clearly **kay** which is translated by Martínez as a proper noun.

[2] There is a town of this name near Mani.

[3] Lizana interpolates. See his translation, p. 129.

[4] Martínez translates this *ciudadano ó el que vivo en el centro ó medio del pueblo* (Ticul, p. 164). He notes that Tancah had been destroyed with Mayapan many years previously.

[5] Martínez writes, " **u-ahom-tše** is the tree of life, *arbol de nuestra subsistencia* and **wa-om-tše** is *picota, horca,* the cross of Jesus, his punishment."

| Tiz.: | kab-e | yum | | ɔ'uni |
|---|---|---|---|---|
| Chu.: | kab-e | yum-e | utš | ɔ'uni to |
| Liz.: | kab-e | yum | | ɔ'uni |
| Mar.: | kab-e | yum | utš | ɔ'uni |
| Tozzer: | the earth, | oh Father | a long time ago | there began |
| Lizana: | the earth, | | | there will be |
| Martínez: | world, | Sirs, | for a long time | there has been |

| Tiz.: | mok-tam-ba | | ɔ'uni |
|---|---|---|---|
| Chu.: | mok-tan-ba | utš | ɔ'uni |
| Liz.: | mok-tan-ba | | ɔ'uni |
| Mar.: | mok-t'an-ba | utš | ɔ'uni |
| Tozzer: | fighting with one another | a long time ago | there began |
| Lizana: | a division | | |
| Martínez: | political divisions | for a long time | there has been |

| Tiz.: | sawinal | ka tal-on | ti pul | tšikul |
|---|---|---|---|---|
| Chu.: | sawinal | ka tal-on | ti pul | tšikul |
| Liz.: | kawinal [1] | ka tal-om | ti pul | tšikul |
| Mar.: | sawinal | ka tal-on | ti pul | tšikul |
| Tozzer: | confusion | when we came | carrying | the sign: |
| Lizana: | among the wills [2] | when is brought | | the sign (in the future) |
| Martínez: | discord | | | |

| Tiz.: | quutšmal | ah qin winik-e | yum | hun-awat [3] hun |
|---|---|---|---|---|
| Chu.: | utšmal-e | ah qin-i winik-e | yum-e | hun-awat hun |
| Liz.: | utšmal | ah qin winik-e | yum | hun-awat hun |
| Mar.: | utšmal-e | ah qin winik-e | yum-e | hun-awat hun |
| Tozzer: | at another time | the priest of the men | the Father | one quarter (of) one |
| Lizana: | before arriving | the priests, men | | a quarter (and) a |
| Martínez: | in that time | ye priests of the idols | | |

| Tiz.: | lub-i | wil | u-tal | | | | |
|---|---|---|---|---|---|---|---|
| Chu.: | lub-i | wil | u-tal | a-wil-ik-eš | mut-e | u-tip'il | yetel |
| Liz.: | lub-i | wil | u-tal | a-wil-k-eš | mut-e | u-t'ipil | yetel |
| Mar.: | lub-i | wil | u-tal | a-wil-k-eš | mut-e | u-tip'il | yetel |
| Tozzer: | league | so that | it comes | you will see | fame | appearing with | |
| Lizana: | league | | | you will see | | appearing | |
| Martínez: | | | | | quetzal bird [4] | | |

---

[1] This reading of Lizana is doubtless due to the omission of the cedilla under the c making it k instead of s.

[2] The Spanish is *voluntades*.

[3] This is literally, one *grito*, a numeral suffix used to count miles and quarters of a league.

[4] The idea, as interpreted by Martínez, is that the quetzal will appear with the Maya cross as it is represented on the bas-reliefs at Palenque.

| Tiz.: | | ahom [1] | wil kab | hun | šaman | hun | tšiqin |
|---|---|---|---|---|---|---|---|
| Chu.: | u-aom-tše | a ho-hom | kab | hun | šaman | hun | tšiqin |
| Liz.: | u-aom-tše | ahom | wil kab | hun | šaman | hun | tšaqin |
| Mar.: | u-ahom-tše | ahom | wil kab | hun | šaman | hun | tšiqin |
| Tozzer: | his cross of wood | illuminate | the earth | one | south | one | west |
| Lizana: | the cross | illuminate | | from | pole | to | pole |

Martínez: the Maya cross will illuminate the world in the four cardinal points.

| Tiz.: | ahom | Itzamna qawil: | tal-el u-kah |
|---|---|---|---|
| Chu.: | ahom | Itzamna qawil | tal-el u-kah |
| Liz.: | ahuom | Itzamna qawil: | tal-el u-ah |
| Mar.: | ahom | Itzamna qabwil: | tal-el u-kah |
| Tozzer: | illuminate | Itzamna,Kabwil [2]; | he is coming |
| Lizana: | | (the worship of) vain gods will cease; | he is coming |

| Tiz.: | a yum Itza | tal-el u-kah | u | sas-kun |
|---|---|---|---|---|
| Chu.: | ka yum Itza | tal-el u-kah | ka | su-kun |
| Liz.: | ka yum Itzaa | tal-el u-kah | a | su-kun |
| Mar.: | ka yum Itza | tal-el u-kah | a | su-kun |
| Tozzer: | your father, Itzas | he is coming | | your brother, |
| Lizana: | your father, oh, Itzas | he is coming | | your brother |
| Martínez: | | they are coming | | your brothers |

| Tiz.: | tan tun-e: | qam | a-wula | ah-meš-ob |
|---|---|---|---|---|
| Chu.: | ah tan tun-e: | qam | a-wula-ob | ah-meš-ob |
| Liz.: | tan tunk: | qama | a-wula | ah-u-meš-ob |
| Mar.: | ah tan kun-e: | qam | a-wula | ah-meš-ob |
| Tozzer: | place him ahead of others; | receive | your guests | the bearded ones |
| Lizana: | oh, Tantunites; | receive | your guests | the bearded ones |

| Tiz.: | | liqin | kab-ob | ah-pul-ob | tu tšikul |
|---|---|---|---|---|---|
| Chu.: | ah | liqin | kab-ob | ah-pul | tu tšikul |
| Liz.: | | liqin | kab-ob | ah-pul | tu tšikul |
| Mar.: | | liqin | kab-ob | ah-pul | tu tšikul |
| Tozzer: | | the east, | the villagers | the carriers | his sign |
| Lizana: | | (of) the east | | (who come) to carry | the sign (of) |

---

[1] ahom from ahal.

[2] Martínez has pointed out in Lizana (1633 ed. 1883, f. 4 ob) the following quotation in reference to this place in the text, "Falso Dios Ytsmat vl, donde pusieron la figura de la mano, que les servia de memoria; y dizen que alli le llevaban los muertos, y enfermos, y que alli resucitaban, y sanaban tocandolos la mano, y este era el que està en la parte del Puniente, y assi se llama y nombra Kal ul, que quiere desir, mano obradora."

| Tiz.: | qu yum | uɔqa | u-t'an | qu ku-tal-el |
| Chu.: | qu-e yum-e | uɔqa | u-t'an | qu ku-tal-el |
| Liz.: | qu-e yum | uɔqa | u-t'an | qu ku-tal-el |
| Mar.: | qu-e yum | uɔka | u-t'an | qu ku-tal-el |
| Tozzer: | God the Lord | to arrange | his word | God who may come |
| Lizana: | God | | | (It is) God who comes, |

| Tiz.: | qiknale | tal-el u-kah | u-t'an-il | u-qin |
| Chu.: | kiknale | təl-el u-kah | | u-qin |
| Liz.: | kiknale | tal-el qa-u-kah | | u-qin |
| Mar.: | yiknale | tal-el u-kah | u-t'an-il | u-qin |
| Tozzer: | in (your) company, | he is coming | (to bring) order | the time |
| Lizana: | (he is) gentle and pious, | he is coming | | the new |
| Martínez: | | | to establish the day | |

| Tiz.: | ka kuš-tal-e | ma a sah-t-ik [1] | yoqol-kab-e [2] | yum |
| Chu.: | ka kuš-tal-e | ma a sah-t-ik | yoqol-kab-e | yum-e |
| Liz.: | ka kuš-tal-e | ma ak a sah-t-ik | yoqol-kab-e | yum |
| Mar.: | ka kuš-tal-e | ma ah sah-t-ik | yoqol-kab-e | yum |
| Tozzer: | again living: | you do not fear him above the earth | | Father, |
| Lizana: | in our life: [3] | you have nothing to fear from | the earth | |
| Martínez: | of resurrection | | | |

| Tiz.: | tetš | hunab qu | tš'ab-t-i | koon uɔ-tum-ba |
| Chu.: | tetš | hunak qu | tš'ab-t-i | kon uh-tun-bak |
| Liz.: | tetš | hunak qu | tšab-t-i | kom u-uɔ-tun-bak |
| Mar.: | tetš | Hunab qu | tš'ab-t-ik | koon uɔ-tan-ba |
| Tozzer: | you | the only God | created | us good for themselves |
| Lizana: | you (are) | the only God (who) | created | us good |

| Tiz.: | u-t'an qu-e | yum | | |
| Chu.: | u-t'an qu-e | yum-e | y(etel) ah-kan-ul | ka |
| Liz.: | u-t'an qu-e | yum | | |
| Mar.: | u-t'an qu-e | yum | ah-kam-ul | ka |
| Tozzer: | his words, God, | Father and | the caretaker (of) | our |
| Lizana: | (are) the words of God [4] | | | |

---

[1] Martínez suggests that this may be read, *a despertar ó iluminar al mundo*, He thinks the rendering given here by Lizana and by the author is more probable however.

[2] Martínez thinks that **yoqol-kab** is simply " the earth " for those who live in it.

[3] Carrillo y Ancona (1883, p. 530) translates this, "*ya viene el tiempo de nuestra vida.*"

[4] Carrillo y Ancona (1883, p. 530) gives this as the translation here. Lizana omits it, probably by mistake.

| Tiz.: | | | | | | | |
|---|---|---|---|---|---|---|---|
| Chu.: | pišan | hemak | bin | qam | u-hatš | okan-ti yole ti kaan |
| Liz.: | | | | | | | |
| Mar.: | pišan | hemak | bin | qam | u-hatš | okan-ti yole ti kaan |
| Tozzer: | souls | he who | goes to | receive | very | true | faith to heaven |

| Tiz.: | | | | | | | |
|---|---|---|---|---|---|---|---|
| Chu.: | u-bin | tu-patš | hewak | u-tšun | ka | qin | winik-il.[1] |
| Liz.: | | | | | | | |
| Mar.: | u-bin | tu-patš | hewak | u-tšun | ka | bin (?) | winik-il. |
| Tozzer: | goes | ahead | but | begins | our | day | of men. |

Lizana:

Martínez: *porque es que fueron los indios, en su compañia el dia de nuestra re-división*, or *sea cuando principiemos por la gracia division a ser hombres nuevamente.*

| Tiz.: | ka | wakunto | u-tšikul | kanal | ka | a wakunto ka |
|---|---|---|---|---|---|---|
| Chu.: | ka | wakunto | u-tšikul | kanal | ka | wakunto |
| Liz.: | ka | wakunto | u-tšikul | kanal | ka | wakunto ka |
| Mar.: | ka | wakunto | u-tšikul | kanal | ka | wakunto ka |
| Tozzer: | We | extol | his sign | on high, | we | extol, we |
| Lizana: | (Let) us | praise | his sign | on high | (let) us | praise it by |

| Tiz.: | pak-te helee | ka | wakunto | u | u-aom-tše |
|---|---|---|---|---|---|
| Chu.: | | | yetel | ua-om-tše |
| Liz.: | pak-te hele | ka | wakunto | yu | a-om-tšek |
| Mar.: | pak-te hele | ka | wakunto | | ua-hom-tše |
| Tozzer: | see (it) now | we | extol | his | cross of wood |
| Lizana: | seeing and adoring it, | we | must praise | | the cross: |

| Tiz.: | num-te tah | u-qeš-ah | oqol | helee | u-hel-tu-patš |
|---|---|---|---|---|---|
| Chu.: | num-te tah | uqaš a | u-hoqol | hele | u-hel-tu-patš |
| Liz.: | num-te tah | uqeš a | tšoqol | hele | u-hel-tu-patš |
| Mar.: | num-te tah (tak) uqeš a | | wolah | hele | u-hel-tu-patš |
| Tozzer: | misery | it changed | discord | now | restore |
| Lizana: | falsehood | in exchange | | to-day | will appear against |

| Tiz.: | u-yaš | tšeel | ka | et sah-om | helel |
|---|---|---|---|---|---|
| Chu.: | u-yaš | tšeel | kab | et sah-an | helel |
| Liz.: | u-yah | tšeel | kab | et kah-an | hele |
| Mar.: | u-yaš | tšeel | kab | et sah-an | hele |
| Tozzer: | the first | tree | of the world: | a demonstration | now |
| Lizana: | the first | tree | of the world | a demonstration | to-day (is made) |

---

[1] These words, given only in the Chumayel, are an interpolation by the copyist of the Chumayel manuscript.

| Tiz.: | ti | bal-kah-e | la u-tšikul | hunab | qu kanal | tal ome |
|---|---|---|---|---|---|---|
| Chu.: | ti | bal-kah-e | la u-tšikul | hunab | qu kanal-e | |
| Liz.: | ti | bal-kal-he | la u-tšiqul | hunab | qu kanal | |
| Mar.: | ti | bal-kah-e | la u-tšikul | hunab | qu kanal | tal emel |
| Tozzer: | to | the world: this his sign | | only | god on high | come, lower |
| Lizana: | to | the world: (there is a) sign | | of a | god on high | |

| Tiz.: | laa | qul teš | ah-Itzaeš | ka | a-qul-te | hele | u-tšitš-il |
|---|---|---|---|---|---|---|---|
| Chu.: | lae | a-qul teš | ah-Itzae | ka | a-qul-te | helel | u-tšikul |
| Liz.: | laak | a-qul teš | ah-Itzaao | ka | a-qul-te | hele | u-tšiqlul |
| Mar.: | la | a-qul teš | ah-Itzae | ka | a-qul-te | hele | u-tšikul |
| Tozzer: | all | reverence you | oh, Itzas | and | reverence | now | his sign, |
| Lizana: | | worship it | oh, Itzas | we | | | |

| Tiz.: | quliqul | kanal-e | kak | qul-te to | | tu | hah-il |
|---|---|---|---|---|---|---|---|
| Chu.: | | kanal-e | ka | a-qul-te to | | tu | hah-il |
| Liz.: | | kanal | ka | a-qul-te to | | tu | hah-ik |
| Mar.: | | kanal-e | ka | qul-te | | tu | hah-il |
| Tozzer: | reverence | on high | and | reverence | | with | true |
| Lizana: | | | | shall reverence | | with | true |
| Martínez: | | | | | | with | all your |
| | | | | | | or with | true |

| Tiz.: | qol-ah | ka a-qul-te | to | ka | hah-al qu-e | |
|---|---|---|---|---|---|---|
| Chu.: | kol-ah | ka qul-te | | | hah-al qu | hehelae |
| Liz.: | kol-ah | ka a-qul-te | | ka | hah-al qak | |
| Mar.: | wol-ah | ka a-qul-te | | ka | hah-al qu-e | |
| Tozzer: | good-will: | and adore | him | our | true | God now |
| Lizana: | good-will: | we shall adore | | our | true | God |
| Martínez: heart or good faith | | | | | | |

| Tiz.: | | okestaba | u-t'an | hunab | qu-e | |
|---|---|---|---|---|---|---|
| Chu.: | yum-e | okestaba | u-t'an | hunab | qu-e yum-e | |
| Liz.: | | okestaba | u-t'an | hunab | qu-e yum | |
| Mar.: | | okcstaba | u-t'an | hunab | qu-e yum | |
| Tozzer: | oh, Father: receive | | his word | only | God | |
| Lizana: | | receive | the word (of) | the true | God | |
| Martínez: | | believe | the commandments ot the only | | God | |

| Tiz.: | tal-i | | kanal | a-wah t'an [1] | ul-e | kuš-kin |
|---|---|---|---|---|---|---|
| Chu.: | tal-i | ti | kaan | a-wah t'an be | | kuš-kin |
| Liz.: | tal-i | ti | kaan | a-wah t'an | u-e | kuš-kin |
| Mar.: | tal-i | ti | kaan | a wah-t'an-e | | kuš-kin |
| Tozzer: | he came | | from on high | the commandments: | | invigorate |
| Lizana: | (who) comes | from heaven | to you speaks: | | | recover |

---

[1] These two words are difficult to translate.   I suggest **halmah-t'an,** commandments.

| Tiz.: | ta-wol-ah | Itza | | ahom [1] |
|---|---|---|---|---|
| Chu.: | ka-a-wol-ah | Itzae | | ahom |
| Liz.: | qa-a-wol-ah | Itzaa | | ah hom |
| Mar.: | ka wol | ah Itzae | | ah hom |
| Tozzer: | your good-will | Itzas | | illuminate |
| Lizana: | your will | (and be one) of the Itzas | | will be enlightened |

| Tiz.: | wilkab-ti-ob | ok-s-ik ti yol itšil | u-yan-al |
|---|---|---|---|
| Chu.: | wilkab-ti-ob | ok-s-ik-ob ti yol-e itšil | u-yan-al |
| Liz.: | wilkab-ti-ob | ok-k-ik-ob ti yol itšil | u-yan-al |
| Mar.: | wilkab-ti-ob | ok-s-ik-ob ti yol itšil | u-yan-al |
| Tozzer: | the earth for them | cause to enter the spirit within | its other |
| Lizana: | | those who believe in | to come |

| Tiz.: | Qatun | wale | yab tuba in t'an |
|---|---|---|---|
| Chu.: | Qatun-e yum-e | | yoq tuba in t'an |
| Liz.: | Qutun | | yoq tuba in t'an |
| Mar.: | Qatun | wale | yok tuba in t'an |
| Tozzer: | Katun, | afterwards: | believe (in) my words |
| Lizana: | the age: | Note | if you care (for what) I say (to you), |

| Tiz.: | ken | Chilam Balam ka | in | ɔol-ah | u-t'an |
|---|---|---|---|---|---|
| Chu.: | ken | Chilam Balam ka | in | ɔol-ah | u-t'an |
| Liz.: | ken | Chilan Balan | kan in | ɔol-ah | u-t'an |
| Mar.: | ken | Chilan Balam ka | in | ɔol-ah | u-t'an |
| Tozzer: | I am | Chilam Balam and I | | interpreted | his word |
| Lizana: | I charge | Chilam Balam | your | interpreter; | I say (that which) |

| Tiz.: | hahal | qu | | | in bin |
|---|---|---|---|---|---|
| Chu.: | hahal | qu | tu sin-il-e | yoqol-kab-e | yabi |
| Liz.: | hahal | qu | | | in bi |
| Mar.: | hahal | qu | tu sin-il-e | yoqol-kab-e | yubi |
| Tozzer: | the true | God | among all | above the earth | to know | I go |
| Lizana: | the true | God | | | ordered |

| Tiz.: | hunak | ɔuk ti kab. |
|---|---|---|
| Chu.: | hunak | ɔuk ti kab-e. |
| Liz.: | hunak | ɔuk ti kah. |
| Mar.: | hunak | ɔuk ti kah-e. |
| Tozzer: | many | portions of the pueblo. |
| Lizana: | *porque dello* | *sea el mundo sabedor.* |

[1] The text from here to the end, according to Martínez, fcrms the "esoteric Maya invocation at the end of the Katuns."

## FREE TRANSLATION

The Prophecy of Chilam Balam, the singer of Cawich Chen of Mani. In the Katun beginning in Ahau 13, the Itzas were in Tancah at this time. Oh, Father, the sign of the only God on high is the cross, the wooden cross. This will be shown to the world so that the world will be enlightened. Oh, Father, a long time ago, there began wranglings and confusion when we came bringing the sign. At another time, the priest of the Indians arrived. From a quarter of a league away you will see fame coming with the cross lighting up all parts of the world, also Itzamna Kabwil. Your Father, oh Itzas, is coming. Your brother is coming. Place him ahead of all. Receive your guests, the bearded men, the villagers from the East, the bearers of the sign of God, the Father. The Lord is coming in your company to promulgate his commandments. He is coming to arrange the day of resurrection. You do not fear him who is above the earth. Oh, Father, you are the only God who created us. Good are the commandments of God, the Father, the caretaker of our souls. He who accepts the true faith, goes upwards to heaven. Our time has come (?). We extol his sign above, we extol it by looking at it, we extol his cross. In exchange for misery and discord restore the first tree of the world. Show this now to the world, the sign of the only God on high. You, oh Itzas, reverence all, reverence the one on high, reverence with true good-will and worship him, our true God. Now, oh Father, receive the commandments of the only God who came from on high. Invigorate your good-will, oh Itzas, the earth is enlightened. The spirit enters in another Katun. Believe my message. I am Chilam Balam. I interpreted the commandments of the true God among all the places of the earth. I go to all parts of the country.

## LIZANA TRANSLATION

"La interpretacion es esta muy á la letra y sentido."

"En el fin de la decima tercia edad estando en su pujanza Ytza y (la ciudad nombrada) Tancah, (que está entre Yacman y Tichaquillo, que oy se llama Ychpaa, que es fortaleza o castillo) vendra la señal de Dios que está en las alturas, y la Cruz se manifestarà ya al mundo con la qual el orbe fue alumbrado, avrá division entre las voluntades quando esta señal sea trayda en tiempo venidero, los hombres Sacerdotes antes de llegar una legua, y aunque un quarto de legua no mas vereis la Cruz que se os aparecerá y os amanecerá de Polo a Polo, cessará luego el culto de vanos dioses ya vuestro padre viene o Ytzalanos, o Tantunites ya viene un hermano, recibid a vuestros guespedes, guespedes barbados del Oriente que vienen a traer la señal de Dios, Dios es que nos viene manso y poderoso, ya viene la nueva de nuestra vida. No teneis que temer del mundo tu eres Dios unico que nos criaste, eres Dios amigable y piadoso, ea ensalcemos su señal en alto ensalcemosla para adorarla y verla, la Cruz emos de ensalçar en oposicion de la mentira se aparece oy en contra del arbol primero del mundo, oy es hecha al mundo demonstracion, señal es esta de un Dios de las alturas, esta adorad o gente Ytzalana, adoremosla con voluntad recta adoremos al que es Dios nuestro y verdadero Dios, recibid la palabra de Dios verdadero que del cielo viene el que os habla cobrad juizio y ser los de Ytza los que creyeren seran alumbrados en la edad que está por venir mirad si os importa lo que os digo y advierto, y encargo yo vuestro interprete y maestro de credito Balam por nombre.[1] Y con esto dixe lo que Dios verdadero me mando, porque dello sea el mundo sebedor."

## 5. CHILAM BALAM DE CHUMAYEL

### Passage, p. 77, 78

This text is to be found in the original document (Gordon, 1913) on p. 77, 78. The translations printed here are to be found in Brinton (1882, p. 180, 181) and in Martínez Hernández (1910). This passage is given to show the differences in the two translations of the same text. The original is obviously incorrect in several places, in one of which Brinton changes it to read in one way and Martínez to read in another. A second point should be noted, the difference in the translation of proper names. Martínez makes a proper name of words which are translated by Brinton. This text, therefore, illustrates some of the difficulties met with in rendering the ancient Maya into English. For purposes of verification I have added the Spanish translation of Martínez.

---

[1] From here to the end, the translation of Carrillo y Ancona (1883, p. 532) reads as follows: "*Y con esto he acabado de decir lo que el Dios verdadero me mandó para que lo oiga el mundo.*"

|  | Kan | Ahau | u-qaba | | Qatun | utš-ki | u-sih-il-ob |
|---|---|---|---|---|---|---|---|
| Brinton: | (The) 4th Ahau | | (was) the | name | (of) the | Katun took place the | |
| | births | | | | | | |
| Martínez: | Four Ahau | is called | | | the Katun | in which | were born |

|  | pawaha [1] | | en [2] | kuh | u-y-ahau-ob: |
|---|---|---|---|---|---|
| Brin.: | were taken possession | | of | the towns | by the rulers: |
| Mar.: | the Pawah | | they | began | the rulers of the years: |

|  | oš-(la)-hunte | ti | Qatun | lik | u-tepal-ob | lai |
|---|---|---|---|---|---|---|
| Brin.: | (It was) the 13th | | Katun | in which | they ruled | these |
| Mar.: | 13 periods of the | | Katun | thus | elapsed [3] | thus |

|  | u-qaba-ob | tamuq u-tepal-ob lae. |
|---|---|---|
| Brin.: | (were) their names | while they ruled. |
| Mar.: | they were called | in the course of time. |

|  | Kan | ahau u-qaba | Qatun | em-ki-ob |
|---|---|---|---|---|
| Brin.: | (The) 4th Ahau | (was) the name | (of) the Katun | in it they arrived |
| Mar.: | (The) 4th Ahau | (was) called | the Katun | in which they arrived |

|  | noh-he-mal | ɔ'ee-mal | u qaba-ob lae. |
|---|---|---|---|
| Brin.: | the great arrival | the less arrival | as they are called. |
| Mar.: | the great descent, | the small descent, | they were called thus. |

|  | Oš la hunte | ti | Qatun | lik | u-tepal-ob | lik u- |
|---|---|---|---|---|---|---|
| Brin.: | (It was) the 13th | | Katun | in which | they ruled | in which |
| Mar.: | 13 periods of the | | Katun | thus | elapsed | thus |

|  | qaba-tik-ob | tii | walak u-kut-ob | lae [4] ošlahun |
|---|---|---|---|---|
| Brin.: | they took names at that time | while they resided | here in the 13th | |
| Mar.: | they were called at that time | they took root | 13 periods | |

|  | kut hi | u-kut-ob lae. |
|---|---|---|
| Brin.: | the residence was continued | they resided here. |
| Mar.: | lasted | their permanency. |

|  | Kan | Ahau | u-Qatun-il | utš-ki | u-kašan-tik-ob |
|---|---|---|---|---|---|
| Brin.: | (The) 4th | Ahau | Katun | (then) took place | the search |
| Mar.: | In the 4th | Ahau | Katun | it happened | that they found |

---

[1] Brinton writes this patš-ah u kah.

[2] Martínez changes this to em-kutš.

[3] In several places Martínez has translated tepalob in two ways. In the translation line by line he translates the word as *gobernaron* whereas in his version given as a whole he translates it as *transcurrieron*. In his line by line translation this sentence reads, *Trece periódos del katun, así gobernaron; así se llamaron mientras gobernaron.* The Martínez translation given here follows that given by him on p. 35–38 (1910).

[4] This word is crossed out in the original MS.

|        | u-Chich'een Itzae. | Tii       | uɔ-kinnabi | makɔil-ti-ob |
| ------ | ------------------ | --------- | ---------- | ------------ |
| Brin.: | for Chichen Itza.  | At that time | they were improved | marvelously |
| Mar.:  | Chichen Itza.      | There     | was modified | their religion |

|        | tumen | u-yum-oobe: | kan ɔuk | luq-ki-ob |
| ------ | ----- | ----------- | ------- | --------- |
| Brin.: | by    | the fathers: | in four divisions | they went forth |
| Mar.:  | by    | their Lords: | four tribes | set out |

|        | kan-ɔukul-kab | u qaba-ob. | Liqul | ti liqin |
| ------ | ------------- | ---------- | ----- | -------- |
| Brin.: | the four territories | which were called. | From | the east of |
| Mar.:  | Cantsuculcabes | called. | From | the east side |

|        | Qin-kolah-peten | bini | hun ɔuki. | Kul šaman |
| ------ | --------------- | ---- | --------- | --------- |
| Brin.: | Kin Cola Peten | came torth | one division. | From the north of |
| Mar.:  | to Kin Cola Peten | went | one tribe. | To the sacred north |

|        | nakok-ob | hoq | hun ɔuk[k]i. |
| ------ | -------- | --- | ------------ |
| Brin.: | Nacocob | came forth | one division. |
| Mar.:  | ascending | set out | one tribe. |

|        | He iš | hoqi | hun ɔuki-e | hol-tun | Suyuua |
| ------ | ----- | ---- | ---------- | ------- | ------ |
| Brin.: |       | Came forth one | division | (from the) gate of | Zuyuua |
| Mar.:  | This other | set out | one tribe | (from the) entrance of | Zuyuah |

|        | ti tšiqin. | Hoqi | hun ɔu[k]ki-e | kan heq |
| ------ | ---------- | ---- | ------------- | ------- |
| Brin.: | to the west. | Came forth | one division | from Can hek |
| Mar.:  | to the west. | Went | one tribe | to the place ot the four |

|        | uiɔ, | bolonte | uiɔ | u-qaba | u-luumil lae. |
| ------ | ---- | ------- | --- | ------ | ------------- |
| Brin.: | the mountains, | the nine | mountains | (as) is called | the land. |
| Mar.:  | hills, | that of the nine | hills | was called | their land. |

|        | Kan | Ahau | u-Qatun-il utš-ki | u-payal-ob |
| ------ | --- | ---- | ----------------- | ---------- |
| Brin.: | (The) 4th | Ahau | Katun then took place | the calling together |
| Mar.:  | (The) 4th | Ahau | Katun it happened | that they were called |

|        | tu kan-ɔuk-[k]il-ob | kan-ɔuk-kul-kab | u-qaba-ob. | [Ka |
| ------ | ------------------- | --------------- | ---------- | --- |
| Brin.: | of the four divisions, | the four territories as they were called. | | |
| Mar.:  | the Cantsuciles | the Cantsuculcabes called. | | When |

|        | emi-ob ti | yum-tal-ob.][1] |
| ------ | --------- | --------------- |
| Briu.: | | |
| Mar.:  | they arrived there (they were received) | as Lords. |

|        | Ka | emi-ob | tu Chich'een Itzae, | ah Itza | tun u-qaba-ob. |
| ------ | --- | ------ | ------------------- | ------- | -------------- |
| Brin.: | And | they arrived | at Chichen Itza, | men of Itzə | they were called. |
| Mar.:  | When | they arrived | at Chichen Itza, | the Itzas | they were called. |

---

[1] The words within the braces are omitted in the Berendt copy of the MS. which was used by Brinton.

|  | Ošlahunte ti | Qatun | lik | u-tepal-ob-i | ka |
|---|---|---|---|---|---|
| Brin.: | [It was the] 13th | Katun | in which | they ruled | then |
| Mar.: | Thirteen periods of the | Katun | thus | elapsed | and |

|  | oki | u-qeban-t'an-ob-i | tumen | Hun nak keeli | ka |
|---|---|---|---|---|---|
| Brin.: | were introduced | the plottings | by | Hunnac Ceel | and |
| Mar.: | took place | the treachery | of | Hunac Ceel | and |

|  | paši (paš-ki) | u-kab-ob. | Ka bini-ob | tan |
|---|---|---|---|---|
| Brin.: | were destroyed | the territories. | Then they went | in the midst ot |
| Mar.: | was abandoned | their towns. | And they went | to the wilderness |

|  | yol-tše | tan | Šuluk-mul u-qaba. | Kan Ahau |
|---|---|---|---|---|
| Brin.: | the forests | in the midst of | Xuluc mul so called. | (The) 4th Ahau |
| Mar.: | forest | to a place | Xuluc mul called. | In the four Ahau |

|  | u-Qatun-il | utš-ki | yawat | pišan-ob-i. |
|---|---|---|---|---|
| Brin.: | Katun | (then) took place | singing | for their happiness. |
| Mar.: | Katun | took place | the cries | of the blessed. |

|  | Ošlahunte ti | Qatun | lik | u-tepal-ob-i | yetel |
|---|---|---|---|---|---|
| Brin.: | (It was the) 13th | Katum | in which | they governed | and (had) |
| Mar.: | Thirteen periods of the | Katum | thus | elapsed | with |

|  | u-numya-ob-i. | Wašak | Ahau u-Qatun-il | utš-ki |
|---|---|---|---|---|
| Brin.: | heavy labor. | The 8th | Ahau Katun | thus it took place (that) |
| Mar.: | their exile. | In the eight | Ahau Katun | thus it took place |

|  | yulel-ob | yala-ob | ah Itza | u-qaba-ob |
|---|---|---|---|---|
| Brin.: | there arrived | the remainder | of the Itza men as they were called; |  |
| Mar.: | arrived | the remainder | of the Itza men | so called |

|  | ka | ul-ob | til | ka walak | u-tepal-ob |
|---|---|---|---|---|---|
| Brin.: | then | they arrived; | and | about that time | they governed |
| Mar.: | as soon as | they arrived |  |  | they took root |

|  | Chakanputune. | Ošlahun | Ahau | u-Qatun-il | u-heɔ'-k-ob |
|---|---|---|---|---|---|
| Brin.: | Chakanputun. | In the 13th | Ahau | Katun | founded |
| Mar.: | at Chakanputun. | In the thirteen | Ahau | Katun | they founded |

|  | kah | Mayapan | Maya | winik | u-qaba-ob. |
|---|---|---|---|---|---|
| Brin.: | the city of | Mayapan | the Maya | men | those called. |
| Mar.: | the pueblo of | Mayapan | Maya | men | they were called. |

|  | Wašak | Ahau | paš-ki | u-cab-ob-i | ka |
|---|---|---|---|---|---|
| Brin.: | (In the) 8th | Ahau | were destroyed | the towns | then |
| Mar.: | (In the) eight | Ahau | were abandoned | the towns | and |

|  | wektšabi [1] | ti peten | tulakal. | Wak | Qatun-i |
|---|---|---|---|---|---|
| Brin.: | they were driven out | of the province | wholly. | (In the) 6th | Katun |
| Mar.: | they disappeared | from the region | whole. | (In the) six | Katun |

---

[1] The original text has wek tša hi. Brinton has wak tša bi.

|  | paš-ki-ob | ka | hawi | u Maya | qaba-ob. |
|---|---|---|---|---|---|
| Brin.: | they were destroyed | and | it was ended | with Maya | those called. |
| Mar.: | they were dispersed | and | they ceased | Maya | calling themselves |

|  | Buluk | Ahau | u-qaba | u-Qatun-il | hau-ki |
|---|---|---|---|---|---|
| Brin.: | (It was the) 11th | Ahau | | Katun. | in which it ended |
| Mar.: | In the eleven | Ahau | | Katun | they ceased |

|  | u-Maya | qaba-ob. | Maya | winik-ob | Christiano |
|---|---|---|---|---|---|
| Brin.: | with Mayas | those called. | The Maya | men | Christians |
| Mar.: | Maya | calling themselves. | Maya | Indians | Christians |

|  | u-qaba-ob | tulakal | u-kutš-kabal | ooma | San Pedro |
|---|---|---|---|---|---|
| Brin.: | were called | all | came under control | | of Saint Peter |
| Mar.: | they called (now) | all | those of the province, | sons | of Saint Peter |

|  | yetel Rey | ah-tepal-e. |
|---|---|---|
| Brin.: | and the king | the rulers. |
| Mar.: | and the king | his Majesty. |

## MARTÍNEZ TRANSLATION

"El cuarto *ahau* se denomina el *katun* en que nacieron los *Pauah*. Comenzaron los regentes de los años. Trece períodos del *katun;* así transcurrieron; [1] así fueron designados en su transcurso. El cuarto *ahau* se llama el *katun* en que llegaron: la gran bajada, la pequeña bajada, así fueron designadas. Trece períodos del *katun;* así transcurrieron; así fueron designados, allí se radicaron; trece períodos duró su permanencia. En el *katun* cuarto *ahau* sucedió que hallaron Chichén Itzá. Allí fué compuesto lo divino en ellos por sus señores. Cuatro tribus salieron llamadas 'cantzuculcabes.' La tribu de lado oriente se dirigió á Kin-colah-petén. Al sagrado norte, ascendiendo, salió una tribu. Esta otra tribu salió de la entrada de Zuyuah al poniente. Una tribu salió hacia el lugar de los cuatro cerros. La de los nueve cerros se llama la tierra de ellos. En el *katun* cuarto *ahau* sucedió que fueron llamados los *cantzuciles*, apellidados *cantzuculcabes.* Cuando llegaron fueron aceptados como señores de la tierra. Cuando llegaron á Chichén Itzá, se llamaron Itzaes. Trece períodos del katun, así transcurrieron y tuvo lugar la traición de Hunac-Ceel. Y fueron abandonados sus pueblos, y fueron á los bosques desiertos á un lugar llamado Xuluc-mul. En

---

[1] It has already been noted that the translation given by Martínez when he is translating line by line differs in several places from the translation he gives as a whole. The latter is more free in several places.

el *katun* cuarto *ahau* tuvo lugar el llanto de los bienventurados. Trece períodos del *katun* transcurrieron, inclusive el período de sus padecimientos. En el *katun* octavo *ahau* llegaron los llamados restos de los Itza: luego que llegaron se radicaron en Chakanputun. En el *katun* trece *ahau* fundaron el pueblo de Mayapan; se llamaron mayas. En el octavo *ahau* fueron abandonadas las poblaciones y se esparcieron por toda la región. En el sexto *katun* fueron dispersos y dejaron de llamarse mayas. En el *katun* once *ahau* cesaron de llamarse mayas. Indios mayas cristianos se llaman hoy todos los de la provincia, hijos de San Pedro y de S. M., el Rey de España."

# PART III

# AN APPRAISEMENT OF WORKS
# RELATING TO THE MAYA LANGUAGE

# PART III

# AN APPRAISEMENT OF WORKS
# RELATING TO THE MAYA LANGUAGE

## INTRODUCTION

In the Bibliography (Part IV) there are listed over 700 different
works, not including second editions, on or in the Maya language
or referring to it in some way. It should be understood that the
language in question is that dialect spoken in the peninsula of
Yucatan and not the Maya linguistic stock which covers a far
more extended area.

The large number of books and manuscripts dating from the
earliest days of the Conquest and continuing down to the present
time indicates the interest taken in this field.

This Appraisement of the works mentioned in the Bibliography,
it is hoped, will serve as an aid to those who desire some idea of
the relative value of the works listed under the various headings.

## HISTORY OF MAYA LINGUISTIC RESEARCH

WRITERS OF THE XVI, XVII, XVIII CENTURIES. The history of
early research in the Maya language centers around the names of
nearly all the authors of the Church who were in Yucatan in the
XVI, XVII, and XVIII centuries. According to instructions from the
Holy See each priest was to learn the language of the country and
was to teach and to preach to the natives in their own languages.[1]
The priests saw at once that a phonetic transcription of the languages was necessary. They accomplished this with no small suc-
cess so that books are found written in the native languages but
with Spanish characters soon after the appearance of the first
white men. In fact, the first books printed in America were trans-

---

[1] See Gomez de Parada, 1722. The titles of all books referred to by author
and date are given in full in Part IV.

lations of the Catechism and sermons in the Nahuatl language of Mexico.

Landa (1864, p. 94), the second Bishop of Yucatan,[1] writing between 1561 and 1566, states that priests were sent to Yucatan from Guatemala and from Mexico and that they established themselves at Campeche, founded in 1541, and at Merida, founded one year later, under the protection of the Adelantado and of his son, both called Francisco de Montejo. A monastery was built at Merida and the priests occupied themselves with learning the Maya language which was difficult. Juan de Herrera was probably the first teacher of Maya written in the Spanish characters.[2]

Villalpando is the first Maya scholar as well as the first author of works in Maya. Landa writes *"El que mas supo fue fray Luis de Villalpando que començo a saberla por señas y pedrezuelas y la reduxo a alguna manera de arte y escrivio una doctrina christiana de aquella lengua."* [3]

Starting with Villalpando, *"el proto-lingüista Maya,"* [4] there is a constant succession of priests, both Spanish and native born, who

---

[1] Carrillo y Ancona (1892–95, p. 318) writes in this connection, *"El Illmo Sr. Landa es en realidad el quinto Obispo de Yucatan, y si suele contárse le como segundo, es solo con respecto á la segunda época de la historia de esta Diócesis."*

[2] Cogolludo (1688, lib. v, cap. v) writes in this connection, *" Fray Iuan de Herrera, aunque Lego, era muy habil, sabia escribir bien, cantar canto llano, y organo, y aprendiendo la lengua, se ocupaba en enseñar la Doctrina Cristiana à los Indios, y en especial à los niños. Para poder mejor lograr su deseo en estos exercicios, puso forma de Escuela, donde acudian todos los muchachos, dandolos sus padres con mucho gusto y voluntad, aprehendian las Oraciones, y a muchos enseñò a leer, escribir, y cantar."*

[3] Garcia Cubas (1888–91, v. 1, p. xv) speaks of Villalpando in the following words: *"En 1546 llegaron directamente de España á la península algunos religiosas franciscanos con el P. Fr. Luis de Villalpando, á fin de afianzar la conquista por medio de la persuasiva y pacífica predicación evangélica."* Lizana (1633, ed. 1893, p. 47 ob.) writes in describing Villalpando, *"A lo qual le ayudaban con gran cuidado sus compañeros Fray Melchor de Benavente, y Fray Angel Maldonado, que eran Sacerdotes, y Fray Juan de Herrera Lego de la Provincia de los Angeles enseñaba la doctrina Christiana a los Indios, y en particular a los niños, poniendoles escuela, y enseñandoles a leer, escribir, y cantar canto llano, y organo, que todo esto sabia el santo baron Lego, Fr. Juan, aunque su estado era de Lego, y con tan santos, y solic'tos trabajadores, etc."*

[4] Carrillo y Ancona (1870; ed. 1872, p. 148) writes, *" Villalpando, pues, debia ser y fué en realidad, como vamos á ver, el proto-lingüista maya, esto es, el que*

devoted themselves to the study of the Maya language, writing grammars, collecting vocabularies, and translating the *Doctrina* into Maya in addition to writing sermons in the native language.[1] After Villalpando the first author of importance is Bishop Diego de Landa whose work entitled *Relación de las cosas de Yucatan*, written between 1561 and 1566, has contributed more to Maya research than any other single book. From this a start was made in deciphering the Maya hieroglyphic writing. Little is known regarding the linguistic work of Landa. He was probably the first to open a school for teaching Maya to the priests in the Monastery of San Antonio at Izamal. Cogolludo (1688, lib. v, cap. xiv) writes *"El que mas presto, y con mayor perfeccion la supo, fue el bendito Padre Fr. Diego de Landa, de quien se dize (no sin admiracion) que à pocos dias la hablada, y predicaba, como si fuera su lengua nativa."*

Solana, who was in Yucatan from 1560 to his death in 1600, is the author of the first dictionary (1580) which has come down to us. Ciudad Real, who died in 1617, is famous for his *Gran Calepino* in six volumes on which he was at work for 40 years.

Gaspar Antonio Xiu, Sanchez de Aguilar and Carlos Mena are some of the natives of Yucatan who are authors of works in the Maya language.[2]

---

*aparece el primero al frente de los que estudian el idioma yucateco, y al frente del catálogo de los escritores que cuenta la civilizacion en este mismo idioma."*

Torquemada, cited by Cogolludo (1688, lib. vi., cap. xii) writes *"Que por ser (el P. Villalpando) el primero que supo la lengua destos naturales, y que la predicò con exemplo de essencial Religioso, es digno de eterna memoria."*

The importance of Villalpando is shown by the fact that he is the only author on Maya mentioned by Bobron (1875).

[1] For excellent accounts of these authorities and their work, see Carrillo y Ancona (1870; ed. 1872).

[2] Carrillo y Ancona (1870; ed. 1872, p. 167–168) gives an interesting account of another author of about this time. He writes, *"El célebre Fr. Bernardino de Valladolid . . . vino á Yucatan siendo aun mas jóven, por el año de 1634, y su aficion al estudio de la lengua maya era como un delirio, una verdadera pasion. Allá por los años de 1641 ó 1642, se celebraron unas funciones literarias ó actos en el convento mayor de San Francisco de esta ciudad de Mérida, pues siguiendo el uso laudable de las universidades y colegios de Europa, ya de algunos años atras acostumbraba celebrarse aquellas funciones en Yucatan en las cátedras de los PP. franciscanos. Por aquella ocasion, pues, Fr. Bernardino, ya tan distinguido y profundo escolar, como perfecto gramático y orador del idioma indígena de su nueva patria, con anuencia del superior de la órden, el R. P. Fr. Antonio Ramirez; y del profesor de lengua yucateca, el P. Fr. Diego Perez, de Mérida,*

Padres Coronel, San Buenaventura and Beltran de Santa Rosa should be mentioned for their excellent work on the Maya grammar.[1] Notice should also be made of the unknown authors of the Motul and San Francisco dictionaries. The work of this early time has hardly been equalled either in quantity or, in some respects, we may add, in quality.

One other writer of these early centuries deserves special mention, Andrés de Avendaño. He is the author of a most important *Relación* (1696) which is fortunately extant. The list of his linguistic works is a long one. These have all disappeared. I pass over the names of many others of the early writers on Maya subjects whose works are listed in the Bibliography. Mention is made of these early efforts under the discussion of the Maya grammars, vocabularies, sermons, the Catechism, etc. A glance at the list of works which are now known only by name (p. 151) shows the fertility of Maya research in the xvi, xvii, and xviii centuries.

There follows a note on the most important modern authors in the field of Maya linguistics with a short account of their work. A detailed list of their manuscripts and books will be found in the Bibliography.

PADRE JOAQUIN RUZ. He was born in Merida in 1785 and died in 1855. He was the first modern author of works on Maya. He was a Franciscan and the most fertile writer on Maya subjects.

*concibió y ejecutó el pensamiento feliz de sostener un acto literario en lengua maya, realzando así el grande mérito que en ella con su continuo estudio habia encontrado. Ademas, al par de las tésis literario-teológicas que sostuvo el célebre actuante, puso una muy notable para la filología, reducida á proponer: que el languaje ó texto bíblico podia vertirse en toda su exactitud característica al idioma maya, de modo que los lugares difíciles de las Sagradas Escrituras podian declararse á la letra en esta lengua.*

*Al principiar una funcion tan extraordinaria y notable como esta, y á que en pos de los hombres de letras fué atraida una gran multitud, así por la singularidad del caso, como por la facilidad de su inteligencia, pues el idioma maya es vulgar entre todas las clases sociales del país, Fr. Bernardino se presenta con las entereza y la modestia de un verdadero sabio, y pronuncia un discurso brillante y sólido (¡lástima que no se hubiese conservado!) original, lleno de propiedad y belleza, en idioma yucateco.*

*Las réplicas, las soluciones, la conferencia toda, fué en el mismo idioma, quedando todos los concurrentes llenos de complacencia y admiracion."*

[1] The relative merit of their works has been discussed exhaustively in Part I (p. 9).

Carrillo y Ancona (1870; ed. 1872, p. 172–179) and Sosa (1884, p. 942–948) give short accounts of his life. The former, quoted also by Sosa (p. 944), most truthfully expresses the number of the works by Ruz when he writes, "*Ninguno de los escritores de la lengua maya se presenta con tan considerable número de volúmenes, debidos á su incansable y sábia pluma, como el R. P. Fr. Joaquin Ruz, que hizo verdaderamente sudar la prensa con la edicion de sus obras en el primer tercio del siglo actual, y precisamente cuando era para el país una cosa rara la publicacion de un libro.*" The writings of Ruz are of little value from the standpoint of the study of Maya linguistics. He did his best to revise the language so that it conformed as far as possible with Latin standards. Brinton (1900, p. 212) writes in this connection, "His style has however been severely criticized by almost all competent scholars as impressing on the native language grammatical forms, terms of expression, and compounds, foreign to its history and character. Ruz was well aware he was making these innovations, but claimed they were called for to elevate and develop the powers of the Maya."

JUAN PIO PEREZ. He was born in Merida in 1798 and died in 1859. He was the first modern Maya scholar. Carrillo y Ancona (1870; ed. 1872, p. 140–145, 179–186), Carrillo Suaste (1875), Ancona (1877), Sosa (1884, p. 803–806), and Martínez Alomía (1906, p. 142–146) are among those giving his biography. Berendt (1871a) describes his work in great detail. He was selected as the Maya interpreter to the Secretary of State at Merida. The successful fulfillment of the duties of this office shows his ability to use the Maya language and the position gave him access to much Maya material. Stephens (1843, v. 2, p. 117) writes, "I had been advised that this gentleman (Perez) was the best Maya scholar in Yucatan, and that he was distinguished in the same degree for the investigation and study of all matters tending to elucidate the history of the ancient Indians. His attention was turned in this direction by the circumstance of holding an office in the department of state, in which old documents in the Maya language were constantly passing under his eyes. Fortunately for the interests of science and his own studious tastes. on account of some political disgust he withdrew from public life, and, during two years of retirement, devoted himself to the study of the ancient chronology of Yucatan."

Perez realized the importance of preserving material on the Maya language which was fast disappearing. He made a collection of original documents in Maya and copies of various manuscripts which he did not personally possess. This collection was copied in great part by Berendt and these copies furnished the foundation for the Berendt Collection. The importance of the Books of Chilam Balam was very early recognized by Perez. The most important parts of his collection were included in a volume entitled "Chilam Balam" (Berendt, 1868, in B. L. C. No. 49)[1] and another called by Carrillo y Ancona, "Codice Perez" (Perez, 2, copy in B. L. C. No. 50).[2] The contents of this volume are treated fully by Carrillo y Ancona (1870; ed. 1872, p. 140-145).

There is another document more properly called the "Codex Perez" (Perez, 1842). This is the famous manuscript given by Perez to Stephens which formed a part of the Chilam Balam de

---

[1] The letters B. L. C. refer to the Berendt Linguistic Collection in the library of the University Museum, Philadelphia. The number refers to the entry in Brinton's Catalogue of this collection. See Brinton, 1900.

[2] This Codice Perez has the following *Advertencia*, written by Carrillo y Ancona and republished by him in his 1870; ed. 1872, p. 140–141: "*Estas apuntaciones son del Sr. D. Juan Pío Perez. Las tomaba ó extractaba de los manuscritos que solia hallar en poder de los indios, y el fin principal que con ellas se proponia era hacer un caudal suficiente de noticias para escribir sobre el Calendario yucateco. Es, pues, muy preciosa esta colección, pues no solo revela mucho de lo que puede apetecerse sobre el cómputo del tiempo, usado por los antiguos yucatecos, sino que servirá tambien para testificar la existencia de muchas obras manuscritas de autores indios, que se han ido perdiendo; pero cuya memoria conservarémos en conjunto en este volúmen, dándole el nombre general de 'Códice Perez,' para perpetuar tambien así el nombre del ilustre yucateco moderno á quien se lo debemos. El 'Codice Perez' será, pues, siempre un importante monumento bibliográfico, de gran trascendencia para la historia, de valor inestimable para los yucatecos, y, por gran fortuna nuestra, una de los mas ricos tesoros de nuestro gabinete particular. — C. C.*"

Carrillo y Ancona (1870; ed. 1872, p. 179) writes: "*Debemos á la pluma del Sr. Perez las siguientes obras: I. 'Opúsculos varios ó notas á las copias y traducciones del yucateco al español, y del español al yucateco, observaciones y apuntaciones sobre diferentes materias, correspondientes á la historia y lengua de Yucatan, esparcida en fragmentos en diferentes manos y países. Mss. inéditos.'* He adds that the first part of this collection is the Codex Perez. The other part of the collection is undoubtedly contained in the several works in manuscript recorded in the Bibliography.

Mani, and is described at length in another place (p. 184). This manuscript made possible the first attempts to synchronize Maya and Christian chronology. His *Cronologia Antigua* (Perez, 1843) has not contributed greatly to the knowledge of the hieroglyphic writing as he made a grave mistake in the interpretation of the length of one of the Maya time periods. Two printed dictionaries bear his name in addition to several important manuscripts not already mentioned, copies of many of which are in the Berendt Linguistic Collection.

FLETCHER, HENDERSON, KINGDON. These three Protestant missionaries were in British Honduras in the second quarter of the last century. There is little that is known regarding the details of their linguistic work and there is, as a consequence, some confusion regarding the authorship of certain books.[1] Richard Fletcher was a Methodist missionary stationed at Corozal and he wrote a catechism in Maya (1865a) for his denomination and a brief series of prayers (1865). The Maya language used by these three Protestant missionaries is very corrupt. Carrillo y Ancona (1870; ed. 1872, p. 191) writes, "*Fletcher se ha apropiado no mas el maya corrompido de hispanismo, ó esa habla amestizada que usa el último vulgo del país, y que no sabemos si llamar mejor un castellano bárbaro ó un maya tristemente degenerado.*"

Alexander Henderson, a Baptist missionary, came to Belize in 1834. John Kingdon came to Belize in 1845 after having served for thirteen years as a missionary in Jamaica. There was constant trouble between these two workers, Kingdon being the more to blame if one is to believe the account of Crowe (1850), another missionary in this field. There are vague notices in this book of the linguistic work of the mission. It would seem as if Henderson devoted most of his time during the first years in this field to work on the Mosquito language. Kingdon (1847) translated the grammar of Ruz and it was he who seems to have been the more energetic in translating portions of the scriptures into Maya. Crowe (1850, p. 493) writes, "Before the close of 1849, Mr. Kingdon had purchased a piece of plantation land on the banks of the Old River

---

[1] Pilling (1885, p. 258) furnishes an interesting letter from Carrillo y Ancona regarding the authorship of various works ascribed to Henderson which were really written by Fletcher.

. . . and thus founded his fifth missionary station, since his arrival four years before. The spot chosen was about twenty miles from Belize, in a very thinly-peopled neighborhood, where his studies and labours in translating Maya would be but little interrupted." The Baptists abandoned their mission in British Honduras in 1850. Henderson evidently stayed on in the country as his *Maia Primer* was published in 1852 and he left in manuscript six volumes of a dictionary of the dialect of Maya spoken in Bacalar (Henderson 1859–66).

BRASSEUR DE BOURBOURG. He was born near Dunkirk in 1814 and died in 1874. He should be remembered not for what he wrote himself but for the manuscripts which he published. He became interested in the Maya field and visited Yucatan in 1865. Carrillo y Ancona (1870; ed. 1872, p. 193–195) and Martínez Alomía (1906, p. 172–175) give short biographies. Mitre (1909–11, v. 1, p. 19–24) sums up his work. The introduction to the Bibliography of Brasseur de Bourbourg (1871, p. vii–xlvii) under the title *Coup d'œil sur les études américaines dans leurs rapports avec les études classiques* serves to show his method of deductions and his fantastic theories.

The importance of the work of Brasseur de Bourbourg from the standpoint of Maya studies is his publication of the Codex Troano (1869–70) and his finding and publishing the manuscript of Landa (1864). In addition to this he published practically the whole of the grammar of San Buenaventura (1869–70, v. 2, p. 1–99). His vocabularies are of no value as will be pointed out later. Berendt (7, in B. L. C. No. 181, fol. 62) has a section marked "Brasseuriana-Troano-Landa" which contains a good criticism of the work of Brasseur de Bourbourg.

CARL HERMANN BERENDT. He was born in Danzig in 1817 and died in Coban, Guatemala, in 1878. He was undoubtedly the greatest scholar of the Maya language although the list of his actual publications is a short one. His biography is given by Brinton (1884–85: 1900, p. 204, note). Berendt came to New York in 1851. He went almost immediately to Central America and, with the exception of occasional visits to the United States, remained in Mexico and Central America until he died in 1878. He made several visits to Yucatan, copying manuscripts and studying the language. He visited all the noted libraries of Middle America collecting material on the Maya language. His monument is the Berendt Linguistic Collection of manuscripts and books in the library of the University Museum of the University of Pennsylvania. Brinton (1900) who purchased this collection and presented it to the Museum has made a catalogue. As already pointed out, the foundation of this library on the Maya side was the copies made by Berendt of the Pio Perez collection the originals of which have now been scattered. Up to the time when Mr. Gates began his photographic reproductions every student of Maya linguistics was absolutely dependent upon this Berendt material.

Berendt's copy of the Motul dictionary with emendations, additions and comparisons with other vocabularies is a monumental work in itself. He brought together for the first time copies of practically everything then known on the Maya languages. His *Lengua Maya Miscelanea* (Berendt, 1868*d*, 3 v. in B. L. C. Nos. 42, 43, 44); and his scrap books (Berendt, 5, 6, 7 in B. L. C. Nos. 179, 180, 181) contain a large mass of important material on the Maya language.[1]

BISHOP CRESCENCIO CARRILLO Y ANCONA. He was born at Izamal, Yucatan in 1837 and died in Merida in 1897. He was the friend of Pio Perez and kept alive the Perez tradition regarding the importance of Maya studies. Carrillo Suaste (1875, p. xi–xx), Sosa (1873: 1884, p. 215), Martínez Alomía (1906, p. 237–244), Rivero Figueroa (1918), and Anon 1897*a*, present biographical notes. The most complete list of his works is published by Rivero Figueroa and Canton Rosado (1918, p. 65–78). Carrillo became the thirty-sixth bishop of Yucatan in 1887. His interest in the early history of the country was great. He founded the archaeological museum at Merida and also started several different literary periodicals. His most important work was on the historical rather than on the linguistic side. Special attention should be called to his *Disertacion sobre la historia de la lengua Maya ó Yucateca* (1870; ed. 1872) and to his main work on the history of the bishops of Yucatan (1892–1895). He was the editor of *El Repetorio Pintoresco* (1863).

---

[1] Bowditch (1908, 1908*a*) and Schuller (1) collated several of the manuscripts in this Berendt Collection. Gates reproduced the Bowditch notes and several of those taken by Schuller. Various unidentified articles should be noted (Berendt 9) together with his copies of various documents of a religious nature (Berendt 1868a in B. L. C. Nos. 46, 47).

DANIEL GARRISON BRINTON. He was born at Thornbury, Pennsylvania, in 1837, and died in Philadelphia in 1899. He was a worthy successor to Berendt. His field of activity was broader than that of Berendt. His great interest in Maya studies caused him to purchase the Berendt Collection and later he presented it to the University of Pennsylvania. Biographical notes are to be found in Brinton (1900b), Martínez Alomía (1906, p. 245–249) and in several transactions of scientific societies of which he was a member. Brinton (1898) sums up his work on American languages. The chief work of Brinton (1882) on Maya linguistics was the publication of an English translation of the chronological parts of several of the Books of Chilam Balam, copies of which he obtained in the Berendt Collection. It is worthy of note that this work, although written almost forty years ago, still remains the most extensive translation from the Maya ever undertaken at one time.

WILLIAM GATES. Mr. Gates of Point Loma, California, is a Maya scholar to whom all students of Maya linguistics owe a deep debt of gratitude. An indefatigable energy, great acumen, and a knowledge of the Middle American field have enabled Mr. Gates to gather together the largest collection of documents on the Maya linguistic stock ever assembled in one place. Moreover, not being satisfied to possess this remarkable collection he desired copies of all available documents on the Maya field owned by libraries and by individuals. With only a few exceptions he now possesses either the original manuscript or the photographic reproduction of all the known documents on the Maya stock, as well as many others on the languages of Southern and Central Mexico. Furthermore, he possesses the only known copies of several printed works on this field. Mr. Gates has made duplicate sets of many of his photographs and he has allowed Mr. Charles P. Bowditch to purchase a set of these. Mr. Bowditch has very generously presented them to the Peabody Museum. The Gates Collection stands, therefore, in the first place.

His photographic reproductions covering the field included in the scope of the present work are mentioned in the Bibliography.[1]  For

---

[1] It should be noted that the bibliographical data on manuscripts photographed by Gates have been taken in general from the reproductions rather than from the original manuscripts themselves. Blank pages in the manu-

convenience a list of them is included here. First place should be given to the Motul and San Francisco dictionaries without which no important work in translation can be done. Anon 5 and 26 are also vocabularies. Next come the unique imprint of the Coronel grammar (1620) and the first editions of the grammars of San Buenaventura (1684) and of Beltran (1746) together with the grammars of Ruz (1844) and Kingdon (1847).

Second place in point of importance should be given to the reproductions of the originals of the Chilam Balam de Calkini, Kaua, Nah, Tekax, and Tizimin and of copies of the Chilam Balam de Calkini, Chumayel, Ixil, Kaua, and Tizimin together with the copy of the Crónica de Chicxulub. The Bowditch notes on Berendt 1868, the Chicxulub, the Mani, and Oxkutzcab manuscripts with the Prophecies, and the Schuller notes on Berendt 1868c and the Mani manuscript come next. The various medical portions of the Books of Chilam Balam should be mentioned, the Judio de Sotuta and Anon, 13, 14, 15, 16, and 19 (Berendt copy). The Ritual of the Bacabs comes here.

The Avendaño manuscript stands alone in importance. The secular manuscripts are as follows: Titulos de Ebtun, Libro de Cacalchen, the Pat Letters, Documentos de Ticul, the Xiu Chronicles, Anon 2 and Anon 8. Finally we also have Gates reproductions of the following religious works: — the Doctrinas of Coronel (1620a), Beltran (1740; ed. 1816), Ruz (1822, 1849, 1851), Fletcher (1865a), Nolasco de los Reyes, and Anon (1803, Berendt copy, 7, 20, 23), together with the sermons of Coronel (1620b), Dominguez y Argaiz, Carvajal (1, Berendt copy), Acosta, Vales, Vela, Oraciones de Teabo, and Anon (21 and 22, Berendt copy).

JUAN MARTÍNEZ HERNÁNDEZ. He was born in Merida in 1866 and educated at Georgetown University, District of Columbia, as a lawyer. He is a descendant of the Adelantado, Don Francisco de Montejo. He has an intimate knowledge of the Maya language as is shown by the list of his published and unpublished works in the Bibliography. He is one of a few gentlemen in Merida who now interest themselves in the study of the language of the natives.

---

scripts have not generally been reproduced so that there may be differences in certain cases in the number of pages in the reproduction and in the manuscript itself.

## BIBLIOGRAPHIES

It is only necessary to note the number of bibliographies mentioned in the following pages to realize the great interest taken in the subject of American languages and, more especially, the languages of Middle America. Little attempt has been made to list the large number of bibliographies which cover the general field of history and travel, although many of these books also contain references to works on the Maya linguistic stock. No bibliography is included here which does not contain books on the Maya language of Yucatan.

BIBLIOGRAPHY OF BIBLIOGRAPHIES. The best list of the bibliographies of Mexico and Central America is that contained in **Mitre (1909–11, v. 1, p. 5–70)**. He discusses at some length most of the important lists of books from this region. **Viñaza (1892, p. xix–xxv)** and the **Bulletin of the New York Public Library (1909, p. 622–624, 810–811)** also give very good lists of bibliographies on Middle America. **Lejeal (1902, p. 5–7)** and **Lehmann (1907)** cover the same ground in a less extensive way.

MISSING AUTHORITIES. There is a long list of works on the Maya language references to which are made in the early histories but many of these books or manuscripts have disappeared in the course of time. It is to be hoped that some of these missing authorities will be found just as the long lost grammar of Coronel (1620) turned up in Mexico in 1912.

Landa who wrote his *Relación de las Cosas de Yucatan* (1864) sometime between 1561 and 1566 mentions Villalpando and his work. No books of this author have survived. Landa himself wrote a grammar and possibly a *Doctrina* which are lost. Other references occur in several of the early works to books, copies of which are now unknown. **León Pinelo (1629)** and **Nicolas Antonio (1672)** list many works which have vanished. **Lizana (1633)** and **Cogolludo (1688, p. 439–440)** refer in their histories to several writers whose manuscripts have disappeared. Cogolludo is especially full on this point. **Clavigero (1780–81)** also gives a short bibliography several entries of which are unknown at the present time. Later notices of missing authorities are usually taken from the lists already mentioned. These lost works are given more or less fully in the bibliographies of **Eguiara (1755)**, **Beristain y Souza (1816–21)**, **Squier (1861)**, **Carrillo y Ancona (1870;** ed. **1872)**, **Civezza (1879)**, **Carrillo y Ancona (1878–82;** ed. **1883**, p. 123–127), **Sanchez (1886)**, and **Medina (1907–12)**. A separate list of these missing authorities is given in **El Registro Yucateco (1845,** p. 358), an almost complete list by **Berendt (1868b)**, and shorter lists by **Brasseur de Bourbourg (1869–70,** v. 2, p. i–iv), **Viñaza (1892,** p. 241 *et seq.*), **Brinton (1897)**, and **Juan Molina (1904–13,** v. 1, p. 327–330).

In the following list of the missing authorities I have tried to arrange the authors in as near a chronological order as possible. The Berendt manuscript (1868b) gives, in several instances, dates for the various manuscripts which I have not been able to find in any other authority. This list compiled from the above sources is as follows:

### List of Missing Authorities

*XVI Century.*

Villalpando: *circa* 1546.

(1) Arte.[1]

(2) Doctrina.

1571 Vocabulario, missing (?).

Landa: in Yucatan, 1549–1579.

(1) Arte (possibly a revised edition of Villalpando (1).

(2) Doctrina (?).

Solana: in Yucatan 1560–1600.

(1) Sermones.

(2) Noticias sagradas.

(3) Apuntaciones sobre las antigüedades (?).

(4) Estudios historicos

(5) Apuntes de las santas escrituras.

(6) Apuntamientos historicos.

Xiu: *circa* 1593.

1582 Relacion sobre las costumbres.

(1) Vocabulario.

---

[1] The number in front of each work refers to the corresponding number in the Bibliography under the author.

Ciudad Real: died, 1617.
(1) Gran calepino (Motul dictionary ?).
(2) Diccionario (?).
(3) Tratado curioso.
(4) Sermones.

Torralva: in Yucatan, 1573–1624.
(1) Sermones.

Nájera, Gaspar de: in Yucatan, *circa* 1579.
(1) Relación de las antigüedades de Yucatan.

Anon.[1]
(28) Vocabulario grande.
(30) Un librillo escrito . . . en el idioma de los Indios.

*XVII Century.*
Sanchez de Aguilar.
(1) Catecismo, 1602 (Berendt).

Acevedo: in Yucatan, 1592–1624.
(1) Gramatica.
(2) Instrucciones catequísticas.

Cuartas: died, 1610.
(1) Arte.

Coronel: in Yucatan, 1590–1651.
(1) Vocabulario.
(2) Doctrina.
(3) Confesionario.

Rincon: died, 1647.
(1) Sermones.

Valladolid: in Yucatan, 1617–52.
(1) Sacramentos.
(2) Dioscórides.
(3) Vocabulario (?).

Mena: died, 1633.
(1) Sermones.

Cardenas:
1639 Relación.

---

[1] Clavigero gives the name of José Dominguez as an author of Maya works.

Vidales: wrote, 1644–48.
(1) Vocabulario.
(2) Sintáxis.
(3) Florílegia medicinal.
Rivas Gastelu.
(1) Gramatica (Lacandone), 1685 (Berendt).
San Buenaventura.
(1) Diccionario, 1695 (Berendt).
*XVIII Century.*
Avendaño: in Yucatan, 1705. 1750 (Berendt).
(1) Arte.
(2) Diccionario.
(3) Diccionario abreviado.
(4) Diccionario botánico.
(5) Diccionario de nombres de personas.
(6) Explicacion de varios vaticinios.
*XIX Century.*
Carvajal.
(2) Collection of proverbs.
Henderson, *circa* 1860.
(1) Book of Genesis in Maya.
(2) Psalms in Maya.
(3) English translation of Beltran (1746), ?
Kingdon, *circa* 1860.
(1) English translation of Beltran (1746), ?
(2) Dictionary.

EARLY HISTORY AND EARLY BIBLIOGRAPHY. No attempt has been made to exhaust the references to books and manuscripts mentioned in the early histories, such as those of **Martyr (1516)**, **Mendieta (1870)**, written about 1590, **Herrera (1601-15)**, **Gregorio García (1607)**, **Torquemada (1613)**, **Remesal (1620)**, **Cogolludo (1688)**, **Villagutierre (1701)**, **Boturini (1746)**, and other similar works. The earliest general bibliographies which mention books on the Maya language are those of **León Pinelo (1629; 2d ed. by Barcia, 1737-38)** and **Nicolas Antonio (1672 and 1696)**, the former a sequel of the latter although published first. **Eguiara (1755)** is the first to give a list composed solely of the books on Latin America. This work was never completed, only the first volume, through C, being printed. Four note-books containing other parts of the manuscript are said to be in the library of the Cathedral of Mexico City.[1] The manuscript bibliography of **Alcedo (1807)** is especially good for biographical details and he gives his opinion of the early bibliographies.[2] **Harrisse (1866, p.** xiii–xlii) also gives a very good discussion of the important bibliographies. **Clavigero (1780–81; ed. 1826, v. 2, p.** 396) gives a *Catálogo de algunos autores Europeos y criollos que han escrito sobre la doctrina y moral cristianas en las lenguas de Anahuac.* This is probably the first attempt to bring together in one place a list of the writings on Mexican linguistics. **Hervás y Panduro (1784; ed. 1800–05, v. 1, p.** 289–290) and **Vater (1815)** are more ambitious attempts at listing linguistic works covering larger areas.

GENERAL AND AMERICAN BIBLIOGRAPHY. There is a long list of general bibliographies many of them specializing on books on America. It is only necessary to give a few of these which contain references to works on Maya linguistics. **Rich (1835), Ternaux-Compans (1837), Leclerc (1867 and 1878), Sabin (1868–92), Andrade, (1869;** Languages, p. 362–368), **Quaritch (1873** *et seq.*), **Field (1873, 1875), Civezza (1879), Murphy (1884)** and **Menéndez y Pelayo (1888)** are a few of the more important general bibliographies.

---

[1] Mitre, 1909–11, v. 1, p. 28–29, probably from *Boletin de Sociedad Mexicana de Geografia y Estadistica,* v. 10, no. 2, p. 77.

[2] Harrisse (1866, p. xxiv) comments as follows on Alcedo's work, " This bulky compilation seems to be based entirely upon Pinelo-Barcia, with the addition of a few biographical notes, which are of interest only when referring to modern American authors. The titles are given in alphabetical order, abridged, and selected with very little discrimination." This is not a fair estimate of the work of Alcedo. The latter gives far more details than Barcia and the biographical notes are very full and refer to the early as well as to the later writers. In a few cases Alcedo is better than Beristain y Souza for biography. It is interesting to note that Alcedo (f. iv *ob*) comments as follows on Barcia, " *Tan lleno de errores en los nombres y apellidos de los autores, en los titulos de las obras y en los años y lugares que se imprimieron, que ó ya fuese por defecto de los copiantes ó del impresor apenas hay articulo sin yerro; por cuya razon es de poquisima utilidad, y no menece el titulo que tiene.*" It is evident that Alcedo did not have access to Cogolludo and therefore he failed to mention several of the early writers.

AMERICAN LINGUISTICS. **Ludewig (1858;** Maya, p. 102–103, 226–227) is an excellent work on American linguistic research. Others are **Icazbalceta (1866)** and **Platzmann (1876: 1903)**. **Winsor (1889,** v. 1, p. 427) has a bibliographical note on American languages. The catalogues of **Hiersemann (1891** et seq.) often contain important material on the Maya language. Special mention should be made of three works which come in this class. The first of these is the most exhaustive list contained in the proof-sheets of **Pilling (1885)**, made in collaboration with librarians of the great collections of Americana. This work is indispensable for investigations on American languages.

The second of these is a bibliography of the *Lenguas Indigenas de América* by **Viñaza (1892)**. He has made use of many of the earlier lists and gives under most of the entries the various early references to the books in question. It is a most useful work.

The third, and perhaps the most valuable general bibliography on American linguistics, is a *Catálogo Razonado* by **Mitre (1909–11, 1912)**. This contains full critical remarks on the different works and often quotes long passages from the various grammars.

**Stein (1897,** p. 261–262) mentions a few of the bibliographies on American linguistics.

MIDDLE AMERICA. GENERAL WORKS. Of the older authorities the first place in this class should be given to the monumental work of **Beristain y Souza (1816–21)** with additions by **Ramirez (1898)**. This is founded on the bibliography of Eguiara (1755), but it is a great improvement in arrangement and it is very much more completo. The biographical notes are especially valuable and are followed by many of the later authorities. Next in importance come the great works of **Medina (1898–1907, 1907–12)**. Next in point of time to Beristain y Souza come two sale catalogues, **Anon (1868)** and **Fischer (1869)**. The latter contains the Berendt books which were not included in those bought by Brinton. The bibliography of **Brasseur de Bourbourg (1871;** Maya, p. 169–172) is a very good one containing a list of many manuscripts as well as printed books. **Pinart (1883)** contains much the same material as that in the Brasseur de Bourbourg list as Pinart bought the greater part of the library of the latter. **Ramirez (1880)** is a well known work, more important for Mexico than for Central

America however. Icazbalceta (1886) has a bibliography of xvi century books with additions by Leon (1902). Beauvois (1899) should be mentioned here. V. de P. Andrade (1899) has an essay on the books of the xvii century, Leon (1902–08) on those of the xviii and Leon (1902a) again on those of the xix century. Lejeal (1902; Languages, p. 31–39) has a very good general bibliography of Middle America. Lehmann (1907) has slight material on the Maya. The Bulletin of the New York Public Library (1909) is a good general working list. The two catalogues of the library of Wilkinson (1914, 1915) include a large number of documents never before noted, together with several unique books. There is also a manuscript list of books by Wilkinson (1). This bibliography is very disappointing as it contains practically no original material. Furthermore, it is far from complete. Medina serves as the main source of the work. The contents are noted in the Bibliography.

The greater part of the rare material in the Bancroft Library at the University of California is included in the notes taken by Tozzer (1918).

MIDDLE AMERICA. LINGUISTICS. Romero (1860) has a list of writers on Mexican languages. The bibliography of Sanchez (1886) gives a few of the early writers on the Maya language. Leon (1905) covers the linguistic field superficially.

CENTRAL AMERICA. GENERAL WORKS. Bandelier (1881) is especially good from the side of early histories. It is of little importance, however, on the subject of languages.

CENTRAL AMERICA. LINGUISTICS. The *Monograph* of Squier (1861) is well known as an excellent second-hand bibliography. He uses the biographical material in Beristain y Souza and Harrisse has noted that the titles are taken from other notices of the books rather than from the books themselves.[1] Haebler (1895; Maya, p. 566–568) is to be especially recommended. Brasseur de Bourbourg (1859) gives a bibliography of the languages of Central America.

---

[1] Squier made use of the works of Beristain y Souza, Remesal, Vasquez, Cogolludo, Villagutierre, Juarros, etc., but he did not use Balbi, Hervas y Panduro, Gilii, Adelung, Vater, and Buschmann as he presumed these were known to investigators.

The Catalogue of the Berendt Linguistic Collection by **Brinton** (**1900**; Maya, p. 204–215) is probably the most valuable printed bibliography of the Maya linguistic stock. It contains material not to be found in any other work, especially as regards manuscripts. Mention has been made in another place of this collection (p. 147). **Gates** (**2**) has prepared a finding list of manuscripts and printed material on the languages of the Maya stock. He also has an excellent essay (**Gates, 1915**) on the unpublished material in the Maya dialects. **Stoll** (**1884**, p. 73–78) contains a short list of books on the Maya family.

YUCATAN. GENERAL WORKS. No attempt is made here to touch upon any material on the ruins of Yucatan. It must not be forgotten also that all the books listed in the previous divisions have something in them on the Maya dialect. There are noted here only those books bearing on the language which are limited in their general contents to Yucatan. **Castillo** (**1866**) published only the first volume of an historical and biographical dictionary which has some good material on the language.[1] **Berendt** (**7** in B. L. C. No. 181) has a fair bibliography of Yucatan in manuscript. **Carrillo y Ancona** (**1868, 1871, 1871a, 1878–82**) gives bibliographical material on the Maya language. **Sosa** (**1884**) and especially **Martínez Alomía** (**1906**) are biographical-bibliographical works of some importance. **Menéndez** (**1906**) has a good list of writers on Yucatan. **Saville** (**1921**) also has a list of works on Yucatan.

YUCATAN. MAYA LINGUISTICS. **Berendt** (**8** in B. L. C. No. 11) and **de Rosny** (**1875**; ed. **1904**) have bibliographical notes limited to the Maya dialect. **Carrillo y Ancona** (**1870**; ed. **1872**) should be mentioned here. **Brinton** (**1882**, p. 72–77) discusses the Maya grammars and dictionaries. **Tozzer** (**1917**, p. 184–186) gives a bibliography covering the Books of Chilam Balam.

BIOGRAPHICAL WORKS. **Alcedo** (**1807**), **Beristain y Souza** (**1816–21**), **Castillo** (**1866**), **Carrillo y Ancona** (**1870**; ed. **1872**), **Sosa** (**1866: 1884**), and **Martínez Alomía** (**1906**) are excellent reference books on the biographies of writers on Maya linguistics.

---

[1] Reference should be made here to another work of **Castillo** (**1861**) which Carrillo y Ancona (1870; ed. 1872, p. 138) considers "*preciosa.*"

SALE CATALOGUES. References have been made to a few of the important sale catalogues containing books on Maya linguistics. No attempt has been made to exhaust this list. The following are noted in the bibliography: **Anon (1868)**, **Fischer (1869)**, **J. M. Andrade (1869)**, **Quaritch (1873** *et seq.*), **Field (1875)**, **Clarke (1878)**, **Ramirez (1880)**, **Maisonneuve (1881: 1897)**, **Trübner (1882)**, **Murphy (1884)**, **Peñafiel (1886)**, **Chadenat (1889** *et seq.*), **Hiersemann (1891** *et seq.*), **Leon (1896)**, **Platzmann (1903)**, **Hamy (1909)**, and **Wilkinson (1914; 1915)**.

PERIODICALS. There is a long list of periodicals printed in Yucatan, principally in Merida and in Campeche. With few exceptions each has had a very short history. The newspaper, **La Revista de Merida,** founded in 1859, has been published continuously up to the present time with the exception of the years 1916, 1917. It often contains important articles on the Maya language. **El Museo Yucateco (1841–42)** was published in Campeche, only two volumes of which appeared. **El Registro Yucateco (1845–49)** only lasted for five years. This publication (1845, p. 233–235) gives a list of the various periodicals appearing in Yucatan from 1813 to 1845. **Medina (1904)** and **Molina (1904–13, v. 3, p. 574)** also give lists. Few of these papers contain anything of interest on our subject. **La Revista Yucateca (1849)**, **El Semanario Yucateco (1878–82)**, and **El Seminario Conciliar** are names of other early serial publications. **Martínez Alomía (1902)** gives a list of the periodicals published in Campeche from 1813 to 1889. The **Calendario de Espinosa,** a modern publication, appearing annually, often contains short articles on the Maya language.

## CLASSIFICATION OF LANGUAGES

GENERAL. The monumental work of the Abbé **Hervás y Panduro (1784;** ed. **1800–05)** is the first attempt at a classification and study of the languages of the world.[1] Hervás (1784) treats of the classification of the languages and v. 1 of the 1800–05 edition considers the languages of America. There is a very brief notice of the Maya language (1800–05, v. 1, p. 289–290).

---

[1] For an excellent discussion of this work and the material used in its preparation, see Mitre 1909–11, v. 1, p. 116–122.

The *Mithridates* begun by **Adelung** (**1806–17**) and continued by
**Vater** is the second great attempt to classify the languages of the
world. The 3d volume, 2d part, treats of the languages of America.
Neither this nor the work of Hervás y Panduro is of much present
use.

MIDDLE AMERICA. The attempts to classify the languages of
America have been many. These classifications are of interest to
us only as they treat the languages of Middle America, especially
those of the Maya stock and particularly those of the Maya dialect.
No attempt has been made to list the numberless minor works
such as *Estadisticas*, etc., printed in Mexico, which often give lists
of languages spoken in the Republic or in the various states.[1]
**Juarros** (**1808**; ed. **1857**, v. 2, p. 35), **Latham** (**1850**, p. 410–411)
and **C. Malte-Brun** (**1862**, p. 59) give imperfect lists of the Maya
dialects. The **Ministerio de Fomento** (**1854**) and **Siliceo** (**1857**),
Secretary of the Ministerio de Fomento, Mexico, both publish brief
accounts of the dialects of Maya. **Brasseur de Bourbourg** (**1857**)
has an incomplete list. **Orozco y Berra** (**1864**, esp. p. 56 and map)
gives one of the best of the earliest classifications. **Malte-Brun**
(**1878**, p. 19–20) republishes this with corrections. **Brasseur de
Bourbourg** (**1865**, p. 127–129,) **Bancroft** (**1874–76**, v. 3, p. 571),
**Berendt** (**1878**, map), **Larrainzar** (**1875–78**, v. 2, p. 407–409, map)
and **Bastian** (**1878–89**, v. 2, p. 343) all give more or less complete
lists of the dialects of the Maya-Quiche stock. **Pimentel** (**1876**)
gives a full list with an interesting arrangement of the dialects as
branches of a tree.

**Stoll** (**1884**, map, and **1886**, p. 300–303) is one of the best writers
on this subject. **Cubas** (**1876**, p. 105–112: **1884**, p. 23) and **Batres**
(**1885**) are less important. **Brinton** (**1891**) and **Cubas** (**1888–91**,
v. 1, p. v, xv; also v. 5, p. 473) are serviceable. **Gerrodette** (**1891–
92**, map), **Charencey** (**1894**, p. 345 346), and **Peñafiel** (**1897**), the
latter arranged by states, are secondary in importance. **Sapper
1893: 1895a: 1897: 1905**) ranks with Stoll as an authority. **Leon**
(**1900**; ed. **1903**, p. 282, map), **Gatschet** (**1900**), and **Keane** (**1901**;
ed. **1911**, v. 2, p. 22) have fairly complete lists. **Peñafiel** (**1900**,
p. 92–97, 216—221, 340—343, 464–469) gives a census of people

---

[1] Two of the most important of these works are those of **Regil** and **Peon**
(**1852**) and **Baqueiro** (**1881**) as they treat solely of Yucatan.

speaking Maya and its various dialects. The work of **Thomas**
(**1902**), amplified and corrected by Swanton, (**Thomas and Swanton, 1911,** map) stands at present as the best discussion of the
different linguistic families of Middle America. **Zayas** (**1908,** p. 160–
164) and **Beuchat** (**1912,** p. 405–406) give brief accounts of the
different Maya dialects. **Joyce** (**1914,** p. 201–202) follows Thomas
and Swanton in the main. Attention should be called to the work
of **Gates** (**1920**), more especially to his map (p. 606). **Wilkinson**
(**1**) has a tentative arrangement of the Maya dialects with their
location.

## AFFINITIES

It is not necessary to treat here the much debated question regarding the possible affiliation between the Maya culture and that
in other parts of the world. For bibliographical purposes it is well
to record the most important discussions regarding the possible connection between the Maya language and that spoken in other parts
of the world. It is hardly necessary to add that these treatises are
of no scientific value. No attempt is made to discuss the possible
affiliation of any features other than language.

EUROPEAN LANGUAGES. The connection between Maya and
several of the languages of the Indo-European and Semitic groups
is discussed by **Brasseur de Bourbourg** (**1869–70,** v. 2, p. i–xlix).[1]
**Douay** (**1900,** p. 94) quotes Brasseur de Bourbourg. The work of
LePlongeon, as described by **Salisbury** (**1877**), and the writings of
**LePlongeon** himself (**1879: 1880: 1880a, 1881: 1881a: 1896**) are
interesting examples of other fantastic ideas regarding the connection between the Maya language and those of the Old World. **Carrillo y Ancona** (**1880b;** ed. **1883,** p. 624–631) refutes the testimony
of LePlongeon of a connection between Maya on the one hand and
Greek and Egyptian on the other. **Ober** (**1884,** p. 102) quotes Le
Plongeon regarding a Chaldean connection. **Ancona** (**1877**) compares some Maya words with Egyptian. **Dusaert** (**1882**) refutes
Brasseur de Bourbourg.[2]

OCEANIC AND ASIATIC LANGUAGES. A belief in a relationship
between Maya and the languages of the Oceanic area is held by

---

[1] See reference to this in Mitre (1909–11, v. 3, p. 63).

[2] See also in this connection the list of comparative vobabularies on p. 293.

**Thomas (1894)**, **Tregear (1898)**, and **Campbell (1898–99)**. **Kennedy (1861, p.** 139) thinks there is some affiliation between Maya and Chinese or Japanese. **Douay (1905)** denies that there is any connection between Maya and Japanese. Books containing comparative vocabularies of Maya and Chinese are discussed on p. 179.

South American Languages. **Douay (1)** discusses the affiliation between the Maya vocabulary and that of Quechua.[1]

Antillian Languages. A connection between Maya and the languages of the Antilles was thought possible from very early times.[2] **Oviedo (1535)**, quoted in turn by **Vater-Adelung (1806–17)** and **Prichard (1843)**, thinks that Cuba and Yucatan were related linguistically. **Bachiller (1883, chap.** 5) states that Cuba was not populated from Yucatan but he compares Maya with the languages of the Antilles. **Douay (1894: 1900)** believes that there are certain lexical similarities between Maya-Quiche and the language of Haiti.

## DESCRIPTION OF LANGUAGE

Apart from the more detailed examination and description of the Maya language given in many of the grammars, there is often a short notice of the dialect in many of the early histories and in a large number of the later works. In the **Colección de Documentos Inéditos (1898–1900, v.** 11, 13) and in other collections of this sort brief reference is often made to the language. The **O'Neil** manuscript **(1795)** probably belongs here. **Barton (1797, p..lxxiii)** quotes Clavigero and mentions the Maya dialect. **F. H. A. von Humboldt (1811, v** 2, p. 246), followed by **J. B. Gordon (1820, p.** 73), has a short statement including the fact that the language is guttural. **Balbi (1826; ed.** 1835, p. xxx), **Ternaux-Compans (1843)**, and **Granado (1845, p.** 167) give very brief notes on the language. **Brasseur de Bourbourg (1855)** gives a short description of the language and **(1857–59, v.** 1, p. 63) mentions the fact that the Maya is undoubtedly the mother of the Tzental of Chiapas.

---

[1] In this connection, he uses the Maya vocabularies of Brasseur de Bourbourg (1869–70) and Charencey both of which are very imperfect.

[2] Peter Martyr in *De Insulis nuper inventis* writes "*Quorum idioma si non idem, consanguineum tamen.*"

Jehán (1864, col. 881) describes the language. Bollaert (1870, p. 291) quotes Beltran regarding Maya diction and Hovelaque (1876, p. 107) classes Maya among the agglutinative languages. Orozco y Berra (1864, p. 155–159) presents almost the first good account of the language outside that of the grammars which are noted in another place. Garcia y Garcia (1865, p. lxxv) is one of the many who states the ease with which Maya is learned by the Spanish-speaking population. Carrillo y Ancona (1865: 1866; ed. 1883, p. 555–561: 1878–82; ed. 1883, p. 101–123) presents his own ideas regarding the language and also quotes freely from the earlier authorities. J. G. Müller (1855) has a very short note. Brinton (1871) has a description of the Maya stock in general. Ancona (1878–1905; ed. 1889, v. 1, p. 112–117) limits his observations to the language of Yucatan. Brinton (1881, p. 623: 1882a, p. 218, note) speaks of the figurative expressions it is possible to make in Maya. In Brinton (1885) the philosophical character of the Maya is described according to an unknown manuscript of von Humboldt. Palma y Palma (1901, p. 108–131) has a very interesting chapter on the richness of expression possible in Maya.

The long description of Brasseur de Bourbourg (1869–70, v. 2, p. i–xlix) is practically worthless. Larrainzar (1875–78, v. 2, p. 407–409) and Rockstroh (1878, p. 1–13) give a general description of Maya. Malte-Brun (1878) has a statement taken from Orozco y Berra (1864). Baeza (circa 1880) has a paper on the Maya language. Short accounts of the language also appear in Winsor (1889, v. 1, p. 427), Juan Molina (1896, p. 332–335), Spencer (1873–1910, div. ii, pt. 1b, p. 51), Mendez (1898), Brinton (1900a, p. 207), and Lehmann (1907). Tozzer (1902–05) makes several general observations on the language. Mitre (1909–11, v. 3, p. 61–64) summarizes the description of the language taken from several sources. Hestermann (1915) has a few scattering observations on the language.

## GRAMMARS

Carrillo y Ancona (1881; ed. 1883, p. 123), quoted by Brinton (1882, p. 72), states that thirteen grammars of the Maya language have been written. This number could be considerably increased at the present time.

XVI CENTURY. Mention has already been made of the early work of Villalpando (§ 1). He was the author of a grammar, according to Landa (1863, p. 94), which was probably printed but no copy is now known. His dictionary, probably founded on the vocabulary contained in the grammar was printed in 1571. The grammar is supposed to have been perfected by **Landa** (§ 1)[1] and to have furnished some of the material for the grammar of Coronel (1620).

XVII CENTURY. It is probable that the first Maya grammar of this century was written by **Acevedo** (§ 1) [2] who came to Yucatan in 1592 and died at the end of the first quarter of the century.[3] Another grammar of about this time is that by **Cuartas** (§ 1). The earliest grammar now available is that of **Coronel (1620)**,[4] the teacher of Cogolludo. The only copy known is in the possession of Mr. Gates. As previously noted (p. 10), it undoubtedly furnished the foundation for the grammar of San Buenaventura. Other grammars of this century, all of which have disappeared, are those written by **Vidales** (§ 2) toward the end of the second quarter of the century [5] and one on the Lacandone dialect by **Rivas Gastelu** (§ 1), a native of Guatemala.

**San Buenaventura (1684**; 2d ed **1888)**, a French Franciscan stationed in Merida, wrote the grammar which has been described elsewhere (p. 10) on or about 1675.[6] This was published in 1684

---

[1] Cogolludo (1688, lib. vi, cap. i) writes, "*Fr. Lorenço de Bienvenida, con no menos feliz despacho, que se presumió de la solicitud de tan gran Religioso, y traxo una Mission de diez Religiosos, que le dió el Rey para esta Provincia, y sabiendo que avian llegado à desembarcar en el Puerto de Zilam, el R. Padre Custodio dió orden al Padre Fr. Diego de Landa, que era Guardian de Merida, para que fuesse al Puerto, y los recibiesse, y llevandolos al Convento de Ytzmal les leyesse el Arte de la lengua de estos naturales, que èl avia perficionado, y que en sabiendole se fuesse à su Convento de Merida.*"

[2] Carrillo y Ancona (1870; ed. 1872, p. 165) writes: "*Vino con la cruz del misionero á la provincia de Yucatan, y entre sus muchos servicios y esclarecidas virtudes, la historia refiere su dedicacion particular al estudio del idioma yucateco, de que escribió un 'Manual ó compendio elemental,' y una como 'Miscelánea Maya,' ó coleccion de escritos varios sobre este idioma y de Tratados morales escritos en él, procurando suplir con estos trabajos el defecto natural de su lengua.*"

[3] See Lizana (1633; ed. 1893, p. 102) for details of his work.

[4] For a full discussion of the grammars of Coronel, San Buenaventura, and Beltran, see Part I, p. 9–14.

[5] Beristain y Souza (1816–21, v. 3, p. 276) states that he wrote from 1644 to 1648. Carrillo y Ancona (1883, p. 124) places this writer among those who worked in the XVI Century.

[6] The *Aprobacion del R. P. Fr. Juan de Torres* is dated May 19, 1675.

with a *fac-simile* edition in 1888. Until a few years ago this was
considered the first of the Maya grammars which had come down
to us. With the appearance of the single copy of Coronel's work
first place in point of time now belongs to that. It has been stated
that San Buenaventura follows Coronel with great, fidelity. It is
quite evident that San Buenaventura's grammar, on the other
hand, furnished the data for grammatical material on the Maya
given by **A von Humboldt** [1] (**1811,** English ed. v. 2, p. 246) and he,
in turn, was followed by **Adelung** (**1806–17,** v. 3, pt. 3, p. 16–23).
**Pimentel** (**1862–65,** v. 2, p. 1–39; ed. **1875,** v. 3, p. 105–138, 230–
275) follows San Buenaventura. **Brasseur de Bourbourg** (**1869–70,**
v. 2, p. 1–84) has printed the greater part of this grammar under a
different arrangement and **Mitre** (**1909–11,** v. 3, p. 64–70) has
given a full outline of this grammar of San Buenaventura. **Bryne**
(**1885,** v. 1, p. 191–193; ed. **1892,** v. 1, p. 195–197) has some grammatical notes after Brasseur de Bourbourg.

XVIII CENTURY. One of the grammars of this century is that
of **Avendaño** (§ **1**) who held the title of *Difinidor* in Yucatan in
1705.[2] This work has disappeared.

**Beltran** (**1746;** 2d ed. **1859**) and his famous grammar come in
this century. As previously noted (p. 10), this grammar, by a
native of Yucatan, seems by far the best of the early works on the
Maya. Brasseur de Bourbourg is altogether too severe in his criticism of this grammar in comparison with that of San Buenaventura. He writes (1871, p. 24), " *Il possédait parfaitement sa
langue: mais il n'en comprit pas le génie comme son prédécesseur,
le père Gabriel de Saint Bonaventure, auquel il emprunta, toutefois,
une partie de son travail; aussi sa grammaire, diffuse et mal conçue,
manque-t-elle de lucidité.*" Seler (1887) is also inclined to favor San
Buenaventura to Beltran.[3] Beltran was a native of Yucatan and

---

[1] **W. von Humboldt (1: 2)** is the author of two manuscripts on the Maya
grammar.

[2] For an excellent account of the missionary labors of this Franciscan, see
his work (**1696**), translated by Mr. Charles P. Bowditch, and collated with
other material by **Means (1917).**

Carrillo y Ancona (1883, p. 125) places Avendaño among the writers of the
xᵥɪɪ Century. Berendt dates these works of Avendaño about 1750.

[3] Gates also regards Beltran's work as inferior to that of the two earlier
writers whose grammars are extant.

a good Maya scholar. He taught Maya in Merida about 1740. His grammar was written in 1742 and printed in 1746 with an excellent reprint in 1859.

Berendt (1867) states that he saw **Henderson** (§ 3) at work in Belize and that the latter made a translation into English of Beltran's grammar. According to Ludewig (1858, p. 227) **Kingdon** (§ 1) made an English translation of the same grammar which is said to be in the possession of the American Bible Society of New York. The present Secretary states that he can find no trace of this manuscript. As previously pointed out, there is much confusion over the authorship of works listed under Henderson and Kingdon.

Much of the material published on the Maya grammar in the last century was taken from Beltran. The list of his followers is a long one. It contains: **Norman (1843,** p. 240–249), **Gallatin (1845,** p. 45–47, 252–268) and **Heller (1853,** p. 381–385). They evidently had access to the first edition. **Brasseur de Bourbourg (1864,** p. 459–478) writes that he obtained his grammatical material from the works of Beltran and Ruz. It is quite evident that he depended very slightly, if at all, on Beltran's treatise. According to Brinton (1900, p. 209), Brasseur de Bourbourg explained to Berendt that when he wrote this book he had never seen the original works either of Beltran or of Ruz but only Gallatin's reference to the former and Kingdon's translation of the latter. **De Rosny (1875,** p. 61–82) and **Bancroft (1874–76,** v. 3, p. 773–776) give some portions of Beltran almost without change. **Charencey (1883–84;** ed. **1885)** uses it in comparing the conjugation of the Maya with that of Quiche. **Larrainzar (1875–78,** v. 2, p. 407–408) mentions Beltran. **Palma y Palma (1901)** follows him quite fully and **Mitre (1909– 11,** v. 3, p. 71–83) gives an outline of the work. **De Rosny (1904,** p. 87–115) has grammatical notes after San Buenaventura, Beltran, and Ruz.

XIX CENTURY, ETC. The next independent work on the Maya grammar was that of **Ruz (1844: 1845).**[1] He was a Franciscan, born in Merida in 1785. He was a prolific writer on Maya sub-

---

[1] Squier (1861, p. 38) gives a Maya grammar by **Narciso (1838).** This is clearly a mistake. The Narciso work is a Spanish grammar by Diego Narciso Herranz y Quiros, translated into Maya by Ruz.

jects as already pointed out. His main grammatical work (1844) is
written in the form of questions and answers in the Maya language
and is really a translation into Maya of the Spanish grammar of
**Herranz y Quiros (1834).** Neither this, his *Cartilla* (**Ruz, 1845;**
2d. ed. **Berendt, 1871**) nor any of his other works are of great importance from a linguistic point of view. An English translation
of his grammar was published by **Kingdon (1847).**[1] **Brasseur de
Bourbourg (1864,** p. 459–478) follows Ruz, as previously stated,
although he claims to have used Beltran as well. Finally, **de
Rosny (1875,** p. 91–93) gives some modern Maya from Ruz.
**Vela (1)** has left a few grammatical notes some of which refer to
the grammar of Ruz.

**Juan Pio Perez (1)** contemplated writing a grammar and collected notes for this work (B. L. C. No. 11). There seems also to
have been some manuscript notes on the language given by **Perez
(1842a)** to Stephens.[2] **Gallatin (1845)** used these in addition to
the grammar of Beltran in preparing his own work. **Perez (1844),**
in a letter written from Peto, makes some very interesting grammatical observations regarding the changes in Maya from the
point of view of time. **Henderson (1852)** published a Maya primer
of no value.

**Berendt (1864** and **5,** § 1, 3–5) has left several incomplete portions of a Maya grammar in manuscript. **Anon (26,** p. 88–98) presents a few grammatical notes. **Shea (1873–76,** v. 1, p. 411) gives
a specimen of Maya grammar. **Sayce (1875,** p. 187, note) has an
example of the Maya noun and adjective taken from the text of
Charencey (1873). **Gabelentz (1881,** p. 368) gives an example of
the possessive. **Charencey (1883: 1896)** should be mentioned
among the writers on Maya grammar although his writings deal
with special features of the language.

---

[1] In a preliminary note to Berendt's copy of the Kingdon translation
(**Berendt, 1865**), Berendt points out that Kingdon mistranslates Ruz's title,
*Gramatica Yucateca* which does not mean a "Yucatan Grammar," but a grammar of the Yucatecan language. He adds: "It seems that Father Kingdon
had only an imperfect knowledge of either Maya or Spanish. We arrive at
this conclusion in view of the many blunders made in his translation, for which
see my notes." (This note given by Brinton, 1900, p. 208).

[2] See Stephens, 1843, v. 2, p. 278. There is another set of manuscript notes
on the grammar by **Perez (10).** It is impossible to judge how much of this
material is contained in Perez (1) and (1842a).

**Brinton (1882,** p. 27–37) gives some brief grammatical notes. He had access to the early works of San Buenaventura and of Beltran. **Seler (1887),** while basing his study entirely on early printed material, presents the grammatical forms in a new light. **Zavala (1896)** has a small grammar, rather badly arranged, and not covering the ground so fully as the early grammarians have done. **Palma y Palma (1901,** p. 83–474), although following Beltran in the main, presents much new and original material of some value. **Romero Fuentes (1910)** and **Pacheco Cruz (1912)** have phrase books which are useful in acquiring a superficial speaking knowlledge of the Maya but they are quite inadequate for a proper understanding of the grammatical forms.

**Lopez Otero (1914)** has a very good grammar founded in part upon the grammar of Beltran and upon the linguistic teachings of the late Señor Don Audomaro Molina. This work ranks next to that of the three early grammarians. It also gives a very good idea of the language as spoken at the present time.

SPECIAL FEATURES. Studies of special phases of the Maya grammar are not numerous. **Adam (1877)** has a study of polysynthesis in Maya and Quiche. **Charencey (1884)** has some pertinent ideas regarding the formation of words in Maya and another paper **(1896)** on the classification of the verb. **Tozzer (1912)** attempts to classify the verb. The Maya pronoun is treated by **Brinton 1885,** p. 35–36), **Charencey (1883,** p. 123–129), and by **Tozzer (1906).** **Rejón García (1905,** p. 19–27) has some remarks of no value on certain particles. **Gates (1)** has an excellent article in manuscript regarding the modern approach to a Maya grammar. He also **(Gates, 1914)** discusses the grammar from a philosophical basis.

COMPARATIVE GRAMMAR. *Maya Stock.* This subject is best treated by **Seler (1887), Charencey (1866: 1883–84;** digest in **Mitre, 1909–11,** v. 3, p. 87–95), and **Charencey (1883,** p. 123–139). The interpretation of the material, gathered from the older authorities, is a distinct contribution to the study of the Maya language as a whole.

Slight comparative grammatical material on the Maya and Quiche is to be found in **Adam (1877). Gallatin (1845)** treats of Maya, Quiche, Pokonchi, and Huastec. **F. Müller (1876–88,** v. 2,

p. 305–313, after Vater) compares Maya, Quiche, Mam, Pokonchi, and Huastec.

*Maya stock and Mexican languages.* **Berendt** (**5** in B. L. C. No. 179) compares Maya with Nahuatl, Otomi, Natchez, Cakchiquel, etc. **Palma y Palma** (**1901,** p. 421–449) has some reflections on Nahuatl and Maya. See also **Adam** (**1878a**) below.

*Maya stock and North American Languages.* **Adam** (**1878**) compares Dakota, Cree and some other North American stocks with Maya and Quiche and **Adam** (**1878a**) treats briefly of Dakota, Nahuatl, Maya, Quiche, as well as two South American stocks.

*Maya stock and South American Languages.* See **Adam** (**1878a**) above.

## PHONETICS

The phonetics of the Maya language are discussed at some length in the grammar of **Beltran** (**1746**) and in several of the other grammars. His list of the sounds is used by **Norman** (**1843,** p. 242) and the latter is copied in turn by **Spence** (**1913,** p. 342). **Juan Molina** (**1896,** p. 335) also quotes from Beltran. **Brasseur de Bourbourg** (**1864,** p. 322, note), followed by **Bollaert** (**1866,** p. 50–51) quote Beltran on the alphabet. The *Analytical Alphabet* of **Berendt** (**1869**) and **Berendt** (**5** in B. L. C. No. 179, § 1) together with **Stoll** (**1884,** p. 39–44) give good discussions of the phonetics of the whole group of Maya languages. **Carrillo y Ancona** (**1880a,** p. 91–95: **1893**) [1] has some words on the pronunciation. **Anon.** (**2,** ff. 9–11) treats of the sounds in Maya. **Perez** (**1842a**) has left some remarks on the various sounds and letters adopted for these sounds as a preliminary notice to his manuscript " Codex Perez " in the library of the New York Historical Society. These notes were used by **Gallatin** (**1845,** p. 252). **Justo Sierra** (**1842–45**) discusses the sounds in Maya. **Gates** (**3**) has a paper in manuscript regarding the pronunciation with an alphabet which he prefers in writing Maya and he describes (**Gates, 1920,** p. 611–613) very carefully the phonetic system of the language. **Tozzer** (**1907,** p. xxiii: **1910,** p. 277) gives a key to the pronunciation of the Maya Sounds.

---

[1] This work introduces the series of manuscript vocabularies from the different towns in Yucatan described on p. 293.

## VOCABULARIES

Carrillo y Ancona (1881; ed. 1883, p. 123), quoted by Brinton (1882, p. 72), states that seventeen dictionaries of the language have been written. This number should be increased if we include all the missing Maya vocabularies.

XVI CENTURY. Villalpando (1571) holds the place of priority regarding the authorship of a Maya dictionary as he does that of a grammar. His dictionary was published in Mexico in 1571.[1] This work is probably based upon the vocabulary contained in his *Arte* (§ 1) which is missing.

Solana (1580), a Franciscan and companion of Landa, is another author of a dictionary in this century. This is in manuscript and is probably in the library of The Hispanic Society of America in New York.[2] Mention should also be made here of a short collection of Maya words given by Oviedo (1535; ed. 1851-55, v. 4, p. 593-607), also in Berendt, (1868d, v. 1, in B. L. C. No. 42-11) and Berendt (6 in B. L. C. No. 180). The Maya words in Landa (1864) have been collected and translated by Bowditch (1).

Another dictionary of this century is that by Gaspar Antonio Xiu (§ 1).[3] He was a Maya Indian and related to the so-called royal family of the Tutul Xius, one of the two reigning families of Mayapan. The manuscript is missing but it is dated toward the close of the century as he is known to have been receiving a pension from the Spanish Government in 1593 and 1599.[4]

---

[1] Brinton (1882, p. 74) states that one copy at least is in existence.

[2] I have been unable to verify this point. For bibliographical purposes several works of Solana are listed in the bibliography although they do not appear to touch upon the Maya language, Solana (§ 3), (§ 4), (§ 5), (§ 6). Nájera (1) should be noted here. The work of Cardonas (1630), although belonging to the next century, may be mentioned as being in the same class.

[3] In the list of missing authorities I have also placed another work by Xiu (1582) although it probably has little to do with Maya linguistics. See Carrillo y Ancona, 1870; ed. 1872, p. 137-138.

[4] A description of his work is given in the *Relación de Quinacama* (*Coleccion de Documentos Ineditos*, v. 11, p. 264). Juan Martínez writes personally as follows, "Antonio Xiu helped everybody in his work. He never wrote a vocabulary: he was not a scholar but an interpreter of the government and had access to the library of the Franciscan Convent in Merida."

Another companion of Landa was Ciudad Real. He came to America in 1573 and died in 1617. He is the author of several works on the Maya language. His *Gran Diccionario ó Calepino* (**Ciudad Real, § 1**) was prepared in two copies neither of which has been found.[1] He is said to have taken forty years to write this. Juan Martínez Hernández identifies the Motul dictionary as this missing work. There is probably another dictionary (**Ciudad Real, § 2**) distinct from the *Calepino*.[2] Cogolludo (1688, p. 513) writes of Ciudad Real, "*Aprendió el idioma de estos Indios con tanta perfeccion que fue el mayor Maestro de èl que ha tenido esta tierra. Como tal predicó, enseñó y escribió Sermones de Santos . . . no solo hizo Vocabularios, que el uno empieça con la lengua Castellana, y el otro con la de los Indios; pero compuso una obra tan insigne, que por su grandeza se llamó Calepino de la lengua Mayo ò Yucatheca.*"

The **Motul Dictionary,** the most famous of all the Maya extant dictionaries, probably goes back to the last quarter of the xvi century.[3] A copy of this manuscript is now in the John Carter Brown Library at Providence, Rhode Island. It is called the Motul Dictionary as there is reason to believe that the first part was written at the Convent of Motul. It is probably a copy of an earlier manuscript. It is impossible to determine the exact date of the original but the author speaks of a comet which he saw in 1577 and "gives other evidence that he was writing in the first generation after the Conquest."[4] The present copy seems to have been made about the close of the xvi century. It consists of two parts:—

---

[1] According to Nicolas Antonio (1672) who copied from Lizana (1633, ed. 1893, p. 100), one copy remained in Yucatan and the other was in the library of the Duque del Infantado in Spain. Brinton (1897, p. 185) tried to trace this library in 1888 and again in 1893. Some volumes were said to have gone to the Real Academia de Historia and the bulk of the collection passed to the Duke de Osuna and was sold by him to the Biblioteca Nacional in Madrid. Inquiries by Brinton in both these institutions met with failure.

[2] Berendt (1868b) gives an *otro diccionario* in his list of missing authorities. Mention is made of another work of **Ciudad Real (§ 3)** although it evidently contained nothing on the language.

[3] Ciudad Real was in Yucatan from 1573 to 1617 which would be about the time this manuscript was written.

For bibliographical note, see **Bartlett (1865–71,** v. 1, p. 226, 2d. ed. **1875–82,** v. 1, p. 446).

[4] **Brinton (1882,** p. 77: **1885a,** p. 32) and **Berendt (7,** in B. L. C. No. 181) also have notes on the Motul. **Bollaert (1866,** p. 54, note) gives information on the Motul taken from **Trübner (1865,** p. 2).

Maya-Spanish and Spanish-Maya, the latter section containing
approximately 11,180 words. This is probably later in date than
the Maya-Spanish part.

Juan Martínez Hernández thinks that the Motul dictionary is
the same work as the *Calepino* of Ciudad Real and refers to Lizana
(1633, ed. 1893, p. 99) who writes, "*Antonio de Ciudad Real . . .
hizo Calepino tan grande, que son seis bolumenes de a dozientos pliegos
cada uno, los dos de su letra sacados en limpios, y los borradores
llenaua dos costales, ocupó 40 años en esta obra, mas es tan buena, y
de tanto peso, y utilidad, que no tiene otro defeto que ser para esta
tierra solamente que a correr esta lengua en todo el mundo solas estas
obras bastauan para dar luz, y claridad a todos los que la aprendiessen,
y alli hallassen quantas frasis, y propiedad se pueden imaginar, sin
que aya falta de una palabra, etc.*"

Berendt made a careful copy of the manuscript in 1864 (B. L. C.
No. 1) with extensive corrections and additions from the other
Maya dictionaries, the Ticul, San Francisco and Pio Perez, copies
of which he possessed. In the preface to his copy he writes, "The
first part of the Providence MS. is written in an extremely small
and badly arranged hand. It shows an author of wide instruction,
with scientific mind, and profound knowledge of the Maya language
and great care and attention. But the copyist was an ignorant
fellow who did not understand what he was writing, not even in the
Spanish part, and in places he shows terrible negligence." [1] It is
needless to add that this dictionary is indispensable for the student
who is working on the translation of old Maya texts. The illustra-
tive sentences after many of the words are most useful. An un-
successful attempt was made by the Bureau of American Ethnology
to publish this manuscript. A portion of it was set up in proof
after having been copied by Miss Thomas. These proofs were being
corrected by Señor Audomaro Molina at the time of his death.[2]
Mr. William Gates is now at work on an edition of the dictionary.

Mention should be made here of the *Vocabulario grande Yucatano*
(**Anon. 28**) mentioned by Cogolludo.[3]

---

[1] This is a translation from the Spanish kindly furnished me by Miss Adela
Breton.

[2] For the work of Miss Thomas and Audomaro Molina, see **Powell (1900**,
p. 67–68), **McGee (1901**, p. 79: **1902**, p. 53–54), and **Holmes (1903**, p. 41).

[3] Carrillo y Ancona (1870; ed. 1872, p. 135) writes: "*La primera obra que
escribieron los indios yucatecos en el siglo mismo de la conquista, usando por*

XVII Century. **Coronel** (§ 1) (*circa* 1620) and **Vidales** (§ 1) (*circa* 1644) are both authors of vocabularies which are missing. **Coronel (1620, p.** 107–110) gives the names of the different parts of the body. **Valladolid** (§ 3) also wrote a dictionary according to Ludewig (1858, p. 103). This may be questioned. The **San Francisco Dictionary** is second in importance to the Motul and probably belongs about the middle of the xvii century. This work was found at the closing of the Convent of San Francisco in Merida in 1820. It bears no date. The original is lost but Perez made a copy (**Perez, 11**) [1] and Berendt made a copy from that of Perez in 1870 (B. L. C. No. 3). **Meneses** (1) made a partial copy. Pio Perez considers that this dictionary is older than the Ticul vocabulary, probably by half a century. Berendt would place it as older than the Motul, basing his decision on some antiquated forms in the San Francisco which appear in the Motul as modernized.[2] Mitre (1909–11, v. 3, p. 71) suggests that this dictionary may have been the work of San Buenaventura (§ 1).[3] In this case the

*primera vez de los caractéres alfabéticos, fué un gran Vocabulario historico que, no habiéndose nunca llegado á imprimir, parece que se ha perdido por completo. Conservábase todavía á mediados del siglo diez y siete, época en que Fr. Diego Lopez de Cogolludo se hallaba en esta Península, pues le vió y aun le servió para componer su Historia, como se ve por estas palabras que se leen en el cap. V del lib. IV, con motivo de hablar aquel autor del nombre que los antiguos Mayas daban á un Dios único é incorpóreo.*"

[1] From Berendt (1871a, p. 60) who writes, " *D. Pio ha copiado tambien este Diccionario, coordinando la parte maya-española por el mismo método que habia empleado en su trabajo anterior,*" it might be inferred that this dictionary was originally arranged in a Spanish-Maya order only and that Perez made the Maya-Spanish part when he copied it in the same way as he had done with the Ticul Dictionary. But in his Preface he states that he received a copy of a part of the Maya-Spanish portion made by Meneses. This seems to show that the original manuscript was in Maya-Spanish and Spanish-Maya.

The Perez copy was found by Martínez Hernández among papers presented by Mrs. Ernesto de Regil to her brother-in-law, José Rafael de Regil of Merida, who is the present owner.

[2] Berendt in the Preface to his copy of v. 2 of the Motul Dictionary (B. L. C. No. 1).

[3] Mitre quotes as follows from Ancona (1877, p. iv), in his introduction to Perez (1866–77): "*En 1848, el mismo Pérez encontró en casa del cura José María Meneses, un diccionario de la lengua Maya, más voluminoso, el cual habia sido de la biblioteca del convento grande de San Francisco, y cuya fecha y autor se ignoraba por faltar á la obra sus primeras páginas. Parece que después de una enfermedad del Señor Meneses el volumen fué extraído de su casa, y Pérez pudo al*

date would presumably be about 1684, the date of his grammar.[1] Mitre is probably incorrect in this supposition. The manuscript is in two parts, Maya-Spanish and Spanish-Maya, the latter portion containing approximately 9160 words. The two parts do not correspond, each portion having terms and acceptations not to be found in the other.

The **Ticul Dictionary** comes at the end of the XVII century. It bears the date of 1690 and was found in 1836 in the Convent of Ticul. The original manuscript is lost. It is in Spanish-Maya, and contains approximately 6190 words. Pio Perez copied it in 1836 and made a second copy in 1847,[2] together with a list of the words arranged as Maya-Spanish (**Perez, 1847a**). From the 1847 copy and the Maya-Spanish arrangement Berendt made his copy in 1870 (B. L. C. No. 2). The manuscript, not including the Maya-Spanish part, was published under the name of **Perez** (**1898**, p. 124–196) by Ignacio Peon who joined it to the vocabulary of Beltran's grammar. The two works do not correspond.

Berendt in the Preface to v. 2 of his copy of the Motul in speaking of the Ticul and the San Francisco vocabularies writes, " The concordance of many Spanish terms and also the identical coordination of their different Maya equivalents and other particulars repeated in the last two works (the Ticul and the San Francisco) give reason to believe that both have the same origin. But as each contains clauses not found in the other, presumably they were copies corrected and amplified by different authors and at different periods."

---

*fin conseguirlo en 1855.*" and Mitre adds "*Este manuscrito era evidentemente el del diccionario Maya de San Buenaventura que según Beristain y Souza se conservaba en el convento de San Francisco de Mérida, el cual servió principalmente de base para el trabajo de Pérez y no se explica sino como ocultación de mala fe,el que se haya omitido mencionar siquiera el nombre del precursor y primer codificador del idioma Maya.*"

[1] Berendt (1868 *b*) places the date of the San Buenaventura dictionary as 1695.

[2] Pio Perez (1844) mentions this Ticul dictionary as having been found with a copy of Coronel's grammar.

**Perez** (**7**, in B. L. C. No. 11, p. 165–84) writes an introduction to this vocabulary. See Perez, 1898.

Juan Martínez writes personally regarding the Ticul as follows, "Said vocabulary is a copy from an older work with innovations of small importance, all copied from a pattern or old vocabulary, a standard authority which is no other than the work of Fray Antonio Ciudad Real."

San Buenaventura (§ 1) (*circa* 1684) is given as the author of a large dictionary toward the end of this century.[1] **Carrillo y Ancona (1)** mentions this vocabulary and the vain search he made for it.

XVIII CENTURY. In this epoch are found the numerous vocabularies of **Avendaño** all of which are missing: — a dictionary (§ 2), a short dictionary of adverbs (§ 3), a botanical and medical dictionary (§ 4), and a list of proper names (§ 5).[2] A single leaf of a vocabulary, probably of this century is in the possession of Mr. Gates (**Anon. 5**).

Mention should be made here of the various vocabularies in the grammar of **Beltran (1746; ed. 1859, p. 209–241)**. These vocabularies are given in the present copy of the **San Francisco** dictionary. The Maya words with their meanings as given by Beltran are all collected and published by **Perez (1898, p. 1–101)**.

XIX CENTURY. The next vocabulary in point of time is that of **Baezo (1832)**, of words in the dialect of Peten, Guatemala.[3] Along with this should go the dialect collected at Sacluk, Peten, by **Berendt (1866–67)** and republished with English translation by **Means, 1917, p. 188–191. Norman (1843, p. 255–263)** gives an English-Maya vocabulary which he may have collected during his sojourn in Yucatan.

**Henderson (1859–66)** has left a manuscript of six volumes, averaging 250 pages each, of a dictionary of the dialect spoken in the District of Bacalar. This is in the collection of manuscripts of the Bureau of Ethnology, Washington.[4] A dictionary by **Kingdon (§ 2)** is reported in the library of the American Bible Society of New York. No trace of this can be found.

Perez was the author of several manuscript vocabularies. He started with the Maya words in Beltran's *Arte* (1746). He amplified this with the words in Beltran's *Doctrina* (1740) and Sermons

---

[1] See note 3 on p. 172–173.

[2] Carrillo y Ancona (1882, p. 125) places these works among those written in the xvii Century.

[3] Ludewig (1858, p. 102) mentions a work by **Malte-Brun (1824)** as containing a Maya vocabulary. I have been unable to find this book. It has been entered in the Bibliography under C. Malte-Brun.

[4] See **Berendt (1867, p. 420)** and **Anon (1900)** for references to this work.

(1740*a*) and Dominguez (1758). In 1836 he obtained possession of the Ticul dictionary which he copied and with this he produced a two volume work (**Perez, 1838**). He treated these manuscripts as rough drafts for future revision. In the same year there is an account of another manuscript vocabulary (**Perez, 1838a**). It is impossible to know whether one of these various works is that (**Perez, 1842b**) noted in Stephens (1843, v. 2, p. 278) who writes that Perez gave him a vocabulary in manuscript containing more than four thousand words in Maya. The manuscript of this is in the library of the New York Historical Society.

Perez (**1845**) left another manuscript containing material for a dictionary. This was presented by his niece to Dr. Berendt and is referred to by **Berendt (1871a, p. 5)**. It is now in the Berendt Linguistic Collection (No. 5). It contains several hundred words not in Perez (1866–77). A partial copy was made by Berendt when the manuscript was still in the possession of Perez. The latter copied the Ticul again (**Perez, 1847**). In this same year he made a Maya-Spanish arrangement of the Ticul (**Perez, 1847a**).

The **Perez** Dictionary (**1866–77**), written as far as the word *ulchahal* by Perez, down to *ven* by Carrillo y Ancona, and completed by Berendt, is the largest dictionary at present in print.[1] It contains about 20,000 words and is Maya-Spanish only. As noted above, Perez used Beltran (1746) in preparing the first drafts of his dictionaries together with Beltran's sermons and *Doctrina*. Later he added the Ticul material. Finally he found the San Francisco and began the work all over again omitting, as antiquated, the examples of Maya construction. The work does not give the parts of the verbs and it is not always useful in explaining many of the old terms. The Ticul is much better in this respect. Brinton (1882, p. 75) rightly complains " that it gives very few examples of idioms or phrases showing the uses of words and the construction of sentences." **Breton (1919)** gives a few relationship terms from Perez.

The second dictionary of **Perez (1898)** was probably written before that of 1866–77 and it is much better for use in translating the old documents. It contains the Ticul Dictionary (p. 124–296) mention of which has already been made.

---

[1] **Gatschet (1879)** has a note on this dictionary. **Gatschet (1883)** again discusses this work together with that of Brinton (1882).

The two vocabularies of **Brasseur de Bourbourg (1864,** p. 480–506 and **1869–70,** v. 2, p. 123–462) are both compilations from various sources: Beltran and San Buenaventura, Cogolludo, Landa Perez, Solis y Rosales, possibly the Motul, and other writers. Neither dictionary is of any great value.[1] Juan Martínez owns an annotated copy of a Brasseur vocabulary made by Berendt which formerly belonged to Rodolfo G. Canton.

**De Rosny (1875,** p. 94–118; ed. **1904,** p. 133–166) has published selections from the vocabulary in Brasseur de Bourbourg (1869–70). The latter (1857–59, v. 1, p. lxxxix) mentions a vocabulary **(Anon, 27)** of 2000 words in Maya, Spanish and English. I have been unable to identify this.

**Waldeck (1838,** p. 79–90, copy in B. L. C. No. 41–1) has published a short list of words in Spanish, French, and Maya and **(1838,** p. 29–33, copy in B. L. C. No. 42–3) he gives the Maya names of many of the pueblos. **Solis y Rosales (1870)** furnished Brasseur de Bourbourg with a manuscript vocabulary.

Berendt has left numerous vocabularies in manuscript:— one in the collection of manuscripts of the Bureau of American Ethnology at Washington **(Berendt, 2),** a list of proper names **(Berendt, 4),** and a large number of comparative vocabularies which will be discussed later.

**Dondé (1876,** p. 229–241) gives a list of plants with their Maya names prepared by Thomas Aznar Barbachano.

**Brinton (1882,** p. 261–279) gives the Maya-English vocabulary of words found in his selections from the Books of Chilam Balam. He published the Maya linear measurements in **1885b** (p. 434–439) and another short vocabulary in **1894** (p. 143–146).[2]

**Charencey (1883a)** has a French-Maya vocabulary of about four thousand words and **Charencey (1891,** p. 247–301) has a Maya-French dictionary of about eighteen hundred words. **DeRosny (1887;** ed. **1888,** p. 71—85) gives a list of Maya divinities.

---

[1] Compare Brinton (1882, p. 75) who writes, "I can say little in praise of the *Vocabulaire Maya-Francais-Espanole*, compiled by the Abbé Brasseur de Bourbourg (1869–70). . . . It contains about ten thousand words but many of these are drawn from doubtful sources, and are incorrectly given; while the derivations and analogies proposed are of a character unknown to the science of language."

[2] **LePlongeon (1896,** p. 202–207) has much to say regarding a controversy with Brinton on the linear measurements of the Mayas.

The Peabody Museum owns a manuscript vocabulary of 250 words from each of the following towns in Yucatan: Peto (**Valez, 1893**), Sotuta (**Anon, 1893**), Valladolid (**Manzano, 1893**), and Tizimin (**Rejón Espínola, 1893**). These were probably collected by Carrillo y Ancona as there is an introduction on the Maya pronunciation by him. A digest of these vocabularies is given in Appendix IV (p. 293).

**Zavala** (**1898**) published a short Spanish-Maya vocabulary. **Palma y Palma** (**1901**, p. 258–269, 307–326) writes instructively on the wealth of material in the Maya vocabularies. In the **Colección de Documentos Inéditos** (**1898–1900**, v. 11, p. 435–436) there is a short list of Maya words to be found in the text.

**Sapper** (*circa* **1895**) collected a small vocabulary from San Luis, Peten, which he was good enough to give the author. **Millspaugh** (**1895–98: 1900: 1903–04**) has works on the flora of Yucatan which give many of the native names of plants. **Pacheco Cruz** (**1919**) has a work on the fauna of Yucatan giving 'the Maya names. Mention should also be made here of the following anonymous vocabularies: — that in the Libreria de San Gregorio de Mexico (**Anon, 25**, after Viñaza, No. 1134), and that owned by Mr. Gates (**Anon, 26**). **Starr** (**1908**, p. 399–404) gives a very few Maya words in his glossary.

DAY AND MONTH NAMES. There are many treatises on the meaning of the names of the days and months in the Maya year and the possible correlation of this meaning with the forms of the hieroglyphs for these days and months. The most comprehensive of these discussions are those by **Seler** (**1888; ed. 1902**, p. 448–503) and by **Bowditch** (**1910**, p. 263–265). The latter collates the meanings given the day names by Perez, Brasseur de Bourbourg, Brinton, Schellhas, and Tozzer. Little need be said in this place regarding the discussion of the linguistic meaning of the Maya hieroglyphics as a whole. The phonetic character of the Maya glyphs is discussed by **Bowditch** (**1910**, p. 254–258) and by many other authors. There is a long series of articles dealing with the supposed phonetic transcription of series of glyphs. These are generally of no value.[1]

---

[1] **Eichhorn** (**1896: 1905**) belongs to this class. **Parisio** is an earlier writer along the same lines.

COMPARATIVE VOCABULARIES. *Maya-Quiche and other Maya dialects.* Galindo (**1834,** p. 63. Copy in B. L. C. No. 42–6) gives a few words in Maya and Punctunc. Berendt (**3**) wrote a manuscript composed of between 600 and 700 words in 24 dialects of the Maya stock. This formed the basis for Stoll (1884). Berendt (**5,** in B. L. C. No. 179–6, fol. 60, 64) gives comparative lists of words in Maya, Putun, Tzental, Cakchiquel, Chontal, etc. Squier (**1857,** p. 179) gives a few words in Maya, Mam, Quiche, and Cakchiquel. Squier (**1858,** p. 552–553) has words in Maya, Cakchiquel, and from Peten. Berendt (**1867a,** in B. L. C. No. 82) has marginal comparisons in Maya and Cakchiquel with Huastec forms in his copy of the dictionary of Tapia Zenteno. Rockstroh (**1878**) gives a comparative vocabulary of the Maya stock. This was probably prepared under the direction of Berendt. Campbell (**1879,** p. 72–73) gives a few Maya and Quiche words.[1]

Stoll (**1884,** p. 46–70, and **1886,** p. 301) gives comparative lists of words of many of the Maya dialects.[2] Brigham (**1887,** p. 276) gives selections from Stoll and Sapper (**1897,** p. 407–436) improves on Stoll. Brinton (**1888,** p. 82–91) gives a comparative vocabulary of Maya dialects and reprints Berendt (**1870a**). Starr (**1901–04**) has a comparative list of words from several Maya dialects and Zoque and Chiapanec.

*Maya and Mexican Languages.* Berendt (**1**) in the Bureau of American Ethnology,[3] Berendt (**5,** in B. L. C. No. 179, fol. 58), and Heller (**1853,** p. 387–388) give comparative lists of words in Maya and Nahuatl. Carrillo y Ancona (**1872**) gives many of the Maya and Nahuatl words used in Spanish. Palma y Palma (**1901,** p. 718–738) has the following: *Voces Aztecas Castellanizadas y sus equivalentes en Maya,* and *Voces Mayas Castellanizadas.* Anon (**1898**) has a short word list in Maya and Nahuatl. Berendt (**5,** in B. L. C., No. 179, fol. 59) has a vocabulary in Maya, Nahuatl and Otomi. Gallatin (**1845,** p. 9–10, 298–304) includes Otomi, Nahuatl, Huastec, and Maya in a comparative vocabulary. Fuertes (**1**) has Zoque, Zapotec, Mixe, and Maya words. **Ternaux-Compans**

---

[1] Ordoñez (**1**), according to Brasseur de Bourbourg (1855–56, p. 292), has the following: *Linguistique du Mexique et de l'Amérique Centrale (une foule d'étymologies tzendales, mayas, itzoziles, quichées, aztèques, etc.*

[2] See Berendt (**3**) above.

[3] Pilling (**1879–80**) has a list of the linguistic manuscripts in the library of the Bureau of Ethnology at Washington.

(**1840–41**; Maya in v. 88, p. 5–37) gives a comparative list of words in the main languages of Mexico. **Prichard** (**1836–47**, v. 5, p. 344) republishes this. **Latham** (**1862, p.** 755) publishes a few words in Maya, Huastec, Nahuatl, and Otomi. - **Ferraz** (**1902,** p. 95) has a short list of words in Maya, Quiche, and Nahuatl.

*Maya and North American languages.* **Adam** (**1878**) has a comparative vocabulary of Cree, Chippewa, Algonkin, Dakota, Hidatsa, Maya, and Quiche. **Berendt** (**5,** in B. L. C. No. 179, fol. 62, 63) gives words in Natchez, Apalachee, and Maya. **Brinton** (**1867**) has a list of words in Natchez, Huastec, and Maya.

*Maya, South American Languages, etc.* **Adam** (**1878a**) gives words from Dakota, Nahuatl, Chibcha, Quechua, Quiche, and Maya. **Douay** (**1894**) has a comparative list of words in Haitian, and Maya. **Douay** (**1900**) gives words in Haitian, Maya, and Quiche, and **Douay** (**1**), in Quechua and Maya. **Nuttall** (**1901,** p. 549–555) gives a comparative vocabulary of Maya, Quechua, and Nahuatl. **Schomburgk** (**1848, p.** 236–237) has a selection of words from American languages and from the languages of the Guianas.

*Maya and Old World Languages.* Comparative vocabularies covering a wider field are in general most unsatisfactory. They are to be found in **Hervás y Panduro** (**1785,** Maya p. 21, 41, 48, 121, Tab. xlix, l, li and **1787a,** Maya, p. 161 *et seq.*) and **Balbi** (**1826;** ed. **1835,** Maya, Tab. xli, No. 676). There is also a class of early works of no present value which give the equivalents for certain common words in many American languages for comparison with the forms in European or Asiatic languages. A few Maya words sometimes appear in the following works: **Vater** (**1810**), **Klaproth** (**1824–28,** v. 2, p. 28–45), **Mérian** (**1828,** p. 185–206) after Vater. **C. Malte-Brun** (**1810–29,** p. 18–21), **Johnes** (**1846**), **Buschmann** (**1853**), and **Clarke** (**1877**). **Nuttall** (**1901,** p. 563–575) gives a list of Maya words and their equivalents in languages of the eastern continent.

**C. Malte-Brun** (**1810–29**), **Latham** (**1860,** p. 398), **Charencey** (**1871,** p. 106), and **Platzmann** (**1871**) give comparative list of words from Chinese and other Asiatic languages and corresponding words from the languages of America including Maya. **Campbell** (**1879,** p. 72–73) compares Maya and Polynesian. **Umery** (**1863**) gives a list of words for "mother" in many languages including Maya.

*Comparative vocabularies of special words.* **Charencey** has two papers (**1882**; Maya, p. 28–30 and **1899**, Maya, p. 117, 166–169) on the names for the points of space in Maya and Quiche. **Charencey** (**1883b**) has another study of the names of the cardinal points and a fourth (**1892**) on the names of the metals in certain Maya dialects. **Brinton** (**1886**; Maya p. 10–13) treats of the word for love in some American languages.

## ETYMOLOGY OF PROPER NAMES

YUCATAN. There has been much discussion regarding the derivation of the names Yucatan and Maya. There is hardly an early history which does not have something to say regarding the origin of the name Yucatan. **Cortés** in his first letter (**1852**; **1866**; ed. **1908**, v. 1, p. 124–125), **Bernal Diaz** (**1632**; ed. **1908–16**, v. 1, p. 32), **Gomara** (**1553**, cap. 52), republished in **Barcia** (**1749**, v. 2), **Lizana** (**1633**, cap. 1), **Landa** (Brasseur de Bourbourg, 1864, p. 6–8, copied by **Malte-Brun** (**1864**, p. 14–15), **Cogolludo** (**1688**, p. 60–61), **Villagutierre** (**1701**, p. 28), all discuss the question of the origin of the word Yucatan. The **Perez Codex** (**Perez, 1842**) and the **Chilam Balam de Chumayel** should be cited here as they contain a variation in the name given to Yucatan.[1] Among the modern authorities to touch upon this question of etymology are: **Waldeck** (**1838**, p. 25), **Stephens** (**1843**, v. 1, p. 139–140), **Prescott** (**1843**, Bk. 2, Chap. 1), **Ternaux-Compans** (**1843**, p. 30–31), **Bollaert** (**1866**, p. 46), **Carrillo y Ancona** (**1868**: **1878–82**; ed. **1883**, p. 133–141: **1890**), **Bancroft** (**1874–76**, v. 5, p. 614–615), **Ancona** (**1881**), and **Zuñiga** (**1**).

MAYA. The best discussion of the derivation of the name Maya is that in **Carrillo y Ancona** (**1883a**, p. 632–634). **Brinton** (**1882**, p. 9–16), **Ancona** (**1878–1905**; ed. **1889**, v. 1, p. 44) and **Rejón García** (**1905**, p. 5–17) also suggest derivations. **Pimentel** (**1860**) discusses the words Mayo and Maya.

MISCELLANEOUS. **Brinton** (**1887**) discusses the origin of the Maya words used in Landa's work. **Rovirosa** (**1888**) and **Douay** (**1891**) mention the etymology of a few Maya names. **Robelo** (**1902**) gives the Maya, Nahuatl and Spanish equivalents of some

---

[1] Compare Carrillo y Ancona, 1890, p. 35–45.

proper names. **Rejón García (1905,** p. 29–78; **1910)** presents several derivations which are in most cases decidedly doubtful in origin.

## NUMERATION

The Maya numeration has already been discussed in the grammatical portion of this work. I mentioned there that practically every publication on the numeration of the Mayas goes back to that given by **Beltran (1746;** ed. **1859,** p. 195–208). Even modern works published in Yucatan seem to rely in general upon the series of numbers given by Beltran. No attempt is made here to list the publications which give the Maya system of numeration as a part of a grammar or as a part of the hieroglyphic writing.[1]

MAYA DIALECT. **Galindo (1832)** gives the numbers from 1 to 10 and **Waldeck (1838,** p. 88, copy in B. L. C. No. 42) gives them from 1 to 100, both of which series were probably collected by the authors themselves. **Baezo (1832)** has some numbers collected at Peten. **Sivers (1861,** p. 290–291) offers a series of numbers in Maya.

**Brasseur de Bourbourg (1869–70,** v. 2, p. 92–99) is the first to give the numeration of Beltran *in extenso* with a French translation.[2] **Bancroft (1874–76,** v. 2, p. 753–754) gives the numbers from 1 to 51 from Brasseur de Bourbourg. **Orozco y Berra (1880,** v. 1, p. 542, 559–569) also follows the same second-hand authority. **Brinton (1882,** p. 37–50), **Molina y Solís (1896,** p. 316–320), and **Perez (1898,** p. 113–120) go back to Beltran. **Pousse (1886)** is of little value. **Nuttall (1903)** gives an excellent translation of the numeral classifiers of Beltran with a suggestion regarding their possible presence in the hieroglyphic inscriptions. This list of suffixes with additions is published in Appendix III (p. 290).

**Valoz (1893), Anon (1893), Manzano (1893),** and **Rejón Espínola (1893)** give several numerals collected in the different towns.[3]

COMPARATIVE LISTS OF NUMBERS. There is a large number of works which present, more or less extensively, comparative series

---

[1] **Charencey (1881),** for example, treats of the numeration by means of bars and dots as shown in the hieroglyphic writing.

[2] There is a copy of the Beltran numeration in the B. L. C. No. 42–8.

[3] These numbers are given in Appendix IV, p. 301.

of numbers from many different peoples. **Hervás y Panduro** (**1786**; Maya, p. 110–111) is the earliest of these works. The best of these comparative lists is that of **Thomas** (**1897–98**) which presents a good discussion of the numeral systems of Mexico and Central America. Other works on numeration covering many of the languages of Middle America are by **Ternaux-Compans** (**1840– 41**, p. 5–37, copy in B. L. C. No. 42–7), followed by **Prichard** (**1836– 47**, v. 5, p. 344), **Gallatin** (**1845**, p. 49–57, Table A), followed by **Pott** (**1847**, p. 93–96, 301), and **Charencey** (**1878**, p. 12). Comparative lists are also given in **Berendt** (**5**, in B. L. C. No. 179–8). Maya and Aztec numerals are given by **Heller** (**1853**, p. 386–388) and **Palma y Palma** (**1901**, p. 447–449), Maya, Quiche, and Aztec by **de Rosny** (**1875a**), several dialects of the Maya by **Charencey** (**1883b**), and Maya and Quiche alone by **Charencey** (**1880, 1882a**).

## TEXTS

There is a large mass of material written in Maya.[1] These texts date from early Spanish times and continue down to the present. They vary in value for linguistic study from the point of view of the time in which they were written and also from the point of view of the individual author. The Books of Chilam Balam furnish the most profitable study of early Maya texts. There are often parallel accounts in several of these Books. The text, however, is corrupt as the present manuscripts are usually copies of earlier documents often made by individuals who did not know Maya. There is far less likelihood of corruption in the legal and political documents, some of which are extant. The Maya texts of sermons, the Catechism, and parts of the Bible vary greatly according to the ability of the individual translator. They are, in general, however, rather poorly done both from a grammatical and a lexical standpoint.

### BOOKS OF CHILAM BALAM

GENERAL. The fullest description of these Maya texts is that by **Tozzer** (**1917**). Other descriptions are by **Carrillo y Ancona** (**1870**: ed. **1872**, p. 138–140), **Melgar y Serrano** (**1873**), **Brinton** (**1882**, p. 67–72), quoted by **Bowditch** (**1910**, p. 1–3), **Brinton**

---

[1] Part II contains several Maya texts. See p. 111 for the discussion of these texts.

(1882b), translated into Spanish by **Aznar** (1882) and **Troncoso** (1883), and **Brinton** (1883a). **Echano** (1758), **Castillo** (1866, p. 255–256), **Rivera** (1878, p. 22–23), **Martínez Alomía** (1906, p. 9–10), and **Beuchat** (1912, p. 407–408) are among those giving short accounts of these Books.

Before considering the bibliographical details of the separate texts it may be well to dwell for a moment on several collections which contain abundant material for the study of the Books of Chilam Balam. Up to a few years ago, for the proper study of the manuscripts one had to depend entirely upon the Maya Chronicles of **Brinton** (1882) which in turn was based upon the Berendt copies of manuscripts collected, for the most part, by Pio Perez (**Berendt, 1868,** in B. L. C. No. 49). This material was augmented by another volume of manuscript material in the possession of Pio Perez and copied by Berendt (**Perez, 2,** in B. L. C. No. 50).

This scarcity of texts no longer holds true. In addition to the University of Pennsylvania reproduction of the original of the Chilam Balam de Chumayel we are fortunate in having the Gates reproductions of the originals of the Tizimin, Kaua, Calkini, Tekax, and Nah, Mr. Gates owning the last two manuscripts. Gates also owns beautiful hand copies of the Chumayel, Tizimin, Ixil, Kaua, and Calkini which he has reproduced.

It does not seem necessary in this paper to give complete references to the frequent use of the chronological parts of the Books of Chilam Balam as a starting point in the attempt to correlate Maya and Christian chronology.[1] The prophecies contained in these manuscripts are considered together.

According to the testimony of Landa, Lizana, Sanchez Aguilar, Cogolludo and other early writers many of these manuscripts were in existence in the xvi century. Several are reported in the xvii century. Most of the manuscripts now known were made in the latter part of the xviii century and were, in some cases, at least, copies of earlier documents.

**Brinton** (1882b) states that there are still in existence sixteen of these Books. **Martínez Alomía** (1906, p. 9) gives a list of eleven.

---

[1] See in this connection **Seler, 1892, 1895, 1895a; Bowditch, 1901, 1901a; Martínez, 1907, 1909a, 1912, 1915, 1918;** and **Morley, 1910, 1911,** and especially **1920,** p. 464–539. For earlier material on this subject which, however, is of little value, see **Perez 2,** in B. L. C. No. 50 and **5,** in B. L. C. No. 44–4.

New ones are appearing at infrequent intervals. Counting the
Mani manuscripts as one, fourteen of these books are listed here,
four of which are known only by name.

CHILAM BALAM DE MANI. The original of the Mani manuscript
is probably lost. It is dated not later than 1595. **Berendt (1868d,**
v. 2, p. 138–184 in B. L. C. No. 43–7) copied from a copy by Pio
Perez certain parts of the manuscript. **Berendt (1868d, v. 2,**
p. 102–106 in B. L. C. No. 43–5) presents a comparison, probably
from the pen of Perez, of the Mani description of the calendar with
that of the Kaua manuscript. **Perez (6),** (or **Berendt 1868d,** v.
3, in B. L. C. No. 44–3) compares the description of the calendar
of the Mani with that of the Tizimin and the Kaua manuscripts.
**Perez (2,** p. 48–49, in B. L. C. No. 50–10) has an entry, *Apuntes
historios del Chilam Balam de Mani.* **Juan Molina (1897,** p. 68–69)
gives a paragraph of this Maya document and a Spanish translation.

Berendt (Brinton, 1882; p. 91) speaks of four Mani manuscripts
dated 1689, 1697, 1755, and 1761 respectively. A portion of one
of them was given by Pio Perez to Stephens. It is well, therefore,
to distinguish between the Mani manuscript proper and that portion given to Stephens which is usually called the "**Perez Codex.**"
A part of the Mani manuscript entitled *Historia de la Doncella
Teodora* is given in **Berendt (1868d, v. 2,** p. 225–239, copy in
B. L. C. No. 43–9). The Kaua has the same story. **Perez (2,**
p. 31–37, copy in B. L. C. No. 50–3) writes, " *La historia que sigue
se halla intercalada entre esta multitud de predicciones que se copiai on
y tradujeron de los antiguos almanaques españoles.*"

PEREZ CODEX (*Lai u tzolan katun*). This is probably the most
widely known example of Maya writing. It gives an outline of
Maya history from the time the Mayas set out from the south to
travel northward down to and including the arrival of the Spaniards. It is a part of the Chilam Balam de Mani and was copied
by Pio Perez from one of the four books of Mani. Perez translated
the Maya into Spanish and wrote an extended commentary on the
Maya text. The whole work was entitled, *Traduccion y juicio
critico de un manuscrito en lengua maya que trata de las principales
epocas de la historia en esta peninsula ante a su conquista. Para el
Sn. D. Juan L. Stephens su amigo Juan Pio Perez, Peto, 5 de Abril*

*de 1842.* As indicated in the title, Perez gave the manuscript to Stephens.[1] **Stephens (1843,** v. 2, p. 465–469) published an English translation with the Maya text but refrained from printing some of the comments made by Perez. He omitted the parts headed *Corrección cronología de manuscrito* and *Recapitulación.* The Stephens copy of the Perez manuscript is now in the library of the New York Historical Society in New York.

The original Perez Codex was owned by Carlos Peon who loaned it to Bishop **Carrillo y Ancona.** The latter (**1868: 1870: 1878–82;** ed. **1883,** p. 48–64) printed the entire manuscript except the Maya text and the *Resúmen* at the end. This feature is given in English in Stephens (p. 468–469).[2]

**Berendt (1868d,** v. 2, in B. L. C. No. 43–1) made a copy of the Perez Codex in the possession of Carrillo y Ancona. This Berendt copy was used by **Valentini (1880,** p. 52–55) who printed the Maya text and translation together with a portion of the comments of Perez. He adds a good discussion of his own regarding the text. **Thomas (1882,** p. 188–192) follows Valentini in printing the text and translation. **Valentini (1896)** also mentions this Perez manuscript. **Perez (6)** has also left a comparison between the Perez Codex and similar portions of the Chilam Balam de Tizimin and the Mani proper. **Mayer (1851,** v. 2, p. 173–177) refers to this manuscript.

**Brasseur de Bourbourg (1855–56,** v. 51, p. 208: **1857–59,** v. 2, p. 2, note) mentions the Stephens edition of the Perez Codex and he (**1864,** p. 420–429) published the Maya text and an attempt at a new translation in French. He took his text from Stephens and his translation is clearly based on that of Stephens as he did not have access to the original Spanish translation. **Charencey (1874)** reprinted the whole from Brasseur de Bourbourg. **Bancroft (1874–76,** v. 5, p. 624–627) follows Stephens. **Ancona (1878–1905; ed. 1889,** v. 1, p. 382–384) gives the Maya text only.

---

[1] See Stephens (1843, v. 2, p. 278–280), where he tells of obtaining it.

[2] The only difference I could find between the text printed by Carrillo y Ancona and the Stephens copy is that in the latter the sub-title is *Corrección cronología de manuscrito* instead of *Juicio analitico del manuscrito* as it is in the Carrillo y Ancona original.

Note some interesting observations on Carrillo y Ancona and the Mani manuscript in **Troncoso, 1883,** notes A. and H.

Brinton (**1882**, p. 89–135) attempts a new translation of the Maya text with extended comments and a comparison of the translations of Perez, and of Brasseur de Bourbourg with his own. **Juan Molina (1896**, p. x, xlviii *et seq.*) and **Seler (1892)** quote sentences from the Brinton translation. **Raynaud (1891–92**, p. 145–149) tries to improve on the translation of Brinton. **Charencey (1896**, p. 13–16) endeavors to correct the translation of a paragraph of Brinton. **Seler (1895)** gives the text and translation of several sentences of the manuscript. **Palma y Palma (1901**, p. 750–753) gives the Spanish only of the Perez manuscript. **Martínez Hernández (1909)** has made the last and most successful attempt to translate the Maya text.

*Perez*: *Cronología antigua de Yucatan.* The Perez Codex (Perez, 1842) and the **Perez (1843)** study of the *Cronología antigua de Yucatan* are sometimes confused.[1] This latter manuscript, although founded on the ancient documents, was entirely written by Pio Perez and has very little to do with the Maya language. It is mentioned here, however, to make a complete record of the different works of Perez.[2] A copy of this manuscript was given by Perez to Stephens who published it in an English translation (**Stephens, 1843**, v. 1, p. 434–459).[3] **Gallatin (1845**, p. 104–114) and **Valentini (1880)** give practically the substance of the entire material contained in the Stephens text. It seems evident that Stephens did not print the entire manuscript as he received it from Perez as the second copy which Perez made contains much more material than was printed by Stephens. This second copy was made for the **Registro Yucateco (1846**, v. 3, p. 281). The same manuscript was printed in the **Diccionario Universal de Historia y Geographia, (1855**, v. 8, *Apéndice, Cronología Yucateca*), and in **Castillo (1866**, p. 31–51). This second copy (4°, 14 ff.) passed into the hands of **Brasseur de Bourbourg** who published it (**1864**, p. 366–419) with a

---

[1] There is also the Codex Peresiano, a pre-Columbian manuscript, which deals with the hieroglyphic writing and does not, therefore, enter into this discussion.

[2] Other material on the chronology by Perez may be mentioned here: — **Perez (3** in B. L. C. No. 43, 5: **9** in B. L. C.).

[3] Stephens (1843, v. 2, p. 117, 277–278) tells of obtaining this manuscript from Perez.

French translation. The Stephens copy is in the possession of the New York Historical Society.[1]

The copy made for the *Registro Yucateco* and published by Brasseur de Bourbourg cannot be located. Pilling states that he saw what may have been this manuscript in the library of Pinart. Many of the items in the Pinart library were purchased from Brasseur de Bourbourg and later these passed into the Bancroft Library now at the University of California. I could find no trace of any manuscript of this kind in the Brasseur de Bourbourg-Pilling-Bancroft Library at Berkeley.

The Peabody Museum has another copy (8°, 20 ff.), said to be from the library of Brasseur de Bourbourg, which follows almost exactly that published in the *Registro Yucateco*.

The original Perez manuscript of his *Cronología* passed into the possession of Carrillo y Ancona along with the other Perez material. Carrillo y Ancona (1878–82; ed. 1883, p. 637–663) published it.[2] There is then the Carrillo y Ancona original, the Stephens, and the *Registro Yucateco*-Peabody Museum texts all differing slightly. The Carrillo y Ancona version is the most complete and has one passage which is in Stephens and not in the Peabody Museum text. The Peabody version follows that of Carrillo y Ancona except for a few omissions in the latter and the passage referred to above. The Stephens text differs in many places both in order and wording, and it is much shorter than that of the other two.

Brasseur de Bourbourg, (1857–59, v. 3, p. 462 *et seq.*), Orozco y Berra (1864, p. 103–108) Bancroft (1874–76, v. 2, 759 *et seq.*), Short (1880, 439 *et seq.*), and many others give the substance of these Perez texts. Carrillo y Ancona (1870; ed. 1872, p. 142) refers to the manuscripts on which Perez founded his *Cronología*.

CHILAM BALAM DE CHUMAYEL. This manuscript is a small quarto of 107 written pages and is dated about 1780. The name

---

[1] This Society also has the original Perez manuscript entitled "An almanac, adjusted according to the chronological calculation of the ancient Indians of Yucatan, for the years 1841 and 1842." Stephens (1843, v. 1, p. 448–458) printed this in an English translation. This article is not included in the Brasseur de Bourbourg-Peabody Museum manuscript.

[2] Carrillo y Ancona gives the title, *Antigua Cronología Yucateca o exposicion sencilla del método que usaban los antiguos habitantes de esta Península de Yucatan para contar y computar el tiémpo.*

of D. Juan José Hoil with the date, January 20, 1782, appears in the manuscript. It is probable that Hoil was the one who compiled the text except for a few insignificant interpolations from earlier documents. The first pages have been lost. The original of the manuscript was owned in Merida.[1] It has been reproduced by the University Museum of the University of Pennsylvania under the editorship of **G. B. Gordon (1913)**. Teoberto Maler had previously (1887) printed several sets of photographs of this manuscript.[2] Gates, the Peabody Museum, and the family of the late Don Audomaro Molina are some of those possessing the Maler photographs. There is a hand copy by **Berendt (1868, p. 1–74, 80, 159–200, in B. L. C. No. 49)**. Gates owns a second copy, contained in ff. 1–55 of a note-book, which has been reproduced by him. Portions of the manuscript are given by **Berendt (1868d, v. 2, p. 25–36, in B. L. C. No. 43–2)**. **Carrillo y Ancona (1870; ed. 1872, p. 145–146)** gives a good description of this work.

**Brinton (1882, p. 152–185)** was the first to make an attempt to translate any large part of the manuscript. He translated those portions relating to the chronology. Berendt had already copied these parts from copies by Pio Perez (Berendt, 1868d, v. 2, in B. L. C. No. 43–2). **Carrillo y Ancona (1890, p. 37–45)** gives a portion of the manuscript containing the name Yucalpetén as given to Yucatan. He also gives in *fac-simile* a portion of p. 63 (Gordon edition). **Seler (1895)** gives the text and translation of a small part of the manuscript. **Juan Molina (1896, p. xxxvii, lviii, etc.)** gives sentences of the Maya text and translation from the Brinton work. **Raynaud (1891–92, p. 153–15?)** attempts an improvement on the translation of Brinton. **Martínez Hernández (1909a: 1912: 1913)** has made successful attempts at translating parts of the manuscript.[3] Martínez has a translation in manuscript

---

[1] Morley (1920, p. 475) writes that he saw the original manuscript in 1913 in the house of Ricardo Figueroa in Merida. Subsequently it was removed to the Cepeda library, Merida. When Morley revisited Yucatan in 1918 he was told that it had disappeared from the library and that its present location was unknown.

[2] Maler (about 1887) also made photographic copies of the Tizimin, Calkini, and Kaua MSS. Gates possesses a complete set of the Maler photographs which he obtained from Seler.

[3] The text, p. 77, 78 and the translation of Brinton and Martínez are given in Part II, p. 130–135.

(**1919**) of p. 102 of the original. The text of a part of p. 85 with translation by **Gates** (**1920b**) is given in Morley (1920, p. 485). **Roys** (**1920**) has a translation of p. 60–62.

The prophecies given in this and other Chilam Balam Books are described in another place (p. 192). The day signs as shown in the original manuscript are given by **Carrillo y Ancona** (**1866**, p. 38; ed. **1871**, p. 257: **1870**; ed. **1872**, p. 144; and **1882**; ed. **1883**, (p. 250). **Carrillo y Ancona** (**1882**; ed. **1883**, p. 605–606) **Riva Palacio** (**1887–89**, v. i, p. 456) or **Chavero** (**1887**, p. 456) give the Chumayel map. **Brinton** (**1882b**; ed. **1890**, p. 266) also gives the drawings of the day signs. The Katun wheel from the Chumayel is reproduced by **Bowditch** (**1910**, fig. 63).[1]

CHILAM BALAM DE TIZIMIN. This manuscript is a quarto of 52 pages formerly owned by Señor Ricardo Figueroa of Merida. Like the Chumayel it has disappeared. This manuscript has been called by Carrillo y Ancona the *Codice Anónimo*. The original has been reproduced by Gates. **Berendt** (**1868**, p. 101–158 in B. L. C. No. 49) made a copy from the original. A second copy (ff. 1–35 in an 8° note-book) is owned by Gates and has been reproduced by him.[2] **Perez** (**6**, in B. L. C. No. 44–3) discusses the historical and chronological portions and compares them with similar parts of the Mani manuscript. **Carrillo y Ancona** (**1870**; ed. **1872**, p. 146) discusses this document. The prophecies of the Tizimin are treated in another place.

**Manuel Luciano Perez** (**1870**, p. 102, in B. L. C. No. 49) has a short letter written from Tizimin to Carrillo y Ancona regarding the sending of the manuscript to the Bishop.[3] The first publication of any portion of the Tizimin text was by **Brinton** (**1882**, p. 136–151) where he presents a translation of the chronological parts. **Raynaud** (**1891–92**, p. 149–152) attempts another translation of those parts given by Brinton. **Seler** (**1895**; ed. **1902**, p. 580: **1898**; ed. **1902**, p. 676) gives sentences with translation from this manuscript.

---

[1] **Perez** (**2**, p. 174–177 in B. L. C. No. 50–31) has a heading *Ruedas cronologicas con su explicación*.

[2] See **Morley, 1920**, p. 470, note.

[3] This letter is discussed with quotations, in **Carrillo y Ancona, 1870**; ed. **1872**, p. 146.

CHILAM BALAM DE CALKINI. This is a quarto manuscript of 30 pages formerly owned by Señor Ricardo Figueroa. It has disappeared. The manuscript is not complete. The pages of the original are numbered 11–40. There is a Gates reproduction of the original and Gates also owns a copy (ff. 55–67 of a note-book) which he has also reproduced. **Martínez Alomía (1906, p.** 14–15) gives a description of this manuscript. **Juan Molina y Solís (1896)** also mentions it.

CHILAM BALAM DE IXIL. This manuscript was also owned by Señor Ricardo Figueroa of Merida. There is no reproduction of the original of this manuscript. **Berendt (1868, p.** 75–79, 97–100 in B. L. C. No. 49) made a copy. Gates also has another copy (ff. 36–60 of a note-book) which has been reproduced by him. **Perez (2, p.** 174–177, in B. L. C. 50–31) gives the Katun wheels from a number of these Chilam Balam Books. That from the Ixil has been reproduced by **Thomas (1881–82, p.** 60), **Carrillo y Ancona (1878–82,** ed. **1883, p.** 252), **Chavero (1887, p.** 440) or **Riva Palacio (1887–89,** v. 1, p. 440), and by **Bowditch (1910,** figs. 61, 62). The prophecies contained in this manuscript are compared with those from the Mani in **Berendt (1868d,** v. 2, p. 107–123, in B. L. C. No. 43–6). **Perez (8,** in B. L. C. No. 44–2) gives a part of this manuscript.

CHILAM BALAM DE OXKUTZCAB (1689). The original of this manuscript has been lost. It was partially copied by Pio Perez and his copy, in turn, copied by **Berendt (1868d,** v. 2, p. 185–224, in B. L. C. No. 43–8). These copies undoubtedly refer only to the chronological portion of the manuscript. It is to be supposed that there were other parts not copied by Perez. **Carrillo y Ancona (1870;** ed. **1872, p.** 147) mentions this document. It is also probably referred to in the *Registro Yucateco* (v. 1, p. 360. **Anon. 1845).**[1]

CHILAM BALAM DE KAUA. This is a quarto manuscript containing 282 pages, also formerly owned by Señor Ricardo Figueroa and now in the Biblioteca Cepeda in Merida. Gates has reproduced the original. There is a partial copy by **Berendt (1868,** p. 81–92, in B. L. C. No. 49). Gates has a second partial copy (to

---

[1] Care should be taken not to confuse this manuscript with the Xiu Chronicles, called by some the *Crónica de Oxkutzcab.*

p. 184 of the original manuscript). This is contained in a note-book (ff. 61—150) and has also been reproduced by him. Parts of this manuscript are given in Berendt (1868d, v. 2, p. 87–101 in B. L. C. No. 43–5). Berendt (1868d, v. 1, in B. L. C. No. 42–13) has the multiplication table from the manuscript. The chronological portions are compared with corresponding parts of the Mani in Berendt (1868d, v. 2, p. 102–106 in B. L. C. No. 43–5). Brinton (1882b; ed. 1890, p. 270–271) gives the day signs from the manuscript. These are copied from Brinton by Troncoso (1883, p. 105). Bowditch (1910, fig. 64) gives a Katun wheel from this manuscript. This manuscript is probably the same as the Chilam Balam de Hocabá.

CHILAM BALAM DE NAH. This is a quarto manuscript of 64 pages, owned by Gates and reproduced by him. It is signed by José María Nah and came from Teabo. Mr. Gates has called it by the name of its signer rather than by the name of the town in which it was found as there are already two collections of documents bearing the name of this town. It is of the calendar type and similar, in general, to the Kaua manuscript. There are entries in a later hand as late as 1871 and 1896.

CHILAM BALAM DE TEKAX. This manuscript is a quarto and consists of 36 written pages. It is incomplete. Gates is the owner and he has reproduced the manuscript. It contains features which place it in the same class as the Chilam Balam de Kaua. The usual medical recipes and a current calendar of the good and bad days are to be found in the manuscript.

CHILAM BALAM DE PETO. There is an obscure reference to the possible existence of a Chilam Balam Book at Peto. Carrillo y Ancona (1878–82: ed. 1883, p. 592) records that Juan Pio Perez writing from Poto in 1840 states, "Literatura quién sabe si la tuvieron; pero sabían escribir con precision. Una es la poesía del pueblo y otra la del sabio y sacerdote; la de éstos no llegó á nosotros, ó serán muy raros los ejemplos."

CHILAM BALAM DE NABULÁ, TIHOSUCO, TIXCOCOB, AND HO-CABÁ. These four manuscripts are known hardly more than by name. The Nabulá has an account of an epidemic which occurred in 1673. Brinton (1883) refers to a manuscript from Tihosuco which he used in preparing his article on " The folk-lore of Yucatan." **Carrillo y Ancona (1870**; ed. **1872**, p. 147–148) and Berendt tried in vain to find the Hocabá manuscript. This latter is probably the same as the Kaua manuscript which formerly belonged to a resident in Hocabá. There is no information available on the Tixcocob document.

## THE PROPHECIES

There has been a great deal of discussion concerning various so-called "Prophecies" contained in several of the Books of Chilam Balam. These prophecies as they now stand clearly foretell the coming of Christianity to the land. The natives of Haiti told Columbus of similar predictions made long before his arrival.[1] As Brinton points out (1868, p. 188) these prophecies were doubtless adapted by the Spanish to proselytizing purposes but they seem fundamentally to have been native accounts of the return of Kukulcan, one of the culture heroes of the Mayas, and corresponding to Quetzalcouatl of the Mexicans.

Gomara, Herrera, Cogolludo, Villagutierre and other early historians give other instances of the prophecy of the arrival of the white race.[2] Several modern authors (**Sierra, 1841**) [3] have tried to prove that these prophecies were pure inventions of the Spanish priests to give a supernatural sanction to their teachings. There is no doubt that the influence of Christian teaching is seen in several of these documents. But the fact that the Mayas and other peoples of Latin America had native tales of the return of their culture heroes is proved by the way the Spanish Conquerors were first received by the natives of Mexico and Peru. They were considered to be the actual deified heroes who the natives had learned were to return.

**Anon (§ 31)** is a discussion of the second return of the Spaniards. Cogolludo (1688, lib. 2, cap. xiv) writes as follows in connection

---

[1] Sahagun, *Historia de la Nueva España*, Lib. xii, Caps. 2, 3.

[2] **Sanchez de Aguilar (1639;** ed. **1892**, p. 95) probably refers to one of these prophecies.

[3] **Vicente Calero** is often mentioned as a writer with Justo Sierra on Maya subjects. **Pablo Moreno** is another author who considered the Prophecies the inventions of the Spanish priests. Le Plongeon expressed the opinion in a private letter that these Prophecies were " pious frauds."

with this work, " *Sin duda se rigió por un librillo escrito de mano,
que ay en el idioma de los Indios, que le escribieron los de muy dentro
de la tierra, despues de su conversion, en que notaron algunas cosas
de aquellos tiempos, desde la segunda venida de los Españoles, y algo
de las guerras referidas.*"

The prophecies under discussion are those of the Maya priests
Napuc Tun, Ah Kuil Chel, Ahau Pech, Natzin Abun Chan, and
Chilam Balam.[1]

The first authority to give these prophecies was Lizana (1633,
parte 2, cap. 1; ed. 1893, p. 37–39). He gives the Maya text and
a translation in Spanish. He probably obtained the Maya from
some early text of a Chilam Balam Book. It was evidently not one
of the Balam Books known at the present time as the text differs
in several places from that in any of the versions of the prophecies
now available. It is interesting to note that there are no two
copies of the same prophecy exactly alike.[2] Cogolludo (1688, lib.
2, cap. 11) gives the Spanish of the five prophecies stating that he
had no room for the Maya. The Avendaño manuscript (§ 6) may
have been an account of these prophecies. Lizana's translation
and text were published by Brasseur de Bourbourg (1857–59, v. 2,
603–606, copy in B. L. C. No. 42–9). Brasseur de Bourbourg
(1869–70, v. 2, p. 103–110) attempts next a French translation but
gives the Maya text together with the translation of Lizana for
comparison. Castillo (1866, p. 256–257) gives the Spanish translation from Cogolludo of the prophecy of Chilam Balam. Perez (2,
p. 65–74, 166–173, in B. L. C. No. 50–13 and No. 50–30) has something on these parts of the Balam Books. Carrillo y Ancona (1870;
ed 1872, p. 142) refers to the text of Perez. Brinton (1868, p. 188–
189) gives an English translation of a portion of the prophecy of
Chilam Balam taken from the Spanish of Lizana and of Brasseur
de Bourbourg. Troncoso (1883, p. 103, 109) gives a few lines of
this prophecy and suggests a connection between the meaning and
the significance of the engraving in Cogolludo. Brinton (1890a,
p. 303) gives the English of a poem by the Priest Chilam.

---

[1] There is a wide variety in the spelling of these proper names. I have followed the spelling given by Lizana for the most part. The prophecy of Chilam
Balam as shown in the Chumayel and Tizimin texts and in Lizana is given
with translation in Part II, p. 120–130.

[2] Compare in this respect the versions given on p. 122 of the Chilam Balam
Prophecy.

Berendt (**1868d,** v. 2) presents the version of the prophecies as given in the Chilam Balam de Mani and Ixil (B. L. C. No. 43–6, p. 107–132), and the versions of the Chilam Balam de Chumayel and again that of Mani (B. L. C. No. 43–3, p. 37–46). As noted above, the same prophecy, as given in different versions, may differ in spelling and also in length. **Nicoli** (**1870,** p. 511) mentions and discusses the prophecy of Napuc Tun but gives neither text nor translation. **Charencey** (**1873**) gives the same prophecy with the Maya text, the translation of Lizana, that of Brasseur de Bourbourg and a new one of his own in French. **De Rosny** (**1875,** p. 85–93; ed. **1904,** p. 120–123) gives the Maya text and his own French translation with comments of the prophecies of Napuc Tun and Ah Kuil Chel. He also gives for comparison the Spanish translation of Lizana and the French of Brasseur de Bourbourg. **Schultz-Sellack** (**1879**) makes a study of the words for east and west as given in the prophecies of Lizana.

Orozco y Berra (**1880,** v. 1, p. 71–73) gives the Spanish of the prophecy of Napuc Tun and portions of the others. **Carrillo y Ancona** (**1878–82;** ed. **1883,** p. 526–532) presents a new translation in Spanish of all five prophecies with the Maya text as foot-notes.

Brinton who formerly had only the Lizana version for study, later came into possession of the Berendt Library so that other versions were available. **Brinton** (**1882,** p. 255–256) gives the Maya and English translation of the prophecy of Ahau Pech. **Troncoso** (**1883,** p. 104) reprints this, also giving the Maya of the Lizana version. **Brinton** (**1882a,** p. 167, 237) refers to the Pech prophecy in the Mani manuscript and **Brinton** (**1882c,** p. xxix) gives the Maya and English translation of the prophecy of Ah Kuil Chel from the Chilam Balam de Chumayel. **Charencey** (**1876;** ed. **1883,** p. 141–150) discusses and translates the same prophecy. Finally, **Brinton** (**1890a,** p. 302) repeats the English translation of Ahau Pech. **Rejón García** (**1905a,** p. 78–84) gives a partial Spanish translation of the prophecy of Ahau Pech. There is a song from one of the Books of Chilam Balam given by **Brinton** (**1882,** p. 126–127). **Charencey** (**1875**) discusses a paragraph from one of the prophecies and **Maclean** (**1883,** p. 442, note) gives an English translation of one of them.

## MEDICAL BOOKS

Libros del Judio. In addition to the medical portions of the Books of Chilam Balam which consider the symptoms and the cure of diseases there are several manuscripts which deal exclusively with the native remedies. These have been classed together under the above heading. They are sometimes called " The Book of the Jew." There was one Ricardo Ossado, *alias*, the Jew, who used herbs and other native remedies for curing disease (see Ossado, 1834). Brinton (1882b; ed. 1890, p. 272–273) and Tozzer (1917, p. 182) describe this class of books.

The first notice of a manuscript dealing exclusively with medicine is the work of Vidales (§ 3) of the xvii century. This is missing. There are several different manuscripts dealing with medicine. They seem to date from the end of the xviii up to the middle of the xix century. These manuscripts include the *Libro del Judio* (Anon, 13) of the Peabody Museum, described with extracts in English by Alice Le Plongeon (1879, p. 92, and 1889, p. 15–17),[1] the *Libro de Medicina* (Anon. 15),[2] the *Libro del Judio de Sotuta*, (Sotuta),[3] and *Medicina Maya* (Anon. 16), all three of which are owned by Gates, and the *Cuaderno de Teabo* (Teabo. Copy in B. L. C. No. 49).

There are two valuable manuscripts dealing with diseases in Spanish. These are the *Noticias de varios plantas* (Anon. 19) a manuscript owned by José Rafael de Regil of Merida, and *El libro de los Medicos* (Anon. 14), a manuscript owned by Gates. Mr. Gates also owns another manuscript (Anon. 1820) on the medicinal plants. It is evidently part of a manuscript of considerable size as the last leaf remaining is numbered 123. It contains brief descriptions of plants with colored sketches.[4] The most valuable

---

[1] This MS. is described as having come from the island of Las Mujeres. Mr. Gates informs me that a physician in Acanceh told him that he had given the MS. to the Le Plongeons.

[2] Gates suggests that this manuscript is very valuable as a supplement to the botanical series of Millspaugh (1895–98: 1900: 1903–04).

[3] The Gates reproduction of this manuscript shows p. 1–26 written in one hand followed by pages numbered 17–26, 33–54 in an entirely different writing. There are evidently two separate documents.

[4] A note in Berendt's hand and signed by his initial states that the MS. was given to him by Rodolfo Cantón in Vera Cruz in 1859.

single manuscript dealing with this subject is probably that of
**Perez (4)** with notes and additions to this manuscript by **Berendt**
(**1870,** in B. L. C. No. 45).

RITUAL OF THE BACABS. This is a most important Maya manuscript, owned by Gates, of 46 medical incantations. **Wilkins**
(**1**), who is at work upon a translation of the text, regards it as the
oldest Maya to which we have access. At the end there are a few
pages of the ordinary medical receipts markedly different from the
main part of the work. All but about ten pages is in one handwriting. These ten pages are in several different hands. The
only mention of anything Christian or Spanish occurs in these
pages. Two of these pages are on the back of a printed Indulgence
of 1779. Wilkins considers the main body of the manuscript of
earlier date. A report and preliminary translation of one chapter
by **Wilkins** (**1919**) was read by Gates at the Cambridge meeting
(1919) of the American Anthropological Association.

## THE CATECHISM

XVI CENTURY. The Catholic Catechism was naturally the first
book to be translated into the native idioms by the Spanish priests.
It is probable that **Villalpando** (§ 2) stands as the first translator
of the Catechism into Maya as he does regarding the authorship
of a Maya grammar and vocabulary. This would have been
written toward the middle of the XVI century.

Sanchez de Aguilar (1639; ed. 1892, p. 35) writing in 1613 states
that all the Indians from childhood learned and knew the whole
Catechism. He adds that the *Doctrina* was translated into Maya
admirably by Bishop **Landa** (§ 2). This was probably done in the
third quarter of the century as Landa died in 1579.[1] The *Noticias
Sagrades* of **Solana** (§ 2) should be mentioned here.

XVII CENTURY. **Sanchez de Aguilar** (§ 1), born in Valladolid
in 1555, a grandson of one of the founders of Merida and a Maya
student under Gaspar Antonio Xiu, wrote a *Doctrina* in Maya
probably toward the beginning of this century. He carried the
manuscript with him to Madrid in 1617 and it was lost on the

---

[1] A *Doctrina* in Maya is listed under the name of **Juan Cruz** (**1571**). This
is probably an error. Squier (1861, p. 29) has a Huastec *Doctrina* by Cruz.

journey. It is said that a copy was left behind in Yucatan in the possession of the Jesuits.

At about the same time **Acevedo,** who was in Yucatan from 1592 to 1624, wrote his *Instrucciones catequísticas* (§ **2**) in Maya. This is missing. The *Doctrina* of **Coronel** (**1620a**) is the first which has come down to us. His larger work *Discursos Predicables* (**1620b**) is also known, three copies of which are said to be in existence, one owned by Gates, another in Puebla, and the third is the Pinart-Pilling copy. **Coronel** (§ **2**) is also the author of a second catechism and, according to Juan de San Antonio in his *Bibliotheca Franciscana,* this is more complete than that of 1620a. The manuscript is supposed to be in the library of the Colegio de San Buenaventura in Seville.

XVIII CENTURY. The *Doctrina* of **Beltran** (**1740**) seems to have been very popular as it has had several editions, the last of which was in 1895. No copy of the first edition is known. Juan Martínez owns the only known copy of the edition of 1816, a product of the first printing press in Yucatan. Gates owns a *Doctrina* in manuscript (**Anon. 7**) of this century.

XIX CENTURY. Ruz made translations of the following works: a Catechism of Abad Fleuri (**Ruz 1822**), one by Ripalda (**1847**), which was issued in another edition by **Charencey** (**1892a**), an explanation of the *Doctrina* by Placido Rico (**Ruz 1847a**), and another edition of the Catechism (**1851**). Mention is also made by Carrillo y Ancona of still another Catechism by **Ruz** (**2**). **Fletcher** (**1865a**) was probably the author of a translation of the Catechism of the Methodist Church.[1] There is a *Doctrina* by **Audomaro Molina** (**1905**) and one in the dialect of Peten (**Anon. 6** in B. L. C. No. 42–10, B. L. C.).

Los SACRAMENTOS. Parts of the Catechism have frequently been translated into Maya. The *Sacramentos* have been translated by **Valladolid** (§ **1**) in a manuscript of the XVII century which is

---

[1] Brinton (1900) gives the author as Richard Fletcher. No author's name appears on the title page but on the Berendt copy that of Richard Fletcher is written in. Brasseur de Bourbourg (1871, p. 81) and Viñaza (1892, § 551) give the author as Henderson. **Carrillo y Ancona** (**2**) definitely establishes the fact that Fletcher was the author of this and other works ascribed by some to Henderson.

missing. He gave the Latin and Maya text. **San Buenaventura** (**1684,** fol. 39–41*ob*.) gives the *Forma administrandi infirmis Sacramentum Eucharistiae.* Gates owns a manuscript of the *Pasion domini* (**Anon. 20**) dating from the end of the XVIII century. **Ruz** (**1846**) in his *Manual Romano* gives the *Sacramentos.* This has been republished in part by **Brasseur de Bourbourg** (**1869–70,** v. 2, p. 121–122).

EL VIÁTICO. This is given in Maya in several places in the Berendt Linguistic Collection, Nos. 42–12 (**Anon. 11**), 42–15 (**Anon. 18**), 42–17 (**Anon. 17**), as well as in **Anon** (**1897**).

VÍA SACRA. This is translated by **Ruz** (**1849**) from the Spanish of José de Herrera Villavicencio. **Nolasco de los Reyes** (**1869**) also translates the *Vía Sacra* which was reissued by **Madier** (**1875**).[1] The manuscript in the Berendt Linguistic Collection, No. 42–17, should be noted in this connection (**Anon, 17**).

ACTO DE CONTRICIÓN. This is given in Maya by **Carrillo y Ancona** (**1866**; ed. **1883,** p. 565). It is also to be found in the Berendt Linguistic Collection, No. 42–14 (**Anon, 1**).

CONFESIÓN. This is given in Maya in an anonymous manuscript (**Anon, 1803**) collected in Campeche by Berendt (B. L. C. No. 26). I saw the *Confesión* in Maya in Merida in 1904 (**Anon, 9**). This may be the same work as **Baeza** (**1883**)[2] although the titles are slightly different. **Coronel** (**§ 3**) is mentioned as having written a *Confesionario* and instructions for new priests.

ACTOS DE FE. These were translated into Maya by **Acosta** (**1851**).[3]

ADMINISTRATION OF THE MASS. This is given in Maya by **Ruz** (**1835**) from the Spanish of Luiz Lanzi.

TRINITATE DEI. This is shown in Maya in an incomplete manuscript owned by Gates (**Anon, 23**).

---

[1] See Carrillo y Ancona (1870; ed. 1872, p. 189–190).

[2] Wilkinson (**Anon, 1883**) gives a Doctrina which is probably the same as that of Baeza.

[3] Carrillo y Ancona (1870; ed. 1872, p. 189) in speaking of this work, writes, "*No hemos podido conseguir ningun manuscrito del Sr. presdítero D. José Antonio Acosta; pero sabemos con certeza que dejó varios, y entre ellos algunas colecciones ó sermonarios.*"

LORD'S PRAYER. In addition to more general works in which
prayers are given, the Lord's Prayer is to be found in several different versions in many places. **Hervás y Panduro (1787,** p.
115–116) gives it and his version is followed by **Adelung (1806–17,** v. 3,
part 3, p. 20–21). **Norman (1843,** p. 68, note), **Auer (1844–47,** part
2, p. 571), and **Anon (1860)** give the same prayer. **Brasseur de
Bourbourg (1864,** p. 478–479) gives it with the Creed after the version by Ruz. **Galindo (1832)** also gives the prayer and Creed.
**Berendt (1869,** p. 8), **Naphegyi (1869,** p. 310–311), **Marietti (1870,**
p. 281), **de Rosny (1875,** p. 83–85; ed. **1904,** p. 116–119), and
**Bancroft (1874–76,** v. 3, p. 776) all print the Lord's Prayer in Maya.
**Carrillo y Ancona (1880)** gives the Maya of two prayers. **Anon.
(1891)** probably has the Lord's Prayer in Maya.

## THE BIBLE

ST. LUKE. The translations into Maya of parts of the Bible are
all comparatively late works. **Ruz (1)** made a translation of
Chapters 5, 11, 15 and 23 of the Gospel of St. Luke. This manuscript, in the handwriting of Ruz with many corrections by him,
was in the library of Bishop Carrillo y Ancona (1870; ed. 1872
p. 177) in Merida. **Ruz (3)** is a second edition of the translation
with a few changes in writing the Maya.

The historical catalogue of the books of the British and Foreign
Bible Society of London states that as early as 1833 the Committee
of the Society had heard that a version of St. Luke in Maya was
being prepared in Central America and some years later they received the manuscript which was published in a tentative edition
in 1862 (?) with no author's name given. John Kingdon arrived
in Belize, British Honduras, in 1845 from Jamaica as a missionary
of the British Missionary Society. It is probable that he was the
author of this edition (**Kingdon, 1862**), as it was published on the
request of the Bishop of Kingston, Jamaica. He may or may not
have used the translation of Ruz.[1] According to the records of

---

[1] Brinton (1882, p. 41) states definitely that Kingdon obtained a copy of
the Ruz MS. which he printed with no acknowledgment of the author. There
is a great deal of confusion regarding the authorship of several of these translations of the Bible. Kingdon and Henderson were Baptist missionaries at
Belize and Fletcher was a Methodist missionary at Corozal, British Honduras.
For the work of Henderson and Kingdon, see **Crowe, 1850.**

the British and Foreign Bible Society, Kingdon completed an edition of the Gospels and the Acts in Maya. This would seem to show that his own translation of St. Luke may have been sent to London to be printed rather than the pirated text of Ruz.

The complete Gospel of St. Luke was published by the Bible Society in 1865 with no name but probably under the same authority as the tentative edition of 1862 (**Kingdon, 1865**). **Henderson (1870)** corrected this text and brought out another edition under the imprint of the Baptist Bible Translation Society of London. Henderson also made a translation of the Book of Genesis (§ **1**) and the Psalms (§ **2**) according to Berendt (1867).

Chapter 6, verses 27–34 of St. Luke have been published by **Bagster** (**1848–51,** p. 386; ed. **1860,** p. 468).

St. John. **Fletcher (1868)**, a missionary at Corozal, British Honduras, brought out a tentative edition of the Gospel of St. John translated into Maya. This was published by the British and Foreign Bible Society as well as the final edition (**Fletcher, 1869**).[1] The latter was printed at Cambridge, England.

Chapter 3, verse 16, of St. John has been published by the **American Bible Society** (**1876,** p. 39), **British and Foreign Bible Society** (**1,** p. 30; 2d ed. **1878,** p. 28) and by the **Pennsylvania Bible Society,** (**1,** p. 39: **2,** p. 28).

St. Matthew and St. Mark. **Fletcher (1900: 1900a)** was also the translator of the Gospels of St. Matthew and St. Mark brought out by the same Society. These translations were probably made at the same time as that of St. John. There seems to be another translation of St. Mark which I cannot identify (**Anon, 12**).

## SERMONS

Not only were the Spanish priests active in spreading the Gospel by means of translations of the Catechism into Maya but again and again one reads that the Spanish missionaries were commanded

---

[1] Brinton (1900, p. 213) makes Alexander Henderson a joint author of this work. This is probably incorrect as Henderson belonged to another denomination. There seems to have been a definitive edition St. John published in 1868 as well as in 1869, according to a record kindly furnished me by the Reverend R. Kilgour, D.D., Librarian of the British and Foreign Bible Society of London. I am also indebted to him for other information concerning the works of these Protestant missionaries. See also Carrillo y Ancona (2).

to learn the languages of the country and to preach in these languages. There are, therefore, references to a large number of sermons written in Maya. The greater part of these are in manuscript although several collections of them have been published.

XVI Century. Mention has already been made of the voluminous writings on Maya vocabularies of Ciudad Real. He was the greatest master of Latin in Yucatan in the xvi century. His sermons in Maya (**Ciudad Real**, § 4) are considered by the early authorities to have been models of excellence. They are unfortunately missing. **Solana** (§ 1) is another *Padre* of this century who wrote sermons. **Torralva** (§ 1) who was in Yucatan from 1573 to 1624 also was the author of a collection of religious treatises in Maya. The copy of a draft of a sermon (**Anon, 4,** copy in B. L. C. No. 42–4), supposedly written by the author of the Motul Dictionary, is to be noted. **Anon** (**30**) should be mentioned here as it is probably the same manuscript as the preceding one.[1]

XVII Century. Among the writers of this century who were the authors of sermons in Maya, mention should be made of **Coronel** (**1620b**), **Rincon**[2] (§ 1), **Mena** (§ 1), and **Valladolid** (§ 2), a native of Yucatan, born in 1617 and dying in 1652. The sermons of the last three writers are missing.

XVIII Century. Writers of discourses of this century include **Beltran** (**1740a,** copy in B. L. C. No. 21), **Dominguez y Argaiz 1758**)[3] and a collection of sermons in manuscript (**Anon, 22,** in B. L. C. No. 47). Mention should also be made here of a second

---

[1] These are probably the two sermons mentioned by LePlongeon in a letter, dated September 26, 1884, to J. R. Bartlett, then Librarian of the John Carter Brown Library. This was written when he returned the Motul Dictionary which he had borrowed to copy. He writes, " Also the two sermons on Maya language which I likewise have copied. One is on Trinity, the Reverend, I am afraid, tried to explain to his hearers what he himself did not understand very clearly for he seems to have become confused, repeating the same thing over and over again. . . . The other is on the faith in the teachings of the Holy Catholic Church."

[2] Cogolludo (1688, lib. 12, cap. xi) writes as follows, " *El R. P. Fr. Antonio del Rincon . . . fue Predicador de Españoles, y muy gran lengua de los naturales, en la cual escribió algunos Sermones, que han aprovechado à otros Ministros.*"

[3] A copy of this together with Carvajal (1) and Anon 22 are in **Berendt 1868a.**

collection of sermons in manuscript belonging to Mr. Gates (**Anon 21**).

XIX CENTURY. **Carvajal (1)** has left a manuscript sermon in Maya.[1] **Carvajal,** (§ 2) also made a collection of proverbs in Maya which has disappeared. These date from the early XIX century. There is a manuscript volume of discourses from **Teabo** owned by Mr. Gates dating from about 1865 to 1884. Toward the middle of the century **Ruz (1846–50)** has a collection of four volumes of sermons in Maya.[2] These are of little real worth as Maya texts. **Vela (1848)** gives a translation of a sermon by Bishop Guerra. **Vela (1848a)** also addresses the *Indios sublevados* in a religious letter in the native language. **Fletcher (1865)** is probably the author of a short sermon for every day of the week.[3] **Vales (1870)** translated into Maya a pastoral sermon of Bishop Gala giving the Spanish and Maya texts. Carrillo y Ancona had the manuscript of two sermons in Maya (**Anon, 1871**) which were copied by Berendt (B. L. C. No. 44–10).

## SECULAR TEXTS

There is a large mass of secular texts in Maya some of which go back to very early Spanish times. It should be remembered that much of the material contained in the Books of Chilam Balam might be considered as secular rather than religious in nature. Reference is here made, however, to purely historical, legal, and political papers.

CRÓNICA DE CHICXULUB.[4] This manuscript, dating from the middle of the XVI century, is also called the Nakuk Pech Manu-

---

[1] This is probably the one referred to by Carrillo y Ancona (1870; ed. 1872, p. 189). He writes: "*Así el Sr. presbítero D. Francisco Carvajal, que floreció en este siglo, escribió en yucateco muchos y muy buenos discursos y sermones, que sin haberse dado á la prensa, los usan los instructores de indios. Varias veces hemos escuchado un elocuente sermon de viérnes santo, de que el anciano Dr. D. Tomás D. Quintana, que conoció y trató íntimamente al P. Carvajal nos testificó ser el MS. obra inédita de este que fué gran orador de la lengua Maya.*"

[2] Pinart (1883, No. 598) mentions three volumes.

[3] Brinton (1900) in his *Catalogue of the Berendt Collection* gives the author of this work as Richard Fletcher. Brasseur de Bourbourg (1871, p. 81) and Viñaza (1892, p. 552) have Alexander Henderson as the author.

[4] The original name of this town was Chacxulubchen.

script, as it deals with the Pech family as well as with the survey of the town. It is a quarto of 26 pages and should still be in existence in the village from which it takes its name. A copy, which is full of errors, was rediscovered by Martínez in 1907. This is owned by José Rafael de Regil of Merida. There is a Gates reproduction of the copy. Berendt (**1868d,** v. 2, p. 47–86, in B. L. C. No. 43–4) copied portions of this manuscript. Avila (**1864**) translated the whole document into Spanish. **Brasseur de Bourbourg (1869–70,** v. 2, p. 110–120) has published the Maya and a French translation of the first five pages of the original together with some other material of the Pech family.[1]

**Brinton (1882,** p. 187–259) describes the manuscript and gives the text and translation of the first document using Avila's Spanish version to some extent. **Charencey (1891)** gives a French translation of Brinton. **Brinton (1882a,** p. 167, note) refers again to the manuscript. **Berendt (1868d,** v. 2, p. 47–86 in B. L. C. No. 43–4) as noted above, made a copy of the manuscript in Yucatan and later he evidently compared his copy with that of Brasseur de Bourbourg and also with that of Avila and Brinton. **Perez (2,** p. 201–258, in B. L. C. No. 50–35) also gives the document. **Fiske (1892,** v. 1, p. 138) refers to the manuscript and **Juan Molina (1897,** p. 467–468) gives a paragraph from this latter document with translation. **Martínez (1918a)** has a paper in manuscript on the chronicle. He found a duplicate manuscript by Ah Naum Pech who is mentioned by Nakuk Pech. The manuscript is practically identical with that of Nakuk Pech.

LEGAL DOCUMENTS. The most important of these non-religious items consist of legal papers. The earliest of these, so far reported, is that dated 1542 (**Anon, 1542**) still preserved according to Brinton. Next in point of time is a collection of legal documents owned by Gates, the first paper of which is dated 1571 (**Anon, 8**).

*Xiu Chronicles* or *Libro de Probanzas.* These date from 1608 to 1817. They are owned by the Peabody Museum and they have been reproduced both by Mr. Gates and by Mr. Bowditch. The Bowditch reproduction has an introduction by Miss Adela C. Breton. This manuscript is probably to be identified as the Ticul Manuscript or the *Crónica de Oxkutzcab* and is the one probably

---

[1] See Brinton, 1882, p. 191–192.

referred to by an anonymous writer in the **Registro Yucateco** (**1845–49,** v. 1, p. 360).[1] This manuscript should be distinguished from the Chilam Balam de Oxkutzcab. This collection contains petitions and evidences and decrees certifying the lordship of the heads of the Xiu family established near Oxkutzcab. The Maya documents are often followed by the substance of the petition given in Spanish. There is also a good map of the region in the vicinity of Ticul and and a genealogical tree of the Xiu family which is published opposite entry No. 472 in the catalogue of **Wilkinson** (**1915**). There is an important page containing data useful in the correlation of Maya and Christian chronology. This page has been reproduced and discussed by **Morley** (**1920**, p. 470 etc.). **Gates** (**1920a**) gives a translation of the same page with notes upon it in Morley (1920, p. 507–509). Parts of the manuscript have been copied by Miss Breton and translated by **Martínez Hernández** (**1920**).

*Titulos de Ebtun.* These compose the largest collection of legal documents, dating from about 1638 to 1829. They have been reproduced by Gates.

*Libro de los Cocomes* or the *Libro de Cacalchen.* This is probably the most interesting series of legal manuscripts from a linguistic point of view. This collection of documents is owned by Gates and dates from 1646 to 1826. It has been reproduced by him. The first 34 leaves contain wills in Maya. The second section is of 41 paragraphs, the first leaf missing, of regulations for the government of the town. It is this section which **Martínez Hernández** (**1920b**) considers to contain copies made in 1729 of original orders (*ordenanzas*) of the *Oidor,* Don Diego Garcia de Palacios,[2] who came to Yucatan in 1583. These orders, in turn, were made by the *Oidor,* Tomás Lopez, in 1552 if we are to believe Cogolludo (1688, p. 401) who writes, " *Las ordenanças, y leyes con que hasta el tiempo presente se estan governando los Indios de esta tierra, son las que hizo este Visitador. Casi todas son renovacion de las que hizo el Oydor Thomàs Lopez, quando visitò esta tierra el año de mil y quinientos y cinquenta y dos, sino que como de aquellas se perdieron co(n) el tiempo*

---

[1] See quotation from this account in Tozzer, 1917, p. 180. This is also given by Carrillo y Ancona 1870; ed. 1872, p. 147.

[2] The same person is mentioned in the Mani and Tizimin manuscripts as Judge Diego Pareja.

*los quadernos, y en el presente son muy pocos que los han visto, dàn por nuevo Autor de ellas à este Visitador* . . . *Traduxeronse en el idioma natural de los Indios, para que mejor las entendiessen, y supiessen, quedando en todos los Pueblos un traslado dellas, para que las leyessen continuamente, como leyes q'avian de observar.*" Miss Adela Breton has pointed out to me that *Ordenanza* 25 is quoted in a *Cedula Real* of 1579 by Palomino in **Juan Molina** (**1904–13**, v. 1, p. 228).[1] Following the *Ordenanzas* are many leaves with lists of minor officials. Later pages have the parish accounts of payments of salaries. It can thus be seen that these documents are of great linguistic value as they offer Maya texts dating from the middle of the XVII century. **Martínez Hernández** (**1920a**) has translated the the will of Andrés Pat (1647) contained in this collection.

*Crónica de Mani.* This is a series of documents, dating from 1556, kept in the *Casa Real* of the town of Mani, according to **Stephens** (**1843**, v. 2, p. 262 268).[2] He gives an English translation from a Spanish version made by **Estanislao Carrillo** (**1**) and corrected by Perez of a portion of these manuscripts. Stephens also reproduces the map of the vicinity of Mani contained in this collection of documents. **Juan Molina** (**1897**, p. 69) gives a paragraph from this manuscript in Maya and Spanish.

Other manuscripts of the same general class are as follows: — *Documentos de Sotuta* (**Perez 2**, p. 187–200, copy in B. L. C. No. 50–34),[3] *Documentos de Ticul* (**Ticul, 1760** *et seq.*) owned by Gates and reproduced by him, *Titulo de Acanceh* (**Acanceh, 1767**, copy in B. L. C. No. 44–7), translated into Maya by **Avila 1864**), and *Papeles de Xtepen* (**Xtepen**, copy in B. L. C. No. 44–8).

POLITICAL PAPERS. These form the next class of secular texts in Maya. The first of these in our list is a collection of letters

---

[1] Gates informs me that this paragraph from Molina is also found in the Xiu Chronicles.

[2] **Morley** (**1920**, p. 473) mentions this manuscript.

[3] Carrillo y Ancona (1870; ed. 1872, p. 144) writes: "*En fin, el libro* (**Perez 2**) *concluye* . . . *con los fragmentos de diferentes manuscritos mayas sobre documentacion de tierras en los pueblos de Sotuta, Yaxcaba y otros. Dichas documentaciones son en parte originalmente obras de nuestro escritor Gaspar Antonio.* . . . *Que esto es así es indudable, pues en la parte maya y en la version española que acompaña el Sr. Perez, aparece por dos veces correspondiendo al año de 1600, la firma de Gaspar Antonio como autor de los documentos.*"

(Anon, 1514–72) in the Archives of the Indies in Seville. Several of these documents are in Maya. A careful search in these Archives would doubtless yield more material in the Maya language. There is a letter in Maya by **Gonçalo Ché** (**1877**) and others, addressed to Philip II, dated 1567, and published in facsimile in *Cartas de Indias*. There is little now known in this line from this early date until the beginning of the xix century. Then, there comes an order of the governor of Yucatan translated into Maya by **Cervera** (**1803,** copy in B. L. C. No. 44–9) and a *Banda* or Proclamation issued by **Artazo y Torredemer** (**1814**), Brigadier and Captain-General, on matters of the insurrection, dangers of war, etc. This is in Maya and Spanish.[1] Next in point of time comes a collection of letters in manuscript written in Maya by **Pat** (**1847,** *circa*) and other leaders of the uprising in 1847. This manuscript is owned by Gates and has been reproduced by him. There follows another proclamation translated by **Perez** (**1848**) and a proposition for an armistice written in Maya by **Chan** (**1850,** copy in B. L. C. No. 44–11) and others.

**Villanueva** (**1864,** in B. L. C. No. 42–17) gives a proclamation in Maya and **Pacheco Cruz** (**1**) translates some of the decrees of Governor Avila. There is also an address to Maximilian in Maya (**Anon. 3,** copy in B. L. C. No. 42–18). A political squib by **Manuel Garcia** (**1856**) should also be noted.

Short portions of secular text are given in **Granado** (**1845,** p. 171) and **Waldeck** (**1838,** p. 90–91, copy in B. L. C. No. 42–2). Mention should also be made of the *Fama diaria* (**Anon. 24,** copy in B. L. C. No. 50–18).

Carrillo y Ancona (1870; ed. 1872, p. 190) writes. " *Hemos visto una especie de circular ó manifiesto de la reina de Inglaterra, ó dado en nombre suyo, á manera de cartelon, con grandes y hermosos caractéres en idioma Maya, el cual fué desprendido de una esquina de calle pública. Modo indirecto de imponer poco á poco y de hecho la dominacion británica sobre los habitantes de nacionalidad yucateca ó mexicana, que hablan el idioma Maya y tienen comercio con aquella colonia inglesa.*" (See **Anon, 10.**)

POEMS, SONGS, FOLK-LORE, ETC. Poems in Maya are given by **Brasseur de Bourbourg** (**1869–70,** v. 2, p. 120–121, copy in B. L. C.

---

[1] Gates regards this as being the first Maya printed in Yucatan. It is No. 10 in Medina (1904) where he calls it Cakchiquel.

No. 44–5), **Hernández (1905)**, and **Rejón García (1905a,** p. 118–
144). Some music and Maya words are given by **Berendt (1868c).**
**Alice LePlongeon (1)** published some Maya music with Maya
words. **Berendt (1866)** has a Maya witch story with translation in
Spanish.[1] **Brinton (1883;** ed. **1890,** p. 171–172) gives this with an
English translation. **Brasseur de Bourbourg (1869–70,** v. 2, p. 101–
102, copy in B. L. C. No. 44–6) gives a short text in Maya and
French entitled *Invocation au Soleil*, which he collected at Xcancha-
kan. An English version is given by **Brinton (1883;** ed. **1890,**
p. 167). **Brasseur de Bourbourg (1869,** p. 10) gives a short sentence in Maya with translation. **Anon (29)** is probably a folk-tale.
**Tozzer (1901)** is a collection of historical and legendary material.[2]

## LACANDONE TEXTS

Finally, mention should be made of the Lacandone text and English translation of fifty-one prayers given by **Tozzer (1907,** p. 169–
189).[3] Incantations, similar in many respects to these, and coming from southeastern Yucatan and British Honduras are given by
**Gann (1918,** p. 46–47).

---

[1] This tale is given in Part II, p. 119–120.
[2] A small part of this manuscript is given in Part II, p. 115–118.
[3] One of these is given with translation in Part II, p. 118–119.

# PART IV

# A BIBLIOGRAPHY OF WORKS RELATING
# TO THE MAYA LANGUAGE

# PART IV

# A BIBLIOGRAPHY OF WORKS RELATING TO THE MAYA LANGUAGE

## INTRODUCTION

It is my intention to give in the accompanying bibliography as complete a list as possible of the writers and their works on and in the Maya language of Yucatan. I do not attempt to give all books which mention this language but those only which describe or treat the language at some length.

It will be noted that following each entry one or more numbers are given. These refer to the page or pages in the critical survey of the literature (Part III) where the book or manuscript in question is discussed. Part III can thus be used in connection with this list as a subject catalogue. A number also follows the names of some of the authors. This refers to the place where the work of the writer in question is discussed as a whole.

A § in front of a date or number indicates that the work referred to is missing.

The anonymous books will be found listed at the end of the bibliography. Wherever possible these are arranged by date; otherwise they are grouped alphabetically by the first word of the title and given consecutive numbers.

I desire at this place to thank once more my friend, William Gates, Esqr., who has given me so much of his valuable time and has been so willing to suggest points which I have overlooked. I wish also to express my appreciation of the kindness of Mrs. Anne Fadil, formerly Librarian of the University Museum, Philadelphia, who was good enough to look up many references for me in the Berendt Collection. Don Juan Martínez Hernández should also be thanked in connection with this bibliography. Professor M. H.

Saville has been good enough to loan me books from his valuable library in addition to giving me several suggestions. Finally, I wish to thank Mr. T. F. Currier, Assistant Librarian of the Harvard College library, who has supervised the verification of many of the references.

# BIBLIOGRAPHY

ACANCEH, TITULO DE
1767 Titulo de un solar y monte en Acanceh (en lengua Maya): Translated into Spanish by Avila. (Copy 12°, 8 p. in Berendt Linguistic Collection, No. 44-7.) **205.**

ACEVEDO, JUAN DE
§ (1) Principios elementales de la gramatica Yucateca: MS. xvii century (missing). (Cogolludo gives the title *Arte de la lengua Yucateca mas breve.*) **163.**
§ (2) Instrucciones catequísticas y morales para los Indios en idioma Yucateco: MS. xvii century (missing). **197.**

ACOSTA, JOSÉ ANTONIO
1851 Oraciones devotas que comprenden los actos de fé, esperanza, caridad. Afectos para un cristiano y una oracion para pedir una buena muerte en idioma Yucateco con inclusion del Santo Dios: Merida, 12°, 16 p. (Maya and Spanish. Gates reproduction.) **198.**

ADAM, LUCIEN
1877 Du polysynthétisme et de la formation des mots dans les langues Quiché et Maya: in *Revue de Linguistique et de Philologie Comparée*, v. 10, p. 34–74. **167 (?)**
1878 Examen grammatical comparé de seize langues américaines: in *Proceedings of the 2d International Congress of Americanists*, Luxembourg (1877), v. 2, p. 161–244. (Published separately, Paris, 1878, 8°, 88 p. 5 folding sheets.) **168, 179.**
1878a Études sur six langues américaines: Dakota, Chibcha, Nahuatl, Kechua, Quiché, Maya: Paris, 8°, viii, 165 p. **168 (3), 179.**

ADELUNG, JOHANN CHRISTOPH
1806-17 Mithridates oder allgemeine Sprachenkunde mit dem Vater unser als Sprachprobe in bey nahe 500 Sprachen und Mundarten. Mit wichtigen Beyträgen zweyer grossen Sprachforscher: Berlin, 8°, 1 v. (with additions by Johann Severin Vater). **159, 161, 164, 199.**

AGUILAR, PEDRO SÁNCHEZ DE
1639 Informe contra idolorum cultores del Obispado de Yucatan: Madrid 4°. (New edition in *Anales del Museo Nacional*, Mexico, v. 6, 1892, p. 15–122.) (This is probably the same work as his *Relación de las cosas de Yucatan y sus ecclesiasticos.*) (See Saville, 1921.) **192.**
§ (1) Catecismo de Doctrina Cristiana en lengua Maya: MS. xvii century (missing). **196.**

ALCEDO Y BEXARANO, ANTONIO DE
1807 Biblioteca americana. Catálogo de los autores que han escrito de la América en diferentes idiomas. Y noticia de su vida y patria, años en que viveron y obras que escribieron: folio, MS. 2 v. vi, 488; 489–1028 ff. (from Lord Kingsborough's library) in John Carter Brown Library, Providence, Rhode Island. (Copy in Sparks Collection, Cornell University, with following note by Sparks, "This volume was copied from the original MS. in the possession of O. Rich of London. The original was found by him in Madrid. Copied, 1843." There is another copy with statement as follows, "Mexico. Copia remitida de Boston por el Señor William H. Prescott, 1854." See criticism of this work by Harrisse, 1866, p. xxiv, and quoted in Spanish by Medina, 1898–1907, v. 6, p. cxvi.) **154, 157.**

AMERICAN BIBLE SOCIETY. Publisher.
1876 Centennial exhibition, 1876. Specimen verses from versions in different languages and dialects in which the Holy Scriptures have been printed and circulated by the American Bible Society and the British and Foreign Bible Society: 16°, 48 p., 2 pls. (Numerous other editions the last of which was in 1919 including specimen verses from 269 different languages.) **200.**

ANCONA, ELIGIO
[1877] Introduction to the Pio Perez Diccionario, 1866–77. (See Perez, 1866–77.) **160.**
1878–1905 Historia de Yucatan: Merida, 8°, 5 v. (4 v. 1878–80. v. 5, edited by José María Pino Suarez, published in 1905. 2d and revised edition of first 4 v. Barcelona, 1889.) **162, 180, 185.**
1881 Compendio de la historia de la peninsula de Yucatan que comprende los estados de Yucatan y Campeche. Obra escrita en forma de diálogo para el uso de las escuelas: Merida, 16°, 84 p. **180.**

ANDRADE, JOSÉ LEOCADIO
1880 See Carrillo y Ancona, 1880.

ANDRADE, JOSÉ MARÍA
1869 Catalogue de la riche bibliothèque de Andrade: Leipzig and Paris, 8°, xi. 368 p. (Sale catalogue.) **154, 158.**

ANDRADE, VICENTE DE PAULA
1899 Ensayo bibliográfico Mexicano del siglo XVII: Mexico, (2d ed.) 8°, vii, 803 p. (1st ed., 1894, in *Memorias de la Sociedad Cientifica "Antonio Alzate,"* never completed.) **156.**

ANON.
For anonymous works, see p. 276–279.

ANÓNIMO, CODICE
See Tizimin, Chilam Balam de

ANTONIO, GASPAR
  See Xiu, Gaspar Antonio
ANTONIO, NICOLAS
  1672 Bibliotheca Hispana sive Hispanorvm, qvi vsqvam vnqvamve
       sive Latinâ sive populari sive aliâ quavis linguâ scripto aliquid
       consignaverunt notitia, his qvæ præcesservnt locvpletior et
       certior brevia elogia, editorum atque ineditorum operum
       catalogum dvabvs par tibvs contiens, etc.: Rome, 4°, 2 v.
       41 ff., 633; 690 p. (2d ed. Madrid, 1783–88.) **150, 153.**
  1696 Bibliotheca Hispana Vetus; sive, Hispanorum qui usquam,
       unquámve scripto aliquid consignaverunt, notitia. Com-
       plectens scriptores omnes, qui, ab Octaviani Augusti imperio,
       usque ad annum M.[1] floruerunt: Rome, 4°, 2 v. (2d ed.
       Madrid, 1788.) **153.**
ARTAZO Y TORREDEMER, MANUEL
  1814 Banda (or Proclamation) Maya and Spanish in parallel columns:
       1 f. **206.**
ASENSIO, JOSÉ MARÍA. Editor.
  See Colección de Documentos, 1898–1900.
AUER, ALOIS
  1844–47. Sprachenhalle: Vienna, 2 parts, folio. **199.**
AVENDAÑO Y LOYOLA, ANDRÉS DE **142.**
  1696 Relación de las dos entradas que hizé a Peten Itza: 4°, MS.
       66 ff. (Gates reproduction. For publication of greater part
       of MS., see Means, 1917. p. 103–174.) **164.**
  § (1) Arte para aprender la lengua de Yucatan: MS. XVIII century
       (missing). **164.**
  § (2) Diccionario de la lengua de Yucatan: MS. XVIII century (miss-
       ing). **174.**
  § (3) Diccionario abreviado de los adverbos de tiempo y lugar de la
       lengua de Yucatan: MS. XVIII century (missing). **174.**
  § (4) Diccionario botánico y medico conforme á los usos y costumbres
       de los Indios de Yucatan: MS. XVIII century (missing). **174.**
  § (5) Diccionario de nombres de personas, idolos, danzas, y otras
       antigüedades de los Indios de Yucatan: MS. XVIII century
       (missing). **174.**
  § (6) Explicacion de varios vaticinios de los antiguos Indios de Yuca-
       tan: MS. XVIII century (missing). **193.**
AVILA, MANUEL ENCARNACION. Translator.
  [1864 circa] [Translation into Spanish of Titulo de Acanceh (1767) and
       Crónica de Chicxulub (1542)]. **203, 205.**
AZNAR Y PEREZ, GABRIEL. Translator.
  1882 Translation of Brinton, 1882b: in Semanario Yucateco: Merida.
       **183.**

---

[1] The M in the title is, of course, a misprint for M.D.

BACABS, RITUAL OF THE
    12°, MS., 237 p. contains 46 incantations.  (Owned by Gates.)
    196.

BACHILLER Y MORALES, ANTONIO
    1883  Cuba primitiva, origen, lenguas, tradiciones e historia de los
          Indios de las Antillas Mayores y las Lucayas: Havana, 8°, 7–
          399 p. 2d ed. Corregida y aumentada.  (Printed first in *La
          Revista de Cuba*.)  (See *Proceedings of the 4th International
          Congress of Americanists*, Madrid, 1882 [1881], p. 315–317.)
          161.

BAEZA, JOSÉ NICOLÁS
    1860  See Beltran, 1740; ed. 1860 and later editions.

BAEZA, SECUNDINO
    [1880 circa]  [Sobre la lengua Yucateca]: in *El Seminario Conciliar*,
          Merida.  162.
    1883  Doctrina necesaria para confesar en el regla.  Dispuesta en
          lengua Maya: Merida. 16°, 24 p. (See Anon, 9.)  198.

BAEZO, PERFECTO
    1832  Vocabulario de las lenguas Castellana y Maya (en el idioma de
          Peten) in *Bulletin de la Société de Géographie de Paris*, v. 18,
          p. 215–217. (Copy in Berendt Linguistic Collection, No. 42–5,
          corrected in Peten by Berendt.)  174, 181.

[BAGSTER, SAMUEL.]  Editor.
    [1848–51]  The Bible of every land.  A history of the sacred scriptures
          in every language and dialect into which translations have been
          made: London, 4°, xxviii, 3, 406, 12 p. maps. (2d ed. London,
          1860, 4°, (28) 32 (3) 475 (5) p.)  200.

BALBI, ADRIEN
    1826  Atlas ethnographique du globe, ou classification des peuples
          anciens et modernes d'après leurs langues, précédé d'un dis-
          cours sur l'utilité et l'importance de l'étude des langues appli-
          quée à plusieurs branches des connaissances humaines, etc.:
          Paris, 1 v. fol. (XLIX pls.). (Another edition, Boston, 1835.)
          161, 179.

BANCROFT, HUBERT HOWE
    1874–76  The native races of the Pacific States of North America: New
          York, 8°, 5 v. (Numerous other editions.)  159, 165, 180, 181,
          185, 187, 199.

BANDELIER, ADOLF F[RANÇOIS ALPHONSE]
    1881  Notes on the bibliography of Yucatan and Central America: in
          *Proceedings of the American Antiquarian Society* (1880) (N. S.)
          v. 1, p. 82–117. (Published separately, Worcester, 1881, 8°,
          39 p.)  156.

BAQUEIRO, SERAPIO
    1881  Reseña geográfica, historica y estadistica del estado de Yucatan:
          Mexico.  159.

BARBACHANO, THOMAS AZNAR
1876   See Dondé, Joaquin, 1876.

BARCIA CARBALLIDO Y ZUNIGA, ANDRÉS GONZÁLEZ DE
1737-38   Epitome de la biblioteca oriental y occidental, nautica y geo-
          gráfica, añadido y enmendado nuevamente en que se contienen
          los escritores de las Indias Orientales, y Occidentales, y reinos
          convecinos, China, Tartaria, Japon, Persia, Armenia, Etiopia,
          y otras partes: Madrid, 4°, 3 v. **153.** This contains:
          Autores que han escrito en lenguas de las Indias (col. 719-
          738). (For 1st ed. see León Pinelo, 1629.)
1749   Historiadores primitivos de las Indias Occidentales que juntò,
          traduxo en parte y sacò à luz, illustrados con eruditas notas y
          copiosos indices: Madrid, 4°, 3 v. (v. 2 contains Gomara,
          1553.) **180.**

BARTLETT, JOHN RUSSELL
1865-71   Bibliotheca Americana. A catalogue of books relating to
          North and South America in the library of John Carter Brown
          of Providence, R. I.: Providence, 8°, 3 pts. (2d ed. 1875-82,
          2 v.). **170.**

BARTON, BENJAMIN SMITH
1797   New views of the origin of the tribes and nations of America:
          Philadelphia, 8°, xii, cix, 83 p. (New edition, 1798.) **161.**

BASTIAN, [PHILLIP WILHELM] ADOLF
1878-89   Die Culturländer des alten America: Berlin, 8°, 3 v. **159.**

BATES, HENRY WALTER. Editor
1878   Central America, the West Indies and South America, edited and
          extended . . . with ethnological appendix by A. H. Keane;
          London, 12°, xviii p. 1 f., 571 p., 20 pls. (Numerous editions.
          For enlarged edition, see Keane, 1901.)

BATRES, LEOPOLDO
1885   Cuadro arqueológico y etnográfico de la República Mexicana:
          New York, 1 folio sheet. **159.**

BEAUVOIS, EUGÈNE
1899   Les publications relatives à l'ancien Mexique depuis une tren-
          taine d'années: Paris, 8°. **156.**

DELTRAN, DE SANTA ROSA MARÍA, PEDRO
1740   Declaracion de la Doctrina Christiana en el idioma Yucateco,
          nuevamente corregida en algunos vocables y periodos: Mexico
          (missing). Ed. 1757, Mexico, 8°, 36 p. (Title p. 1, p. 2–22
          *Advertencias*, p. 18 incorrectly numbered 81.) Later editions
          have title *Declaracion de la Doctrina Christiana en el idioma
          Yucateco por el. . . . Añadiendole el acto de contricion en verso:*
          Merida, 1816, 12°, 2 ff. 3–20 p. (Gates reproduction); Merida,
          1860, 24°, 23 p. (revised by J. N. Baeza with *Acto de contricion
          en prosa.*) Later editions follow this: Merida, 1866, 16°, 23 p.
          and Merida, 1895, 16°, 16 p. **197.**

BELTRAN, DE SANTA ROSA MARÍA, PEDRO (*continued*).

1740*a* Novena de Christo crucificado con otras oraciones en lengua
Maya: Mexico, 27 ff. (Copy by Berendt, 12°, 105 p. in
Berendt Linguistic Collection, No. 21.) **201.**

1746 Arte de el idioma Maya reducido a succintas reglas y semi-
lexicon Yucateco: Mexico 8°, 8 ff. 188 p. (Gates reproduction.) (2d ed. Merida, 1859. 1739 is date given by some as
that of 1st ed., this is incorrect.) (See Kingdon 1, and Henderson 3.) **164, 168, 174, 181.**

1859 Second edition of 1746: Merida, 8°, 8 ff., 242 p. (The editor,
Espinosa, has a second impression of his edition with a Preface
and notes at bottom of page.) **164, 168, 174, 181.**

BERENDT, CARL HERMANN **146.**

1864 Notas gramaticales sobre la lengua Maya de Yucatan: Incomplete MS. 4°, 40 p. (Berendt Linguistic Collection, No. 12).
**166.**

1865 [Annotated copy of Kingdon, 1847, which, in turn, is a translation of Ruz, 1844]: 12°, MS. in Berendt Linguistic Collection,
No. 14. **166.**

1866 Ein feen Märchen der Maya; (Maya and Spanish) Peten. MS.
in Berendt Linguistic Collection. (Published in Brinton, 1883;
ed. 1890, p. 171–72). **207.**

1866–67 Vocabulario del dialecto (de Maya) de Peten: MS. (Berendt
Linguistic Collection, No. 42–5. English translation by Means
(1917) in *Papers of the Peabody Museum*, v. 7, p. 188–191).
**174.**

1867 Report of explorations in Central America: in *Report of the
Smithsonian Institution*, Washington p. 420–426. **174.**

1867*a* Diccionario Huasteco-Español estractado de la Noticia de la
lengua Huasteca con Catecismo y Doctrina Christiana y con
un copioso Diccionario por Carlos de Tapia Zenteno: 8°, MS.
288 p. (Copy of the Tapia Zenteno dictionary with numerous
additions and marginal comparisons of Huastec words with
others in Maya and Cakchiquel. About 3000 words, in B. L. C.
No. 82.) **178.**

1868 Chilam Balam. Artículos y fragmentos de manuscritos antiguos
en lengua Maya, colectados y copiados en facsimile: 4°, MS.
200 p. (Berendt Linguistic Collection, No. 49. Notes taken
on this MS. by C. P. Bowditch (1908*a*). Gates reproduction
of notes). **144, 183.** This contains the following:
Chilam Balam de Chumayel, p. 1–74, 80, 159–200. **188.**
Chilam Balam de Ixil, p. 75–79, 97–100. **190.**
Chilam Balam de Kaua, p. 81–92. **190.**
Chilam Balam de Tizimin, p. 101–158. **189.**
Cuaderno de Teabo, p. 93–96. **195.**

1868a Coleccion de platicas, doctrinales y sermones en lengua Maya por
diferentes autores: 16°, MS. 257 p. (Berendt Linguistic Collection, Nos. 46, 47). **147, 201.** This contains the following:
Dominguez y Argaiz (1758) p. 1–76.
Carvajal (1) p. 77–116.
Sermones (Anon. 22) p. 119–229.
Modo de confesar (Anon 1803) p. 231–257.
(P. 37, 77–257 reproduced by Gates.)

1868b Literatura de la lengua Maya, obras que parecen perdidas: MS.,
written in Merida (Berendt Linguistic Collection). **151.**

1868c Canciones en lengua Maya: MS., collected in Merida, in Berendt
Linguistic Collection. (Partial copy by Schuller, 8°, 13 p,
reproduced by Gates.) **207.**

1868d Lengua Maya. Miscelanea: 12°, MS. 3 v. **147.** The contents
of these volumes are entered in this bibliography under the
following headings:
Vol. 1 (Berendt Linguistic Collection, No. 42).
No. 1. Waldeck, 1838, p. 79–90.
2. Waldeck, 1838, p. 91.
3. Waldeck, 1838, p. 29–30.
4. Anon (4).
5. Baezo, 1832.
6. Galindo, 1832.
7. Ternaux-Compans, 1840–41.
8. Numerales: in Beltran, 1748; ed. 1859, p. 195–201.
9. Las Profecias: in Brasseur de Bourbourg, 1857–59, v.
2, p. 603–606. **192.**
10. Anon (6).
11. Oviedo, 1535; ed. 1851–55, v. 4, p. 593–607. **169.**
12. Anon (11).
13. Tabla de multiplicar: in Chilam Balam de Kaua. **191.**
14. Anon (1).
15. Anon (18).
16. Anon (17).
17. Villanueva (1).
18. Anon (3).
Vol. 2 (Berendt Linguistic Collection, No. 43).
No. 1. Epocas de la historia de Yucatan: in Perez, 1842. **185.**
2. The same: in Chilam Balam de Chumayel **188.**
3. Las Profecias: in Chilam Balam de Mani y de Chimayel. **194.**
4. Crónica de Chicxulub. **203** (2).
5. Fragmentos sobre la cronologia (Perez, 3). (Mainly
the Chilam Balam de Kaua.) **184, 191** (2).
6. Las Profecias: in Chilam Balam de Ixil and Mani.
**190, 194.**

BERENDT, CARL HERMANN—1868d, Vol. 2 (*continued*).
   No. 7. Chilam Balam de Mani. **184.**
      8. Chilam Balam de Oxkutzcab. **190.**
      9. Historia de la Doncella Teodora. **184.**
   Vol. 3 (Berendt Linguistic Collection, No. 44).
   No. 1. Perez (9).
      2. Perez (8).
      3. Perez (6).
      4. Perez (5).
      5. Canción amorosa: in Brasseur de Bourbourg, 1869–70, v. 2, p. 120–121. **206.**
      6. Invocation au soleil: in Brasseur de Bourbourg, 1869–70, v. 2, p. 101–102. **207.**
      7. Titulo de Acanceh. **205.**
      8. Papeles de Xtepen. **205.**
      9. Cevera, 1803.
    10. Anon, 1871.
    11. Chan, 1850.
1869  Analytical alphabet for the Mexican and Central American languages: New York, 16°, 8, 6 p. (Published by American Ethnological Society.) **168, 199.**
1870  Extractos de los recetarios de Indios en lengua Maya, notas, y añadiduras [á MS. de Pio Perez]: See Pio Perez (4). (In Berendt Linguistic Collection, No. 45). **196.**
1870a Apuntes sobre la lengua Chaneabal. Con un vocabulario: 8° MS. 7, 25 ff. (See Brinton, 1888.) (In Berendt Linguistic Collection. No. 96.) **178.**
1871  2d edition of Ruz, 1845, revised and edited: Merida, 16°, 14 p. **166.**
1871a Los trabajos linguisticos de Don Juan Pio Perez: Mexico, in *Boletin de la Sociedad de Geografía y Estadistica de la Republica Mexicana* (2d Series), v. 3, p. 58–61. (Published separately. Mexico, 1871, 8°, 6 p. Original MS. in Berendt Linguistic Collection. No. 11, p. 137–163. See Perez, 1.) **143, 175.**
1878  Remarks on the centres of ancient civilization in Central America and their geographical distribution: in *Bulletin of the American Geographical·Society*, (1876) v. 8, p. 132–145 (Published separately, New York, 1876). **159.**
1878a See Rockstroh 1878.
   (1) Comparative vocabulary of Mexican or Nahuatl and Maya languages: 4°, MS. 10 ff. in Collection Linguistic MSS., Bureau of Ethnology, Washington. **178.**
   (2) Vocabulary of the Maya language; 200 words: fol. MS. 6 ff. in Collection Linguistic MSS., Bureau of Ethnology, Washington. **176.**
   (3) Vocabulario comparativo de las lenguas pertenecientes á la familia Maya-Quiche: 600–700 words in 24 dialects: MS.

(formerly in possession of Rockstroh, published, in part, in Stoll, 1884). **178.**

(4) Nombres proprios en lengua Maya: folio, MS. 150 ff. (in Berendt Linguistic Collection, No. 48). **176.**

(5) Miscellanea Maya. Folio scrap-book: (Berendt Linguistic Collection, No. 179). **147.** This book contains the following:
  1. Gramatica.
     Analytical alphabet, 11 p. fol. 4. **168.**
     Comparative alphabet of the Maya, 2 p. fol. 5. **168.**
  2. Languages.
     Alfabeto de las lenguas Metropolitana, 4 p. fol. 14.
     Charakter der americanischen Sprachen, 2 p. fol. 22.
  3. Wortbildungen Maya, 17 p. fol. 24. **166.**
  4. Maya moderna y dialectos, 2 p. fol. 34. **166.**
  5. Grammar. **166.**
     Formacion del plural, 4 p. fol. 36.
     Adjectivos, 2 p. fol. 39.
     Pronombres, 4 p. fol. 42.
     Prepositiones, etc. 3 p. fol. 45.
     Verbos, 19 p. fol. 47.
     Partes sexuales, 6 p.
     Korpertheile, 5 p.
     Nombres de parentesco, 3 p.
     Plantas; mais; medidas, 12 p. fol. 54.
     Bebida y comida; Mammalia, 7 p.
     Pajaros; Beleuchtung, Insects, Aves, 13 p. fol. 55.
     Conversazione, 10 p. fol. 57.
  6. Vocabulario de la lengua Maya, del Putun, del Tzental, del Chontal, etc. **178.**
     Maya und Nahuatl, 56 p. fol. 58. **178.**
     Mexicano-Maya-Otomi, 30 p. fol. 59. **178.**
     Maya-Cakchiquel, 4 p. fol. 60. **179.**
     Maya-Natchez, 13 p. fol. 62. **170.**
     Maya-Apalahchi, fol. 63. **179.**
     Maya-Chontal-Quiche-Cakchiquel-Zutuhil-Huasteca-Mame-Poconchi, 2 p. fol. 64. **179.**
  7. Gramatical comparativos de las lenguas de la Familia Maya, 5 p. fol. 66. **168.**
  8. Vergleichende Uebersicht d. Zahlu'tr, 14 p. fol. 67. **182.**
  9. Locuciones varios en Maya, 8 p. fol. 71.
  10. Ethnologia, fol. 76.
     Caracter de los indios de Yucatan.
     Costumbres de los indios, fol. 77.
     Calendarios, fol. 79.
     Jeroglificos, fol. 86.
     Antiqüedades, fol. 89.
     Maya ethnologia, fol. 92.

BERENDT, CARL HERMANN, (continued).
(6) Miscellanea Centro-Americana. Folio scrap-book: (Berendt Linguistic Collection, No. 180). **147.** Among other items, this volume contains:
A bibliography of no value for Maya linguistics.
100 words with translation from Oviedo. **169.**
(7) Miscellanea historica et linguistica. Folio scrap-book: (Berendt Linguistic Collection, No. 181). **147.** Among other items, this volume contains:
A note on the Motul dictionary. **170.**
A bibliography of Yucatan. **157.**
Brasseuriana. **146.**
(8) Historia de la lexicografia de la lengua Maya. Original MS. (in Berendt Linguistic Collection, No. 11, p. 185–188. See Perez 1). **157.**
(9) [Unidentified articles in *Deutsch-Amerikanisches Conversations-Lexikon, Correspondenzblatt für Anthropologie, Ethnologie und Urgeschichte, La Revista de Merida*, etc.] **147.**

BERISTAIN Y [MARTIN DE] SOUZA, JOSÉ MARIANO
1816–21 Biblioteca hispano-americana septentrional (ó Catálogo y noticia de los literatos): Mexico, 3 v. (2d edition, Amecameca, 1883, sm. 12°, 3 v. and 1 v. Santiago de Chile, 1897. Latter has sub-title, Ó catalogo y noticia de los literatos que ó nacidos ó educados ó florecientes en la América septentrional han dado á luz algún escrito ó lo han dejado preparado para la prensa). (See Ramirez, 1898.) **151, 155, 157.**

BEUCHAT, HENRI
1912 Manuel d'archéologie américaine (Amérique préhistorique. Civilisations disparues): Paris, 8°, xli, 773 p. **160, 183.**

BOBAN, E[UGÈNE]. Editor.
1885 See Batres, 1885.

BOLLAERT, WILLIAM
1866 Maya hieroglyphic alphabet of Yucatan: In *Memoirs of the Anthropological Society of London*, v. 2 (1865–66), p. 46–54. **168, 170, 180.**
1870 Examination of Central American hieroglyphs: Of Yucatan — including the Dresden Codex, the Guatémalien of Paris, and the Troano of Madrid: the hieroglyphs of Palenqué, Copan, Nicaragua, Veraguas, and New Granada; by the newly discovered Maya alphabet: in *Memoirs of the Anthropological Society of London*, v. 3 (1867–69), p. 288–314. **162.**

BOTURINI BENADUCCI, LORENZO
1746 Idea de una nueva historia general de la America Septentrional. Fundada sobre material copioso de figuras, symbolos, caractères, y geroglificos, cantares y manuscritos de autores indios, ultimamente descubiertos: Madrid, 4°, 20 ff., 167, [8], 96 p. (2d ed. Mexico, 1887.) **153.**

BOWDITCH, CHARLES P[ICKERING]
1901  Memoranda on the Maya calendars used in the Books of Chilam
      Balam: in *American Anthropologist* (N. S.) v. 3, p. 129–138.
      **183.**
1901a On the age of the Maya ruins: in *American Anthropologist* (N. S.)
      v. 3, p. 697–700. **183.**
1908  Collation of Berendt 1868d, v. 2: in Berendt Linguistic Collec-
      tion No. 43. (Gates reproduction.) **147.**
1908a Collation of Berendt, 1868: in Berendt Linguistic Collection, No.
      49. (Gates reproduction.) **147.**
1910  The numeration, calendar systems, and astronomical knowledge
      of the Mayas: Cambridge, 8°, xviii, 340 p. , xix pls.  **177** (2),
      **182, 189, 190, 191.**
  (1) List of Maya words in Landa and elsewhere with translation.
      4°, MS. 17 ff.  **169.**

BRASSEUR DE BOURBOURG, CHARLES ETIENNE  **146.**
1851  Lettres pour servir d'introduction à l'histoire primitive des na-
      tions civilisées de l'Amérique Méridionale, à M. le duc de
      Valmy: Mexico, 4°, 76 p. (This is the 1st ed. of his 1855–56.)
1855  Notes d'un voyage dans l'Amérique Centrale. Lettres à M.
      Alfred Maury, Bibliothécaire de l'Institut: in *Nouvelles Annales
      des Voyages et des Sciences Géographiques*, Paris, (6th series),
      v. 1, p. 129–158.  **161.**
1855–56 Nouvelles découvertes sur les traditions primitives conservées
      chez les anciens habitants de l'Amérique, d'après leurs livres
      et la lecture de leurs hiéroglyphes: in *Annales de Philosophie
      Chrétienne*, Paris, v. 50, p. 278–296, 325–341; v. 51, p. 199–
      220, 477–491; v. 52, p. 62–79, 112–117.  **185.**
1857  Essai historique sur les sources de la philologie Mexicaine: in
      *Archives de la Société Américaine de France*, v. 1, p. 5–32.  **159.**
1857–59 Histoire des nations civilisées du Mexique et de l'Amérique-
      centrale, etc.: Paris, 8°, 4 v. xcii, 440; 010; 092, 851 p.  **101,
      185, 187, 193.**
1859  Essai historique sur les sources de la philologie mexicaine et sur
      l'ethnographie de l'Amérique Centrale: in *Revue Orientale et
      Américaine, Mémoires de la Société d'Ethnographie*, (Series 1),
      Paris, v. 1, p. 354–380, v. 2, p. 64–75.  **156.**
1864  Relation des choses de Yucatan de Diégo de Landa . . . avec
      une grammaire et un vocabulaire abrégés Français-Maya:
      Paris, 8°, cxii, 516 p.  **168, 169, 180.**  This also contains:
      Lizana (1633, caps 1–4) with French translation, p. 348–365.
      Perez (1843) with French translation, p. 366–419.  **186.**
      Perez (1842) with French translation, p. 420–429.  **185.**
      Esquisse d'une grammaire de la langue Maya; d'après celles
      de Beltran et de Ruz, p. 459–478.  **165, 166.**

Brasseur de Bourbourg, Charles Etienne, 1864 (*continued*).
    Les prières en Maya et en Français d'après le P. Joaquin
      Ruz, p. 478–479. **199.**
    Vocabulaire Maya-Français d'après divers auteurs anciens
      et modernes, p. 480–506. (Annotated copy by Berendt
      in Berendt Linguistic Collection, No. 7.) **176.**

1865  Esquisses d'histoire, d'archéologie, d'ethnographie et de linguis-
      tique pouvant servir d'instructions générales: in *Archives de
      la Commission Scientifique du Mexique*, Paris, v. 1, p. 85–136.
      **159.**

1869  Lettre à M. Léon de Rosny sur la découverte de documents
      relatifs à la haute antiquité américaine, et sur le déchiffrement
      et l'interprétation de l'écriture phonétique et figurative de la
      langue Maya: in *Mémoires de la Société d'Ethnographie de
      Paris* (2d Series), v. 1. (Published separately: Paris, 1869,
      8°, 20 p.) **207.**

1869–70  Manuscrit Troano. Études sur le système graphique et la
      langue des Mayas: Paris, 4°, 2 v. Mission Scientifique au
      Mexique et dans l'Amérique Centrale. V. 2 contains:
    Introduction aux éléments de la langue Maya, p. i–xlix. **160,
      162, 151.**
    Grammaire et chrestomathie de la langue Maya (after San
      Buenaventura), p. 1–84. **164.**
    Observations du traducteur sur l'orthographe de quelques
      mots, p. 85–87.
    Résumé des désinences verbales, p. 87–91.
    Tables des noms de nombre, manières de compter, etc.
      d'après Beltran, p. 92–99. **181.**
    Chrestomathie ou choix de morceaux de littérature Maya,
      p. 101–122. **207.**
    Invocation au soleil (collected at Hacienda de Xcanchakan),
      p. 101–102. Copy in Berendt Linguistic Collection, No.
      44–6. **207.**
    Les cinq prophéties sibyllines d'après Lizana, p. 103–110.
      **193.**
    Titre antique concernant la famille de Nakuk Pech, p. 110–
      120. **203.**
    Chant d'amour. Recueilli à Izamal au mois de décembre,
      1864, p. 120–121. (Copy in Berendt Linguistic Collection,
      No. 44–5.) **206.**
    Ruz, 1846, p. 121–2. **198.**
    Vocabulaire général, Maya-Français et Espagnol, p. 123–
      462. **176.**

1871  Bibliothèque Mexico-Guatémalienne précédée d'un coup d'œil
      sur les études américaines dans leurs rapports avec les études
      classiques et suivie du tableau par ordre alphabétique des
      ouvrages de linguistique américaine contenus dans le même

volume, rédigée et mise en ordre d' après les documents de sa
collection américaine: Paris, 8°, xlvii, 183 p. **146, 155.**

1872 Dictionnaire, grammaire et chrestomathie de la langue Maya
précédés d' une étude sur le système graphique des indigènes
du Yucatan (Méxique): Paris, 4°, xlix, 464 p. (Reissue with
new title page of his 1869–70, v. 2.)

BRETON, ADELA C.
1919 Relationships in Central America: in *Man*, v. 19, article 94,
London. **175.**
1920 See Martínez Hernández, 1920, 1920a, 1920b.

BRIGHAM, WILLIAM T[UFTS]
1887 Guatemala, the land of the quetzal: New York, 8°, xv, 453 p.
**178.**

BRINTON, DANIEL GARRISON **148.**
1867 The Natchez of Louisiana, an offshoot of the civilized nations of
Central America: in *Historical Magazine*, New York, (2d
series), v. 1, p. 16–18. **179.**
1868 The myths of the New World: a treatise on the symbolism and
mythology of the red race of America: New York, 12°,
viii, 307 p. (2d ed., New York, 1876; 3d ed., Philadelphia,
1896.) **193.**
1871 Remarks on the nature of the Maya group of languages: in *Proceedings of the American Philosophical Society*, (1869), v. 11,
p. 4–6. **162.**
1881 The names of the gods in the Kiche myths, Central America:
in *Proceedings of the American Philosophical Society*, v. 19,
p. 613–647. (Published separately, Philadelphia, 1881, 8°,
37 p.) **162.**
1882 Maya chronicles: Philadelphia, 8°, 279 p.: in *Library of Aboriginal American Literature*, No. 1. **148, 183.** Among other items,
this book contains the following:
The name "Maya," p. 0–16. **180.**
Maya linguistic family, p. 17–20.
Grammar, p. 27–37. **167.**
Numeral system, p. 37–50. **181.**
Books of Chilam Balam, p. 67–72, 81–88. **182.**
Grammars and dictionaries, p. 72–77. **157, 170.**
Extracts with translations: —
Mani MS., p. 89–135. **186, 194.**
Tizimin MS., p. 136–151. **189.**
Chumayel MS., p. 152–185. **188.**
Pech MS., p. 187–259. **194, 203.**
Vocabulary, p. 261–279. **176.**
1882a American hero-myths, a study in the native religions of the
western continent: Philadelphia, 8°, 251 p. **162, 194, 203.**

BRINTON, DANIEL GARRISON (continued)

1882b The books of Chilam Balam, the prophetic and historic records of the Mayas of Yucatan: in *Penn Monthly*, v. 13, p. 261–275. (Republished in his 1890, p. 255–273, also printed separately, Philadelphia, 1882, 8°, 19 p. Spanish translations by Aznar y Perez, 1882, and Troncoso, 1883, in *Anales del Museo Nacional*, Mexico, v. 3, p. 92–109.) **183** (2), **189, 191, 195.**

1882c The graphic system and ancient records of the Mayas. Originally published as the Introduction to Cyrus Thomas: "Study of the Manuscrit Troano " in *Contributions to North American Ethnology:* Washington, v. 5, 4°, p. xvii–xxxvii. (Republished with additions as "The writing and records of the Ancient Mayas" in his 1890, p. 230–254.) **194.**

1883 The folk-lore of Yucatan: in *Folk-Lore Journal*, London, v. 1, p. 244–256. (Republished in his 1890, p. 163–180.) **191, 207** (2).

1883a Aboriginal American authors and their productions; especially those in the native languages. A chapter in the history of literature: Philadelphia, 8°, viii, 9–63 p. **183.**

1884 Catalogue of the Berendt Linguistic Collection: 4°, MS. 1 p. 79 ff. (For printed edition, see his 1900.)

1884–85 Memoir of Dr. C. H. Berendt: in *Proceedings of the American Antiquarian Society*, 1883, (N. S.) v. 3, p. 205–210. **146.**

1885 The philosophic-grammar of American languages, as set forth by Wilhelm von Humboldt; with the translation of an unpublished memoir by him on the American verb: in *Proceedings of the American Philosophical Society*, v. 22, p. 306–354. (Published separately, Philadelphia, 1885, 8°, 51 p. This is reprinted in an altered form in his 1890, p. 328–348.) **162, 167.**

1885a American languages and why we should study them: in *Pennsylvania Magazine of History and Biography*, v. 9, p. 15–35. (Published separately.) **170.**

1885b The lineal measures of the semi-civilized nations of Mexico and Central America: in *Proceedings of the American Philosophical Society*, v. 22, p. 194–207. (Published separately, Philadelphia, 1885. 8°, 14 p. Republished in his 1890, p. 433–451.) **176.**

1886 The conception of love in some American languages: in *Proceedings of the American Philosophical Society*, v. 23, p. 546–561. (Published separately. Philadelphia, 1886, 8°, 18 p. and republished in his 1890, p. 410–432.) **180.**

1887 Critical remarks on the editions of Diego de Landa's writings: in *Proceedings of the American Philosophical Society*. v. 24, p. 1–8. (Published separately, Philadelphia, 1887, 8°, 8 p.) **180.**

1888   On the Chane-abal (four language) tribe and dialect of Chiapas:
       in *American Anthropologist*, v. 1, p. 77–96. (Contains Berendt's
       comparative vocabulary (1870a) in Berendt Linguistic Collec-
       tion, No. 96.) **178.**
1890   Essays of an Americanist: Philadelphia, 8°, 489 p. This con-
       tains, among other items, the following articles: his 1882b,
       1882c, 1883, 1885, 1885b, 1886, 1890a.
1890a  Native American poetry: in his 1890, p. 284–304. **193, 194.**
1891   The American race. A linguistic classification and ethnographic
       description of the native tribes of North and South America:
       New York, 8°, xvi, 392 p. (Another edition, Philadelphia,
       1901.) **159.**
[1894] A primer of Maya hieroglyphics: Boston, 8°, vi, 9, 152 p. in
       *Publications of the University of Pennsylvania Series in Philos-
       ophy, Literature and Archaeology*, v. 3, n. 2. **176.**
1897   The missing authorities on Mayan antiquities: in *American
       Anthropologist*, v. 10, p. 183–191. **151.**
1898   A record of study in aboriginal American languages: Media
       (Pa.), 8°, 24 p. **148.**
1900   Catalogue of the Berendt linguistic collection: in *Bulletin of
       the Free Museum of Science and Art*, Philadelphia,v. 2, n. 4.
       p. 203–234. **146, 157.**
1900a  Indians of Central America: in (*Appleton's*) *Universal Cyclo-
       pædia* (New edition), New York, 4°, v. 6, p. 206–208. **162.**
1900b  Brinton Memorial meeting. Report of the memorial meeting
       held January 16, 1900, under the auspices of the American
       Philosophical Society . . . in honor of the late Daniel Garri-
       son Brinton, M.D.: Philadelphia, 8°, 67 p. (Bibliography of
       Brinton by Stewart Culin, p. 42–67). **148.**

BRITISH AND FOREIGN BIBLE SOCIETY
   (1) St. John III, 16, in most of the languages and dialects in which
       the British and Foreign Bible Society has printed or circulated
       the Holy Scriptures: London, 12°, 3–20 p. (Enlarged ed.
       London, 1878, 16°, 48 p. 1 f.) **200.**

BUSCHMANN, JOHANN KARL EDUARD
1853   Über den Naturlaut: in *Philologische und historische Abhand-
       lungen der Königlichen Akademie der Wissenschaften zu Berlin*
       (1852), p. 391–423. **179.**

BYRNE, JAMES
1885   General principles of the structure of language: London, 8°, 2 v.
       xxx, 504; xvii, 396 p. (2d ed. London, 1892, 8°, xxx, 510;
       xvii, 404 p.) **164.**

CACALCHEN, LIBRO DE
       [Collection of legal documents in Maya dating from about 1646
       to 1826.] 4°, MS., 164 p. (Owned by Gates and reproduced
       by him.) **204.**

CALERO, VICENTE and JUSTO SIERRA
[Articles in *Museo Yucateco* and *Registro Yucateco*.] **192.**
CALKINI, CHILAM BALAM DE
4°, MS., 15 ff. (Gates reproduction. He owns a copy, 8°, 13 p.
also reproduced by him.) **190.**
CAMPBELL, JOHN
1879 On the origin of some American Indian tribes: in *Proceedings of
the Natural History Society of Montreal*, (N. s.) v. 9, p. 65–80,
193–212. **178, 179.**
1898–99 Decipherment of the hieroglyphic inscriptions of Central
America: in *Transactions of the Canadian Institute*, v. 6, p.
101–244. **161.**
CANTÓN ROSADO, FRANCISCO
See Rivero Figueroa, 1918.
CARDENAS, FRANCISCO
§ 1639 Relación de la conquista y sucesos de Yucatan, para el uso del
Cronista Mayor de las Indias, D. Tomás Tamayo de Vargas:
(missing). **169.**
CARRILLO, ESTANISLAO
(1) [Translation of portion of Crónica de Mani: see Stephens, 1843,
v. 2, p. 265.] **205.**
CARRILLO Y ANCONA, CRESCENCIO **147.**
1863 El Repertorio Pintoresco ó Miscelanea instructiva y amena con-
sagrada á la religion, la historia del pais, la filosofia, la industria
y las bellas letras. . . . Redactor D. Crescencio Carrillo:
Merida, 8°, 586 p. **147.**
1865 Estudio histórico sobre la raza indígena de Yucatan: Vera Cruz,
8°, 26 p. **162.**
1866 Disertacion sobre la literatura y civilizacion antigua de Yucatan:
Merida, 4°, 38 p. (Republished in *Boletin de la Sociedad de
Geografía y Estadistica de la Republica Mexicana* (2d series),
1871, v. 3, p. 257–271, and in his 1883, p. 555–590.) **162, 189,
198.**
1868 Manuel de historia y geografía de la península de Yucatan: in
*La Península*, Merida, parts 1–5, p. 1–162. (Part republished
in his 1883.) **157, 180, 185.**
1870 Disertacion sobre la historia de la lengua Maya ó Yucateca: in
*La Revista de Merida* (Año II). Republished in *Boletin de la
Sociedad de Geografía y Estadistica de la Republica Mexicana*,
(2d series) 1872, v. 4, p. 134–195. **147, 151, 157 (2), 182, 185,
187, 188, 189 (3), 190, 192, 193.**
1871 Compendio de la historia de Yucatan, precedido del de su geografía y dispuesto en forma de lecciones: Merida, 16°, xii,
432 p. **157.**
1871a Compendio historico de Yucatan. Resúmen: Merida, 8°, 64 p.
**157.**

1872 Catálogo de las principales palabras Mayas usadas en el Castellano que se hable en el estado de Yucatan. (This forms the second part (p. 57–75) of Mendoza, 1872.) **178.**

1878–82 Historia antigua de Yucatan: in *Semanario Yucateco,* Merida. (Other editions with additions, Merida, 1881 and 1883. **151, 157, 162, 180, 185, 187, 190, 191, 194.**

1880 Quilich xocbil-u-payalchi ti c-colebil x-Zuhuy Maria, yetel u chucaan payalchiob ualkezahantacob ti maya-dtan tumen Don Hozé Leocadio Andrade u-mektan-pixnal katunil etel huntul yetkinil: Ho (Merida), 16°, 31 (1) p. (This was written in collaboration with José Leocadio Andrade.) **199.**

[1880a] Catecismo de historia y de geografía de Yucatan: Merida, 16°, 95 p. (This is an abbreviated edition of his 1871. See also 1871a and 1887.) This also contains:
Geografía de Yucatan (p. 1–28). (In 1887 ed. Audomaro Molina is given as the author.)
Nota sobre la ortologia de Yucatan (p. 91–95). **168.**

1880b Sobre la historia del idioma Yucateco o Maya: Republished in his 1883, p. 624–631. **160.**

1881 Bibliotheca de autores Yucatecos. Tomo I. Historia antigua de Yucatan. . . . Segunda de las disertaciones del mismo autor relativas al proprio asunto: Merida, sm. 4°, 504 + p. (This is a reissue with changes of several previous works: 1866; 1868; 1878–82. For 2d edition see his 1883.)

1882 Geografía Maya: in *Anales del Museo Nacional,* Mexico, v. 2, p. 435–438. (Republished in his 1883, p. 603–611.) **189 (2).**

1883 Historia Antigua de Yucatan: Merida, 16°, 670 p. (This is another edition of his 1881.) **151, 160, 162, 168, 180, 185, 187, 189 (2), 190, 191, 194, 198.**

1883a Maya. Etimologia de este nombre: in his 1883, p. 632–634. **180.**

1887 Compendio de la historia de Yucatan por Carrillo y Ancona. Compendio de la geografía de Yucatan por Audomaro Molina: Merida, 16°, 96 p. (This is an enlarged edition of 1880a without the *Nota de ortologia.* There is an edition of the *Compendio de la historia:* Merida, 1904, 16°, 72 p.) (Compare Ancona, 1881.)

1890 Estudio filologico sobre el nombre de America y el de Yucatan: Merida, 8°, 54 p. (Much the same material as in Chap. 5 in his 1883, p. 133–141.) **180, 188.**

1892–95 El obispado de Yucatan. Historia de su fundacion y de sus obispos desde el siglo XVI hasta el XIX seguida de las constituciones sinodales de la diocesis y otros documentos relativos. (Edicion ilustrada): Merida, 4°, 2 v. 1–521, 522–1102 p. (Supplements, 1896–97, 28 p.) (First published in *La Guirnalda.*) **147.**

[1893?] Pronunciacion de las letras del alfabeto en lengua Maya, según el Sr. Obispo de Yucatán: Copy, 4°, MS., 2 ff. in Peabody Museum. **168.**

CARRILLO Y ANCONA, CRESCENCIO (*continued*).
1897 Homenajes funebres. See Anon, 1897*a*.
(1) Galeria biografica-litografica de los Señores Obispos de Yucatan. Merida. **174.**
(2) [Portion of a letter written to Pilling regarding the authorship of works attributed to Henderson and Fletcher]: in Pilling, 1885, p. 258. **197.**

CARRILLO SUASTE, FABIAN
[1875] D. Juan Pio Perez. Memoria biografica: in Perez, 1866–77, p. i–xx. **143.**

CARVAJAL, FRANCISCO
(1) Discurso para el descendimiento del Señor (en Maya): Early XIX century MS. in Merida. (Copy by Berendt, 1868*a*, p. 77–116 in Berendt Linguistic Collection, No. 46. Reproduction by Gates of Berendt copy.) **202.**
(2) [Collection of proverbs in Maya.] Early XIX century MS. (unlocated). **202.**

CASTILLO, GERÓNIMO
1861 Efemérides hispano-mexicanas ó calendario-histórico Yucateco: in *Repertorio Pintoresco*, Merida. **157.**
1866 Diccionario historico, biografico y monumental de Yucatan, desde la conquista hasta el ultimo año de la dominacion Española en el pais: Merida, v. 1, A–E, 12°, vii, 9–315 p. (Only volume published.) **157** (2), **183, 186, 193.**

CERVERA, JOSÉ TIBURCIO. Translator.
1803 Una orden (por Benito Perez) de Gobierno de Yucatan respecto del despacho puntual de los correos, traducida en lengua Maya. (Copy, 12°, 6 p. in Berendt Linguistic Collection, No. 44–9.) **206.**

CHACXULUBCHEN, CRÓNICA DE
See Chicxulub, Crónica de

CHADENAT, CHARLES. Editor.
1889 *et seq.* Le bibliophile américain. Catalogue de livres, etc. relatifs à . . . l'Amérique. Archéologie, histoire, géographie, ethnographie, linguistique, voyages, etc. Bulletin trimestriel. (Numerous sale catalogues.) **158.**

CHAN, FLORENCIO and others
1850 Propositiones de los Indios sublevados para un armisticio y tratado de paz en carta dirigida al Cura de Chimax. MS. Cruzctun. (Copy, 12°, 15 p. from original in *Colección de Documentos para la Historia de la Guerra*, formerly in possession of Carrillo y Ancona, in Berendt Linguistic Collection No. 44–11.) **206.**

CHARENCEY [CHARLES FÉLIX HYACINTHE GOUHIER] COMTE DE
1866  Introduction à une étude comparative sur les langues de la famille
        Maya-Quiche: Paris (in *Avant Propos*, p. 32–37.) **167.**
1871  Le mythe de Votan. Étude sur les origines asiatiques de la civili-
        sation américaine: in *Actes de la Société Philologique*, Paris,
        v. 2, ii, 7–144 p. (Published separately.) **179.**
1873  Recherches sur une ancienne prophétie en langue Maya (Napuc-
        tun): in *Revue de Linguistique et de Philologie Comparée*, v. 6,
        p. 42–61. **194.**
1874  Essai d'analyse grammaticale d'un texte en langue Maya: in
        *Mémoires de l' Académie Nationale des Sciences, Arts et Belles-
        Lettres de Caen*, p. 142–161. (Published separately, Le Havre,
        1875, 8°, 9 p.) **185.**
1875  Fragment de chrestomathie de la langue Maya antique: in
        *Revue de Philologie et d'Ethnographie*, v. 1, p. 259–264. (Pub-
        lished separately, Paris, 1875, 8°, 8 p.) **194.**
1876  Étude sur la prophétie en langue Maya d'Ah Kuel-Chel: in
        *Revue de Linguistique et de Philologie Comparée*, v. 8, p. 320–
        332. (Published separately, Paris, 1876, 8°, 15 p. Republished
        in his 1883, p. 141–150.) **194.**
1878  Des animaux symboliques dans leur relation avec les points de
        l'espace chez les Américaines: Paris, 8°, 19 p. **182.**
1880  Des explétives numérales dans les dialectes de la famille Maya-
        Quichée: in *Revue de Linguistique et de Philologie Comparée*,
        v. 13, p. 339–386. (Published separately, Paris, 1880.) **182.**
1881  Des signes de numération en Maya: in *Actes de la Société Philolo-
        gique*, v. 8, p. 230–234. (Published separately, Alençon, 1881,
        8°, 7 p.) **181.**
1882  Recherches sur les noms des points de l'espace: Caen, 8°, 86 p.
        **180.**
1882a Du système de numération chez les peuples de la famille Maya-
        Quiché. in *Le Muséon. Revue des Sciences et des Lettres*, Paris,
        v. 1, p. 256–261. (Published separately, Louvain, 1882, 8°,
        8 p. Republished in his 1883, p. 151–157.) **182.**
1883  Mélanges de philologie et de paléographie américaines: Paris:
        8°, 2, 195 p. **166, 167.** Among other items, this volume con-
        tains the following.
        Sur le système de numération (see 1882a).
        Étude sur la prophétie (see 1876).
        Sur le pronom personnel dans les idiomes de la famille Maya-
            Quiché, p. 123–139. **167.**
        Sur les lois phonétiques dans les idiomes de la famille Mame-
            Huastèque, p. 89–121.
1883a Vocabulaire Français-Maya: in *Actes de la Société Philologique*,
        v. 13, p. 1–87. (Published separately, Alençon, 1884, 8°,
        87 p.) **176.**

# 232 BIBLIOGRAPHY

CHARENCEY [CHARLES FÉLIX HYACINTHE GOUHIER] COMTE DE (*contin'd*).

1883*b* Recherches sur les noms de nombres cardinaux dans la famille Maya-Quiché: in *Revue de Linguistique et de Philologie Comparée*, v. 16, p. 325–339. (Published separately, Paris, 8°, 15 p.) **180, 182.**

1883–84 De la conjugaison dans les langues de la famille Maya-Quiche: in *Le Muséon. Revue des Sciences et des Lettres*, Paris, v. 2, 1883, p. 575–595; v. 3, 1884, p. 40–72, 280–293, 464–488. (Published separately, Louvain, 1885, 8°, 130 p.) **165, 167.**

1884 De la formation des mots en langue Maya: in *Proceedings of the 5th International Congress of Americanists*, Copenhagen (1883), p. 379–426. (Published separately, Copenhagen, 1884.) **167.**

1891 Chrestomathie Maya d'après la chronique de Chac-Xulub-Chen. Extrait de la " Library of Aboriginal American Literature " de M. le Dr. D. G. Brinton. Texte avec traduction interlinéaire, analyse grammaticale et vocabulaire maya-française: in *Actes de la Société Philologique*, v. 19, 20. (Published separately, Paris, 1891, 8°, viii, 301 p.) **176, 203.**

1892 Les noms des métaux chez différents peuples de la Nouvelle Espagne: Paris, 8°, 14 p. (Republished, in part, in his 1894, p. 346–349.) **180.**

1892*a* 2d edition of Ruz, 1847; in *Actes de la Société Philologique*, (1891) v. 21, p. 157–207. (Published separately, Alençon, 1892, 8°, 51 p.) **197.**

1894 Le folklore dans les deux mondes: Paris, 8°. 424 p. **159.**

1896 Mélanges sur quelques dialectes de la famille Maya-Quichée: in *Journal de la Société des Américanistes*, Paris, v. 1, p. 43–60. (Published separately, Paris, 1897.) **166.** Among other items this paper contains the following:

Rectification d' un texte en langue Maya. **186.**

Des voix verbales en Maya. **167.**

1899 Noms des points de l'espace dans divers dialectes américains: in *Journal de la Société des Américanistes*, Paris, v.2, p.109–178. **180.**

CHAVERO, ALFREDO.

1887 Historia antigua y de la conquista. See Riva Palacio, 1887–88, v. 1. **189, 190.**

CHÉ, GONÇALO and others.

1877 Carta de diez caciques de Nueva España, á S. M. el Rey Don Felipe II, pidiendo de la órden de San Francisco, Yucatan, 11 de febrero de 1567: in *Cartas de Indias*, Madrid, folio, p. 307–308 and facsimile. **206.**

CHICXULUB, CRÓNICA DE

1542–62 4°, MS. 26 p., copy owned in Merida (Gates reproduction). (Notes on this MS. in Berendt Linguistic Collection, No. 43–4, copied by C. P. Bowditch, reproduced by Gates. Other notes in Berendt Collection No. 50–35. See Perez (2). This MS. written by Nakuk and Pablo Pech.) **202.**

CHUMAYEL, BOOK OF CHILAM BALAM OF
1913  Sm. 4°, MS. 107 p.  Published in *Anthropological Publications of
the University of Pennsylvania*, v. 5, Philadelphia. George
Byron Gordon, editor. (There is a copy by Berendt, 1868, in
the Berendt Linguistic Collection, No. 49. Gates owns a
second copy, 8°, 55 ff., reproduced by him.) **180, 187.**

CIUDAD REAL, ANTONIO DE
§ (1)  Gran diccionario ó calepino de la lengua Maya de Yucatan: MS.
4°, 6 v. XVI century (missing). **170.**
§ (2)  Diccionario de la lengua Maya: MS. XVI century (missing).
**170.**
§ (3)  Tratado curioso de las grandezas de Nueva España: MS. XVI
century (missing). **170.**
§ (4)  Sermones de Santos en lengua Maya: MS. XVI century (missing).
**201.**

CIVEZZA, MARCELLINO DA
1879  Saggio di bibliografía, geografica, storica, etnografica, San Fran-
cescana: 4°, xv, 698 p. (This is the geographical part of
Wadding and Sboralen's *Scriptores ordinis minorum*). **151, 154.**

CLARKE, HYDE
1877  The Khita and Khita-Peruvian epoch: Khita, Hamath, Hittite,
Canaanite, Etruscan, Peruvian, Mexican, etc.: London, 8°,
vii, 88 p. **179.**

CLARKE AND CO., ROBERT. Editors.
1878  Bibliotheca Americana; catalogue of a valuable collection of
books and pamphlets relating to America: Cincinnati, 8°.
(4), 262, (2), 64 p. Other sale catalogues, 1879, 1883, etc. **158.**

CLAVIGERO, FRANCESCO SAVERIO
1780–81  Storia antica del Messico, cavata da' migliori storici spagnuoli
e da' manoscritti e dalle pitture antiche degl' Indiani; divisa in
dieci libri e corredata di carte geografiche e di varie figure e
dissertazioni sulla terra, sugli animali e sugli abitatori del
Messico; Cesena, 4°, 4 v. vii, 302 p. 4 pls.; 276 p. 17 pls.;
260 p. 1 pl.; 331 p. Spanish ed. London, 1826, 8°, 2 v. Among
other editions, London, 1787, (English), 4°, 2 v.; Leipzig, 1789,
(German); Richmond, Va.; 1806, London, 1807, Philadelphia
1817, (English); London, 1826, (Italian); Mexico, 1844 and
1853; Jacapa, 1868, (Spanish). 1st ed. v. 4 (1781) p. 262–263
has the following:
*Catologo d'alcuni autori Europei e Creogli, che hanno scritto
della dottrina e morale christiana nelle lingue della Nuova Spagna.*
Ed. 1826, v. 2, p. 396 and later Spanish editions have the
following:
*Catalogo de algunos autores Europeos y Criollos que han escrito
sobre la doctrina y moral cristianas en las lenguas de Anahuac.*
**150, 154.**

Cocomes, Libro de los
    See Cacalchen, Libro de
Codice Anómino
    See Tizimin, Chilam Balam de
Cogolludo, Diego Lopez
    1688 Historia de Yucathan: Madrid, 4°, 15, 760 (31) p. (2d ed. with
        title. *Los tres siglos de la dominacion española en Yucatan ó
        sea historia de esta provincia desde la conquista hasta la inde-
        pendencia*, etc.: Campeche, 1842, Merida, 1845, 8°, 2 v.,
        (Justo Sierra, editor): 3d ed. with title, *Historia de Yucatán,
        escrita en el siglo xvii*. Merida, 1867–68, 8°, 2 v.) **150, 153,
        180, 193.**
Colección de Documentos
    1898–1900 Colección de documentos inéditos relativos al descubri-
        miento, conquista y organizatión de las antiguas posesiones
        Españoles de Ultramar. (2d series), v. 11, 13. Relaciones de
        Yucatan: Madrid, 8°, xl, 436; xvi, 414 p. (José María Ascen-
        sio, editor.) **161, 177.**
Coronel, Juan
    1620 Arte en lengua de Maya recopilado y enmendado: Mexico, 24°,
        54 ff. [Gates reproduction.] **163, 172.**
    1620a Doctrina Christiana en lengua de Maya: Mexico, 16°, 27 ff.
        (Gates reproduction, 4 ff. at end contain contents of Coronel,
        1620b.) **197.**
    1620b Discursos predicables, con otras diversas materias espirituales,
        con la Doctrina Christiana, y los articulos de la Fe, recopilados
        y enmendados [en lengua Yucateca]: Mexico, 16°, 8, 240 ff.
        (ff. 73–80 are mispaged as 83–90). (Gates reproduction.) **197,
        201.**
    § (1) Vocabulario Maya: MS. xvii century (missing). **172.**
    § (2) Doctrina Christiana, MS. xvii century (missing ?). **197.**
    § (3) Confesionario ó instrucciones para los nuevos ministros, en lengua
        Maya: MS. xvii century (missing). **198.**
Cortés, Hernando
    1852 Cartas [1st letter lost.] In its place the letter of the Municipality
        of Vera Cruz, dated July 10, 1519, may be substituted. This
        printed in *Colección de Documentos Inéditos para la Historia de
        España*, v. 1, and in *Historiadores primitivos de Indias:* Madrid
        1852, v. 1. (See MacNutt ed. of letters, New York, 1908,
        8°, v. 1, p. 123–182.) **180.**
    1866 Cartas y relaciones al Emperador Carlos V: Paris, 8°, li, 575 p.
        (Best edition by MacNutt, New York and London, 1908, 8°,
        2 v. xi, 354; vii, 374 p.) **180.**
Crowe, Frederick
    1850 The Gospel in Central America; containing a sketch of the
        country . . . a history of the Baptist mission in British Hon-
        duras, etc.: London, 12°, xii, 588 p. **199.**

CRUZ, JUAN
1571   Catecismo en lengua Maya: Mexico (also 1639 ed.) [?]   **196.**
CUBAS, ANTONIO GARCÍA
        See García Cubas, Antonio
CUARTAS, JULIAN DE
§ (1)   Arte compendiado de la lengua Maya: MS. XVII century, (missing).   **163.**
D. Do
        [Initials of writers on Maya language in *Repertorio Pintoresco*, of Merida].
DIAZ DEL CASTILLO, BERNAL
1632   Historia verdadera de la conquista de la Nueva-España, escrita por el Capitan Bernal Diaz del Castillo, uno de sus conquistadores: Madrid, 4°, 6 p. 254 ff. (11) p. (Numerous other editions, the best of which is that by Maudslay, published by the Hakluyt Society, London, 1908–16, 8°, 5 v.)   **180.**
DICCIONARIO HISTORICO, BIOGRAFICO Y MONUMENTAL DE YUCATAN.
        See Castillo, 1866.
DICCIONARIO UNIVERSAL DE HISTORIA Y GEOGRAPHIA.   **186.**
DOMINGUEZ, JOSÉ
        [Given by Clavigero as a writer on Maya.]   **152.**
DOMINGUEZ Y ARGAIZ, FRANCISCO EUGENIO
1758   Platicas de los principales mysterios de nuestra Santa Fee, con una breve exortación al fin del modo con que deben excitarse al dolor de las culpas. Hechas en el idioma Yucateco: Mexico, 8°, 5 ff., 24 p. 1 f. (Gates reproduction. Copy by Berendt in 1868a, p. 1–76.)   **201.**
DONDÉ, JOAQUIN Y DONDÉ, JUAN
1876   Lecciones de Botanica, arregladas segun los principios admitidos por Guibourt Richard Duchartre, etc.: Merida, 8°, xxiii, 259 p. (Maya names prepared by Thomas Aznar Barbachano.)   **176.**
DOUAY, LÉON
1891   Études etymologiques sur l'antiquité américaine: Paris, 8°, 158 p.   **180.**
1894   Affinités lexicologique du Haitien et du Maya: in *Proceedings of the 10th International Congress of Americanists*, Stockholm, p. 191–208.   **161, 179.**
1900   Nouvelles recherches philologiques sur l'antiquité américaine: Paris, 8°, 188 p.   **160, 161, 179.**
1905   De la non-parenté de certaines langues de l'ancien monde (en particulier du japonais) avec celles du Nouveau, et spécialement, du groupe Maya: in *Proceedings of the 13th International Congress of Americanists*, New York (1902), p. 245–247.   **161.**
(1)   Mémoire sur les affinités du Maya avec certaines langues de l'Amérique Méridionale: 8°, 17 p. (reprint).   **161, 179.**

DUSAERT, [ÉDOUARD] LE COLONEL
1882   La carie américaine, mère, en civilisation de l'antique Égypte
       d'après les documents de M. l'Abbé Brasseur de Bourbourg:
       Paris, 8°, 64 p. **160.**

EBTUN, TITULOS DE
4°, Mssel. MSS. en lengua Maya. 324 p. dating from about 1638
to 1829. (Gates reproduction.) **204.**

ECHANO, AGUSTIN DE
1758   Aprobacion: in Dominguez, 1758. **183.**

EGUIARA ET EGUREN, JUAN JOSÉ DE
1755   Bibliotheca Mexicana, sive eruditorum historia virorum, qui
       in America Boreali nati, vel alibi geniti in ipsam domicilio aut
       studijs asciti, quavis linguâ scripto aliquid tradiderunt: v. 1,
       A. B. C.: Mexico, 4°, 80 ff., 543 p. (Other portions exist
       in manuscript.) **151, 153.**

EICHHORN, ALBERT
1896   Naual; oder Die hohe Wissenschaft (scientia mirabilis) der
       architectonischen und künstlerischen Composition bei den
       Maya-Völkern, deren Descendenten und Schülern: Berlin, 4°,
       126 p. **177.**
1905   Die Hieroglyphen-Bildschrift der Maya-Völker in ihrer stufen-
       weisen Entwickelung bis zur Ornamentbildschrift dargestellt
       und an den Hieroglyphen der 20 Monatstage erläutert: Berlin,
       4°, iv. 236 (2), p. **177.**

ESPINOSA, CALENDARIO DE
Annual publication, Merida. **158.**

FERRAZ, JUAN FERNANDEZ
1902   Lengua Quiché. Sinopsis de constitutiva gramatical, 1897–1902:
       San José de Costa Rica, 12°, 153 p. **179.**

FIELD, THOMAS WARREN
1873   An essay towards an Indian bibliography. Being a catalogue of
       books, relating to the history, antiquities, languages, customs,
       religion, wars, literature, and origin of the American Indians,
       etc.: New York, 8°, iv, 430 p. **154.**
1875   Catalogue of his library: New York, 8°, viii, 376 p. (Sale cata-
       logue.) **154, 158.**

[FISCHER, AUGUSTIN]
1869   Bibliotheca Mejicana. A catalogue of an extraordinary collec-
       tion of books relating to Mexico and North and South America,
       from the first introduction of printing in the New World, A.D.
       1544 to A.D. 1868. Collected during 20 years' official residence
       in Mexico: London, 8°, 312 p. (p. 229 has title: Valuable
       books relating to the history, literature, and dialects of North
       and South America, comprising the libraries of the late Dr.
       Berendt of Vera Cruz, and that of an official personage for
       many years resident in the West Indies). (Sale catalogue.)
       **155, 158.**

FISKE, JOHN
1892 The discovery of America with some account of ancient America and the Spanish Conquest: Boston and New York, 12°, 2 v. (Other editions.) **203.**

[FLETCHER, RICHARD] **145.**
1865 Breve devocionario para todos los dias de la semana. Payalchioob utial tulacal le u kiniloob ti le semana: London, 16°, 17 ff. **202.**

1865a Catecismo de los Metodistas. No. 1, Para los niños de tierna edad. Catecismo ti le metodistaoob. No. 2, Utial mehen palaloob: London, 16°, 17 ff. (Gates reproduction.) **197.**

1868 [A tentative edition in Maya of St. John's Gospel, published by the British and Foreign Bible Society.] (See Fletcher, 1869.) **200.**

1869 Leti u ebanhelio Hezu Crizto Hebix Huan: London, 16°, 83 p. **200.**

1900 Leti u ebanhelio Hezu Crizto Heliz Marcoz: London, 16°, 67 p. **200.**

1900a Leti u ebanhelio Hezu Crizto Hebix Mateo: London, 16°, 104 p. **200.**

FUERTES, E. A.
(1) Vocabularies of the Chimalapa or Zoque: Guichicovian, or Mixe; Zapoteco; and Maya; 200 words each, accompanied by grammatic notes: 1°, MS. 17 ff. in Bureau of Ethnology MSS. Collection, Washington. (Copy by Berendt.) **178.**

GABELENTZ, [HANS] GEORG [CONON] VON DER
1881 Die Sprachwissenschaft, ihre Aufgaben, Methoden und bisherigen Ergebnisse: Leipzig, 8°, xx, 502 p. **166.**

GALA, LEANDRO RODRIGUEZ DE LA
See Vales, 1870.

GALINDO, JUAN
1832 Mémoire de M. Galindo, officier supérieur de la République de l'Amérique Centrale, adressé à M. le Secrétaire de la Société de Géographie de Paris: in *Bulletin de la Société de Géographie de Paris*, v. 18, p. 198–214. (Copy in Berendt Linguistic Collection, No. 42–6.) **181, 199.**

1834 Description of the river Usumasinta in Guatemala: in *Proceedings of the Royal Geographical Society*, v. 3, p. 59–64, (1833). (French trans. In *Nouvelles Annales des Voyages*, 3d series: Paris, 1834, v. 3, p. 147–151. **178.**

GALLATIN, ALBERT
1845 Notes on the semi-civilized nations of Mexico, Yucatan and of Central America; in *Transactions of the American Ethnological Society*, v. 1, p. 1–352. **165, 166, 167, 168, 178, 182, 186.**

GANN, THOMAS W. F.
1918 The Maya Indians of southern Yucatan and northern British Honduras: in *Bureau of Ethnology*, Washington. Bulletin 64, 8°, 146 p. 28 pls. **207.**

238 BIBLIOGRAPHY

GARCÍA, GENARO
1898  See Spencer, 1873–1910.
GARCÍA, GREGORIO
1607  Origen de los Indios de el Nuevo Mundo e Indias Occidentales
averiguado con discurso de opiniones por el padre presentado
fray Gregorio Garcia de la orden de Predicadores. Tratanse en
este libro varias cosas, y puntos curiosos, tocantes a diversas
ciencias y facultades, con que se haze varia historia, de mucho
gusto para el ingenio y entendimiento de hombres agudos y
curiosos: Valencia. (2d ed. Madrid, 1729, 26, 336, (80) p.)
**153.**
GARCÍA, [MANUEL]
1856  El toro de Sinkeuel. Leyenda hipica, politico-tauromaquica:
Merida, 24°, 32 p.  **206.**
GARCÍA CUBAS, ANTONIO
1876  The Republic of Mexico in 1876. A political and ethnographical
division of the population, character, habits, costumes, and
vocations of its inhabitants. Translated into English by
George E. Henderson: Mexico, 8°, 130 p.  1 f. 8 p. of music,
8 pls. map.  **159.**
1884  Cuadro geográfico, estadístico, descriptivo é histórico de los
Estados Unidos Mexicanos: Mexico, 8°, xxxi, 474, iii p. 1
map, 1 pl., 3 tab. (Another edition, Mexico, 1885.)  **159.**
1888–91  Diccionario geográfico, histórico, y biográfico de los Estados
Unidos Mexicanos: Mexico, 4°, 5 v.  **159.**
GARCÍA Y GARCIA, APOLINAR
1865  Historia de la guerra de castas en Yucatan: Merida, 4°.  **162.**
GARCÍA ICAZBALCETA, JOAQUÍN
See Icazbalceta, Joaquín García.
GATES, WILLIAM [E.]  **148.**
1914  Concepts linguistiques dans l'Amérique ancienne: in *Compte
Rendu, Congrès International d'Anthropologie et d'Archéologie
Préhistoriques*, 14th Session, Geneva (1912), v. 2, p. 341–348.
**167.**
1915  The unpublished material in the Mayance and southern Mexican
languages: 8°, MS. 22 ff. (Prepared for the meeting of the
Archaeological Institute of America. San Francisco, 1915.)
**157.**
1920  The distribution of the several branches of the Mayance linguistic stock: in Morley, 1920. Appendix 12, p. 604–615.  **160,
168.**
1920a  [Transcription and translation with notes of page 66 of the
Crónica de Oxkutzcab]: in Morley, 1920, p. 507–509.  **204.**
1920b  [Transcription and translation of p. 85 of the Chilam Balam de
Chumayel]: in Morley, 1920, p. 485.  **189.**
(1)  Apuntes para el arte de la lengua Maya: 4°, MS. 7 ff.  **167.**

(2) [Finding list of MSS. and printed material on the languages of the Maya stock]: 4°, MS. 56 ff. **157.**

(3) [Maya pronunciation and alphabet]: 4°, MS. 5 ff. **168.**

(4) Photographic reproductions of Maya manuscripts and books. For list, see p. 148–149.

GATSCHET, ALBERT S[AMUEL]
1879 Perez' Maya-Spanish dictionary: in *American Antiquarian*, v. 2, p. 30–32. **175.**
1883 Native American languages: in *The Critic*, New York, v. 3. No. 61, p. 96–97. (Review of Perez, 1866–77 and Brinton, 1882.) **175.**
1900 Central-Amerikas Sprachstämme und Dialekte: in *Globus*, v. 77, n. 5, p. 81–84. **159.**

GERRODETTE, FRANK HONORÉ
1891–92 The linguistic stocks of the Indians of Mexico and Central America: sm. 4°, MS. 320 p. Index and map. (In Peabody Museum.) **159.**

GÓMARA, FRANCISCO LOPEZ DE
1553 Hispania Victrix. Primera y segvnda parte de la historia general de las Indias cō todo el descubrimiento, y cosas notables que han acaescido dende que se ganaron hasta el año de 1551: Medina del Campo, folio, cxxii, cxxxix ff. (There was evidently another edition, with slightly different title, published in Zaragoza in 1553. Also numerous other editions.) (See Barcia, 1749.) **180.**

GOMEZ DE PARADA, JUAN
1722 Constituciones Sinodales dispuestas por el orden de Libros y Titulos y Santos Decretos del Concilio Mexicano III para el Obispado de Yucatan por su Obispo el Yll^mo. S^or. D^v. D^n Juan Gomez de Parada del Conséjo de su Mag^d. en el Sinodo que comenzo en su Yglecia Catedral, el dia seis de Ag^to. de mil setecientos veinte y dos, y se finalizo el dia primero de O^bre. del mismo año: fol. 454 p. **139.**

GORDON, GEORGE BYRON. Editor.
1913 See Chumayel, Book of Chilam Balam of

GORDON, JAMES BENTLEY
1820 An historical and geographical memoir of the North American continent, its nations and tribes: Dublin, 4°, civ, x, 305 p. **161.**

GRANADO BAEZA, BARTOLOMÉ JOSÉ
1845 Los indios de Yucatan. Informe dado por el cura de Yaxcabá en contestacion al interrogatorio de 36 preguntas, etc.: in *Registro Yucateco*, v. 1, p. 165–178. (Written in 1813.) **161, 206.**

GUERRA, JOSÉ MARÍA
See Vela, 1848.

240 BIBLIOGRAPHY

HAEBLER, KARL
1895 Die Maya-Litteratur und der Maya-Apparat zu Dresden: in
Centralblatt für Bibliothekswesen, v. 12, part 12, p. 537–576.
156.

[HAMY, ERNEST THÉODORE]
1909 Catalogue de la bibliothèque de feu M. le Docteur E. T. Hamy:
Paris, 8°, 118 p. (Sale catalogue.) 158.

HARRISSE, HENRY
1866 Bibliotheca americana vetustissima. A description of works relating to America published between the years 1492 and 1551:
New York, l. 8°, liv, 519 p. (Additions, Paris, 1872, l. 8°, xl,
199 p.) 154.

HELLER, CARL BARTHOLOMAEUS
1853 Reisen in Mexiko in den Jahren 1845–48: Leipzig, 8°, xxiv,
432 p. 1 pl. 1 map. 165, 178, 182.

HENDERSON, ALEXANDER 145.
[1852] The Maia primer: Birmingham, 16°, 12 p. (Berendt, 1867, gives
the date as 1863.) 166.
1859–66 A Maya dictionary of the language as spoken in the District
of Bacalar, Yucatan. MS. 6 v. averaging 250 pages each. 3 v.
Maya-English; 3 v. English-Maya: in Bureau of Ethnology
library. (See note in American Anthropologist (N. S.) 1900.
v. 2, p. 403–404. 174.
1870 Ebanhilio Hezu-Clizto hebix Zan Lucaz: London, 16°, 14 p.
(Four chapters of St. Luke as translated by Ruz, 1, published
by Kingdon, 1865, and corrected by Henderson.) 200.
§ (1) Book of Genesis in Maya. MS. (according to Berendt, 1867,
p. 420). [?] 200.
§ (2) The Psalms in Maya. MS. (according to Berendt, 1867, p. 420).
[?] 200.
§ (3) Translation of Beltran's grammar into English. (According to
Berendt, 1867, p. 420. [?] See Kingdon, 1.) 165.

HERNÁNDEZ, PEDRO M.
1905 De los primeros habitantes de la venturosa Yucateca, traducido
de la Maya al Castellano: Merida, 8° (5 parts in one. Maya
and Spanish text). 207.

HERRANZ Y QUIROS, DIEGO NARCISO
1834 Compendio mayor de gramatica Castellana para uso de los niños
que concurren à las escuelas: Madrid. (9th ed. Madrid, 1858.)
(This is the Spanish grammar translated into Maya by Ruz,
1844. See Narciso, 1838.) 166.

HERRERA, ALFONSO L. and CICERO, RICARDO E.
1895 Catálogo de la coleción de anthropología del Museo Nacional de
Mexico: Mexico, 8°, viii, 164 p.

HERRERA [Y TORDESILLAS], ANTONIO DE
1601–15. Historia general de los hechos de los Castellanos en las islas
i tierra firme del mar océano en quatro decadas desde el año
de 1492 hasta el de 1531: Madrid, 4°, 8 pt. (Other editions.)
The original edition contains the following:
Los Autores impresos, y de mano, que han escrito cosas
particulares de las Indias Occidentales. **153.**

HERVÁS Y PANDURO, LORENZO
1784 Catalogo delle lingue conosciute e notizia delle loro affinità e
diversità . . . : Cesena, 4°, 260 p. (V. 17. *Idea dell'Universo.*) **154, 158.**
1785 Origine, formazione, meccanismo, ed armonia degl' idiomi:
Cesena, 4°, 180 p. 18 ff. (V. 18. *Idea dell'Universo.*) **179.**
1786 Aritmetica delle nazioni e divisione del tempo fra l'Orientali:
Cesena, 4°, 206 p. (V. 19. *Idea dell'Universo.*) **182.**
1787 Saggio pratico delle lingue con prolegomeni, e una raccolta di
orazioni Dominicali in più di trecento lingue, e dialetti con cui
si dimostra l'infusione del primo idioma dell'uman genere, e la
confusione delle lingue in esso poi succeduta, e si additano la
diramazione, e dispersione della nazioni con molti risultati
utili alla storia: Cesena, 4°, 256 p. (V. 21. *Idea dell' Universo.*) **199.**
1787a Vocabolario poligloto con proligomeni sopra più di CL. lingue.
Dove sono delle scoperte nuove, ed utili all'antica storia
dell'uman genere, ed alla cognizione del meccanismo delle
parole: Cesena, 4°, 247 p. (V. 20. *Idea dell' Universo.*) **179.**
1800–05 Catálogo de las lenguas de las naciones conocidas, y numer-
acion, división y clases de éstas, según la diversidad de sus
idiomas y dialectos: Madrid, 4°, 6 v. (An enlarged, corrected,
and selective edition of Hervas, 1785, 1786, 1787, 1787a.) **154,
158.**

HESTERMANN, P. FERDINAND
1915 Die Maya-Kultur Mittelamerikas (Sprache, Schrift, Literatur,
Kalender und Bauwerke): in *Mitteilungen der Anthropolo-
gischen Gesellschaft, Sitzungsberichte:* Vienna, v. 45, p. [8]–[9].
**102.**

HIERSEMANN, KARL WILHELM. Editor.
1891 *et seq.* Amerikanische Sprachen. (Numerous sale catalogues,
1891, Nos. 70, 82, 87; 1893, No. 119; 1895, No. 143; 1897,
No. 179; 1898, No. 200; 1904, No. 301; etc.) **155, 158.**

HOCABA, CHILAM BALAM DE
See Chilam Balam de Kaua. **191.**

HOIL, JUAN JOSÉ
Chilam Balam de Chumayel (see under Chumayel).

HOLMES, WILLIAM HENRY
1903  Report of the Bureau of American Ethnology: in *Smithsonian Institution, Annual Report*, Washington, [1904], p. 34–48. **171.**

HOVELAQUE, ABEL
1876  La linguistique: in *Bibliothèque des Sciences Contemporaines*, Paris, v. 2, 16°, xi, 365 p. (2d ed. Paris, 1877, 8°, xiv, 435 p.) **162.**

HUMBOLDT, [FRIEDRICK HEINRICH] ALEXANDER VON
1811  Essai politique sur le royaume de la Nouvelle-Espagne, etc. Paris, 8°, 5 v. (Many other editions among them, English ed. London, 1811, 8°, 5 v. Spanish ed.: Paris, 1822, 8°, 4 v.) **161, 164.**

HUMBOLDT, [KARL] WILHELM VON
(1) Ueber das Verbum in den amerikanischen Sprachen: MS. 40 p. (in Humboldt's writing, 13 p. notes by ?). **164.**
(2) Maya Grammatik: folio MS. 135 p. (36 p. in Humboldt's writing, 82 p. and table in writing of his secretary, 15 p. notes and list of affixes in Humboldt's writing.) **164.**

ICAZBALCETA, JOAQUÍN GARCÍA
1866  Apuntes para un catálogo de escritores en lenguas indígenas de América; Mexico, 16°, xiii, 157 p. (Republished in his *Obras*, Mexico, 1898, v. 8, p. 1–181.) (134 titles reprinted in *Polémica entre el Diario Oficial y la Colonia Española*, Mexico, 1875.) **155.**
1870  See Mendieta.
1886  Bibliografía mexicana del siglo XVI. Primera parte. Catálogo razonado de libros impresos en México de 1539 á 1600 con biografías de autores y otras ilustraciones; precedido de una noticia acerca de la introducción de la imprenta en México: Mexico, 4°, xxix, 419, p. (3) ff. (See León, 1902.) **156.**

IXIL, CHILAM BALAM DE
MS. owned in Merida. (There is a Berendt copy, 1868, in the Berendt Linguistic Collection, No. 49. Gates owns a second copy, 8°, 25 ff. reproduced by him.) **190.**

JÉHAN, LOUIS FRANÇOIS
1864  Dictionnaire de linguistique et de philologie comparée. Histoire de toutes les langues mortes et vivantes, traité complet d'idiomographie etc.: in Migne's *Troisième et Dernière Encyclopédie Théologique*, v. 34, Paris, 4°, 1448 columns (two to a page.) **162.**

JOHNES, ARTHUR JAMES
1846  Philological proofs of the original unity and recent origin of the human race. Derived from a comparison of the languages of Asia, Europe, Africa and America. Being an inquiry how far the differences in the languages of the globe are referrible to causes now in operation: London, 8°, lx, 172, 103 p. **179.**

JOYCE, THOMAS A[THOL]
1914  Mexican archaeology, an introduction to the archaeology of the
      Mexican and Mayan civilizations of pre-Spanish America:
      New York and London, 8°, xvi, 371 p. 30 pls. **160.**

JUARROS, DOMINGO
1808  Compendio de la historia de la ciudad de Guatemala. . . .
      Tomo I. Que comprende los prelimminaires de dicha historia.
      Tomo II. Contiene un cronicon del Reyno de Guatemala:
      Guatemala, 4°, 2 v.  (Numerous other editions including an
      English one by Baily, London, 1823, 8°, viii, 520 p. maps, and
      a Spanish ed. of 1857.)  **159.**

JUDIO, LIBRO DE
      See Anon (13–16), Ossado, 1834, Perez (4) and Berendt 1870.  **195.**

KAUA, CHILAM BALAM DE
      4°, MS. 282 p. owned in Merida (Gates reproduction.)  (There is
      a partial Berendt copy, 1868, in the Berendt Linguistic Collec-
      tion, No. 49.  Gates has a second (partial) copy, 8°, 99 ff., also
      reproduced by him).  (Sometimes referred to as the Hocaba
      MS.)  **190.**

KEANE, AUGUSTUS HENRY
1901  Central and South America:  London, 12°, 2 v. edited by Sir
      Clements Markham.  (2d ed., London, 1909 11, 2 v.  This
      work and that of Bates, 1878, form part of Stanford's "Com-
      pendium of geography and travel.")  **159.**

KENNEDY, JAMES
1861  Essays ethnological and linguistic: London, 8°, vi p. (1) f. 230 p.
      (Edited by C. M. Kennedy.)  This contains:
          Supplementary notices of the American Indians, the Mayas,
          the Caribs, the Arrawaks and the Mosquitos (p. 124–
          152).  **161.**

KINGDON, JOHN  **145.**
1847  A Yucatecan grammar: translated from the Spanish into Maya
      and abridged for the instruction of the native Indians by the
      Rev. J. Ruz, of Merida.  Translated from the Maya into
      English: Belize, 8°, 68 p.  (Gates reproduction.)  (See Ruz,
      1844 and Berendt, 1865.)  **166.**
1862 [?]  [A tentative edition in Maya of chaps. v, xi, xv, xxiii of St.
      Luke's Gospel, published by the British and Foreign Bible
      Society: London].  (See Kingdon, 1865.)  **199.**
1865  Leti u cilich Evangelio Jesu Cristo hebix San Lucas: London,
      16°, 90 p, published by the British and Foreign Bible Society.
      **200.**
§ (1)  [Beltran's grammar translated into English].  MS. [?]  (Ludewig,
      1858, p. 227 states that there is a translation of Beltran's gram-
      mar into English in possession of American Bible Society,
      New York.  Present officers deny this.  See Henderson, 3.)
      **165.**

KINGDON, JOHN (*continued*).
§ (2)   Dictionary Maya-Spanish-English and English-Spanish-Maya:
        MS. [?].  (Ludewig, 1858, p. 227 states this is in possession of
        the American Bible Society, New York.  Present officers deny
        this.)  **174.**

KLAPROTH, JULIUS
1824–28  Mémoires relatifs à l'Asie contenant des recherches histo-
         riques, géographiques et philologiques sur les peuples de
         l'Orient: Paris, 12°, 3 v.  **179.**

LANDA, DIEGO DE  **141.**
1864     See Brasseur de Bourbourg, 1864.  (2d edition, Appendix to the
         Delgado edition of de Rosny, *Essai sur le déchiffrement de
         l'écriture hiératique de l'Amérique Centrale*, Madrid, 1884;
         and a 3d edition in *Colección de Documentos Inéditos* (2d
         series): Madrid, 1900, v. 13, p. 265–411).
§ (1)    Arte perfeccionado de la lengua Maya: MS. XVI century (miss-
         ing).  **162.**
§ (2)    Doctrina en la lengua Maya [?].  (See Aguilar, 1639; ed. 1892,
         p. 35.)  **196.**

LARRAINZAR, MANUEL
1875–78  Estudios sobre la historia de America, sus ruinas y anti-
         güedades, etc.: Mexico, 8°, 5 v.  **159, 162, 165.**

LATHAM, ROBERT GORDON
1850     The natural history of the varieties of man: London, 8°, xxviii
         574 p.  **159.**
1860     Opuscula.  Essays chiefly philological and ethnographical: Lon-
         don, 8°, vi, 418 p.  **179.**
1862     Elements of comparative philology: London, 8°, xxxii, 774 p.  **179.**

LECLERC, CHARLES
1867     Bibliotheca americana.  Catalogue raisonné d'une très-précieuse
         collection de livres anciens et modernes sur l'Amérique et les
         Philippines: Paris, 8°, vii, 407 p.  **154.**
1878     Bibliotheca americana.  Histoire, géographie, voyages, archéo-
         logie et linguistique des deux Amériques et des îles Philippines:
         Paris, 8°, xx, 737 p.  (Enlarged edition of 1867.)  (Maya, Nos.
         2279–2294, 2468, 2609.)  (Supplements appeared in 1881 and
         1887.)  **154.**

LEHMANN, WALTER
1907     Ergebnisse und Aufgaben der mexikanistischen Forschung: in
         *Archiv für Anthropologie* (N. S.) v. 6, p. 113–168.  (English
         translation by Seymour de Ricci, Paris, 1909, 12°, 127 p.)  **150,
         156, 162.**

LEJEAL, LÉON
1902     Les antiquités mexicaines (Mexique, Yucatan, Amérique-cen-
         trale): Paris, 8 , 79 p.  (Published by the *Société des Études
         Historiques.  Bibliothèque de bibliographies critiques.*)  **150, 156.**

León, Nicolás
1896 Biblioteca mexicana. Catálogo para la venta de la porcion mas
     escogida de (su) biblioteca: Mexico, 16°, 37 p. (Sale cata-
     logue.) **158.**
1898 See Ramirez, 1898.
1900 Familias lingüisticas de México: in *Memorias de la Sociedad
     Cientifica de "Antonio Alzate,"* v. 15, p. 275–284. (Republished
     in *Anales del Museo Nacional,* Mexico, 1903, v. 7, p. 279–309,
     map.) **159.**
1902 Adiciones á la Bibliografía mexicana del siglo xvi: in *Boletin del
     Instituto Bibliográfico Mexicano,* Part 1, p. 43 *et seq.* (See
     Icazbalceta, 1886.) **156.**
1902a La bibliografía in México en el siglo xix; in *Boletin del Instituto
     Bibliográfico Mexicano,* Part 3, p. 55–66. **156.**
1902–08 Bibliografía mexicana del siglo xviii: Mexico, sm. 4°, 5 parts.
     (Parts 1–3 in *Boletin del Instituto Bibliográfico Mexicano,*
     Nos. 1, 4, 5, 7.) **156.**
1905 Las lenguas indígenas de Mexico en el siglo xix, Nota biblio-
     gráfica y crítica: in *Anales del Museo Nacional,* Mexico, (2d
     epoca), v. 2, p. 180–191. (French edition in *L'Année Linguis-
     tique, publiée sur les auspices de la Société de Philologie.* Paris,
     1904, v. 2, p. 249–281. **156.**
León Pinelo, Antonio Rodriguez de
1629 Epitome de la biblioteca oriental i occidental, nautica i geo-
     gráfica: Madrid, 8°, 44 ff., 186, xii p. 1 f. This contains:
     Autores que han escrito en lenguas de las Indias (p. 104–110).
     (See Barcia, 1737–38 for 2d ed.) **150, 153.**
Le Plongeon, Alice [Dixon]
1879 Notes on Yucatan: in *Proceedings of the American Antiquarian
     Society* (1878), p. 77–106. (Published separately with other
     papers, Worcester, 1879, p. 69–98.) **195.**
[1839] Here and there in Yucatan. Miscellanies. New York, 12°,
     146 p. **195.**
(1) Maya melodies of Yucatan. Taken from Indian airs of Alice
     Dixon LePlongeon with musical settings by Susanne V. R.
     Lawton. **207.**
Le Plongeon, Augustus
1877 See Salisbury, Stephen, 1877.
1879 Letter addressed to the Right Rev. Bishop Courtenay, Bishop of
     Kingston [on the Maya language]: in *Proceedings of the Ameri-
     can Antiquarian Society,* p. 113–117. **160.**
1880 Ensayo sobre la antigüedad de la lengua Maya: in *La Revista
     de Merida.* (Republished in *El Republicano,* Mexico.) (See
     Carrillo y Ancona, 1880b.) **160.**
[1880a?] [Comparative study of the Maya language.] (A letter in
     Spanish addressed to the Right Reverend Bishop Courtenay of
     Kingston, Jamaica): in *La Revista de Merida.* **160.**

LE PLONGEON, AUGUSTUS (*continued*).

1880*b* [Letter on the antiquity of the Mayas addressed to the Right
Rev. Bishop Courtenay, Bishop of Kingston]: in *The Present
Century*, New York, v. 2. No. 22. (This is probably the same
as 1880*a*.)

1881  Mayapan and Maya inscriptions: in *Proceedings of the American
Antiquarian Society*, (N. S.), v. 1, p. 246–282.  **160.**

1881*a* Vestiges of the Mayas, or, Facts tending to prove that communi-
cations and intimate relations must have existed, in very
remote times, between the inhabitants of Mayab and those of
Asia and Africa: New York, 8°, 68 p.  **160.**

1896  Queen Moo and the Egyptian Sphinx: New York, 8°, lxv, 277 p.
68 pls. (2d ed. 1900.)  **160, 176.**

LIZANA, BERNARDO DE

1633  Historia de Yucatan. Devocionario de Nuestra Señora de Izmal
y conquista espiritual; Valladolid. (Another edition, Mexico,
1893, 8°, (12 ff.), 127 ff. (1) f. Parts of first four chapters published in Brasseur de Bourbourg, 1864, p. 348–364, with French
translation. Extracts in Carrillo y Ancona, 1870; ed. 1872,
p. 155–160.)  **150, 180, 193.**

LOPEZ OTERO, DANIEL

1914  Gramatica Maya. Metodo teorico practico: Merida, 8°, 130 p.
(Founded, in part, on notes by Audomaro Molina.)  **167.**

LUDEWIG, HERMANN ERNST

1858  The literature of American aboriginal languages. With additions and corrections by Professor Wm. W. Turner. Edited
by Nicolas Trübner: London, 8°, xxiv, 258 p. (This is v. 1
of Trübner's *Bibliotheca Glottica*.)  **155.**

MC GEE, W. J.

1901  Report of the Bureau of American Ethnology: in *Smithsonian
Institution, Annual Report*, Washington, [1902], p. 65–84.  **171.**

1902  Report of the Bureau of American Ethnology: in *Smithsonian
Institution, Annual Report*, Washington, [1903], p. 39–57.  **171.**

MACLEAN, J. P.

1883  Maya literature: in [some magazine for] October, (N. S.) v. 20,
p. 438–448. (Pilling, No. 2392*a* after Brinton.)  **194.**

MACNUTT, FRANCIS AUGUSTUS

1908  See Cortés, Hernando.

1912  See Martyr d'Anghera.

MADIER DE MONTJAU, ÉDUARD

1875  Textes Mayas: in *Archives de la Société Américaine de France*
(2d ser.) v. 1, p. 373–378. (This is an edition of Nolasco de los
Reyes, 1869.)  **198.**

MAISONNEUVE ET CIE. Editors.
1881   Bibliotheca americana. Histoire, géographie, voyages, archéologie, et linguistique des deux Amériques: Paris, 8°, 105 p.
(This is a supplement to Leclerc, 1878. Another appeared
in 1887.) **158.**
1897   Catalogues des livres de fonds et en nombre. Histoire, archéologie, voyages, mythologie, religions, ethnographie et linguistique, etc., de l'Amérique et de l'Océanie: Paris, 8°, 2, 134 p.
(Sale catalogue.) **158.**

MALTE-BRUN, CONRAD
1810–29   Précis de la géographie universelle, ou description de toutes
les parties du monde, sur un plan nouveau, d'après les grandes
divisions naturelles du globe; Précédée de l'histoire de la
géographie chez les peuples anciens et modernes, etc.: Paris,
8°, 8 v. atlas, 4°. (2d ed. corrigée, Paris, 1812–29, 8°, 8 v.)
**179.** This contains:
Tableau de l'enchaînement géographique des langues américaines et asiatiques (v. 5, p. 227–234.) (Numerous other
editions.) **179.**
1824   Gemälde von Amerika und seinen Bewohnern. Uebersetzt von
Greipel: Leipzig, 8°, 2 v. (Fischer, 1869, No. 1016 has *Neuestes
Gemälde von Amerika und seinen Bewohnern*, Leipzig, 1819.)
**174.**
1862   Le Méxique illustré, histoire et géographie. Récit des événe-
ments militaires qui s'y sont passées jusqu'à ce jour com-
prenant en outre l'histoire et la géographie illustrées des
États-Unis: Paris, 4°, 72 p. **159.**

MALTE-BRUN, V[ICTOR] A[DOLPH]
1864   Un coup d'œil sur le Yucatan: Paris, 8°, 34 p. **180.**
1878   Tableau de la distribution des langues au Mexique: in *Proceedings of the 2d International Congress of Americanists*, Luxembourg (1877), v, 2, p. 10–44. (Published separately, Nancy,
1878, 8°, 35 p. 1 map.) **159, 162.**

MANI, CHILAM BALAM DE
1595 *circa*. [Portions of this MS. called Perez Codex (*q. v.*), other parts
copied by Berendt in *Berendt Linguistic Collection*, No. 43–7,
p. 133–183, etc. Notes on this copy by C. P. Bowditch and by
Schuller, reproduced by Gates.] **184.**

MANI, CRÓNICA DE
1556 *et seq*. [MS. in Maya described by Stephens, 1843, v. 2, p. 262–
268.] **205.**

MANZANO, L.
1893   Vocabularios comparativos del estado de Yucatan. 250 palabras en la lengua Maya y Castellano de la ciudad de Valladolid: Copy, 4° MS., 4 ff. in Peabody Museum. **177, 181.**

248 BIBLIOGRAPHY

MARIETTI, PIETRO. Editor.
1870 Oratio Dominica in CCL. lingvas versa et CLXXX charactervm formis vel nostratibvs vel peregrinis expressa cvrante Petro Marietti, etc.: Rome, 4°, 5 ff. xi–xxvii, 319 p. 4 ff. **199.**

MARTÍNEZ ALOMÍA, GUSTAVO
1902 Introducción de la imprenta en Campeche y cien portadas de impresos Mexicanos: in *Boletin del Instituto Bibliográfico Mexicano*, Part 3, p. 1–25. **158.**
1906 Historiadores de Yucatan. Apuntes biográficos y bibliográficos de los historiadores de esta península desde su descubrimiento hasta fines del siglo xix: Campeche, 8°, xii, 360 p. (Originally published in *La Revista de Merida*.) **157** (2), **183** (2), **190.**

MARTÍNEZ HERNÁNDEZ, JUAN **149.**
1907 [Essay on Maya calendar]: in *El Calendario de Espinosa.* **183.**
1909 El Chilam Balam de Maní ó Códice Pérez: Merida, 12°, 18 p. (Published originally in *El Calendario de Espinosa*.) **186.**
1909a Las crónicas Mayas. Revision y traducción del texto de las crónicas de Chicxulub, de Mani, de Tizimin, de Chumayel: MS. **183, 188.**
1912 Los grandes ciclos de la historia Maya según el manuscrito de Chumayel: in *Proceedings of the 17th International Congress of Americanists*, Mexico (1910), p. 180–213. (Published separately, Merida, n. d. 8°, 42 p.) **183, 188.**
1913 La creación del mundo según los Mayas. Páginas inéditos del manuscrito de Chumayel: in *Proceedings of the 18th International Congress of Americanists*, London (1912), p. 164–171. **188.**
1915 La muerte de los " Ahpulhaob." Retaliación de Nachi Cocom á Tutul Xiu por la destrucción de Mayapan: MS. **183.**
1918 Correlación entre la cronología Maya y la cristiana. Correlación por katunes desde el ciclo noveno hasta la fundación de Merida. Correlación de todas las fechas determinadas en los monumentos arqueológicos Mayas: MS. **183.**
1918a La crónica de Yaxkukul por Ah Macan Pech y Ah Naum Pech. Revisión y traducción del texto: MS. **203.**
1919 El juicio final. (Translation into Spanish of p. 102 of the Chumayel.) 4°, MS. 2 p. **189.**
1920 Petición de Juan Xiu (from Xiu Chronicles): Translation. MS. (In collaboration with Adela C. Breton.) **204.**
1920a Testamento de Andrés Pat (from Libro de Cacalchen. 1647): Translation. MS. (In collaboration with Adela C. Breton.) **205.**
1920b Ordenánzas de Don Diego García Palacios (from Libro de Cacalchen, 1583): Translation. MS. (In collaboration with Adela C. Breton.) **204.**

MARTYR D'ANGHERA, PETER
1516   De orbe nouo decades: Alcalá, folio, (65), 16 ff. (Numerous other
       editions. Best edition by MacNutt, New York and London,
       1912, 8°, 2 v., vii, 414; v, 448 p.)   **153.**

MAUDSLAY, ALFRED PERCIVAL.   Editor.
1908–16   See Diaz del Castillo.

MAYER, BRANTZ
1851   Mexico. Aztec, Spanish and Republican . . . with . . . his-
       torical sketch of the late war: and notices of New Mexico and
       California: Hartford, 8°, 2 v. 433, 398 p. (Other editions.)
       **185.**

MEANS, PHILIP AINSWORTH
1917   History of the Spanish conquest of Yucatan and of the Itzas: in
       *Papers of the Peabody Museum*, v. 7, Cambridge, 8°, xvi,
       206 p. **164, 174.**

MEDINA, JOSÉ TORIBIO
1893   La imprenta en México. Epítome (1539–1810). Seville 8°,
       291 p. (See ed. 1907–12.)
1898–1907   Biblioteca Hispano-Americana (1493–1810): Santiago de
       Chili, 4°, 7 v. **155.**
1904   La imprenta en Mérida de Yucatán (1813–21). ·Notas biblio-
       gráficas: Santiago de Chile. 8°, xii, 13–32 p. **158.**
1907–12   La imprenta en México (1539–1821). Santiago de Chile, 4°,
       8 v. **151, 155.**

MELGAR Y SERRANO, JOSÉ MARÍA.
1873   Juicio sobre lo que servio de base a las primeras teogonias. Tra-
       ducción del manuscrito Maya perteneciente al Señor Miró:
       Vera Cruz. **182.**

MENA, CARLOS
§ (1)   Sermon y opúsculos piadosos en lengua de Yucatan: MS. xvii
       century (missing). **201.**

MENDEZ, SANTIAGO
1898   Noticias sobre las costumbres, trabajos, idioma, industria, fisono-
       mia de los Indios de Yucatan: in *Boletin de la Sociedad de
       Geografía y Estadistica de la Republica Mexicana*. (Repub-
       lished in *El Reproductor Campechano*, 1899.) **162.**

MENDIETA, GERÓNIMO DE
1870   Historia eclesiástica indiana, obra escrita á fines del siglo xvi.
       . . . La pública por primera vez Joaquín García Icazbalceta:
       Mexico, 4°, xlv, 790 p. (Written about 1590.) **153.**

MENDOZA, EUFEMIO
1872   Apuntes para un catálogo razonado de las palabras Mexicanas
       introducidas al Castellano: Mexico, 8°, 88 p. This contains:
       Carrillo y Ancona, 1872 (p. 56–88).

MENÉNDEZ, RODOLFO
1906 [Bibliographical note]: in Martínez Alomía, 1906, p. i–iv. **157.**

MENÉNDEZ Y PELAYO, MARCELINO
1888 Inventario bibliográfico de la ciencia española: in *Ciencia Española*, Madrid, v. 3, p. 125–445. (It is v. 64 in *Colección de Escritores Castellanos*.) **154.**

MENESES, JOSÉ MARÍA
1848 See Perez, 1848.
(1) [Copy of Diccionario de San Francisco, Maya-Spanish, A–K, 4°, MS., 54 ff. with *Advertencia preliminar*]. **172.**

MÉRIAN [FALKACH, ANDRÉ ADOLPHE] BARON DE
1828 Principes de l'étude comparative des langues par le baron de Mérian, suivis d'observations sur les racines des langues sémitiques par M. Klaproth: Paris, 8°, viii, 240 p. **179.**

MIGNE, JACQUES PAUL. Editor.
1864 Dictionnaire de linguistique (Troisième et Dernière Encyclopédie Théologique, v. 34): Paris, 4°. (See Jéhan, 1864.)

MILLSPAUGH, CHARLES FREDERICK
1895–98 Contributions 1–3 to the flora of Yucatan: in *Field Museum Publications*, 4, 15, 25. *Botanical Series*, v. 1, p. 1–56, i–vii, 281–339; 345–410. **177, 195.**
1900 Plantæ Utowanæ: in *Field Museum Publications*, 43, 50. *Botanical Series*, v. 2, p. 1–135. **177, 195.**
1903–04 Plantæ Yucatanæ: in *Field Museum Publications*, 69, 92. *Botanical Series*, v. 3, p. 1–151, 1 f. **177, 195.**

MINISTERIO DE FOMENTO, ANALES DE
1854 Mexico, v. 1, 8°, 726 p. 1 map. (See also Siliceo, 1857.) **159.**

MITRE, BARTOLOMÉ
1909–11 Catálogo razonado de la sección lenguas Americanas: Buenos Aires, 8°, 3 v. xliii, 409 p. 1 f.; 325 p. 1 f.; 318 p. 1 f. **150, 155, 162, 164, 165, 167.**

1912 Museo Mitre. Lenguas americanas. Catálogo ilustrado de la sección X de la biblioteca. Con muchos facsimiles de portadas: Buenos Aires, 8°, 182 p. **155.**

MOLINA Y SOLÍS, AUDOMARO
1887 Compendio de la geografía de Yucatan. (See Carrillo y Ancona, 1887, p. 1–31).
1905 U molcabthanil camathan. Catecismo de la Doctrina Cristiana Merida, 46 p. (Published without name of author.) **197.**
1914 See Lopez Otero, 1914.

MOLINA Y SOLÍS, JUAN FRANCISCO
1896 Historia del descubrimiento y conquista de Yucatan con una reseña de la historia antigua de esta peninsula: Merida, 8°, lx, 911 p. **162, 168, 181, 186, 188, 190.**
1897 El primer Obispado de la nacion Mejicana. Articulos publicados sobre esta materia y sobre otros puntos de nuestra historia: Merida, 8°, 475 p. **184, 203, 205.**
1904–13 Historia de Yucatan durante la dominacion Española: Merida, 8°, 3 v. iv, 359; iii, 455; 658 p. **151, 158, 205.**

MORENO, PABLO
[Writer on Maya subjects, after Castillo, 1866, p. 255.] **192.**

MORLEY, SYLVANUS GRISWOLD
1910 The correlation of Maya and Christian chronology: in *American Journal of Archaeology* (2d series), v. 14, p. 193–204. **183.**
1911 The historical value of the Books of Chilam Balam: in *American Journal of Archaeology* (2d series), v. 15, p. 195–214. **183.**
1920 The inscriptions at Copan: Washington, 4°, xii, 643 p. 33, 1 pls. (Carnegie Institution Publication, No. 219.) **183, 189, 204, 205.**

MOTUL, DICCIONARIO DE
MS. XVI century (missing). Copy, 16°, in John Carter Brown Library, Providence, Rhode Island: Maya-Spanish, 465 ff. Spanish-Maya, 236 ff. (ff. 83–104, 161, 171–174, 209–216, 233 missing), (Gates reproduction, 8°.) (Copy by Berendt, 4°, 2 v., viii, 1565, 508 p. with 1 v. of Additions and Corrections, about 600 p. Berendt Linguistic Collection, No. 1. Copy (partial) by Le Plongeon in 1884 and copy (partial) by Miss Thomas, 1900 *et seq.* in Bureau of Ethnology. Note of this dictionary by Berendt in Berendt Linguistic Collection, No. 181.) **170.**

MÜLLER, FRIEDRICH
1876–88 Grundriss der Sprachwisseuschaft: Vienna, 8°, 4 v. V. 2, part 1 (1882) contains:
Die Sprachen der schlichthaarigen Kassen. Die Maya-Sprachen (p. 305–313). **167.**

MÜLLER, J[OHANN] G[EORG]
1855 Geschichte der amerikanischen Urreligionen: (2d ed., Basel, 1867, 8°, vii, 706 p.) **162.**

[MURPHY, HENRY CRUSE]
1884 Catalogue of the magnificent library of . . . consisting almost wholly of Americana or books relating to America: New York, 8°, viii, 434 p. (Sale catalogue.) **154, 158.**

MUSEO YUCATECO, EL
1841–42 Redactado por D. Justo Sierra y D. Vicente Calero Quintana; considerado como la piedra miliar en que descansa el edificio, levantado á literatura en la península: Campeche, 8°, 2 v. **158.**

NABULÁ, CHILAM BALAM DE
[MS. known only by name.] **191.**

NAH, CHILAM BALAM DE
4°, MS. 64 p. Signed by José María Nah. (Owned by William
Gates and reproduced by him.) **191.**

NÁJERA, GASPAR DE
§ (1) Relación de las antigüedades de Yucatan: MS. XVI century
(missing). **169.**

NAPHEGYI, GABOR
1869 The album of language illustrated by the Lord's Prayer in one
hundred languages, with historical description of the principal
languages, interlinear translation and pronunciation of each
prayer, a dissertation on the languages of the world and tables
exhibiting all known languages, dead and living: Philadelphia, fol. 4, 11–323, (1) p. **199.**

NARCISO, J.
[1838 Arte de la lengua Maya]. (This is mentioned by Squier, p. 38
but it is clearly a mistake. The work is the Spanish grammar
of Diego Narciso Herranz y Quiros, translated into Maya by
Ruz.) **165.**

NEW YORK PUBLIC LIBRARY, BULLETIN OF
1909 List of works in New York Public Library relating to Mexico:
v. 13, n. 10–12, New York, p. 622–662, 675–737, 748–829.
**150, 156.**

NICOLI, JOSÉ P.
1870 Las ruinas de Yucatan y los viajeros: in *Boletin de la Sociedad
de Geografía y Estadistica de la Republica Mexicana.* (2d
series), v. 2, p. 510–524. **194.**

[NOLASCO DE LOS REYES, PEDRO]
1869 El ejercicio del santo via crusis puesto en lengua Maya y
copiado de un antiguo manuscrito: Lo da á la prensa con superior permiso el Dr. D. J. Vicente Solís Rosales quien desea
se propágue esta devocion entre los fieles, principalmente de
la clase indígena. Va corregida por el R. P. Fr. M. Antonio
Peralta: Mexico, 16°, 31 p. (Gates reproduction.) (See
Madier de Montjau, 1875, and Anon. 17.) **198.**

NORMAN, B[ENJAMIN] M[OORE]
1843 Rambles in Yucatan including a visit to the remarkable ruins of
Chi-Chen, Kabah, Zayi, Uxmal, etc.: New York, 8°, 304 p.
(Other editions.) **165, 168, 174, 199.**

NUTTALL, ZELIA.
1901 Fundamental principles of old and new world civilizations: in
*Papers of the Peabody Museum,* v. 2, Cambridge, 602 p. **179** (2).
1903 A suggestion to Maya scholars: in *American Anthropologist,*
(N. S.) v. 5, p. 667–678. **181.**

OBER, FREDERICK A[LBION]
1884  Travels in Mexico and life among the Mexicans: Boston, 8°, xxii, 672 p. **160.**

O'NEIL ó O'KELLY, ARTURO
1795  Descripcion, poblacion, y censo de la Provincia de Yucatan en la Nueva España: MS. (Copy in Library of Cathedral of Mexico City according to Beristain y Souza, 1816–21, v. 2, p. 355). (Name of author is written "Oneil ú Oneylli".) **161.**

ORDOÑEZ RAMON DE
(1)  Historia de la creacion del ciclo y de la tierra, conforme al systema de la gentilidad Americana, etc.: MS. 253 ff. (Copied by Brasseur de Bourbourg in 1848 and 1849.) Part 2, 50 p. incomplete. (See Brasseur de Bourbourg, 1871, p. 112–113.) **178.**

OROZCO Y BERRA, MANUEL
1864  Geografía de las lenguas y carta etnográfica de México, precedidas de un ensayo de clasificacion de las mismas lenguas y de apuntes para las inmigraciones de las tribus: Mexico, 4°, xiv, 392 p. 1 map. **159, 162, 187.**
1880  Historia antigua y de la conquista de México: Mexico, 8°, 4 v. ix, 584; 603; 527; 694 p. and atlas, fol. **181, 194.**

OSSADO, RICARDO, alias EL JUDIO
1834  Conocimiento de yerbas Yucatecas, etc.: Merida, 16°, 80 p. (Unique imprint owned by Gates.) **195.**

OVIEDO Y VALDÉS, GONZALO FERNANDEZ DE
1535  La historia general de las Indias, etc.: Seville. 4°. (French trans. of first 10 books. Paris, 1555. Ed. Madrid, 1851–55. 4°, 4 v.). (Berendt copy of Maya words in Oviedo in Berendt Linguistic Collection Nos. 42–11, and 180.) **161, 169.**

OXKUTZCAB, CHILAM BALAM DE
1689  Pronosticos de los ahaues del libro de Chilam Balam de Oxkutzcab. (This is a partial copy from Perez collection, copied by Berendt, 1868d, in Berendt Linguistic Collection, No. 43–8, p. 185–224. Notes on this copy taken by C. P. Bowditch. These reproduced by Gates.) **190.**

OXKUTZCAB, CRÓNICA DE
See Xiu Chronicles.

PACHECO CRUZ, SANTIAGO
1912  Compendio del "Idioma Yucateco": Merida, 12°, 122 (3) p. (2d ed. Aumentada, corregida y reformada. Merida, 12°, 5 entregas.) **167.**
1919  Lexico de la fauna Yucateca: Merida, 12°, 76 p. **177.**
(1)  Traducción literal de los descretos del Gobernador E. Avila, á la lengua Maya. **206.**

PALMA Y PALMA, EULOGIO
1901 Los Mayos (Disertaciones historico-filológicas): Motul (Yucatan), 8°, viii, 753, (2) p. Among other items this book contains:
Arqueología e historia, p. 1–63.
Filología, gramatica, y escritura, p. 83–474. **162, 165, 167, 168, 177, 182.**
Disquisiciones historicas, p. 475–712.
Voces aztecas castellanizadas y sus equivalentes en Maya, p. 718–735. ' **138.**
Voces mayas castellanizadas, p. 735–738. **178.**
Dioses y genios malignos de la mitología maya, p. 742–749.
La serie de los katunes (Perez, 1842). **186.**

PARISIO, NICOLA
(1) De' pretesi elementi fonetici nelle antiche scriture del Messico e del Yucatan: Rassegna Storica Napolitana di Lettere et Arte. v. 1, pts. 3–5, p. 17–34, 65–82, Naples. **177.**

PAT, JACINTO and others
1847 [circa] Cartas particulares (en la lengua Maya )de la sublevacion de 1847. Mssel. MSS. (owned by Gates and reproduced by him, 4°, 9 p.). **206.**

PECH MANUSCRIPT
See Chicxulub, Crónica de

PEÑAFIEL, ANTONIO
1886 Libros mexicanos antiguos y modernos. Catálogo descriptivo de la biblioteca del Dr Peñafiel. **158.**
1897 Division y clasificación de las lenguas y dialectos que usaron los antiguos habitantes del actual territorio Mexicano. Su estado presente: in Proceedings of the 11th International Congress of Americanists, Mexico, (1895), p. 91–96. **159.**
1900 Censo general de la Republica Mexicano, verificado el 20 de Octubre de 1895: Mexico. (Published by the Ministerio de Fomento, Direccion General de Estadistica.) **159.**

PENNSYLVANIA BIBLE SOCIETY,
(1) Specimen verses in 164 languages and dialects in which the Holy Scriptures have been printed and circulated by the Pennsylvania Bible Society: Philadelphia, 18°, 46 p. **200.**
(2) Specimen verses in 215 languages and dialects in which the Holy Scriptures have been printed and circulated by the Pennsylvania Bible Society: Philadelphia, 16°, 48 p. **200.**

PERALTA, ANTONIO
1869 See Nolasco de los Reyes, 1869.

PEREZ, BENITO
1803 See Cervera, José Tiburcio.

PEREZ, JUAN PIO **143.**

1836 [Copy of the Diccionario de Ticul.] (Missing.) **173.**

1838 Tomo 2°, de la coordinacion alfabética de las palabras reunidas en los apuntes ó cuadernos hechos para la formacion de un diccionario de la lengua Maya (Letras L-O): 4° MS. 108 ff. (The first volume has no title nor date. It contains letters A–K, 84 ff.) **175.**

1838a Diccionario de la lengua Maya, ó mas bien, apuntes para la formacion de un diccionario de la lengua Maya y Española: 4°, MS. 1108 (4) ff. **175.**

[1840] Carta á Don Vicente Calero Quintana sobre la literatura de los Indios. Written at Peto: in *Registro Yucateco*, v. 2. (Republished in Carrillo y Ancona, 1883, p. 591–592.) **191.**

1842 Principales epocas de la historia antigua de Yucatan: (Original MS., a part of the Chilam Balam de Mani, copied and translated by Perez, Peto, 1842. His copy (8°, 13, 2 p.) given to Stephens (1843, v. 2, p. 465–469) who published it and presented the MS. to the New York Historical Society. Copy in Berendt Linguistic Collection, No. 43–1). (See Mani, Chilam Balam de.) (Also called the Codex Perez.) **144, 180, 184.**

[1842a] Notas sobre la lengua Maya [pronunciation of various Maya sounds and letters adopted for these sounds. MS. given to Stephens (1843, v. 2, p. 178) and now in the New York Historical Society as a preliminary notice to the Codex Perez]. **166, 168.**

[1842b] [Dictionary of 4000 Maya words. MS. given to Stephens (1843, v. 2, p. 278) and now in the New York Historical Society.] **175.**

1843 Cronologia antigua de Yucatan y exámen del método con que los Indios contaban el tiempo, sacados de varios documentos antiguos: English translation in Stephens, 1843, v. 1, p. 434–459. There is a Brasseur de Bourbourg-Pilling copy with the following title: *Explicacion | del Calendario y de la cronologica | antiqua de Yucatan, | escrita por D. Pio Perez, | juos que fué de Peto:* folio, MS. 14 ff. There is also a copy in the Peabody Museum with the following title: *Cronologia antigua | de Yucatan | y examen del método con que los Indios contaban el tiempo. | Sacada de varios documentos antiguos, por D. Juan Pio Perez | jefe politico de Peto, Yucatan:* 8°, MS. 20 ff. (See Pilling, 1885, No. 2950.) **145, 186.**

[1844] Carta á Don Vicente Calero Quintana (sobre el idioma Maya). Peto: in Carrillo y Ancona, 1870; ed. 1872, p. 182–185. **166.**

1845 Apuntes del diccionário de la lengua Maya, compuestos en vista de varios catálogos antiguos de sus voces y aumentado con gran suma de las de uso comun y otras que se han extractado de manuscritos antiguos por un Yucateco aficionado á la lengua: 4°, MS. 4, 468 p. 8 ff. in Berendt Linguistic Collection, No. 5. (A partial copy was made by Berendt.) **175.**

PEREZ, JUAN PIO (*continued*).

1847 [2d copy of the Diccionario de Ticul: 4°, MS. 146 p.] **175.**

1847*a* Coordinacion alfabética de las palabras Mayas que se hallan en la anterior parte Castellana: 4°, MS. 133 p. (This is the Diccionario de Ticul arranged by Perez in Maya-Spanish order. Copied by Berendt in Berendt Linguistic Collection, No. 2, v. 2.) **173, 175.**

1848 Una proclama destinada á los Indios sublevados. (Translated into Maya by Perez and Meneses.) **206.**

1866–77 Diccionario de la lengua Maya: Merida, 4°, x, xx, 437 p. (Maya-Spanish). **175.**

1898 Coordinacion alfabetica de las voces del idioma Maya que se hallan en el arte y obras del Padre Fr. Pedro Beltran de Santa Rosa, con las equivalencias castellanas que en las mismas se hallan: Merida, 8°, vi, 296 p. (p. 123–296 contain the Ticul dictionary). **173, 174, 175, 181.**

(1) Apuntes para una gramática Maya, etc., copia de los fragmentos en poder de D. Pedro Regil: Merida, 12°, MS., 144 p. (Copied by Berendt from notes of Perez in Berendt Linguistic Collection, No. 11.) This is a note-book with pages numbered 45 to 188. It contains:

Apuntes para una gramatica, p. 45–132, 173–179. **166.**

Indice alfabetico, p. 132.

Berendt (1871*a*), p. 137–163.

Perez (7), p. 165–184.

Berendt (8), p. 185–188.

(2) Chilam Balam. Articulos y fragmentos de manuscritos antiguos en lengua Maya colectados por Perez: MS. (Copy by Berendt (1870), 4°, vi, 258 p. in Berendt Linguistic Collection, No. 50.) **144, 183 (2), 205.**

This volume contains the following:

Parte primera.

1. Calendario español para todos los dias del año en relacion con el calendario yucateco, con pronosticos para todos los dias y todos los meses; p. 1.

2. Relaciones astrologicos entre los siete planetas y los dias de la semana; p. 25.

3. Historieta de le Donsella Teodora; p. 31. **184.**

4. Influencias planetarias; p. 38.

5. Influencias de los signos del zodiaco; p. 39.

6. Indicaciones sobre sangrias; p. 39.

7. Pronósticos de los años segun comienzan con uno ú otro dia de la semana; p. 41.

8. Pronósticos de los signos del zodiaco; p. 43.

9. Nota de D. Pio Perez; p. 47.

10. Apuntes historias del Chilam Balam de Mani; p. 48. **184.**

11. Relacion del año yucateco con el español; p. 50.
12. Calendario español para todos los dias del año en su relacion al calendario yucateco; p. 51.
Parte segunda.
13. Las profecias de los sacerdotes mayas; p. 65. **193.**
14. Los Ahaues; p. 75.
15. Explicacion de la cronologia antigua; p. 90.
16. Tabla del numero de horas en el dia y en la noche para todos los meses del año; p. 93.
17. Los dias del mes maya en relacion a cientos Santos del calendario cristiano; p. 93.
18. U mutil vinc zanzamal (fama diaria del hombre); p. 94.
19. Los Katunes; p. 95.
20. Calendario maya para cuatro meses; p. 95.
21. Rueda para el computo del calendario maya; p. 99 *bis.*
22. Explicacion del calendario maya en español (1595); p. 100.
23. Cuceb. Explicacion de la cronologia antigua; p. 101.
24. Explicaciones de la cronologia antigua; p. 122.
25. Las épocas de la historia antigua de Yucatan; p. 134.
Parte tercera.
26. Tabla de años con los dias en que cae 7 poop; p. 138.
27. Tabla de correspondencia de los dos calendarios; p. 139.
28. Calendario español en su relacion con el yucateco con pronósticos para todas los dias; p. 140.
29. Pronósticos de los Ahaues; p. 152.
30. Las profecias de los sacerdotes mayas; p. 166. **193.**
31. Ruedas cronologicas con su explicacion; p. 174. **189, 190.**
32. Bukxok. Tabla para el computo de fechas del año maya con explicacion de D. Pio Perez (no concluida y completada por el copiante); p. 178.
Apéndice.
33. Documento sobre un convenio entre varios pueblos de la Sierra Alta; p. 181.
34. Documentos de tierras del pueblo de Sotuta; p. 187. **205.**
35. Documentos de tierras del pueblo Chacxulubchen; p. 201. **203.**
(3) Fragmentos sobre la cronologia de los Mayas. Tomados de la colección de MSS. en lengua Maya de Pio Perez. (Copy by Berendt in Berendt Linguistic Collection, No. 43–5, p. 87–106. Notes on this MS. by C. P. Bowditch reproduced by Gates.) **186.**
(4) Recetarios de Indios en lengua Maya. Indices de plantas medicinales y de enfermedades coordinados: 4°, MS., 85 ff. (Berendt made extracts, notes and additions to this. See Berendt, 1870. Gates has a copy.) **196.**

PEREZ, JUAN PIO, (*continued*).

(5) Los años de la era Cristiana arreglados al computo de los Mayas: 4°, MS. 13 ff. (Copy 12°, 79 p. in Berendt Linguistic Collection, No. 44–4.) **183.**

(6) Las epocas de la historia antigua de Yucatan. Texto del Códice Perez confrontado con el del Codice de Tizimin, Chilam Balam de Mani; 12°, MS., 18 p. (in Berendt Linguistic Collection, No. 44–3). **184, 185, 189.**

(7) Extractos de la introduccion que puso á su transcripcion del diccionario de Ticul: (See Perez, 1898, p. 123–127. Copy by Berendt in Berendt Linguistic Collection, No. 11, p. 165–184). **173.**

(8) Fragmentos de la historia sagrada traducido en lengua Maya y copiado de un libro de Chilam Balam que fue hallado en el Pueblo de Ixil: 4°, MS. cuaderno, 4 p. (Copy by Berendt, 12°, 7 p. in Berendt Linguistic Collection, No. 44–2.) **190.**

(9) Predicciones de los meses. Fragmento de un calendario antiguo del año 1701 en lengua Maya: 4°, MS. cuaderno, 20 p. (Copy by Berendt 12°, 22 p. in Berendt Linguistic Collection, No. 44–1.) **186.**

(10) Estudios de la gramática. Unos fragmentos: 8°, ·MS. 48 p. (This probably contains some of the same material that is in Perez, 1.) **166.**

(11) [Copy of the San Francisco Dictionary]: 4°, Introduction, v. p. Maya-Spanish, 93 ff. Beltran's vocabularies, 8 p. Adiciones marginales que se hallan en la parte Maya, p. 9–10: Spanish-Maya, 87 ff. Complemento del diccionario, 87*a*, 87*b*, 87*c* ff. Adiciones marginales del diccionario, 88–101 ff. (Gates reproduction. Copy by Berendt, 1870, 4°, 2 v., vii, 364; 386 p. in Berendt Linguistic Collection, No. 3.) **172.**

PEREZ, MANUEL LUCIANO

1870 Carta á Carrillo y Ancona: in *La Revista de Merida*, p. 128. (This relates to sending the Tizimin MS. to Carrillo y Ancona. Quoted in Carrillo y Ancona, 1870; ed. 1872, p. 146. Partial copy in Berendt Linguistic Collection, No. 49, p. 102. English translation in Pilling, 1885, p. 161–162.) **189.**

PEREZ CODEX.

See Perez, Juan Pio, 1842.

PETO, CHILAM BALAM DE [?]

(See Pio Perez, 1840, in Carrillo y Ancona, 1883, p. 592.) **191.**

PILLING, JAMES CONSTANTINE

1879–80 Catalogue of linguistic manuscripts in the library of the Bureau of Ethnology, Washington: in *1st Annual Report* [1881] of the *Bureau of Ethnology*, Washington, p. 553–577. **178.**

1885 Proof-sheets of a bibliography of the languages of the North American Indians: Washington, l. 4°, xl, 1135 p. (Publication of the Bureau of Ethnology.) **145, 155.**

PIMENTEL, FRANCISCO
1860 Algunas observaciones sobre las palabras Mayo y Maya: in
*Boletin de la Sociedad de Geografía y Estadistica de la Republica
Mexicana.* (Republished in Pimentel, 1862–65, v. 2, p. 35–38;
ed. 1874–75, v. 3, p. 133–137.) **180.**
1862–65 Cuadro descriptivo y comparativo de las lenguas indígenas
de México: Mexico, 8°, 2 v. lii, 539 p.; vi., 427 p., 2 ff.
(2d edition, 3 v. Mexico, 12°, 1874–75, xvi, 426; 472; 570,
p. 1f.) (German ed. by Epstein, New York, 1877.) **164.**
1876 Cuadro sinoptico de las lenguas indígenas de México. **159.**

PINART, ALPHONSE LOUIS
1883 Catalogue de livres rares et précieux, manuscrits et imprimés,
principalement sur l'Amérique et sur les langues du monde
entier, composant la bibliothèque de M. A. L. P., et compre-
nant . . . la bibliothèque mexico-guatémalienne de M. l'abbé
Brasseur de Bourbourg: Paris, 8°, viii, 248 p. **155.**

PLATZMANN, JULIUS
1871 Amerikanisch-asiatische Etymologien via Behring-Strasse "from
the east to the west": Leipzig, 8°, (3) ff., 112 p. map. **170.**
1876 Verzeichniss einer auswahl amerikanischer Grammatiken, Wör-
terbücher, Katcchismen, u. s. w.: Leipzig, 8°, (6) 38 p. **155.**
1903 Verzeichniss der werthvollen an Seltenheiten reichen Bibliothek
des verstorbenen Amerikanisten Dr Julius Platzmann welche
nebst einigen anderen linguistischen Beiträgen am 10 bis 13
Juni 1903 in Leipzig versteigert werden soll: Leipzig, 8°, 112 p.
(Sale catalogue.) **155, 158.**

POTT, AUGUST FRIEDRICH
1847 Die quinare und vigesimale Zählmethode bei Völkern aller Welt-
theile nebst ausführlicheren Bemerkungen über die Zahl-
wörter indogermanischen Stammes, und einem Anhange über
Fingernamen: Halle, 8°, viii, 304 p. **182.**

POUSSE, A.
1886 Sur les notations numériques dans les manuscrits hiératiques de
Yucatan: in *Archives de la Société Américaine de France* (2d
series), v. 4, p. 97–110. **181.**

POWELL, JOHN WESLEY
1900 Report of the Director of the Bureau of American Ethnology: in
*Smithsonian Institution, Annual Report,* Washington [1901],
p. 58–72. **171.**

PRESCOTT, WILLIAM H[ICKLING]
1843 History of the conquest of Mexico with a preliminary view of the
ancient Mexican civilization and the life of the conqueror,
Hernando Cortés: New York, 8°, 3 v. (Numerous other
editions.) **180.**

PRICHARD, JAMES COWLES
1836–47 Researches into the physical history of mankind: London, 8°, 5 v. (Enlarged edition of 1826, London, 8°, 2 v. Numerous other editions.) **179, 182.**
1843 Natural history of man, etc.: London, 8°, xvi, 556 p. (Numerous other editions.) **161.**

PROFECIAS DE LOS MAYAS, LAS
[These are found in several of the Books of Chilam Balam. They first appeared in Lizana, 1633. Those from Mani, Ixil, and Chumayel MSS. are in Berendt Linguistic Collection, Nos. 43–3, 43–6. Notes by C. P. Bowditch, reproduced by Gates.] **192.**

QUARITCH, BERNARD. Editor.
1873 et seq. (Numerous sale catalogues. For list, see Mitre, 1909–11, v. 1, p. 62–63.) **154, 158.**

R. Y.
[Initials of writer on Maya language in *Repertorio Pintoresco* of Merida.]

RAMÍREZ, JOSÉ FERNANDO
1880 Bibliotheca Mexicana: or, A catalogue of the library of rare books and important manuscripts relating to Mexico and other parts of Spanish America: London, 8°, iv, 165 p. (Sale Catalogue.) **155, 158.**
1898 Biblioteca Hispano-Americana Septentrional. Adiciones y correcciones que á su fallecimiento dejó manuscritas el Sr. lic. D. José Fernando Ramírez, y son las que cita con el nombre de " Suplemento "; ó " Adición " en las apostillas que pasó á su ejemplar de la Biblioteca hispano-americana del Dr. D. J. Mariano de Beristain y Souza: Mexico, 12°, xlvii, (4), 662 p. (Nicolas León, Editor.) (See Beristain y Souza, 1816–21.) **155.**

RAYNAUD, GEORGES
1891–92 L'histoire Maya d'après les documents en langue Yucateque (Chilam Balam): in *Archives de la Société Américaine de France* (N. s.) v. 7, p. 145–159. **186, 188, 189.**

REGIL, JOSÉ MARÍA and PEON, A. M.
1852 Estadistica de Yucatan. Publícarse por acuerdo de la R. Sociedad de Geografía y Estadistica, de 27 de Enero de 1853: in *Boletin de la Sociedad de Geografía y Estadistica de la Republica Mexicana*, v. 3, p. 237–340. **159.**

REGISTRO YUCATECO
1845–49 Periodico literario (edited by Justo Sierra): Merida and Campeche. **151, 158, 186, 204.**

Rejón Espínola, Francisco
1893 Vocabularios comparativos del estado de Yucatan. 250 palabras en la lengua Maya y Castellano de la villa de Tizimin: Copy, 4°, 4 ff. in Peabody Museum. **177, 181.**

Rejón García, Manuel (Marcos de Chimay)
1905 Los Mayas primitivos. Algunos estudios sobre su orígen, idioma y costumbres: Merida, 16°, 124 p. 1 f. **167, 180, 207.**
1905a Supersticiones y leyendas Mayas: Merida, 16°, 147 p. **181, 194.**
1910 Etimologías Mayas. Los nombres de varias poblaciones Yucatecas. Algo sobre su orígen: Merida, sm. 4°, vi, 75 p. **181.**

Remesal, Antonio de
1620 Historia general de las Indias Ocidentales y particular de la governacion de Chiapa, y Guatemala, escrivese juntamente los principios de la religion de nuestro glorioso padre Santo Domingo, y de las demas religiones: Madrid, 4°, 6 ff., 784 p. (1619 on eng. tp. There is a second title, *Historia de la Provincia de S Vicente de Chyapas y Guatemala de la orden de Santo Domingo*). **153.**

Repertorio Pintoresco
1863 See Carrillo y Ancona, 1863:

Revista de Merida, La
1859–1915, 1918– [A newspaper of Merida often publishing articles on the Maya language.] **158.**

Revista Yucateca, La
1849 Periodico politico y noticioso sedienta de saber la inteligencia abarca el universo en su gran vuelo: Merida, 2 v. **158.**

Rich, Obadiah
1835 Bibliotheca Americana Nova; or, A catalogue of books in various languages relating to America, printed since the year 1700: London, 8°, 2 ff. 424 p. (Numerous other catalogues by Rich.) **154.**

Rincon, Antonio del
§ (1) Sermones en la lengua de los naturales: MS. xvii century (missing). **201.**

Ripalda, Gerónimo de
See Ruz, 1847 and Charency, 1892a.

Riva Palacio, Vicente. Editor.
1887–89 México a través de los siglos: historia general y completa del desenvolvimiento social, político, religioso, militar, artístico, científico y literario de México desde la antigüedad más remota hasta la época actual; obra única en su género: Mexico, fol. 5 v. (v. 1, author, Alfredo Chavero, subtitle of volume, *Historia antigua y de la conquista*). **189, 190.**

RIVAS GASTELU, DIEGO
§ (1) Gramática de la lengua de los Lacandones (de Guatemala):
MS. XVII Century (missing). **163.**

RIVERA AGUSTIN
1878 Compendio de la historia antigua de Mexico; desde los tiempos
primitivos hasta el desembarco de Juan de Grijalva: San Juan
de los Lagos, 8°, v. 1, 447 p. **183.**

RIVERO FIGUEROA, JOSÉ DOLORES
1918 Dos vidas ejemplares. Ensayos biográficos del Ilmo. Sr. Obispo
de Yucatan, Don Crescencio Carrillo y Ancona y de Monseñor
Norberto Domínguez: Havana, 8°, 86 p. (Francisco Cantón
Rosado, joint author.) **147.**

ROBELO, CECILIO A.
1902 Toponimia Maya-Hispano-Nahoa: Cuernavaca, 8°, 81 p. **180.**

ROCKSTROH, EDWIN and BERENDT, C. H.
1878 Los indígenas de la America Central y sus idiomas, reseña ethno-
grafica, compilado de los escritos y apuntes dél Doctor C.
Hermann Berendt. Edicion de la Sociedad Economica,
Guatemala. (Only the first 16 p. were ever completed).
Copy in Berendt Linguistic Collection. This copied by
Schuller and reproduced by Gates.) **162, 178.**

ROMERO, JOSÉ GUADALUPE
1860 Noticia de las personas que han escrito algunas obras sobre idiomas que se hablan en la República: in *Boletin de la Sociedad de
Geografía y Estadistica de la Republica Mexicana*, p. 374–386.
**156.**

ROMERO FUENTES, LUIS C.
1910 La lengua Maya. Al alcance de todos. Manuel que contiene 34
lecciones compuestas de las frases más usuales, presentadas
con un método sencillo para facilitar su aprendizaje: Merida,
12°, 100 p. and *errata*. **167.**

ROSNY, LÉON [LOUIS LUCIEN PRUNOL] DE
1875 L'interprétation des anciens textes Mayas, suivie d'un aperçu de
la grammaire Maya, d'un choix de textes originaux avec traduction et d'un vocabulaire: Paris, 8°, 70 p. 1 f. (Originally
published in *Archives de la Société Américaine de France*, 2d.
series, v. 1, p. 53–118. Spanish edition with notes by Juan
de Dios de la Rada y Delgado, Madrid, 1881. Republished in
de Rosny, 1904, p. 75–166.) **157, 165, 166, 176, 194, 199.**
1875a Mémoire sur la numération dans la langue et dans l'écriture
sacrée des anciens Mayas: in *Proceedings of the 1st International Congress of Americanists*, Nancy, v. 2, p. 439–458.
(Republished in his 1904, p. 167–192.) **182.**

1887 Codex Peresianus. Manuscrit hiératique des anciens Indiens de l'Amérique Centrale conservé à la Bibliothèque Nationale de Paris, publié en couleurs: 4°, 94 p. 28 pls. (2d ed. Paris, 1888, without colors.) **176.**
1904 L'Amérique pré-Colombienne. Études d'histoire, de linguistique & de paléographie sur les anciens temps du Nouveau-Monde: Paris, 8°, xiv, 376 p. (This contains reprints of his 1875, 1875a, etc.) **157, 165, 176, 194, 199.**

ROVIROSA, JOSÉ N.
1888 Nombres geográficos del estado de Tabasco: Mexico, 8°, 36 p. **180.**

ROYS, RALPH L.
1920 A Maya account of creation (pls. 60–62, Chilam Balam de Chumayel): in *American Anthropologist* (N. S.) v. 22, p. 360–366. **189.**

RUZ, [JOSÉ] JOAQUIN [FRANCISCO CARRILLO DE]. **142.**
1822 Catecismo histórico ó compendio de la istoria sagrada y de la Doctrina Cristiana. Con preguntas, y respuestas, y lecciones seguidas por el Abad Fleuri; y traducidos del Castellano al idioma Yucateco con un breve exhorto para el entrego del Santo Cristo á los enfermos: Merida, 16°, 3 ff., 3–186 p., 2 f. (Gates reproduction. Title and 2 p. (185, 186) and *errata* missing.) **197.**
1835 El devoto instruido en el Santo Sacrificio de la Misa; por el P. Luiz Lanzi. Traduccion libre al idioma Yucateco con unos afectos: Merida, 4°, 9 ff. (MS. copy, 16°, 62 p., made by Berendt in 1873, in Berendt Linguistic Collection, No. 32.) (León gives an edition of 1839.) **198.**
1844 Gramática Yucateca — formada para la instruccion de los indígenas, sobre el compendio de D. Diego Narciso Herranz y Quiros: Merida 16°, (7), 8–119 p. (Gates reproduction.) (English ed. by Kingdon, 1847.) **165.**
1845 Cartilla ó silabario de lengua Maya para la enseñanza de los niños indígenas: Merida, 24°, 16 p. (2d ed. Berendt, 1871. Another ed. Merida, 1882.) (Pilling has an edition of 1845, 12°, 20 p.) **165, 166.**
1846 Manual Romano Toledano y Yucateco para la administración de los Santos Sacramentos: Merida, 8°, 9 ff., 6–191 p. (Portion published by Brasseur de Bourbourg, 1869–70, v. 2, p. 121–122.) **198.**
1846–50 Colección de sermones para los domingos de todo el año, y Cuaresma, tomados de varios autores, y traducidos libremente al idioma Yucateco: Merida, 8°, 4 v. **202.** The contents are as follows:
    v. 1 (11, 145 p. 1846) contiene las domínicas desde adviento hasta quincuagésima.

Ruz, [José] Joaquin [Francisco Carrillo de] (continued).
1846–50 Colección de sermones, etc. (continued).
    v. 2 (268 p. 1849) contiene desde ceniza, viérnes de cua-
    resma y domínicas hasta pentescotés.
    v. 3 (254 p. 1850) contiene desde pentescotés hasta la
    domínica vigésimacuarta.
    v. 4 (228 p. 1850) contiene las festividades principales del
    Señor, de Nuestra Señora, de algunos Santos, y cuatro
    pláticas de ánimas, sobre el dogma.
1847 Catecismo y exposition breve de la Doctrina Cristiana por el P.
    Maestro Gerónimo Ripalda, de la compañia de Jesus. Tra-
    ducida al idioma Yucateco, con unos afectos para socorrer á
    los moribundos: Merida, 16°, 88 p. (2d ed. published by
    Charency, 1892a.) **197.**
1847a Explicacion de una parte de la Doctrina Cristiana: Instrucciones
    dogmatico-morales en que se vierte toda la Doctrina del Cate-
    cismo romano, por el R. P. M. Fr. Plácido Rico Frontaura:
    se amplian los diferentes puntos que el mismo Catecismo remite
    á los párrocos para su extencion: y se tratan de nuevo otros
    importantes, traducido al idioma Yucateco: Merida, part I,
    8°, 390, 3 p. (Part II never published.) **197.**
1847b See Kingdon, 1847.
1849 Via Sacra del Divino Amante Corazon de Jesús dispuesta por las
    cruces del Calvario, por el Presbítero José de Herrera Villa-
    vicencio . . . traducida al idioma Yucateco: Merida, 24°,
    34 p. (Gates reproduction.) **198.**
1851 Análisis del idioma Yucateco, al Castellano: Merida, 16°, 16 p.
    (Gates reproduction.) **197.**
  (1) Leti u cilich Evangelio Jesu Cristo hebix San Lúcas. MS. 106 p.
    in Merida. (Original translation of chaps. 5, 11, 15, 23 of St.
    Luke. See Kingdon, 1862, 1865, and Henderson, 1870.) **199.**
  (2) Catecismo explicado en treinta y nueve instrucciones, sacadas del
    romano: 1ª parte, Merida, 4°, about 200 p. (This is given by
    Carrillo y Ancona and León, 1905, p. 188. Pilling, 1885, No.
    3427 suggests that this is the same as his 1822.) **197.**
  (3) Ebanhelio Hezu Clizto (Zan Lucas): No title, p. 1–14, 16.
    (This is taken with few changes from his 1.) **199.**

Sabin, Joseph
1868–92 A dictionary of books relating to America; from its discovery
    to the present time: New York, 8°, 20 v. **154.**

Salisbury, Stephen
1877 Dr Le Plongeon in Yucatan [containing letter written to Mr.
    Salisbury by Le Plongeon from Island of Cozumel, June 15,
    1877]: in Proceedings of the American Antiquarian Society,
    Worcester, p. 70–119. (Letter originally published in Boston
    Daily Advertiser, September 3, 4, 1877.) **160.**

SAN BUENAVENTURA, GABRIEL DE
1684   Arte de la lengua Maya: Mexico, 8°, (8) ff. 4 p. 5–9, (2), 10–41 ff.
       (Gates reproduction. Copy in Berendt Linguistic Collection,
       No. 8. For 2d ed. see 1888.)  (Ludewig notes an edition of
       1560. This is a mistake.)  **163, 198.**
1888   Facsimile reprint of 1684 edition: Mexico, (8) ff. 4 p. 5–9, (2),
       10–41 ff., viii p. (Icazbalccta, editor.)
§ (1)  Diccionario Maya-Hispano é Hispano-Maya, medico-botánico
       regional; 3 v. about 500 ff. MS. xvii century (missing.) **174.**

SANCHEZ DE AGUILAR, PEDRO
       (See Aguilar.)

SANCHEZ, JESUS
1886   Lingüistica de la Republica Mexicana: in *Anales del Museo
       Nacional*, Mexico, v. 3, p. 279–280. **151, 156.**

SAN FRANCISCO, DICCIONARIO DE
       MS, xvii century (missing). (Copy by Perez: 4°, MS. Maya-
       Spanish, v p. 93 ff. 10 p.; Spanish-Maya, 101 ff., extra leaves
       at 87a, 87b, 87c. (Gates reproduction. Copy by Berendt,
       1870, 4°, 2 v., vii, 364; 386 p. in Berendt Linguistic Collection,
       No. 3. See Perez, 11 and Meneses, 1.) **172, 174.**

SAPPER, KARL
1893   Beiträge zur Ethnographie der Republik Guatemala: in *Peter-
       mann's Mitteilungen*, Gotha, v. 39, p. 1–14, pl. 1. **159.**
[1895, circa.] La lengua de San Luis (Peten): 16°, MS. note book, 6 ff.,
       in possession of author of this work. **177.**
1895a  Beiträge zur Ethnographie von Südost-Mexiko und Britisch-
       Honduras: in *Petermann's Mitteilungen*, Gotha, v. 41, p. 177–
       186, pl. 12. **159.**
1897   Das nördliche Mittel-Amerika nebst einem Ausflug nach dem
       Hochland von Anahuac. Reisen und Studien aus den Jahren
       1888–95. Braunschweig, 8°, xii, 436 p., 8 maps. **159.** Ap-
       pendix 4 (p. 407–436) contains:
            Vergleichendes Vocabulár culturgeschichtlich interessanter
            Wörter der Mayasprachen. Nach eigenen Vocabularen
            und Stoll's Ethnographie zusammengestellt. **178.**
1905   Der gegenwärtige Stand der ethnographischen Kenntnis von
       Mittelamerika: in *Archiv für Anthropologie* (n. f.) v. 3, p 1–
       38, pls. i–vii, map. **159.**

SAVILLE, MARSHAL H[OWARD]. Editor.
1921   Reports on the Maya Indians of Yucatan: in *Indian Notes and
       Monographs of the Museum of the American Indian, Heye
       Foundation*, New York, v. 9, p. 137–226. This volume con-
       tains the following English translations:
            Santiago Mendez: The Maya Indians of Yucatan in 1861.
            Sanchez de Aguilar: Notes on the superstitions of the
            Indians of Yucatan (1639).

SAVILLE, MARSHAL H[OWARD]. Editor (continued).
1921 Reports, etc. (continued).
Francisco Hernandez: On the religious beliefs of the Indians
of Yucatan in 1545 (from Las Casas).
Glossary of Maya terms.
Bibliography. 157.

SAYCE, ARCHIBALD HENRY
1875 The principles of comparative philology: (2d ed. revised and
enlarged, London, 1875, 16°, xxx, (1) f., 416 p. Numerous
other editions.) 166.

SCHOMBURGK, ROBERT H[ERMANN]
1848 Contributions to the philological ethnography of South America:
in Proceedings of the Philological Society of London, v. 3, p. 228–
237. This contains:
Affinity of words in Guinau with other languages and dialects of America (p. 236–237). 179.

SCHULLER, RUDOLPH R. Collator.
(1) [Collation of various documents in Berendt Linguistic Collec-
tion.] (Gates reproduction.) 147. This volume includes:
Rockstroh, 1878.
Utzolan u Xocol from Mani MS. 184.
Canciones en lengua Maya (Berendt, 1868c), etc.

SCHULTZ-SELLACK, CARL
1879 Die amerikanischen Götter der vier Weltgegenden und ihre
Tempel in Palenque: in Zeitschrift für Ethnologie, v. 11, p. 209–
229. 194.

SELER, EDUARD
1887 Das Konjugationssystem der Maya-Sprachen: Leipzig, 8°,
51 p. (Republished in his Gesammelte Abhandlungen zur
Amerikanischen Sprach- und Alterthumskunde, Berlin, v. 1,
1902, p. 65–126.) 167 (2).
1888 Die Tageszeichen der aztekischen und der Maya-Handschriften
und ihre Gottheiten: in Zeitschrift für Ethnologie, v. 20, p. 10–
97. (Republished in his Gesammelte Abhandlungen, etc. v. 1,
p. 417–503.) 177.
1892 On Maya chronology: in Science, v. 20, n. 496. (Republished in
his Gesammelte Abhandlungen, etc., v. 1, p. 557.) 183, 186.
1895 Die wirkliche Länge des Katun's der Maya-Chroniken und der
Jahresanfang in der Dresdener Handschrift und auf den
Copan-Stelen: in Zeitschrift für Ethnologie, v. 27, p. (441)–(449).
(Republished in his Gesammelte Abhandlungen, etc., v. 1,
p. 577–587. 183, 186, 188, 189.
1895a Bedeutung des Maya-Kalenders für die historische Chronologie:
in Globus, v. 68, p. 37–41. (Republished in his Gesammelte
Abhandlungen, etc., v. 1, p. 588–599.) 183.

1898 Quetzalcouatl-Kukulcan in Yucatan: in *Zeitschrift für Ethnologie*, v. 30, p. 377–410. (Republished in his *Gesammelte Abhandlungen*, etc., v. 1, p. 668–705.) **189.**

SEMANARIO YUCATECO, EL
1878–82 [A periodical published in Merida, often containing articles on the Maya language.] **158.**

SEMINARIO CONCILIAR, EL
[A periodical published in Merida.] **158.**

SHEA, JOHN GILMARY
1873–76 Languages of the American Indians: in *American Cyclopædia* (Ripley G. and Dana, C. A. editors), New York, 8°, v. 1, p. 407–414. **166.**

SHORT, JOHN T[HOMAS]
1880 The North Americans of antiquity. Their origin, migrations, and type of civilization considered: New York, 8°, 544 p. (2d ed. 1880). **187.**

SIERRA, JUSTO
1841 [?] Profetas Yucatecas: in *Museo Yucateco*. (Republished in 1842 edition of Cogolludo, 1688.) **192.**

1842–45 2d ed. of Cogolludo (1688). (This contains in Appendix a discussion of the Maya sounds. This is reprinted in the 3d ed. 1867–1868, v. 1, p. 595.) **168.**

SIERRA, JUSTÓ and VICENTE CALERO
[Articles in *El Museo Yucateco* and *El Registro Yucateco*.]

SILICEO, MANUEL
1857 Memoria de la Secretaria . . . de Fomento: Mexico, folio, map. **159.**

SIVERS, JEGÓR VON
1861 Ueber Madeira und die Antillen nach Mittelamerika. Reisedenkwürdigkeiten und Forschungen: Leipzig, sm. 8°, xii, 388 p. **181.**

SOBRON, FELIX C.
1875 Los idiomas de la América Latina. Estudios biografico-bibliográficos: Madrid, 12°, 137 p. **141.**

SOLANA, ALONSO DE **141.**
1580 Vocabulario muy copioso en lengua Española e Maya de Yucatan. sm. 4°, MS. 115 ff. XVI century: in Library of the Hispanic Society of America, New York. [Hispanic MS. may be a XVII century copy of the XVI century original.] **169.**

§ (1) Sermones de dominicas y Santos en lengua Maya: MS. XVI century (missing). **201.**

§ (2) Noticias sagradas y profanas de las antigüedades y conversion de los Indios de Yucatan: MS. XVI century (missing). **196.**

§ (3) Apuntaciones sobre las antigüedades Mayas o Yucatecas: MS. XVI century (missing.) (Probably a variant title for 2. Molina,

SOLANA, ALONSO DE, (3) (*continued*).
  1904–10, v. 1, p. 329, gives a third variant *Historia de las antigüedades de los Indios Mayas y de la predicación de la fe en Yucatán*). **169.**
  § (4)  Estudios historicos sobre los Indios, MS. xvi century (missing). **169.**
  § (5)  Apuntes de las Santas Escrituras: MS. xvi century (missing). (Molina, 1904–10, v. 1, p. 329 gives a variant title, *Vidas de varones apostólicos*.) **169.**
  § (6)  Apuntamientos historicos y sagrados de la promulgacion del Evangelio en Yucathan, y sus misiones: MS. xvi century (missing). (After Alcedo.) **169.**

SOLIS Y ROSALES, JOSÉ VICENTE
  1869  See Nolasco de los Reyes, 1869.
  1870  Vocabulario de la lengua Maya compuesto y redactado por el uso del Sr. Abate Brasseur de Bourbourg: Folio MS. 18 ff. **176.**

SOSA [ESCALANTE], FRANCISCO
  1866  Manuel de biografia Yucateca: Merida, 12°, 228 p. **157.**
  1873  Don Crescencio Carrillo. Ensayo biografico: in *Boletin de la Sociedad de Geografía y Estadistica de la Republica Mexicana* (Series 3), v. 1, p. 733–742. **147.**
  1884  Biografias de Mexicanos distinguidos: Mexico, 8°, xii, 1115, 8 p. **157** (2).

SOTUTA, DOCUMENTOS DEL PUEBLO DE
  [Various papers in Maya.] (Copy in Berendt Linguistic Collection, No. 50–34, p. 187–200. See Perez (2). Gaspar Antonio Xiu, possible author.) **205.**

SOTUTA, LIBRO DEL JUDIO DE
  4°, MS. en lengua Maya (incomplete), 58 p.; (owned by Gates and reproduced by him). **195.**

SPENCE, LEWIS
  [1913]  The myths of Mexico and Peru: New York, 8°, xiii, 366 p. **168.**

SPENCER, HERBERT
  1873–1910  Descriptive sociology or groups of sociological facts classified and arranged: London and New York, folio, 10 v. (Partial Spanish ed. by Genaro Garcia, *El antiguo Yucatan*: Mexico, 1898, 8°, 153 p.) **162.**

SQUIER, EPHRAIM GEORGE
  1857  Nouvelles découvertes d'antiquités monumentales dans l'Amérique Centrale: in *Nouvelles Annales des Voyages et des Sciences Géographiques*, Paris, v. 153, p. 175–182. (This communication introduces a letter from J. A. Urrutia, p. 182–186.) **178.**

1858　The states of Central America; their geography, topography, climate, population, resources, productions, commerce, political organization, aborigines, etc.: New York, 8°, xvi, 17–782, maps, pls. (German ed. Leipzig, 1865.) **178.**

1861　Monograph of authors who have written on the languages of Central America, and collected vocabularies or composed works in the native dialects of that country: New York, 8°, xvi, 17–70 p. (Another ed., London, 1861.) **151, 156.**

STARR, FREDERICK

1901–04　Notes upon the ethnography of southern Mexico: in *Proceedings of the Davenport Academy of Sciences*, Davenport, Iowa, v. 8, p. 102–198; v. 9, p. 63–162, pls. (Published separately.) **178.**

1908　In Indian Mexico. A narrative of travel and labor: Chicago, 8°, xi, 425 p. **177.**

STEIN, HENRI

1897　Manuel de bibliographie générale. (Bibliotheca bibliographica nova): Paris, 8°, xx, 895 p. This contains:
Philologie Amérique (p. 261–262). **155.**

STEPHENS, JOHN L[LOYD]

1843　Incidents of travel in Yucatan: New York, 8°, 2 v. xii, 9–459; xvi, 9–478 p. (Other editions with slight variations in imprint are: New York, 1847, 1848, 1855, 1856, 1858, 1860, 1868. English ed. London, 1843. Spanish ed. by Justo Sierra, Campeche, 1848 50. German ed. by Meissner, Leipzig, 1853.) **180, 185, 186, 205.**

STOLL, OTTO

1884　Zur Ethnographie der Republik Guatemala: Zürich, 8°, 175, 5 p. map. **157, 159, 168, 178.**

1886　Guatemala. Reisen und Schilderungen aus den Jahren 1878–83, Leipzig, 8°, xii, 519 p., 2 maps. **159, 178.**

SWANTON, JOHN R. and THOMAS, CYRUS

1911　See Thomas, Cyrus and Swanton, John R.

TAPIA ZENTENO, CARLOS

1767　For copy with marginal words in Maya, see Berendt, 1867a.

TEABO, CUADERNO DE

(Copy by Berendt, 1868, p. 93–96, in Berendt Linguistic Collection, No. 49.) **195.**

TEABO, ORACIONES DE

12°, MS. en la lengua Maya, 30, 76 p. *circa* 1865–1884. (Owned by Gates and reproduced by him.) **202.**

TEKAX, CHILAM BALAM DE

4°, MS. 36 p. (incomplete). (Owned by Gates and reproduced by him.) **191.**

TEODORA, HISTORIA DE LA DONCELLA
    (Copiado del Chilam Balam de Mani por Juan Pio Perez. Copy
    by Berendt, 1868*d*, v. 2, p. 225–240 in Berendt Linguistic Col-
    lection, No. 43–9. See also Perez, 2., p. 31–37, in Berendt
    Linguistic Collection, No. 50–3. Same is found in Chilam
    Balam de Kaua.) **184.**

TERNAUX-COMPANS, HENRI
1837  Bibliothèque américaine ou Catalogue des ouvrages relatifs à
    l'Amérique qui ont paru depuis sa découverte jusqu'à l'an
    1700: Paris, 8°, viii, 191 p. **154.**
1840–41  Vocabulaire des principales langues du Mexique: in *Nouvelles
    Annales des Voyages et des Sciences Géographiques*, Paris, v. 88,
    p. 5–37, v. 92, p. 257–287. (Copy of numerals in Berendt Lin-
    guistic Collection, No. 42–7.) **178, 182.**
1843  Notice sur le Yucathan tirée des écrivains españols: in *Nouvelles
    Annales des Voyages et des Sciences Géographiques:* Paris, v. 97,
    p. 30–52. **161, 180.**

THOMAS, CYRUS
1881–82  Notes on certain Maya and Mexican manuscripts: in *Bureau
    of Ethnology*, Washington, 3d Report, p. 7–65, pls. i–iv. **190.**
    This contains:
      Symbols of the cardinal points, p. 37–65.
1882  Study of the manuscript Troano: in *Contributions to North
    American Ethnology*, Washington, v. 5, 4°, xxxvii, 237 p. 8 pls.
    (Introduction by D. G. Brinton.) **185.**
1894  The Maya language: in *American Antiquarian*, v. 16, p. 244.
    **161.**
1897–98  Numeral systems of Mexico and Central America; in *Bureau
    of Ethnology*, Washington, 19th Report, part 2, p. 853–956.
    **182.**
1902  Provisional list of linguistic families, languages, and dialects of
    Mexico and Central America: in *American Anthropologist*
    (N. S.) v. 4, p. 207–216. **160.**

THOMAS, CYRUS and SWANTON, JOHN R[EED]
1911  Indian languages of Mexico and Central America and their
    geographical distribution: in *Bureau of Ethnology*, Bulletin 44,
    Washington, 8°, vii, 108 p. map. **160.**

TIBURCIO CERVERA, JOSÉ
    [Writer on Maya language in *Repertorio Pintoresco* of Merida.]

TICUL, DICCIONARIO DE
1690  MS. Spanish-Maya, 154 ff. Original MS. missing. Copy by
    Perez (1836) missing. Another copy by Perez (1847, 146 p.).
    Printed in Perez (1898, p. 123–296), with following title *Co-
    ordinacion alfabética de la coleccion de voces de la lengua Maya,
    compuesta por varios autores, hallada en el Archivo de Libros
    Bautismales del Pueblo de Ticul en el año de 1836, copiada en*

*dicho año por Juan Pío Perez y arreglada en 1847 por el mismo.*
(Rearranged in Maya-Spanish order by Perez (1847*a*), 133 p.
Copy by Berendt (1870) of Maya-Spanish and Spanish-Maya:
4°, 2 v. 268; 241 p. in Berendt Linguistic Collection, No. 2.
See Perez, 1836: 1847: 1847*a*: 1898: 7.) **173.**

Ticul, Documentos de
1760 *et seq.* MS. collection of deeds and legal papers. 4°, 62 p.
(owned by Gates and reproduced by him). **205.**

Ticul, Manuscrito de
See Xiu Chronicles.

Tihosuco, Chilam Balam de
[MS. known only by name.] **191.**

Tixcocob, Chilam Balam de
[MS. known only by name.] **191.**

Tizimin, Chilam Balam de
4°, MS., 52 p. (Gates reproduction.) (There is a Berendt copy,
1868, in the Berendt Linguistic Collection, No. 49. Gates
owns second copy, 8°, 35 ff., also reproduced by him.) (This
MS. is also called the *Codice Anónimo.*) **189.**

Torquemada, Juan de
1613 Los veinte i un libros rituales i monarchia Indiana, con el
orígen y guerras de los Indios occidentales, de sus poblaçiones,
descubrimiento, conquista, conversion, y otras cosas maravil-
losas de la mesma tierra: Madrid. (2d ed. by Barcia, Madrid,
1723, 4°, 3 v. 768; 623; iv, 634 p. Other editions.) **153.**

Torralva, Francisco de
§ (1) Sermones de Dominicas y Santos, para predicar á los Indios todos
los dias, en lengua Maya ó Iucateca, mui clara i elegante:
MS. xvi–xvii century (missing). **201.**

Tozzer, Alfred M[arston].
1901 Modern Maya texts with Spanish translation and grammatical
notes, collected near Valladolid, Yucatan: 8°, MS. 175 p. **207.**
1902–05 Reports of the Fellow in American Archaeology of the Archaeological Institute of America: in *American Journal of
Archaeology* (2d series), Supplements, v. 6, p. 2–4; v. 7, p. 45–
49; v. 8, p. 54–50, v. 9, p. 45 17. **162.**
1906 Notes on the Maya pronoun: in *Boas Anniversary Volume*, New
York, p. 85–87. **167.**
1907 A comparative study of the Mayas and the Lacandones: New
York, 8°, 195 p., xxix pls. **168, 207.**
1910 The animal figures in the Maya codices: in *Papers of the Peabody
Museum*, Cambridge, v. 3, p. 272–372, 39 pls. (Glover M.
Allen, joint author.) **168.**
1912 A classification of Maya verbs: in *Proceedings of the 17th International Congress of Americanists*, Mexico (1910), p. 233–237.
**167.**

TOZZER, ALFRED M[ARSTON] (continued).
1917 The Chilam Balam books and the possibility of their translation:
in Proceedings of the 19th International Congress of Americanists, Washington (1915), p. 178–186. **157, 182, 195.**

1918 Bibliographical notes on the linguistic and other material from
Middle America in the Bancroft Library of the University of
California, Berkeley: 4°, MS. 101 ff. **156.**

TREGEAR, EDWARD
1898 Notes on Maya and Malay: in Journal of the Polynesian Society,
v. 7, p. 101–108. **161.**

T[RONCOSO], F[RANCISCO DEL] P[ASO Y] Translator.
1883 Los Libros de Chilam Balam: (Translation of Brinton, 1882b,)
in Anales del Museo Nacional, Mexico, v. 3, p. 92–109, (with
many original notes). **183, 185, 191, 193, 194.**

TRüBNER, NICOLAS
1858 Editor of Ludewig, 1858.
1865 American literary intelligence: in American and Oriental Literary
Record, No. 1, London. **170.**

TRÜBNER AND Co. Editors.
1882 Catalogue of dictionaries and grammars of the principal languages and dialects of the world: London, 2d. ed. 12°, viii,
170 p. (Sale catalogue.) (Also many previous catalogues.)
**158.**

UMERY, J.
1863 Sur l'identité du mot mère dans les idiomes de tous les peuples:
in Revue Orientale et Américaine, Mémoires de la Société d'Ethnographie, Series 1, Paris, v. 8, p. 335–338. **179.**

URRUTIA, J. A.
1857 See Squier, 1857.

VALENTINI, PHILIPP J[OHANN] J[OSEF]
1880 The katunes of Maya history: in Proceedings of the American
Antiquarian Society, (1879), p. 71–117. (Published separately,
Worcester, 1880.) **185, 186.**

1896 Das geschichtliche in den mythischen Städten "Tulan": in
Zeitschrift für Ethnologie, v. 28, p. 44–55. **185.**

VALES, JOSÉ PILAR. Translator.
[1870] U ɔibhuun hach noh tzicbenil Ahaucaan Ahmiatz Leandro
Rodriguez de la Gala ti ú hach yamailoob mohenoob yanoob
tu nachilcahtaliloob Nohol y Chíkin ti le luumcabil Yucatan
laa: Ho (Merida), 8°, 8 p. (Pastoral sermon translated into
Maya.) (Gates reproduction.) **202.**

VALEZ, MANUEL A.
1893 Vocabularios comparativos del estado de Yucatan, 250 palabras
en la lengua Maya y Castellano del pueblo de Sotuta: Copy,
4°, MS., 4 ff. in Peabody Museum. **177, 181.**

VALLADOLID, BERNARDINO DE **141.**
§ (1)   Conclusiones de todas las materias de los Sacramentos en Latin
y en Yucateco: MS. xvii century (missing). **197.**
§ (2)   Dioscórides en lengua de Yucatan, con adiciones et conciones
theologicas en idioma Yucateco: MS. xvii century (missing).
**201.**
§ (3)   Vocabulario: MS. xvii century, [?] missing. (After Ludewig,
1858, p. 103.) **172.**

VATER, JOHANN SEVERIN
1806–17   See Adelung.
1810   Untersuchungen über Amerika's Bevölkerung aus dem alten
Kontinente dem Herrn Kammerherrn Alexander von Humboldt: Leipzig, 8°, xii, 212 p. **179.**
1815   Linguarum totius orbis index alphabeticus, quarum grammaticæ,
lexica, collectiones vocabularum recensentur, patria significa-
tur historia adumbratur: Berlin, 8°, 10,259 p. (Text in German
and Latin. This contains the bibliographical notices in first
two volumes and the first part of v. 3 of Adelung, 1806–1817.
German edition by B. Jülg, Berlin, 1847.) **154.**

VELA, JOSÉ CANUTO.   Translator.
1848   Pastoral del Ilustrísimo Señor Obispo (José María Guerra) dirigida á los indígenas de esta diocesis: Merida, 16°, 8 p. in Maya
and Spanish. (Gates reproduction.) (There is possibly a
later edition of this. See Carrillo y Ancona, 1870; ed. 1872,
p. 186.) **202.**
1848a   Carta que yo presidente de la Mision evangelica dirijo á los
caudillos de los Indios sublevados del Sur y Oriente de esta
peninsula de Yucatan, Ven Tekax, 23 de febrero de 1848: 1
leaf, Merida. **202.**
(1)   [Some grammatical notes on the Maya language. MS. once
owned by Carrillo y Ancona. See his 1870; ed. 1872, p. 187.]
**166.**

VIDALES, LUIS
§ (1)   Vocabulario Hispano-Maya y Maya-Hispano: MS. xvii century
(missing). **172.**
§ (2)   Sintáxis de la lengua Maya: MS. xvii century (missing). **163.**
§ (3)   Florílegia medicinal propio de la provincia de Yucatan: MS.
xvii century (missing?). **195.**

VILLAGUTIERRE Y SOTOMAYOR, JUAN
1701   Historia de la conquista de la provincia de el Itza, reduccion y
progressos de la de el Lacandon y otras naciones de Indios
barbaros, de la mediacion de el reyno de Guatimala, a las
provincias de Yucatan, en la America Septentrional; Primera
parte. 4°, Madrid, 33 ff., 660 p., 17 ff. **153, 180.**

VILLALPANDO, LUIS DE **144.**
1571 Diccionario de la lengua Maya: Mexico, 4° (see 1). (Brinton, 1882, p. 74, states one copy at least is in existence.) **169.**
§ (1) Arte de la lengua Maya: MS. XVI century (missing). **162, 169.**
§ (2) Doctrina Cristiana en idioma Yucateco ó Maya: MS. XVI century (missing). **196.**

VILLANUEVA, JUAN JOSÉ. Translator.
1864 Proclama del Comisario. Traducida en lengua Maya. Impresso en hoja suelta. (Copy, 12°, 5 p. by Berendt in Berendt Linguistic Collection, No. 42–17.) **206.**

VIÑAZA, [CIPRIANO MANZANO], CONDE DE LA
1892 Bibliografía Española de lenguas indígenas de América: Madrid, 8°, xxv, 1 f. 427, (5) p. **150, 151, 155.**

WALDECK, FRÉDÉRIC
1838 Voyage pittoresque et archéologique dans la Province d'Yucatan (Amérique Centrale), pendant les années 1834 et 1836: Paris, folio, x, 110 p. map, pls. This contains:
Vocabulaire Maya avec les noms de nombre et quelques phrases à l'usage des voyageurs (Spanish, French, Maya), p. 79–80. (Copy in Berendt Linguistic Collection, No. 42–13.) **176 (2), 180, 181, 206.**

WILKINS, E. PERCIVAL
1919 [Report and translation of one chapter of Ritual of the Bacabs, read by Gates at meetings of the American Anthropological Association, Cambridge, December, 1919]. **196.**
(1) Ritual of the Bacabs. (Text and translation in preparation.) **196.**

[WILKINSON, PAUL]
1914 The library of . . . scarce books, manuscripts and other material relating to Mexico: New York, 8°, 81 p. (Sale catalogue.) **156, 158.**
1915 Illustrated catalogue of books, maps and documents relating to Mexico, Central America and the Maya Indians of Yucatan: New York, 8°, 483 nos. (Sale catalogue.) **156, 158, 204.**
(1) Bio-bibliographical accounts of the writers on Yucatan and Central America with special relation to those who have treated of the Maya race and "Mayaland": 4°, MS. contained in a loose-leaved note-book in the Library of Congress, Washington (Handbook of manuscripts, p. 265). **156.** Among other items this volume contains:
An incomplete list of the works of Acosta, Berendt, Brasseur de Bourbourg, Brinton, Carrillo y Ancona, Las Casas, Cortes, Bernal Diaz, Juan Diaz, Gage, Gomara, Herrera, Martyr, Oviedo, Perez, Ruz, Solis, and Squier.
List of the *Relaciones* (from *Colección de Documentos Inéditos* (1898–1900).

Tentative arrangement of the Maya dialects. **160.**
Definition of Spanish terms, such as *adelantado, audiencia,* etc.
Article on Folk-Lore.
List of Maya codices.
List of Books of Chilam Balam and Maya prophecies.
List of Chronicles.
Bibliographies of bibliographies.
Special bibliographies such as Bandelier and Haebler.
General bibliographies such as León Pinelo and Nicolas Antonio.
Bibliography of general works such as Fiske and Winsor.
Bibliography of writers on Maya inscriptions (four entries only).
Entries regarding Columbus.
Books on the discovery of America.
Early maps and navigation.
Early suggestions and accounts of Yucatan.
The main body of the manuscript is taken up with a general bibliography, arranged chronologically, of books and manuscripts dating from 1524 to 1912. The entries are taken, for the most part, from Medina (1898–1907), Martínez Alomía (1906), Squier (1861), Beristain y Souza (1816–21), and Gates (2).

WINSOR, JUSTIN
1889 Narrative and critical history of America. Boston, l. 8°, 8 v. **155, 162.**

XIU, GASPAR ANTONIO [also called CHI or HERRERA]
§ 1582 Relacion sobre las costumbres de los indios de Yucatan (missing) **169.**

§ (1) Vocabulario Maya ó de la lengua de Yucatan: MS. XVI century (missing). **169.**
See also Sotuta, Documentos de.

XIU CHRONICLES
1608 *et seq.* 4°, MS. 1608–1817, 164 p., owned by Peabody Museum. (Reproduced by Gates and by C. P. Bowditch, latter with introduction by A. C. Breton.) (Also called the Ticul MS. and the Crónica de Oxkutzcab.) **203.**

XIU DE OXKUTZCAB
See Oxkutzcab, Chilam Balam de

XTEPEN, PAPELES DE
Dos piezas de las papeles de la Hacienda Xtepen de Don Joaquin Hübbe (en lengua Maya). (Copy, 12°, 2 p. in Berendt Linguistic Collection No. 44–8.) **205.**

ZAVALA, M.
1896 Gramatica Maya: Merida, 8°, 94 p. **167.**

ZAVALA, M. and MEDINA, A.
1898  Vocabulario Español-Maya: Merida, 8°, 72 p. **177**.

ZAYAS ENRÍQUEZ, RAFAEL DE
1908  El estado de Yucatán, su pasado, su presente, su porvenir: New York, 8°, 366 p. **160**.

ZÚÑIGA, P.
(1)  [MS. formerly in Carrillo y Ancona collection regarding derivation of word Yucatan.]  **180**.

ANON.
1514-72  Un libro que contiene varias cartas escritas á S. M. por los governadores, obispos, oficiales reales, caciques, é indios de la provincia de Yucatan: 4°, MS. in *El Archivo General de Indias*, Sevilla. (Several of the letters are in the Maya language.) **206**.

1542  [Official document in Maya still preserved on authority of D. G. Brinton.] **203**.

1803  Modo de confesar en lengua Maya: 12°, MS. from Campeche, 38 ff. in Berendt Linguistic Collection, No. 26. (Copy by Berendt in Berendt, 1868a, p. 231-257. This copy reproduced by Gates.) **198**.

1820  Apuntes sobre algunas plantas medicinales de Yucatan, escritos por un fraile franciscano de Campeche: 4°, MS., 20 ff. (Owned by Gates.) **195**.

1845  Manuscrito antiguo (probably the Chilam Balam de Oxkutzcab): in *Registro Yucateco*, v. 1, p. 360. **190**.

1860  Colección polidiómica Mexicana que contiene la Oración Dominical vertida en cincuenta y dos idiomas indígenos de aquella República: Mexico, l. 8°, vii, 52 p. (Reprint in *Boletin de la Sociedad Geografía y Estadistica de la Republica Mexicana* (Ser. 4), v. 1, 1888, p. 151-179.) (Pilling mentions an earlier ed. of 1859.) **199**.

1868  Bibliotheca Mexicana. Catalogue d'une collection de livres rares (principalement sur l'histoire et la linguistique) réunie au Mexique par M. * * * : Paris, 8°, 47 p. **155, 158**.

1871  Dos oraciones en lengua Maya. (Copiados de una hoja suelta numerada 21, que es de alguno libro: MS. en poder de Carrillo y Ancona. Copy, 12°, 4 p., in Berendt Lingüistic Collection, No. 44-10). **202**.

1883  Doctrina anónima (en lengua Maya): Merida (with approval of Bishop de la Gala by Secretary, Carrillo y Ancona). (See Baeza, 1883.) **198**.

1891  The Lord's Prayer in three hundred languages: London. **199**.

[1893]  Vocabularios comparativos del estado de Yucatan. 250 palabras en la lengua Maya y Castellano del pueblo de Sotuta: Copy, 4°, MS., 4 ff. in Peabody Museum. **177, 181**.

1897 Modo de administrar los santos Sacramentos de Sagrada Viático Matrimonio Extrema Uncion en lengua Maya con una breve explicacion acerca del examen de Conciencia y la Comunion: Merida, 16°, 52 p. **198.**

1897a Homenajes fúnebres tributados a la memoria del Ilustrisimo Señor Doctor Don Crescencio Carrillo y Ancona, Obispo de Yucatan, con motivo de su muerte, acaecida el 19 de Marzo de 1897: Merida. **147.**

1898 Vocabulario de las palabras de las lenguas Maya y Mejicana usadas y explicadas de las relaciones: in *Colección de Documentos Inéditos*, (2d series), v. 11, p. 435–436. **178.**

1900 The Henderson Maya dictionary: in *American Anthropologist* (N. S.) v. 2, p. 403–404. (See Report, Smithsonian Institution, Washington, 1867, p. 420–421.) **174.**

1905 See Audomaro Molina, 1905.

(1) Acto de Contricion en Maya: 12°, MS., 38 ff. (" Copiado de un cuadernito ms. . . . en poder de D. J. Dolores Espinoza, Merida," by Berendt in Berendt Linguistic Collection, No. 42–14.) **198.**

(2) Algunos apuntes sobre la historia antigua de Yucatan: 16°, MS. 14 ff. in Bibliothèque Nationale, Paris. (Gates reproduction.) **168.**

(3) Alocucion de Indios Mayas á Maximilian (en lengua Maya.) (Copy by Berendt, 12°, 2 p., in Berendt Linguistic Collection, No. 42–18.) **206.**

(4) Borrador de un sermon (en lengua Maya): 12°, MS., 4 p. (" MS. del autor del Vocabulario en lengua de Maya en Providence " (Motul dictionary): in Berendt Linguistic Collection, No. 42–4). (See Anon, 30.) **201.**

(5) Diccionario de la lengua Maya: 12° MS. xviii century, 1 f. No. 277 " va." Owned by Gates and reproduced by him. **174.**

(6) Doctrina en el dialecto de la Montaña de Holmul (Peten): 4°, MS. 12 ff. (Berendt copy, Sacluc, 1867, in Berendt Linguistic Collection, No. 42–10.) **197.**

(7) Doctrina en lengua Maya: 8°, MS. xviii century, 34 p. (Owned by Gates and reproduced by him.) **197.**

(8) Documentos en la lengua Maya desde el año 1571, 1663, etc.: Mssel. MSS. (mostly 4°). (Owned by Gates and reproduced, 4°, 101 p., by him.) **203.**

(9) Doctrina necesaria para confesarse en la regla. Dispuesta en lengua Maya: Merida, 24 p. (This is probably the same work as Baeza, 1883.) **198.**

(10) " Especie de circular ó manifiesto de la reina de Inglaterra . . . á manera de cartelon, con grandes y hermosos caractéres en idioma Maya, el cual fué desprendido de una esquina de calle pública." (Mentioned by Carrillo y Ancona, 1870; ed. 1872, p. 190.) **206.**

ANON. (*continued*).

(11) Forma de administrar el Viatico en lengua Maya. ("Copia [12°, 12 p.] tomada de un ms. moderno de principios de este siglo, en poder de Presbitero D. Crescencio Carrillo, Merida, September, 1868 " by Berendt in Berendt Linguistic Collection, No. 42–12.) **198.**

(12) Hari va vuh ru lokolah evangelio cheri Kanim Ahauh, Kanima Kolonel, Jesu Christo Incheel Tantzibatal Rome San Marco: 16°, 79 p. **200.**

(13) Judio, Libro del: 16°, MS. en lengua Maya, 156 p. (Original in Peabody Museum, Gates reproduction.) **195.**

(14) El libro de los medicos, yervateros de Yucatan ó noticias sobre yervas y animales medicinales Yucatecos sacados de los antiguos libros Mayas de Chilam Balam, calendarios y demas copias curiosas. 8°, MS., 72–117 ff. of a note book. (Gates reproduction.) **195.**

(15) Medicina, Libro de: 12°, MS. en lengua Maya, 176 p. (Owned by Gates and reproduced by him.) **195.**

(16) Medicina Maya. 4°, MS. in lengua Maya. 94, 2 ff. (ff. 8, 52–57, 60–73, 75–92 missing. Owned by Gates and reproduced by him). **195.**

(17) Modo de administrar el sagrado viatico en lengua Maya. Copiado del Via Crusis: 12°, MS. 2 p. (in Berendt Linguistic Collection, No. 42–16. See Nolasco de los Reyes, 1869). **198** (2).

(18) Modo de administrar el Santissimo Sacramento de la Eucaristia como viatico (en lengua Maya). MS. (copy 12°, 7 p. by Berendt in Berendt Linguistic Collection, No. 42–15). **198.**

(19) Noticias de varias plantas y sus virtudes (de Yucatan). MS. in Merida (copy by Berendt, 16°, 29 p. Reproduction by Gates of Berendt copy). **195.**

(20) Pasion domini en la lengua Maya: 12°, MS., 44 p. (Owned by Gates and reproduced by him.) **198.**

(21) Sermones en la lengua Maya: 4°, MS., 144 p. (Owned by Gates and reproduced by him.) **202.**

(22) Sermones en la lengua Maya: 4°, MS., 196 ff., XVIII century. (Copy by Berendt, 1868*a*. p. 119–229: in Berendt Linguistic Collection, No. 47. Reproduction by Gates of Berendt copy.) **201.**

(23) De Trinitate Dei en la lengua Maya ó del Ser de Dios: 8°, MS., incomplete, 12 p. (Gates reproduction.) **198.**

(24) U mutil vinc zanzamal (fama diaria del hombre): MS. 1 p.: in Berendt Linguistic Collection, No. 50–18. (See Perez, 2, p. 94.) **206.**

(25) Vocabulario de la lengua Maya: 8°, MS., (in la Libreria de San Gregorio de Mexico, after Viñaza, No. 1134). **177.**

(26) Vocabulario de la lengua Maya (with a short list of grammatical forms): 8°, MS. modern, 98 p. (Owned by Gates and reproduced by him.) **166, 177.**

(27)  Vocabulaire de la langue Maya en Anglais, d'environ deux mille
      mots, travail moderne, très-incomplet fait à Bélize. (MS. once
      belonging to Brasseur de Bourbourg. See his 1857–59, v. 1,
      p. lxxxix.)  **176.**

§(28)  Vocabulario grande Yucatano (after Cogolludo lib. iv. cap. vi.)
      **171.**

(29)  Cuento de vieja. U tzichbal xnuc: Broadside, 1 sheet. Parallel
      columns, Spanish and Maya. Merida. **207.**

(30)  [Two sermons in Maya] 16°, MS. 6 ff. in John Carter Brown
      Library, Providence. (This is probably the same as Anon, 4.)
      **201.**

§(31)  Un librillo escrito . . . en el idioma de los Indios. MS. xvi cen-
      tury (missing, after Cogolludo, lib. 2, cap. xiv.) **192.**

HARVARD UNIVERSITY
May 21, 1921

# APPENDICES

# APPENDIX I

## PARADIGMS
### Verb Classification

**Class Ia.** *Verbs of action or state.*

Transitive

| | | |
|---|---|---|
| Present | tin (tan-in) het-ik | I am opening something, my opening something |
| Future | hēn (he-in) het-ik-e | I shall open something |
| | kin (ki-in) het-ik | I may open something |
| | bin in het-e | I am going to open something |
| Past | tin (t-in) het-ah | I opened something |
| | ɔ'in (ɔ'on-in) het-ah | I have just opened something |
| | in het-m-ah | I opened something a long time ago |
| Imperative | het-e | open it |

Intransitive

| | | |
|---|---|---|
| Present | tin (tan-in) het-el or het-el-in-kah (het-l-in-kah) | I am performing the act of opening |
| Future | hēn (he-in) het-el-e | I shall open |
| | bin-het-ăk-en | I am going to open |
| Past | het-en or t'-het-en | I performed the act of opening, I opened |
| | ɔ'in het-el | I have just opened |
| Imperative | het-en | open |

Passive

| | | |
|---|---|---|
| Present | tun (tan-u) het-s-el | it is being opened, its being affected by someone causing it to open |
| Future | hu (he-u) het-s-el-e, or bin het-s-ăk-i | it will be opened |
| Past | het-s-ah-b-i, or het-s-ah-n-i | it was opened |

**Class Ib.** *Verbs of action or state with causal*

Transitive

| | | |
|---|---|---|
| Present | tin (tan-in), kim-s-ik | I am killing something, my causing death to something |
| Future | hēn (he-in) kim-s-ik-e | I shall kill something |
| | kin (ki-in) kim-s-ik | I may kill something |
| | bin in kim-s-e, or bin in kim-e-s | I am going to kill something |
| Past | tin (t-in) kim-s-ah | I killed something |
| | ɔ'in (ɔ'ok-in) kim-s-ah | I have just killed something |
| | in kim-s-m-ah | I killed something a long time ago |
| Imperative | kim-s-e or kim-e-s | kill it |

CLASS IB. *Verbs of action or state with causal* (continued).

### Intransitive

| | | |
|---|---|---|
| Present | tin (tan-in) kim-il, or kim-il-in-kah (kim-l-in-kah) | I am dying, my being affected by death |
| Future | hēn (he-in) kim-il-e | I shall die |
| | bin kim-ăk-en | I am going to die |
| Past | kim-i, or t'-kim-i | he died |
| | ɔ'u kim-i | he has just died |
| Imperative | kim-en | die |

### Passive

| | | |
|---|---|---|
| Present | tin (tan-in) kim-s-il | I am being killed, my being affected by someone causing my death |
| Future | hēn (he-in) kim-s-il-e, or | I shall be killed |
| | bin kim-s-ăk-en | I am going to be killed. |
| Past | kim-s-ah-b-i, or kim-s-ah-n-i | he was killed |

CLASS II. *Verbs in t-al, "endowed with."*

| | | |
|---|---|---|
| Present | tin (tan-in) kuš-t-al | I am living |
| Future | hēn (he-in) kuš-t-al-e | I shall be living |
| | bin kuš-tal-ăk-en | I am going to live |
| Past | kuš-t-al-ah-en or kuš-l-ah-en | I lived |
| Imperative | kuš-t-en or kuš-t-al-en | live |

CLASS IIIA. *Nominal verbs*

### Transitive

| | | |
|---|---|---|
| Present | tin (tan-in) ɔ'on-ik | I am shooting something, my gunning something |
| Future | hēn (he-in) ɔ'on-ik-e | I shall shoot something |
| | kin (ki-in), ɔ'on-ik | I may shoot something |
| | bin in ɔ'on-e | I am going to shoot something |
| Past | tin (t-in) ɔ'on-ah | I shot something |
| | ɔ'in (ɔ'ok-in) ɔ'on-ah | I have just shot something |
| | in ɔ'on-m-ah | I shot something a long time ago |
| Imperative | ɔ'on-e | shoot it |

### Intransitive

| | | |
|---|---|---|
| Present | tin (tan-in) ɔ'on (ɔ'on-in-kah) | I am shooting or my gunning |
| Future | hēn (he-in) ɔ'on-e | I shall shoot |
| | bin ɔ'on-ăk-en | I am going to shoot |
| Past | ɔ'on-n-ah-en | I shot |
| | ɔ'in (ɔ'ok-in) ɔ'on | I have just shot |
| | ɔ'on-n-ah-ah-en | I shot a long time ago |
| Imperative | ɔ'on-en | shoot |

### Passive

| | | |
|---|---|---|
| Present | tin (tan-in) ɔ'on-ol | I am being shot, I am affected by a gun |
| Future | hēn (he-in) ɔ'on-ol-e | I shall be shot |
| Past | ɔ'on-ah-b-en or ɔ'on-ah-n-en | I was shot, I was gunned |

CLASS IIIʙ. *Nominal verbs with agent*

## Transitive

| | | |
|---|---|---|
| Present | tin (tan-in) ɔ'ib-t-ik | I am writing something, my writing something |
| Future | hēn (he-in) ɔ'ib-t-ik-e | I shall write something |
| | kin (ki-in) ɔ'ib-t-ik | I may write something |
| | bin in ɔ'ib-t-e | I am going to write something |
| Past | tin (t-in) ɔ'ib-t-ah | I wrote something |
| | ɔ'in (ɔ'ok-in) ɔ'ib-t-ah | I have just written something |
| | in ɔ'ib-t-m-ah | I wrote something a long time ago |
| Imperative ɔ'ib-t-e | | write it |

## Intransitive

| | | |
|---|---|---|
| Present | tin (tan-in) ɔ'ib | I am writing, my writing |
| Future | hēn (he-in) ɔ'ib-e | I shall write |
| | bin ɔ'ib-n-ăk-en | I am going to write |
| Past | ɔ'ib-n-ah-en | I wrote |
| | ɔ'in (ɔ ok-in) ɔ'ib | I have just written |
| | ɔ'ib-n-ah-ah-n-en | I wrote a long time ago |
| Imperative ɔ'ib-en | | write |

## Passive

| | | |
|---|---|---|
| Present | tun (tan-u) ɔ'ib-t-il or ɔ'ib-t-al | it is being written |
| Future | hu (he-u) ɔ'ib-t-il-e | it will be written |
| Past | ɔ'ib-t-ah-b-i, or ɔ'ib-t-ah-n-i | it was written |

CLASS IV. *Verb "to be"*

| | | |
|---|---|---|
| Present | winik-en | I am a man |
| Future | hēn (he-in) winik-tal-e, or | I shall be a man, I shall become a man |
| | winik-tšal-e | |
| | bin winik-tal-ăk-en | I am going to become a man |
| Past | winik-h-en | I was a man |

# APPENDIX II

## PARADIGMS FROM BELTRAN, SAN BUENAVENTURA, CORONEL, LOPEZ, AND TOZZER[1]

### FIRST CONJUGATION; nakal, ascend, climb

| | BELTRAN | SAN BUENAVENTURA | CORONEL | LOPEZ[2] | TOZZER |
|---|---|---|---|---|---|
| **Intransitive, Indicative** | | | | | |
| Present | nakal in kah | nakal in kah | nakal in kah | ten kin nakal or nakal in kah | tin nakal or nakal in kah |
| Imperfect | nakal in kah kutši | nakal in kah kutši | nakal in kah kutši | nakal in kah katši | nakal in kah utši (?) |
| Preterit | naken | naken | naken (naaken) | naken, ɔ'ok in nakal (§106) | naken, ɔ'in nakal |
| Pluperfect | naken ili kutši | naken ili kutši | naken ili kutši | ɔokili in nakal | |
| Future | bin nakaken | bin nakaken | bin nakaken | bin nakaken or he in nakale (§107) | hēn nakale or bin nakāken |
| Fut. perf. | naken ili kotšom | naken ili kutšom | naken ili kutšom | | |
| **Imperative** | | | | | |
| Present | naken | naken | naken | naken | naken |
| Future | kat nakaketš | kat nakaketš | kat nakaketš | | |
| **Participle** | | | | | |
| Pres, fut., | ah nakal | ah nakal | ah nakal | | H nakal |
| Preterit | nakan | nakan | nakan | nakaan | nakan |
| Passive | naksabal | | | | naksabal |
| Pas. stem | naksal | | | | naksal |

[1] See note, p. 52.

[2] The verb ḣanal is used by Lopez (§77) for forms corresponding to this conjugation.

## SECOND CONJUGATION; kambesah, show

| | BELTRAN | SAN BUENAVENTURA | CORONEL | TOZZER |
|---|---|---|---|---|
| **Transitive, Indicative** | | | | |
| Present | ten kambesik | kambesah in kah | kambesah in kah | tin kambesik |
| Imperfect | ten kambesik kuˀši | kambesah in kah kutši | kambesah in kah kutši | tin kambesik utši (?) |
| Preterit | in kambesah | in kambesah | in kambesah | tin kambesah |
| Pluperfect | in kambesah ili kutši | in kambesah ili kutši | in kambesah ili kutši | |
| Future | bin in kambes | bin in kambes | bin in kambes | hēn kambesike, bin in kambes(e) |
| Future perfect | in kambesah ili kotšom | in kambesah ili kotšom | in kambesah ili kutšom | |
| **Imperative** | | | | |
| Present | kambes | kambes | kambes | kambes(e) |
| Future | | kat a kambes | kat a kambes | |
| **Participles** | | | | |
| Present | a kambesah | ah kambesah | ah kambesah | H kambes |
| Passive | ah kambesabil | ah kambesabal | ah kambesabal | kambesabal |
| Preterit | kambesahan or kambesan | kambesan or kambesahan | kambesan | kambesan |
| Passive stem | kambesabal | kambesabal | kambesabal | kambesal |

## THIRD CONJUGATION; ɔlk, obey

| | BELTRAN | SAN BUENAVENTURA | CORONEL | TOZZER |
|---|---|---|---|---|
| **Transitive, Indicative** | | | | |
| Present | ten ɔlkik | ɔlk in kah | ɔlk in kah | tin ɔlkik |
| Imperfect | ten ɔlkik kutši | ɔlk in kah kutši | ɔlk in kah kutši | tin ɔlkik utši (?) |
| Preterit | in ɔlkah | in ɔlkah | in ɔlkah | tin ɔlkah |
| Pluperfect | in ɔlkah ili kutši | in ɔlkah ili kutši | in ɔlkah ili kutši | |
| Future | bin in ɔlke or ɔlkib | bin in ɔlkib | bin in ɔlkib | hên ɔlkike (ɔlke), bin in ɔlke |
| Future perfect | in ɔlkah ili kotšom | in ɔlkah ili kotšom | in ɔlkah ili kutšom | |
| **Imperative** | | | | |
| Present | ɔlke | ɔlki | ɔlki | ɔlke |
| Future | | kat a ɔlkib | kat a ɔlkib | |
| **Participle** | | | | |
| Present | ah ɔlk | ah ɔlk | ah ɔlk | H ɔlk |
| Preterit | ɔlkan | ɔlkakan | ah ɔlkil | ɔlkakan |
| Passive | ah ɔlkbil or ah ɔlkil | ah ɔlkil | ɔlkil | ɔlkabal |
| Passive stem | ɔlkil | ɔlkil | | ɔlkil |
| **Intransitive, Indicative** | | | | |
| Present | ɔlk in kah (§63) | ɔlknen (p. 6 ob) | | tin ɔlk or ɔlk in kah |
| Preterit | ɔlknahen (§113) | bin ɔlknaken | | ɔlknahen |
| Future | bin ɔlknaken | | | hên ɔlke or bin ɔlknaken |

## FOURTH CONJUGATION; kanan, protect

| | BELTRAN | SAN BUENAVENTURA | CORONEL | LOPEZ [1] | TOZZER |
|---|---|---|---|---|---|
| **Transitive, Indicative** | | | | | |
| Present | ten kanantik | kanan in kah | kanan in kah | ten kin kanantik | tin kanantik |
| Imperfect | ten kanantik kutši | kanan in kah kutši | kanan in kah kutši | ten kin kanantik katši | tin kanantik utši (?) |
| Preterit | in kanantah | in kanantah | in kanantah | ten tin kanantah | tin kanantah |
| Pluperfect | in kanantah ili kutši | in kanantah ili kutši | in kanantah ili kutši | ɔ'okɨl in kanantik | |
| Future | bin in kanante | bin in kanante | bin in kanante | bin in kanante, he in kanantike (§107) | hên kanantike, bin in kanante |
| Fut. per. | in kanantah ili kotšʊm | in kanantah ili kotšom | | | |
| **Imperative** | | | | | |
| Present | kanante | kanante | kanante | kanante | kanante· |
| Future | | kat a kanante | kat a kanante | | |
| **Participle** | | | | | |
| Present | ah kanan | ah kanan | | | H kanan |
| Pres. pas. | ah kanantabal | ah kanantabal | | kanantabal kanantaan or kanantahan | kanantabal |
| Preterit | kanan, kanantan or kanantahan | kananan or kanan-ahan | | | kananan |
| Pas. stem | kanantabal | kanantabal | | kanantaal or kanantabal kanantal | |

[1] The verb hantik is used by Lopez (§ 82) for forms corresponding to this conjugation.

# APPENDIX III

## LIST OF NUMERAL CLASSIFIERS [1]

**Ak.**  For canoes, boats, houses, lots, seats, earthen vessels, churches, altars, caves, holes or pits, troughs, villages, or maize fields.

**Ahau.**  For the twenty-year groups of the Maya calendar, which are like our indictions, although they consist of a larger number of years than these. The native century or era contained 13 **ahaues,** or 260 years.

**Awat.**  For distances; miles or quarters of leagues.

**Baq.**  For 400; because just as we count by thousands, the Indians counted by 400, sayinq **hunbaq, kabaq,** etc.

**Bal.**  For ends of ropes, of thread, etc.
For things [z].

**Balatš.**  For strokes, of measurements made by rule, line or compass.

**Balaq.**  For the turns given to cords laid in circles, or to similar things which are twisted or twined.  (Compare **Koɔ'.**)

**Ban.**  For things in heaps.  The same as **banab,** which also serves for counting small flocks or herds of animals.

**Em.**  For births.

**Kat.**  For quadrupeds [z].

**Kot.**  For quadrupeds.

**Koɔ.**  For lengths of threads, cords, rods or staffs; for " pieces " of time.

**Koɔ'.**  For rolls or circular twists, " a roll of cord " (made of native vines). Compare **Balaq.**

**Kuk.**  For elbow measurements.

**Kutš.**  For loads.

**Kul.**  For shrubs, young trees, maize plants, and balls or lumps of dough.

**Qan.**  For rope.

**Qas.**  For closets, rooms, etc.

**Tšatš.**  For handfuls of herbs or hair.

**Tšinab.**  For what is measured by *gemes*, i.e., the space from the end of the thumb to the end of the forefinger extended.

**Tš'iik.**  For incised wounds made by arrows, lances, knives, sticks, etc., which are thrown and remain sticking in the flesh.

**Tš'ot.**  For counts of skeins of thread.

**Tš'ui.**  For bunches of fruit, strings of beads, necklaces, braids, bags, and things which are carried hanging from the hand.

**Hah.**  For splinters [z].

---

[1] This list was originally published by Beltran (1746; ed. 1859, p. 203–208). An English translation was made by Nuttall (1903, p. 674–678).  Several additions have been made from Zavala (indicated by Z) and from the author's own investigations.

**Hat.** For mantles or " *pati* " for *piernas* of mantles or *pati*; also for splinters of wood.

**Hau.** For gourd vessels split into halves, pages of writing, quarters of dead animals, and slices of fruit.

**Heb, Hebal, Hebél.** For *piernas* of mantles or *pati;* also for the counting of provinces.

**Hetš.** For hours and pages of books. Also used in counting strings of bells.

**Heq.** For branches or bunches.

**Lat'.** For dishes of food.

**Lat'abqin.** For hours; **hun lat'abqin** " one hour."

**Lem.** For times; **hun lem** " once." (Compare **Mal** and **Muk.**)

**Lot.** For counting in pairs, such as **kan lot** " four pairs."

**Lub.** For counting leagues.

**Mal.** For counting numbers of times. (Compare **Lem.**)

**Muk.** For the same count of times and for duplications, such as paying " twice as much " " three times as much," etc.

**Mutš'.** For small heaps of seeds, stones, earth, or for crowds of animals, birds, and people.

**Mol.** For things that are united or congregated.

**Nab.** For handbreadths as a measure.

**Nak.** For things that are close to each other, such as jugs, staffs, or seated men.

**Nakat.** For recumbent living beings.

**Num.** For times, when expressed by ordinal numbers.

**Ok.** For things measured by handfuls.

**Paak.** For mantles or *patics* of four edges (i.e., square pieces of stuff).

**Paq.** For blows, times, years.

**Patš.** For birds and other animals; employed from number 9 to 19, after which the expression **hun tab,** " twenty " is used.

**Pai.** For things which are long and not thin, such as beehives, canoes, seaboats, wooden beams, bales of cloth, and skeins of thread.

**Pek.** For circular things, such as consecrated wafers, maize-cakes, and others which are flat.

**Pet.** For maize-fields and for pastures.

**Peɔ'.** For chapters of books and for orations and songs.

**Pis.** For years, days, months, and coin currency (a *real* or *peso* or dollar).

**Pitš'.** For pieces of a thing cut off and for mouthfuls.

**Poq.** For fish, birds, and animals.

**Pul.** For lashes given with a whip or blows dealt with the flat side of the blade of a sword.

**P'eel.** For all inanimate things in general.

**P'ik.** For a written chapter or articles of faith; or for rows of stones, each row or stone being above the other.

**P'is.** For any kind of measure or weight. At the same time this particle usually expresses a *fanega* or measure consisting of twelve *almudes*.

**P'otš.** For bunches of fruit.

**P'uuk.** For plants and trees. The particle **šek** is more popularly used.

**P'uk.** For mouthfuls of food or swallows of liquid.

**Sap.** For counts of arm's lengths; each contains two yards.

**Šek.** For trees and other plants.

**Tas.** For things which follow each other in order or in line; also for heavens.

**Té.** For counts of years, months, days, leagues, cocoa, eggs, and calabashes or squashes.

**Ten, Tenak.** For numbers of times, and **tenak** for past times. **Tenel** is also used for times, but with the particle **bahun** or **bahunš** or another.

**Tenel.** For number of times in questions. (z)

**Tuk.** For heaps of things.

**Tul.** For men, women, angels, and souls.

**T'il, ɔool.** For things placed in order or file and for the subdivisions of a house.

**T'ol.** For lines, furrows, ditches, or trenches, and for pages, printed columns, naves of churches, etc.

**Ɔiil.** For the selvage of mantles or cloths and for folds of paper or the leaves of books.

**Ɔuk.** For towns, paragraphs, articles, chapters, notices, heaps or piles, divisions of a whole in various parts.

**Ɔ'ak.** For steps, grades, crowns, or things which are placed one over the other, or for something that succeeds another, such as one governor after another. It is then an ordinal number.

**Ɔ'am.** For consecrated wafers, pamphlets, shoes, and of all things which are counted in pairs.

**Ɔ'ik.** For persons, this particle being specially dedicated to the persons of the Holy Trinity. It is also employed for counting fingers as well as for the husbands or wives that a person has had.

**Ɔ'it.** For candles; cane pipes; long fruits, such as bananas; also alligator pears, ears of corn, the mamey fruit, etc.

**Wal.** For leaves of tobacco, of banana trees, etc.

**Waɔ'.** For counting journeys or the number of times a person goes and comes in performing some business.

**Wol.** For balls of dough, bundles of cotton or of wool, balls of thread and other round things.

**Wuɔ'.** For folded cloths and similar things.

**Yal.** For sheaths or things that are brought together.

# APPENDIX IV

## COMPARATIVE VOCABULARIES

### Introduction

THE following vocabulary is made up, first of all, of a collection of Maya words gathered in 1893 from various towns in Yucatan. The document, which is a typewritten copy of the original lists of words, was purchased from Paul Wilkinson in the sale of his library by Mr. Charles P. Bowditch and presented by him to the Peabody Museum. This manuscript has an introduction on Maya pronunciation by Crescencio Carrillo y Ancona. It is probable that the collection of words was made for a contemplated work by him on the Maya language.

The vocabulary from Peto was made by Presbítero D. Manuel A. Valez, that from Valladolid by Licenciado L. Manzano, that from Tizimin by Francisco Rejón Espínola, and that from Sotuta is unsigned. These towns are widely separated. Valladolid is the most eastern town in the settled portion of the peninsula, Tizimin is almost directly north of Valladolid, about half way to the coast, Peto is in the south-central part of Yucatan, and Sotuta is north of Peto about a third of the way to the northern coast.[1]

A careful study of these words together with grammatical forms collected in the same areas would probably show slight dialectical differences in the language.[2]

In order that a comparison may be made between these modern vocabularies and those of early date, corresponding terms are given, wherever possible, from the Motul, the San Francisco, and the Ticul dictionaries. These early works probably date from the end of the xvi to the end of the xvii century.

There are comparatively few cases where words of the three early authorities differ entirely from those of the four modern

---

[1] It is well to point out that there is a Book of Chilam Balam from Tizimin and a collection of documents in Maya from Sotuta as well as a *Libro del Judio* from the same locality.

[2] See note by Palma y Palma, Part I, p. 14.

lists. It is much more common to find the earlier terms for the same word differ among themselves and the later words agreeing some with one and some with others of the older lists. Of the later vocabularies, the words in the Peto, Tizimin, and Valladolid lists are much more frequently in agreement than the corresponding words from the Sotuta collection.

In words where there is a possibility for single or double vowels, the Peto collector is more inclined to use the double vowels than any of the others. In the Sotuta and Ticul vocabularies, on the other hand, the single vowel occurs most frequently. The Peto list, for example, uses eight single to seventeen double vowels while the Sotuta uses fifteen single to six double vowels and the Ticul eleven single to three double vowels.[1]

In the Valladolid and the Tizimin lists the use of **n** in place of **m** is common. There is also often a different usage in the earlier vocabularies in this respect, the Motul and the Valladolid using **šinbal,** and all the others have the more common form, **šimbal.** In the later lists, the Peto, the Sotuta, and the Valladolid use **hun,** the Tizimin alone using **hum.**

The use of the fortis forms differs greatly. In the Peto and Sotuta vocabularies one finds ɔ**a,** or ɔ**ah,** to give; in all the others the form is ɔ**'a** or ɔ**'ah.**

The differences in many of the verbal forms are due to the fact that in some cases the verb is understood in a transitive sense and in others as an intransitive.

Disregarding the failure to recognize the proper form of the verb, the use of the semi-vowels, **w** and **y,** before vowel stems, and the use of the masculine and feminine prefixes, there is a surprising agreement between the earlier and later vocabularies. It is only fair to point out, however, that the words given in the lists are common every-day terms and one would not expect to find many changes in these. Words for spring, summer, autumn, and winter are given in the later vocabularies except the Tizimin, the author of which notes, quite properly, that there are no words in Maya exactly corresponding to these terms. The words for ice and snow are naturally not found in the earlier lists.

---

[1] Note the discussion of the use of the double vowel in Part I, p. 30.

## VOCABULARIES [1]

| | |
|---|---|
| abdomen, | naq, p, s, v, z : m.  homtan-il, s.  qo, m. |
| afternoon, | o-qin, m, f, t,  o-qin-al, z.  o-qn-al, z.  o-qin-il, z.  okan-qin, p, v.  sis-qin, s. |
| all, | lah —, z.  tulakal, all.  tu-sin-il, m, f. |
| arch (arco), | pun, s.  p'un, z.  p'um, p : m, t.  uɔ'-bil-tše, v. |
| arm, | qab, s, z : m, f, t.  noh-qab, p.  ɔ'ik-qab, p.  ɔ'it-qab, v. |
| armadillo, | wetš, p, z.  h-wetš, s, v.  ibatš, t. |
| arrow, | hul, s, v, z.  hul-eb, p.  hal-al, t. |
| autumn, | itš-ha-ha-lil, p.  qini-yaš-le, v.  no word, z. |
| axe, | baat, all. |
| bad, | lob, s, v : m, f, t.  qas, p, s, z.  ma patan, m. |
| bark (ladrar), | tši-bal, p, z.  ha-hai-tši-bal, s.  awat-tši-bal, v.  yawat-peq, m, f.  u qeyah-peq, m. f. |
| bark (corteza), | sool, z.  sol-tše, s.  sool-tše, p.  patš, v.  boš, f, t.  boš-el-tše, f. |
| bat, | soɔ', p, s, v, z : t. |
| bear (oso), | san-hool, p.  saan-hool, z.  sam-hol, t.  kab-noh, m, f. |
| beard, | notš, s.  nootš, p, v, z.  meš, m.  meeš, f, t.  keb, m. |
| bird, | tš'itš', s : m, f, t.  tšiitš, v.  tš'iitš, p.  tš'iitš', z. |
| black, | boš, p, s, v, z : f, t.  eq, z : f.  eeq, p : f. |
| blood, | qiq, s : m, f, t.  qiiq, p, v, z. |
| blue, | yaš, z.  ya-yaš, t.  yaš-kab, m, f.  yaš-kaben, f.  yaš-top'en, f.  yaš-sak-nohen, v.  yaš-il-kaan, z.  sak-yaaš, p. |
| boar (jabali), | kitam, s, z.  qas-i-qeqen, p, v.  qaš-il-qeqem, s. |
| body, | winkil, p.  winklil, s, z.  h-wiklil, v.  kukut, m, f, t. |
| bone, | bak, all. |
| boy, | pal, z.  paal, m.  ši-pal, p, s, v, z.  šibi-pal, z. |
| breast, | ɔem, p, s, v, z.  tan, m, f. |
| breasts of woman, | im, p, s, z.  yim, v. |
| brother, elder, | sukun, s : m, t.  sukuun, p, z : f.  nohotš sukun, v. |
| brother, younger, | iɔ'in, s : m, f, t.  wiɔin, p.  wiɔ'in, p, z.  h-wiɔ'in, v. |
| buzzard, | tš'om, p, s, v, z. |
| canoe, | tšem, p, s, v, z.  tš'em, p. |
| chatter (charlar), | ɔik-bal, p.  ban-kab-klu-bal, s.  tš'o-tš'op-tši, v.  sakatš-t'an, z.  t'an-t'an-ah, z. |
| chief, | holil, p.  noh-tšil, p.  halatš winik, s, z.  yun-ɔil, v.  H-meq-tan, z.  kutš-kab, z.  meq-tan-kah, z. |
| child, | tšam-pal, p, v.  tšan-tšan-pal, m, f, t.  tšan-ši-pal, s.  tšan-tš'u-pal, s.  mehen-pal, m, f. |

---

[1] The letters following the Maya words refer to the various vocabularies where the terms occur: p, Peto; s, Sotuta; v, Valladolid; z, Tizimin; m, Motul; s, San Francisco; and t, Ticul. A colon separates the older from the later authorities.

| | |
|---|---|
| chile, | ik, p, z : t. iq, s, v. |
| cigarette, | tšamal, z. tš'utš'-lem, f. tšutš-lem, t. |
| cold, | sis, s : t. siis, p, z. keel, p, v : m, f. keel-en, t. |
| come, | tal, z : m, f. tal-el, p, s : m, f, t. u-tal, v. |
| corn, | išim, s : m, f, t. šiim, p, v, z. išiim, p, z. |
| coyote, | u-peqil-qaaš, p. h-wayu, v. |
| cradle (cuna), | tas-tše-qan, p. qu-pal, s. kutš-il u ɔ'a-bal pal-al tan tu sihil, v. qu-tšam-pal, z. |
| crow (cuervo), | tšom, s. tš'om, v, z. tšim-toq, p. |
| crow (cacarear), | qo-qoan-kil, z. qo-qoan-kil u-lum, t. tokan-kil u kal u lun, m. to-tokan-kil u kal u lum, f. to-tok-t'ere, p, s. tša-tšak t'oloan-kil, z. awat u lun, m. awat u lum, f. |
| cry out (gritar), | awat, all. ta-tah-awat, m. |
| dance, | oqot, all. |
| daughter, by father, | š-mehen, z. iš-mehen, m, f, t. wiš-mehen, p, z. š-tš'upu-iš-mehen, s. ts'up-lal, v. |
| daughter, by mother, | al, m, f. wal, z. tšu-pal, t. tšup-lal, m. tš'u-pal, p. tš'up-lal, f. š-tšup-wal, s, z. tšupu-al, v. |
| day, | qin, all. sasil-qin, s. sasil, t. |
| dead, | kimen, all. |
| deer, | keh, v, z : f, t. keeh, p. šibil-keh, s. |
| dog, | peq, all. |
| drink, | uq-ul, all. |
| drop (gotear), | tš'ah, v, z. tš'ah-al, p. tš'ah-al-haa, m. tšah-al-haa, f. t'ah-al, t. t'ah-al-haa, m, f. t'unul-haa, m, f. tš'ab-il, s. |
| duck, | kuɔ-a, f. kuɔ-ha, p, z : t. kuɔ-haa, s. patuš-ha, p. |
| ear, | šikin, p, v, z : m, f, t. lee šikin, s. |
| earth (tierra), | lum, s : m. luum, p, v, z : f, t. kab, z. |
| eat, | han-al, all. ɔentah-ba, z. |
| eel, | kan-il-ha, p. |
| egg, | he, p, v, z : f, t. hee, s. eel, s, z. |
| eye, | itš, s, z : m, f, t. witš, v. tuq-nel-itš, p. |
| face, | itš, p, s, z : m, f, t. witš, v. tan-itš, p. |
| far, | natš, s, z : f. naatš, p, v, z. natš-il, z. |
| father, | yum, s, z : m, f, t. llum, p. yum-bil, t. tata, v. tat, z. |
| feather, | qu-qum, all. |
| finger, | al-qab, z. yal-qab, p, s, z. ts'il-bi-qab, v. motš, z: m. motš-qab, m. motš'-qab, f, t. |
| finger-nail, | its'ak, p, s, v, z. |
| fire, | qaq, s, z : m, f. qaaq, p, v. |
| fish (pez), | kai, p, s, v, z : m, t. ɔaqin, f. yiɔ, f. tš'a, f. |
| fish (bobo), | sohol-kai, v. |
| fish (bagre), | lu, p, v, z. lun, s. boš-kai, p. |
| fly, | yaš-katš, s, v, z : m, f. yaaš-katš, p. |
| foot, | ok, all. |

| | |
|---|---|
| forehead, | lek, s, z : m, f, t.  lek-tši, z.  tši-lek, p, v. |
| forest, | qaš, m.  qaaš, p, s, v, z.  pok-tš'e, m.  tš'en-tše, m. |
| forget, | tub-ul, s : m, t.  tub-olal, z.  tub-sa, v.  tub-sah, p : f. |
| | tub-esah, m. |
| friend, | etool, p.  etail, z : m, f, t.  yukunah winik, s.  yukuna |
| | h-winik, v.  nup-t'an, m, f.  hun-pel u lak, f.  hun- |
| | p'el u lak, m. |
| frijol, | buul, all. |
| fox (zorra), | otš, p, s, v.  tšomac, z.  tšamak, m.  tš'amak, f. |
| girl, | š-ts'u-pal, s, v, z.  š-tš'upu-pal, z.  tš'up-lal-paal, f. |
| | tšup-lal-paal, m. |
| give, | ɔa, p.  ɔah, s.  ɔ'a, m, f, t.  ɔ'ah, p, z.  u-ɔ'a-bal, v. |
| | hah, s. |
| go, | bin, p, v.  bin-el, p, s, z : t.  ben, m, f.  ben-el, m, f, t. |
| god, | qu, all.  kitš-kelem-yum, s. |
| gold, | qan-maskab, p.  qan-qan-taqin, m, f, t. |
| good, | uɔ, all.  mal-ob, p, s, z.  tibil, m, f, t. |
| goodness, | uɔ-il, p, z : m, f.  yuɔ-il-in-puqsiqal, v.  tibil uɔ-il, f. |
| goose (ganso), | yak-bok, p. |
| gourd, | qum, s, z.  quum, p, v : m, f. |
| grave, | muk-nal, p, s, v, z : t.  muk-sah, f.  muk-kimen, f. |
| green, | yaš, s.  yaaš, p. v, z : m, f, t.  ya-yaš, m, f.  yaašil-kaaš, |
| | z.  (" se confunden el verde y el azul " z). |
| groan (bramar), | akan, all. |
| hair, | ɔooɔ, all.  ɔoɔ-el, z. |
| hand, | qab, p, v, z : m, f, t.  tan-qab, s. |
| he, | le, p, z.  leti, p, s, v, z. |
| head, | pol, p, s, v, z : m, t.  hool, p, z : m, f, t. |
| heart, | pusiiq, z.  puksiqal, all. |
| herb, | šiu, all. |
| here, | wai, z : m.  waye, p, v, z : t.  tela, s, z. |
| hill, | puuk, p, z : f, t.  wiɔ, s.  mul, z.  muul, v.  noh-muul, |
| | v.  qaaš, p. |
| horse, | ɔimin, all. |
| house, | na, p, v, z : m, f, t.  nah, s.  ototš, z : m, f. |
| house of palm, | šani-na, v.  šanil-na, p, s, z.  pasel, z.  yukil-na, z. |
| husband, | itšam, m, f.  h-witšam, v.  witšam, p, s, z. |
| I, | ten, p, s, v, z. |
| ice, | yeeb, p.  noh-tat-yeeb, p.  bat, s, v, z. |
| indian, | masewal, p, v, z.  H-maya-bil, z. |
| island, | peten, z.  petem, s.  ɔukub-luum, p.  hay luum itš ha, v. |
| kettle, | maskab-kum, p, z : f.  kum maskab, t.  u-kutšil, v. |
| | lokansa-ha, v. |
| kill, | kim-sah, p, s, z : m, f.  kin-sah, v. |
| knife, | qupeb, p.  šoteb, p, s, z.  tšan-qab-maskab, v. |
| lake, | šoɔ-ha, v.  ɔ'aɔ', z.  aqal, p, z.  tši-tšan-qanaab, p. |
| large, | noh, m, f, t.  nohotš, p, s, v, z : t. |

| | |
|---|---|
| laugh, | tšeh, v. tšeeh, p. z : f, t. muqluk u tšeeh, m. tšek, s. |
| laziness, | ma-qol, m. ma-qobal, s. ma-qolal, v, z : f, t. ma-qolil, p. |
| leaf, | le, p, v, z : m, f. u-leh tše, t. leh tše, s. |
| leg, | ok, s : f. muq-ok, p. p'ul-ok, v, z. ɔelek, z. |
| lie (mentir), | tus, all. |
| lightning, | lemba, t. lemba-kaan, m, f. lemba-tšak, p, s. lemba-tšaak, z. |
| living, | ku-šan, s, z. ku-šaan, p, v. |
| lizard, | tolok, p, z. iš-metš, m. iš-me-metš, s, z : f. meretš, v. iš-be-betš, s. š-selutš, s. pikuneil, z. silwoh, z. iš-tulub, s, z. |
| love (amar), | yakuna, v. yakunah, p, z : m, f, t. yakunah-il, s. |
| love (amor), | yukuna, v, z. yakunah, p, s : m, f, t. |
| man, | winik, z : m, f, t. bal-kab winik, m. šib, v, s. H-šib, p, z. |
| many, | yab, s. yaab, p, v, z : m, f. |
| meat, | baq, all. |
| memory, | qah-sa, v. qah-sah, p, z : f. qah-lai, s, z : m. |
| moon, | u, all. |
| morning, | samal, p, z : m, f. haɔ-kab, v, z. haɔ-kab-qin, s. |
| mosquito, | qaš-ol, m. qoš-ol, p, s, v, z : f. |
| mother, | na, p, z. naa, m, t. nah, s. na-il, z. mama, v. |
| mouse, | ts'o, p, v, z : m, f, t. ts'oo, s. |
| mouth, | tši, p, v, z : m, f. tšii, s : t. |
| name, | qaba, all. |
| near, | naɔ-ti, p. naɔ'-ti, s, v, z. naq-lik, z. |
| neck, | kal, all. |
| night, | aqab, all. |
| no, | ma, p, s, v, z : m. maa, f. matan, m, f. |
| nose, | ni, p, v, z : m. nii, s : f, t. |
| ocean, | qab-nab, s, v. qa-naab, p. qaq-nab, m. qaq-nab-e, m. qaq-naab, z. |
| old, | noh-šib, f, t. nu-šib, p, s, v, z. lab, z. utšben, z. |
| people, | maak, p, z. winik, s, v. |
| pigeon, | ukum, s, z : m, f, t. kastran-ukum, p. kastlan-ukum, z. sak-pakal, z. ku-kut-kib, z. ɔuɔui, z. |
| pine, | hu-hub, p. |
| pipe, | hobon-tše, v. |
| plain (llano), | taš-kab, p, z. ta-taš-luum, s. uɔi-luum, v. |
| priest, | ah-qin, m, f. H-qin, p, s, z. yun-qin, v. yun-h-qin, z. pišnal-yum-ɔil, s. ah-meqtan-pišan, z. iq-kab, z. |
| puma, | koh, v : m, f. tšak-koh, p. qan-koh, z. balam, t. tšak-bolai, m. |
| rabbit, | t'ul, s, v : m, f, t. t'uul, p, z. |
| rain (lluvia), | ha, p. kašal-ha, s, z. kašal-haa, m. ha-hal, v. haa-haal, m. tšaak, p, z. |

| | |
|---|---|
| rain (*lloviznar*), | tos-ha, p, s, v, z : t. tos-haa, f, m. to-tos-ha, p. tosol-ha, z. ɔabal-ha, f. ɔabal-haa, m. |
| rain water, | tšulub, z. tšulub-ha, z : t. tšakil-haa, m. tšakiqal-haa, f. kanil-haa, m. kaanil-haa, f. |
| rattle-snake, | ɔab-kan, p, s, v, z. ahau-kan, z. |
| reason, | naat, m, f. toh-t'an, p, s. kušolal, z : m, f, t. u nuk-t'an, v. |
| red, | tšak, p, v, z : m, f. tša-tšak, p, z : m, f, t. tšu-tšak, s. |
| river, | bekan, z. bekan-ha, p. hai-ha, v. yatš-ha, z. yok-ha, f, t. yok-haa, m. |
| rob, | okol, p, s, v, z. koɔ, m, f, t. paa-koɔ, m, f. |
| run, | alkab, all. |
| salt, | taab, all. |
| sandal (*guarache*) | šanab, p, z. šanab-kewel, p, s, v, z. |
| scorpion, | sinan, s. sinaan, p, v, z : m, f. |
| see, | ilah, s, z. ilmah, (*permitir*) m, f, t. pakat, p, v. |
| silver, | sak-maskab, p. sak-taqin, m, f, t. |
| sing, | qai, all. |
| sister, elder, | kik, p, s, z : f, t. kiik, m. nohotš kik, v. |
| sister, younger, | iɔ'in, m, f, t. wiɔ'in, p, z. tšup-iɔ'in, s. tšupu-iɔ'in, v. |
| sit, | kutal, p, s, v, z. šekba, z. |
| sky, | kaan, all. |
| sleep, | wen-el, all. |
| small, | tši-tšan, p, s, v, z. tšan-tšan, m, t. ma-tšan-tšan, m, f. manob, m. mehen, m, f. ɔ'eɔ', t. |
| soldier, | qatun, m, f, t. H-qatun, z. qaatun, v. qatun-maak, s. bateel, p. batel-naal, p. H-batel, z. boteel, m. H-p'isba, z. holkan, f. |
| snake, | kan, v, z : m, f, t. qanal-kan, s. quqi-kan, p, v. quqil-kan, s. |
| snow, | yeeb, p, s, v. |
| son, by mother, | al, m, f, t. wal, p, z. šibi-al, s, v. šibi-bal, z. |
| son, by father, | mehen, p, z : m, f, t. laq-pal, v, z. šibi-iš-mehen, s. |
| speak, | t'an, s, v, z : m, f, t. lelau, p. |
| spring, | yaš-qin, m. itš-yaš-qin, p. yaš-tšun-hab, v. no word, z. |
| squirrel, | kuuk, p, s, v, z. |
| stand (*pararse*), | watal, all. |
| star, | eq, all. |
| stone, | tun, p. tunitš, all. buq-tun, z. |
| strong, | t'a, s. tšitš, p, v, z. qaam, z. um-qan, v. mu-qaan, z. |
| summer, | yaš-qin, p. qin-un-yabil, t. qin tun yaabil, m, f. qini-qil-kab, v. lub-tšak, p. no word, z. |
| sun, | qin, all. |
| tejon, | tšab, p. šib, s. emutš, v. |
| temple, | quna, p, v, z : m, f. qunah, s. yototš qu, m, f. |
| that, | le — e, z. lai, s. lailo, z. le letieele, p. leti-wale, v. helo, m. |

| | |
|---|---|
| there, | te, f. telo, v, z. tel-lo, t. tlo, z. tolo, p, s, z. lelo, p. — o, z. |
| they, | leti-ob, v, z. le-ob-ti, p, s, z. te-ob-ti-ob, p. |
| this, | le, z. lela, z. le — a, z. letiela, p, s, v. |
| thought, | tukul, all. |
| thumb, | na-qab, p, v, z : m, f, t. naa-qab, s. |
| thunder, | kil-ba, v. kil-bal, p. amba, z. ambah, s. |
| thunder-clap, | tšaak, z. amba-tšak, s. hum-tšaak, p, z. u pek-tšak, t. yakan-tšak, v. |
| tiger (tigre) | balam, s : m. balam-tšak-eqel, z. tšak-mool, p, v, z. tšak-eqel, s, z. |
| time, | qin, z : t. qin-il, p, s, z. u-qin-il, v : m, f. |
| toad, | mutš, all. uo, p, s. |
| tobacco, | quɔ, s, v, z : f. quuɔ, p. |
| to-day, | hele, f. be-hele, z. be-hela, z. be-helae, z. be-helak, v. ba-hele, p, s. |
| toe, | al-ok, z. yal-ok, p, s. tšil-bi-ok, v. sau, m. |
| to-morrow, | samal, p, s, v, z. haɔ-kab, v : m, f. |
| tongue, | aq, p, s, z : m, f, t. hu-aq, v. |
| tooth, | ko, all. |
| tree, | kul, z. kulul-tše, p. watal-tše, s. wiklil un p'el tše, v. ts'e, m. tše, t. tše-el, f. |
| true, | ha, s. hah, v, z : m, f, t. ha-hil, p, z. ha-hi-lil, p. |
| turkey, | ɔo, p, z. ɔoo, s. ɔun, s. ulum, v, z. tuš, z. |
| turtle, | ak, m, f, t. aak, p, s, v, z. |
| valley, | qop, m, f, t. qoop, z. qom, m, f, t. tša-qan, p. taɔ-luum, v. hem-lum, t. |
| village, | kah, all. noh-kah, s. tan-kah, p. tšan-kah, s. kah-talil, p. noh-kab, p. ka-kab, z. |
| walk, | šimbal, p, s, z : f, t. šinbal, v : m. |
| warble (gorjear), | qai, z : m. qo-qo-qai, p. hum, m, awat, m. |
| warm, | tšoko, p, s, z. tšokoh, v. tšakau, m, f. |
| water, | ha, p, v, z : t. haa, s : m, f. |
| we, | toon, p, s, v, z. |
| who, | mak, m, f. makš, t. maš, s, z. maaš, p, v. he-maš, z. heken-maaš, z. |
| white, | sak, p, s, v, z : f, t. sasak, p, z : f, t. |
| wife, | watan, p, s, z. h-waten, v. |
| will (voluntad), | olah, p, s, z. u sihil tin puqsiqal, v. |
| wind, | iq, all. |
| wing, | siq, all. |
| winter, | itš-kelil, p. qini-keel, v. aq-yebil (tiempo de aguas), m, f, t. no word, z. |
| wolf (lobo), | kab-koh, p, s. |
| woman, | š-tš'up, p, s, v, z. tšup-lal, f. tš'up-lal, m. |
| wood, | tše, all. |

work,             meya, v.   meyah, p, z.   menyah, s : m, f, t.
world,            yoqol-kab, z : m, f, t.   baal-kah, f.   bal-kal, t.   baal-
                  kal, m.
yellow,           qan, p, v, z : m, f, t.   qan-qan, p, z : m.   qun-qan, s.
yes,              bei, p, v.   bai, p.   la, s, z.
yesterday,        holhe, p, s, v, z : f, t.   holohe, p.
you (plural),     teeš, p, s, z.   toon, v.   mulanil, v.
you,              tetš, p, s, v, z.
young,            tan-kelem, p, s, v, z.

## NUMERATION [1]

| | Peto | Sotuta | Tizimin | Valladolid |
|---|---|---|---|---|
| 1. | hun | hun | hum | un |
| 2. | ka | ka | ka | ka |
| 3. | oš | oš | oš | oš |
| 4. | kam | kan | kan | kan |
| 5. | ho | ho | ho | hok |
| 6. | wak | wak | wak | wak |
| 7. | ušuk | wuk | wuk | huk |
| 8. | wašak | wašak | wašak | wašak |
| 9. | bolom | bolon | bolon | bolon |
| 10. | la-hun | la-hun | la-hun | la-hun |
| 11. | buluk-hun | buluk | buluk | buluk |
| | | | | un la-hun |
| 12. | lah-ka | lah-ka | lah-ka | ka-la-hun |
| 20. | hun-qaal | hun-qal | hun-qal | un-qal |
| 30. | la-hun-ka-qaal | la-hu-ka-qal | la-hun-ka-qal | oš-qal [3] |
| 40. | ka-qaal | ka-qal | ka-qaal | kan-la-hun |
| 50. | la-hun-yoš qaal | la-hu-yoš-qal | la-hu-yoš-qaal | la-hun-yoš-qal |
| 60. | oš-qaal | oš-qal | oš-qal | un-la-hun-yoš-qal |
| 70. | la-hun-kan-qaal | la-hu-kan-qal | la-hun-kan-qaal | ka-la-hun-yoš-qal |
| 80. | kan-qaal | kan-qal | kan-qaal | kan qal |
| 90. | la-hun-ho-qaal | la-hu-yo-qal | la-hun-ho-qaal | un kan la hun qal |
| 100. | ho-qaal | ho-qal | ho-qal | ho-qal |
| 1000. | pik | hum-pik | la-hun-oš-baaq | un-pik |
| | | | hum-pik [2] | |

---

[1] The numbers given here may be compared with those of Beltran on p. 99–100.

[2] The author of the Tizimin list states that anciently **pik** means 8000. See the statement regarding the present use of the term **pik** in Part I, p. 103.

[3] Many of the terms from this point onward are obviously incorrect.

A CATALOGUE OF SELECTED DOVER BOOKS
IN ALL FIELDS OF INTEREST

# A CATALOGUE OF SELECTED DOVER BOOKS
## IN ALL FIELDS OF INTEREST

THE NOTEBOOKS OF LEONARDO DA VINCI, edited by J.P. Richter. Extracts from manuscripts reveal great genius; on painting, sculpture, anatomy, sciences, geography, etc. Both Italian and English. 186 ms. pages reproduced, plus 500 additional drawings, including studies for Last Supper, Sforza monument, etc. 860pp. 7⁷/₈ x 10¾.                              USO 22572-0, 22573-9 Pa., Two vol. set $15.90

ART NOUVEAU DESIGNS IN COLOR, Alphonse Mucha, Maurice Verneuil, Georges Auriol. Full-color reproduction of Combinaisons ornamentales (c. 1900) by Art Nouveau masters. Floral, animal, geometric, interlacings, swashes — borders, frames, spots — all incredibly beautiful. 60 plates, hundreds of designs. 9³/₈ x 8¹/₁₆ .                              22885-1 Pa. $4.00

GRAPHIC WORKS OF ODILON REDON. All great fantastic lithographs, etchings, engravings, drawings, 209 in all. Monsters, Huysmans, still life work, etc. Introduction by Alfred Werner. 209pp. 9¹/₈ x 12¼.                              21996-8 Pa. $6.00

EXOTIC FLORAL PATTERNS IN COLOR, E.-A. Seguy. Incredibly beautiful full-color pochoir work by great French designer of 20's. Complete Bouquets et frondaisons, Suggestions pour étoffes. Richness must be seen to be believed. 40 plates containing 120 patterns. 80pp. 9³/₈ x 12¼.                              23041-4 Pa. $6.00

SELECTED ETCHINGS OF JAMES A. McN. WHISTLER, James A. McN. Whistler. 149 outstanding etchings by the great American artist, including selections from the Thames set and two Venice sets, the complete French set, and many individual prints. Introduction and explanatory note on each print by Maria Naylor. 157pp. 9³/₈ x 12¼.                              23194-1 Pa. $5.00

VISUAL ILLUSIONS: THEIR CAUSES, CHARACTERISTICS, AND APPLICATIONS, Matthew Luckiesh. Thorough description, discussion; shape and size, color, motion; natural illusion. Uses in art and industry. 100 illustrations. 252pp.
                              21530-X Pa. $3.00

TEN BOOKS ON ARCHITECTURE, Vitruvius. The most important book ever written on architecture. Early Roman aesthetics, technology, classical orders, site selection, all other aspects. Stands behind everything since. Morgan translation. 331pp.
                              20645-9 Pa. $3.75

THE CODEX NUTTALL. A PICTURE MANUSCRIPT FROM ANCIENT MEXICO, as first edited by Zelia Nuttall. Only inexpensive edition, in full color, of a pre-Columbian Mexican (Mixtec) book. 88 color plates show kings, gods, heroes, temples, sacrifices. New explanatory, historical introduction by Arthur G. Miller. 96pp. 11³/₈ x 8½.                              23168-2 Pa. $7.50

CREATIVE LITHOGRAPHY AND HOW TO DO IT, Grant Arnold. Lithography as art form: working directly on stone, transfer of drawings, lithotint, mezzotint, color printing; also metal plates. Detailed, thorough. 27 illustrations. 214pp.
21208-4 Pa. $3.50

DESIGN MOTIFS OF ANCIENT MEXICO, Jorge Enciso. Vigorous, powerful ceramic stamp impressions — Maya, Aztec, Toltec, Olmec. Serpents, gods, priests, dancers, etc. 153pp. 6⅛ x 9¼.
20084-1 Pa. $2.50

AMERICAN INDIAN DESIGN AND DECORATION, Leroy Appleton. Full text, plus more than 700 precise drawings of Inca, Maya, Aztec, Pueblo, Plains, NW Coast basketry, sculpture, painting, pottery, sand paintings, metal, etc. 4 plates in color. 279pp. 8⅜ x 11¼.
22704-9 Pa.$5.00

CHINESE LATTICE DESIGNS, Daniel S. Dye. Incredibly beautiful geometric designs: circles, voluted, simple dissections, etc. Inexhaustible source of ideas, motifs. 1239 illustrations. 469pp. 6⅛ x 9¼.
23096-1 Pa. $5.00

JAPANESE DESIGN MOTIFS, Matsuya Co. Mon, or heraldic designs. Over 4000 typical, beautiful designs: birds, animals, flowers, swords, fans, geometric; all beautifully stylized. 213pp. 11⅜ x 8¼.
22874-6 Pa. $5.00

PERSPECTIVE, Jan Vredeman de Vries. 73 perspective plates from 1604 edition; buildings, townscapes, stairways, fantastic scenes. Remarkable for beauty, surrealistic atmosphere; real eye-catchers. Introduction by Adolf Placzek. 74pp. 11⅜ x 8¼.
20186-4 Pa. $3.00

EARLY AMERICAN DESIGN MOTIFS, Suzanne E. Chapman. 497 motifs, designs, from painting on wood, ceramics, appliqué, glassware, samplers, metal work, etc. Florals, landscapes, birds and animals, geometrics, letters, etc. Inexhaustible. Enlarged edition. 138pp. 8⅜ x 11¼.
22985-8 Pa. $3.50
23084-8 Clothbd. $7.95

VICTORIAN STENCILS FOR DESIGN AND DECORATION, edited by E.V. Gillon, Jr. 113 wonderful ornate Victorian pieces from German sources; florals, geometrics; borders, corner pieces; bird motifs, etc. 64pp. 9⅜ x 12¼.
21995-X Pa. $3.00

ART NOUVEAU: AN ANTHOLOGY OF DESIGN AND ILLUSTRATION FROM THE STUDIO, edited by E.V. Gillon, Jr. Graphic arts: book jackets, posters, engravings, illustrations, decorations; Crane, Beardsley, Bradley and many others. Inexhaustible. 92pp. 8⅛ x 11.
22388-4 Pa. $2.50

ORIGINAL ART DECO DESIGNS, William Rowe. First-rate, highly imaginative modern Art Deco frames, borders, compositions, alphabets, florals, insectals, Wurlitzer-types, etc. Much finest modern Art Deco. 80 plates, 8 in color. 8⅜ x 11¼.
22567-4 Pa. $3.50

HANDBOOK OF DESIGNS AND DEVICES, Clarence P. Hornung. Over 1800 basic geometric designs based on circle, triangle, square, scroll, cross, etc. Largest such collection in existence. 261pp.
20125-2 Pa. $2.75

150 MASTERPIECES OF DRAWING, edited by Anthony Toney. 150 plates, early 15th century to end of 18th century; Rembrandt, Michelangelo, Dürer, Fragonard, Watteau, Wouwerman, many others. 150pp. 8⅜ x 11¼.                21032-4 Pa. $4.00

THE GOLDEN AGE OF THE POSTER, Hayward and Blanche Cirker. 70 extraordinary posters in full colors, from Maîtres de l'Affiche, Mucha, Lautrec, Bradley, Cheret, Beardsley, many others. 9⅜ x 12¼.                22753-7 Pa. $5.95

SIMPLICISSIMUS, selection, translations and text by Stanley Appelbaum. 180 satirical drawings, 16 in full color, from the famous German weekly magazine in the years 1896 to 1926. 24 artists included: Grosz, Kley, Pascin, Kubin, Kollwitz, plus Heine, Thöny, Bruno Paul, others. 172pp. 8½ x 12¼.                23098-8 Pa. $5.00
23099-6 Clothbd. $10.00

THE EARLY WORK OF AUBREY BEARDSLEY, Aubrey Beardsley. 157 plates, 2 in color: Manon Lescaut, Madame Bovary, Morte d'Arthur, Salome, other. Introduction by H. Marillier. 175pp. 8½ x 11.                21816-3 Pa. $4.00

THE LATER WORK OF AUBREY BEARDSLEY, Aubrey Beardsley. Exotic masterpieces of full maturity: Venus and Tannhäuser, Lysistrata, Rape of the Lock, Volpone, Savoy material, etc. 174 plates, 2 in color. 176pp. 8½ x 11.   21817-1 Pa. $4.50

DRAWINGS OF WILLIAM BLAKE, William Blake. 92 plates from Book of Job, Divine Comedy, Paradise Lost, visionary heads, mythological figures, Laocoön, etc. Selection, introduction, commentary by Sir Geoffrey Keynes. 178pp. 8½ x 11.
22303-5 Pa. $4.00

LONDON: A PILGRIMAGE, Gustave Doré, Blanchard Jerrold. Squalor, riches, misery, beauty of mid-Victorian metropolis; 55 wonderful plates, 125 other illustrations, full social, cultural text by Jerrold. 191pp. of text. 8⅛ x 11.
22306-X Pa. $6.00

THE COMPLETE WOODCUTS OF ALBRECHT DÜRER, edited by Dr. W. Kurth. 346 in all: Old Testament, St. Jerome, Passion, Life of Virgin, Apocalypse, many others. Introduction by Campbell Dodgson. 285pp. 8½ x 12¼.                21097-9 Pa. $6.00

THE DISASTERS OF WAR, Francisco Goya. 83 etchings record horrors of Napoleonic wars in Spain and war in general. Reprint of 1st edition, plus 3 additional plates. Introduction by Philip Hofer. 97pp. 9⅜ x 8¼.                21872-4 Pa. $3.50

ENGRAVINGS OF HOGARTH, William Hogarth. 101 of Hogarth's greatest works: Rake's Progress, Harlot's Progress, Illustrations for Hudibras, Midnight Modern Conversation, Before and After, Beer Street and Gin Lane, many more. Full commentary. 256pp. 11 x 14.                22479-1 Pa. $7.95

PRIMITIVE ART, Franz Boas. Great anthropologist on ceramics, textiles, wood, stone, metal, etc.; patterns, technology, symbols, styles. All areas, but fullest on Northwest Coast Indians. 350 illustrations. 378pp.                20025-6 Pa. $3.75

CATALOGUE OF DOVER BOOKS

MOTHER GOOSE'S MELODIES. Facsimile of fabulously rare Munroe and Francis "copyright 1833" Boston edition. Familiar and unusual rhymes, wonderful old woodcut illustrations. Edited by E.F. Bleiler. 128pp. 4½ x 6⅜. 22577-1 Pa. $1.50

MOTHER GOOSE IN HIEROGLYPHICS. Favorite nursery rhymes presented in rebus form for children. Fascinating 1849 edition reproduced in toto, with key. Introduction by E.F. Bleiler. About 400 woodcuts. 64pp. 6⅞ x 5¼. 20745-5 Pa. $1.50

PETER PIPER'S PRACTICAL PRINCIPLES OF PLAIN & PERFECT PRONUNCIATION. Alliterative jingles and tongue-twisters. Reproduction in full of 1830 first American edition. 25 spirited woodcuts. 32pp. 4½ x 6⅜. 22560-7 Pa. $1.25

MARMADUKE MULTIPLY'S MERRY METHOD OF MAKING MINOR MATHEMATICIANS. Fellow to Peter Piper, it teaches multiplication table by catchy rhymes and woodcuts. 1841 Munroe & Francis edition. Edited by E.F. Bleiler. 103pp. 4⅝ x 6. 22773-1 Pa. $1.25

THE NIGHT BEFORE CHRISTMAS, Clement Moore. Full text, and woodcuts from original 1848 book. Also critical, historical material. 19 illustrations. 40pp. 4⅝ x 6. 22797-9 Pa. $1.35

THE KING OF THE GOLDEN RIVER, John Ruskin. Victorian children's classic of three brothers, their attempts to reach the Golden River, what becomes of them. Facsimile of original 1889 edition. 22 illustrations. 56pp. 4⅝ x 6⅜. 20066-3 Pa. $1.50

DREAMS OF THE RAREBIT FIEND, Winsor McCay. Pioneer cartoon strip, unexcelled for beauty, imagination, in 60 full sequences. Incredible technical virtuosity, wonderful visual wit. Historical introduction. 62pp. 8⅜ x 11¼. 21347-1 Pa. $2.50

THE KATZENJAMMER KIDS, Rudolf Dirks. In full color, 14 strips from 1906-7; full of imagination, characteristic humor. Classic of great historical importance. Introduction by August Derleth. 32pp. 9¼ x 12¼. 23005-8 Pa. $2.00

LITTLE ORPHAN ANNIE AND LITTLE ORPHAN ANNIE IN COSMIC CITY, Harold Gray. Two great sequences from the early strips: our curly-haired heroine defends the Warbucks' financial empire and, then, takes on meanie Phineas P. Pinchpenny. Leapin' lizards! 178pp. 6⅛ x 8⅜. 23107-0 Pa. $2.00

ABSOLUTELY MAD INVENTIONS, A.E. Brown, H.A. Jeffcott. Hilarious, useless, or merely absurd inventions all granted patents by the U.S. Patent Office. Edible tie pin, mechanical hat tipper, etc. 57 illustrations. 125pp. 22596-8 Pa. $1.50

THE DEVIL'S DICTIONARY, Ambrose Bierce. Barbed, bitter, brilliant witticisms in the form of a dictionary. Best, most ferocious satire America has produced. 145pp. 20487-1 Pa. $1.75

THE BEST DR. THORNDYKE DETECTIVE STORIES, R. Austin Freeman. The Case of Oscar Brodski, The Moabite Cipher, and 5 other favorites featuring the great scientific detective, plus his long-believed-lost first adventure — 31 New Inn — reprinted here for the first time. Edited by E.F. Bleiler. USO 20388-3 Pa. $3.00

BEST "THINKING MACHINE" DETECTIVE STORIES, Jacques Futrelle. The Problem of Cell 13 and 11 other stories about Prof. Augustus S.F.X. Van Dusen, including two "lost" stories. First reprinting of several. Edited by E.F. Bleiler. 241pp.
20537-1 Pa. $3.00

UNCLE SILAS, J. Sheridan LeFanu. Victorian Gothic mystery novel, considered by many best of period, even better than Collins or Dickens. Wonderful psychological terror. Introduction by Frederick Shroyer. 436pp. 21715-9 Pa. $4.50

BEST DR. POGGIOLI DETECTIVE STORIES, T.S. Stribling. 15 best stories from EQMM and The Saint offer new adventures in Mexico, Florida, Tennessee hills as Poggioli unravels mysteries and combats Count Jalacki. 217pp. 23227-1 Pa. $3.00

EIGHT DIME NOVELS, selected with an introduction by E.F. Bleiler. Adventures of Old King Brady, Frank James, Nick Carter, Deadwood Dick, Buffalo Bill, The Steam Man, Frank Merriwell, and Horatio Alger — 1877 to 1905. Important, entertaining popular literature in facsimile reprint, with original covers. 190pp. 9 x 12. 22975-0 Pa. $3.50

ALICE'S ADVENTURES UNDER GROUND, Lewis Carroll. Facsimile of ms. Carroll gave Alice Liddell in 1864. Different in many ways from final Alice. Handlettered, illustrated by Carroll. Introduction by Martin Gardner. 128pp. 21482-6 Pa. $2.00

ALICE IN WONDERLAND COLORING BOOK, Lewis Carroll. Pictures by John Tenniel. Large-size versions of the famous illustrations of Alice, Cheshire Cat, Mad Hatter and all the others, waiting for your crayons. Abridged text. 36 illustrations. 64pp. 8¼ x 11. 22853-3 Pa. $1.50

AVENTURES D'ALICE AU PAYS DES MERVEILLES, Lewis Carroll. Bué's translation of "Alice" into French, supervised by Carroll himself. Novel way to learn language. (No English text.) 42 Tenniel illustrations. 196pp. 22836-3 Pa. $3.00

MYTHS AND FOLK TALES OF IRELAND, Jeremiah Curtin. 11 stories that are Irish versions of European fairy tales and 9 stories from the Fenian cycle — 20 tales of legend and magic that comprise an essential work in the history of folklore. 256pp. 22430-9 Pa. $3.00

EAST O' THE SUN AND WEST O' THE MOON, George W. Dasent. Only full edition of favorite, wonderful Norwegian fairytales — Why the Sea is Salt, Boots and the Troll, etc. — with 77 illustrations by Kittelsen & Werenskiöld. 418pp.
22521-6 Pa. $4.50

PERRAULT'S FAIRY TALES, Charles Perrault and Gustave Doré. Original versions of Cinderella, Sleeping Beauty, Little Red Riding Hood, etc. in best translation, with 34 wonderful illustrations by Gustave Doré. 117pp. 8⅛ x 11. 22311-6 Pa. $2.50

EARLY NEW ENGLAND GRAVESTONE RUBBINGS, Edmund V. Gillon, Jr. 43 photographs, 226 rubbings show heavily symbolic, macabre, sometimes humorous primitive American art. Up to early 19th century. 207pp. 8⅜ x 11¼.
21380-3 Pa. $4.00

L.J.M. DAGUERRE: THE HISTORY OF THE DIORAMA AND THE DAGUERREOTYPE, Helmut and Alison Gernsheim. Definitive account. Early history, life and work of Daguerre; discovery of daguerreotype process; diffusion abroad; other early photography. 124 illustrations. 226pp. 6⅙ x 9¼. 22290-X Pa. $4.00

PHOTOGRAPHY AND THE AMERICAN SCENE, Robert Taft. The basic book on American photography as art, recording form, 1839-1889. Development, influence on society, great photographers, types (portraits, war, frontier, etc.), whatever else needed. Inexhaustible. Illustrated with 322 early photos, daguerreotypes, tintypes, stereo slides, etc. 546pp. 6⅛ x 9¼. 21201-7 Pa. $6.00

PHOTOGRAPHIC SKETCHBOOK OF THE CIVIL WAR, Alexander Gardner. Reproduction of 1866 volume with 100 on-the-field photographs: Manassas, Lincoln on battlefield, slave pens, etc. Introduction by E.F. Bleiler. 224pp. 10¾ x 9.
22731-6 Pa. $6.00

THE MOVIES: A PICTURE QUIZ BOOK, Stanley Appelbaum & Hayward Cirker. Match stars with their movies, name actors and actresses, test your movie skill with 241 stills from 236 great movies, 1902-1959. Indexes of performers and films. 128pp. 8⅜ x 9¼. 20222-4 Pa. $3.00

THE TALKIES, Richard Griffith. Anthology of features, articles from Photoplay, 1928-1940, reproduced complete. Stars, famous movies, technical features, fabulous ads, etc.; Garbo, Chaplin, King Kong, Lubitsch, etc. 4 color plates, scores of illustrations. 327pp. 8⅜ x 11¼. 22762-6 Pa. $6.95

THE MOVIE MUSICAL FROM VITAPHONE TO "42ND STREET," edited by Miles Kreuger. Relive the rise of the movie musical as reported in the pages of Photoplay magazine (1926-1933): every movie review, cast list, ad, and record review; every significant feature article, production still, biography, forecast, and gossip story. Profusely illustrated. 367pp. 8⅜ x 11¼. 23154-2 Pa. $7.95

JOHANN SEBASTIAN BACH, Philipp Spitta. Great classic of biography, musical commentary, with hundreds of pieces analyzed. Also good for Bach's contemporaries. 450 musical examples. Total of 1799pp.
EUK 22278-0, 22279-9 Clothbd., Two vol. set $25.00

BEETHOVEN AND HIS NINE SYMPHONIES, Sir George Grove. Thorough history, analysis, commentary on symphonies and some related pieces. For either beginner or advanced student. 436 musical passages. 407pp. 20334-4 Pa. $4.00

MOZART AND HIS PIANO CONCERTOS, Cuthbert Girdlestone. The only full-length study. Detailed analyses of all 21 concertos, sources; 417 musical examples. 509pp. 21271-8 Pa. $6.00

THE FITZWILLIAM VIRGINAL BOOK, edited by J. Fuller Maitland, W.B. Squire. Famous early 17th century collection of keyboard music, 300 works by Morley, Byrd, Bull, Gibbons, etc. Modern notation. Total of 938pp. 8³/₈ x 11.
ECE 21068-5, 21069-3 Pa., Two vol. set $15.00

COMPLETE STRING QUARTETS, Wolfgang A. Mozart. Breitkopf and Härtel edition. All 23 string quartets plus alternate slow movement to K156. Study score. 277pp. 9³/₈ x 12¼. 22372-8 Pa. $6.00

COMPLETE SONG CYCLES, Franz Schubert. Complete piano, vocal music of Die Schöne Müllerin, Die Winterreise, Schwanengesang. Also Drinker English singing translations. Breitkopf and Härtel edition. 217pp. 9³/₈ x 12¼.
22649-2 Pa. $5.00

THE COMPLETE PRELUDES AND ETUDES FOR PIANOFORTE SOLO, Alexander Scriabin. All the preludes and etudes including many perfectly spun miniatures. Edited by K.N. Igumnov and Y.I. Mil'shteyn. 250pp. 9 x 12. 22919-X Pa. $6.00

TRISTAN UND ISOLDE, Richard Wagner. Full orchestral score with complete instrumentation. Do not confuse with piano reduction. Commentary by Felix Mottl, great Wagnerian conductor and scholar. Study score. 655pp. 8¹/₈ x 11.
22915-7 Pa. $11.95

FAVORITE SONGS OF THE NINETIES, ed. Robert Fremont. Full reproduction, including covers, of 88 favorites: Ta-Ra-Ra-Boom-De-Aye, The Band Played On, Bird in a Gilded Cage, Under the Bamboo Tree, After the Ball, etc. 401pp. 9 x 12.
EBE 21536-9 Pa. $6.95

SOUSA'S GREAT MARCHES IN PIANO TRANSCRIPTION: ORIGINAL SHEET MUSIC OF 23 WORKS, John Philip Sousa. Selected by Lester S. Levy. Playing edition includes: The Stars and Stripes Forever, The Thunderer, The Gladiator, King Cotton, Washington Post, much more. 24 illustrations. 111pp. 9 x 12.
USO 23132-1 Pa. $3.50

CLASSIC PIANO RAGS, selected with an introduction by Rudi Blesh. Best ragtime music (1897-1922) by Scott Joplin, James Scott, Joseph F. Lamb, Tom Turpin, 9 others. Printed from best original sheet music, plus covers. 364pp. 9 x 12.
EBE 20469-3 Pa. $7.50

ANALYSIS OF CHINESE CHARACTERS, C.D. Wilder, J.H. Ingram. 1000 most important characters analyzed according to primitives, phonetics, historical development. Traditional method offers mnemonic aid to beginner, intermediate student of Chinese, Japanese. 365pp. 23045-7 Pa. $4.00

MODERN CHINESE: A BASIC COURSE, Faculty of Peking University. Self study, classroom course in modern Mandarin. Records contain phonetics, vocabulary, sentences, lessons. 249 page book contains all recorded text, translations, grammar, vocabulary, exercises. Best course on market. 3 12" 33¹/₃ monaural records, book, album. 98832-5 Set $12.50

MANUAL OF THE TREES OF NORTH AMERICA, Charles S. Sargent. The basic survey of every native tree and tree-like shrub, 717 species in all. Extremely full descriptions, information on habitat, growth, locales, economics, etc. Necessary to every serious tree lover. Over 100 finding keys. 783 illustrations. Total of 986pp.
20277-1, 20278-X Pa., Two vol. set $9.00

BIRDS OF THE NEW YORK AREA, John Bull. Indispensable guide to more than 400 species within a hundred-mile radius of Manhattan. Information on range, status, breeding, migration, distribution trends, etc. Foreword by Roger Tory Peterson. 17 drawings; maps. 540pp.
23222-0 Pa. $6.00

THE SEA-BEACH AT EBB-TIDE, Augusta Foote Arnold. Identify hundreds of marine plants and animals: algae, seaweeds, squids, crabs, corals, etc. Descriptions cover food, life cycle, size, shape, habitat. Over 600 drawings. 490pp.
21949-6 Pa. $5.00

THE MOTH BOOK, William J. Holland. Identify more than 2,000 moths of North America. General information, precise species descriptions. 623 illustrations plus 48 color plates show almost all species, full size. 1968 edition. Still the basic book. Total of 551pp. 6½ x 9¼.
21948-8 Pa. $6.00

HOW INDIANS USE WILD PLANTS FOR FOOD, MEDICINE & CRAFTS, Frances Densmore. Smithsonian, Bureau of American Ethnology report presents wealth of material on nearly 200 plants used by Chippewas of Minnesota and Wisconsin. 33 plates plus 122pp. of text. 6⅛ x 9¼.
23019-8 Pa. $2.50

OLD NEW YORK IN EARLY PHOTOGRAPHS, edited by Mary Black. Your only chance to see New York City as it was 1853-1906, through 196 wonderful photographs from N.Y. Historical Society. Great Blizzard, Lincoln's funeral procession, great buildings. 228pp. 9 x 12.
22907-6 Pa. $6.95

THE AMERICAN REVOLUTION, A PICTURE SOURCEBOOK, John Grafton. Wonderful Bicentennial picture source, with 411 illustrations (contemporary and 19th century) showing battles, personalities, maps, events, flags, posters, soldier's life, ships, etc. all captioned and explained. A wonderful browsing book, supplement to other historical reading. 160pp. 9 x 12.
23226-3 Pa. $4.00

PERSONAL NARRATIVE OF A PILGRIMAGE TO AL-MADINAH AND MECCAH, Richard Burton. Great travel classic by remarkably colorful personality. Burton, disguised as a Moroccan, visited sacred shrines of Islam, narrowly escaping death. Wonderful observations of Islamic life, customs, personalities. 47 illustrations. Total of 959pp.
21217-3, 21218-1 Pa., Two vol. set $10.00

INCIDENTS OF TRAVEL IN CENTRAL AMERICA, CHIAPAS, AND YUCATAN, John L. Stephens. Almost single-handed discovery of Maya culture; exploration of ruined cities, monuments, temples; customs of Indians. 115 drawings. 892pp.
22404-X, 22405-8 Pa., Two vol. set $9.00

CONSTRUCTION OF AMERICAN FURNITURE TREASURES, Lester Margon. 344 detail drawings, complete text on constructing exact reproductions of 38 early American masterpieces: Hepplewhite sideboard, Duncan Phyfe drop-leaf table, mantel clock, gate-leg dining table, Pa. German cupboard, more. 38 plates. 54 photographs. 168pp. 8⅜ x 11¼. 23056-2 Pa. $4.00

JEWELRY MAKING AND DESIGN, Augustus F. Rose, Antonio Cirino. Professional secrets revealed in thorough, practical guide: tools, materials, processes; rings, brooches, chains, cast pieces, enamelling, setting stones, etc. Do not confuse with skimpy introductions: beginner can use, professional can learn from it. Over 200 illustrations. 306pp. 21750-7 Pa. $3.00

METALWORK AND ENAMELLING, Herbert Maryon. Generally coneeded best all-around book. Countless trade secrets: materials, tools, soldering, filigree, setting, inlay, niello, repoussé, casting, polishing, etc. For beginner or expert. Author was foremost British expert. 330 illustrations. 335pp. 22702-2 Pa. $4.00

WEAVING WITH FOOT-POWER LOOMS, Edward F. Worst. Setting up a loom, beginning to weave, constructing equipment, using dyes, more, plus over 285 drafts of traditional patterns including Colonial and Swedish weaves. More than 200 other figures. For beginning and advanced. 275pp. 8¾ x 6⅜. 23064-3 Pa. $4.50

WEAVING A NAVAJO BLANKET, Gladys A. Reichard. Foremost anthropologist studied under Navajo women, reveals every step in process from wool, dyeing, spinning, setting up loom, designing, weaving. Much history, symbolism. With this book you could make one yourself. 97 illustrations. 222pp. 22992-0 Pa. $3.00

NATURAL DYES AND HOME DYEING, Rita J. Adrosko. Use natural ingredients: bark, flowers, leaves, lichens, insects etc. Over 135 specific recipes from historical sources for cotton, wool, other fabrics. Genuine premodern handicrafts. 12 illustrations. 160pp. 22688-3 Pa. $2.00

DRIED FLOWERS, Sarah Whitlock and Martha Rankin. Concise, clear, practical guide to dehydration, glycerinizing, pressing plant material, and more. Covers use of silica gel. 12 drawings. Originally titled "New Techniques with Dried Flowers." 32pp. 21802-3 Pa. $1.00

THOMAS NAST: CARTOONS AND ILLUSTRATIONS, with text by·Thomas Nast St. Hill. Father of American political cartooning. Cartoons that destroyed Tweed Ring; inflation, free love, church and state; original Republican elephant and Democratic donkey; Santa Claus; more. 117 illustrations. 146pp. 9 x 12.
22983-1 Pa. $4.00
23067-8 Clothbd. $8.50

FREDERIC REMINGTON: 173 DRAWINGS AND ILLUSTRATIONS. Most famous of the Western artists, most responsible for our myths about the American West in its untamed days. Complete reprinting of *Drawings of Frederic Remington* (1897), plus other selections. 4 additional drawings in color on covers. 140pp. 9 x 12.
20714-5 Pa. $5.00

HOW TO SOLVE CHESS PROBLEMS, Kenneth S. Howard. Practical suggestions on problem solving for very beginners. 58 two-move problems, 46 3-movers, 8 4-movers for practice, plus hints. 171pp. 20748-X Pa. **$3.00**

A GUIDE TO FAIRY CHESS, Anthony Dickins. 3-D chess, 4-D chess, chess on a cylindrical board, reflecting pieces that bounce off edges, cooperative chess, retrograde chess, maximummers, much more. Most based on work of great Dawson. Full handbook, 100 problems. 66pp. 7⅞ x 10¾. 22687-5 Pa. **$2.00**

WIN AT BACKGAMMON, Millard Hopper. Best opening moves, running game, blocking game, back game, tables of odds, etc. Hopper makes the game clear enough for anyone to play, and win. 43 diagrams. 111pp. 22894-0 Pa. **$1.50**

BIDDING A BRIDGE HAND, Terence Reese. Master player "thinks out loud" the binding of 75 hands that defy point count systems. Organized by bidding problem—no-fit situations, overbidding, underbidding, cueing your defense, etc. 254pp. EBE 22830-4 Pa. **$3.00**

THE PRECISION BIDDING SYSTEM IN BRIDGE, C.C. Wei, edited by Alan Truscott. Inventor of precision bidding presents average hands and hands from actual play, including games from 1969 Bermuda Bowl where system emerged. 114 exercises. 116pp. 21171-1 Pa. **$2.25**

LEARN MAGIC, Henry Hay. 20 simple, easy-to-follow lessons on magic for the new magician: illusions, card tricks, silks, sleights of hand, coin manipulations, escapes, and more —all with a minimum amount of equipment. Final chapter explains the great stage illusions. 92 illustrations. 285pp. 21238-6 Pa. **$2.95**

THE NEW MAGICIAN'S MANUAL, Walter B. Gibson. Step-by-step instructions and clear illustrations guide the novice in mastering 36 tricks; much equipment supplied on 16 pages of cut-out materials. 36 additional tricks. 64 illustrations. 159pp. 6⅝ x 10. 23113-5 Pa. **$3.00**

PROFESSIONAL MAGIC FOR AMATEURS, Walter B. Gibson. 50 easy, effective tricks used by professionals —cards, string, tumblers, handkerchiefs, mental magic, etc. 63 illustrations. 223pp. 23012-0 Pa. **$2.50**

CARD MANIPULATIONS, Jean Hugard. Very rich collection of manipulations; has taught thousands of fine magicians tricks that are really workable, eye-catching. Easily followed, serious work. Over 200 illustrations. 163pp. 20539-8 Pa. **$2.00**

ABBOTT'S ENCYCLOPEDIA OF ROPE TRICKS FOR MAGICIANS, Stewart James. Complete reference book for amateur and professional magicians containing more than 150 tricks involving knots, penetrations, cut and restored rope, etc. 510 illustrations. Reprint of 3rd edition. 400pp. 23206-9 Pa. **$3.50**

THE SECRETS OF HOUDINI, J.C. Cannell. Classic study of Houdini's incredible magic, exposing closely-kept professional secrets and revealing, in general terms, the whole art of stage magic. 67 illustrations. 279pp. 22913-0 Pa. **$3.00**

THE MAGIC MOVING PICTURE BOOK, Bliss, Sands & Co. The pictures in this book move! Volcanoes erupt, a house burns, a serpentine dancer wiggles her way through a number. By using a specially ruled acetate screen provided, you can obtain these and 15 other startling effects. Originally "The Motograph Moving Picture Book." 32pp. 8¼ x 11. 23224-7 Pa. $1.75

STRING FIGURES AND HOW TO MAKE THEM, Caroline F. Jayne. Fullest, clearest instructions on string figures from around world: Eskimo, Navajo, Lapp, Europe, more. Cats cradle, moving spear, lightning, stars. Introduction by A.C. Haddon. 950 illustrations. 407pp. 20152-X Pa. $3.50

PAPER FOLDING FOR BEGINNERS, William D. Murray and Francis J. Rigney. Clearest book on market for making origami sail boats, roosters, frogs that move legs, cups, bonbon boxes. 40 projects. More than 275 illustrations. Photographs. 94pp. 20713-7 Pa $1.50

INDIAN SIGN LANGUAGE, William Tomkins. Over 525 signs developed by Sioux, Blackfoot, Cheyenne, Arapahoe and other tribes. Written instructions and diagrams: how to make words, construct sentences. Also 290 pictographs of Sioux and Ojibway tribes. 111pp. 6⅛ x 9¼. 22029-X Pa. $1.75

BOOMERANGS: HOW TO MAKE AND THROW THEM, Bernard S. Mason. Easy to make and throw, dozens of designs: cross-stick, pinwheel, boomabird, tumblestick, Australian curved stick boomerang. Complete throwing instructions. All safe. 99pp. 23028-7 Pa. $1.75

25 KITES THAT FLY, Leslie Hunt. Full, easy to follow instructions for kites made from inexpensive materials. Many novelties. Reeling, raising, designing your own. 70 illustrations. 110pp. 22550-X Pa. $1.50

TRICKS AND GAMES ON THE POOL TABLE, Fred Herrmann. 79 tricks and games, some solitaires, some for 2 or more players, some competitive; mystifying shots and throws, unusual carom, tricks involving cork, coins, a hat, more. 77 figures. 95pp. 21814-7 Pa. $1.50

WOODCRAFT AND CAMPING, Bernard S. Mason. How to make a quick emergency shelter, select woods that will burn immediately, make do with limited supplies, etc. Also making many things out of wood, rawhide, bark, at camp. Formerly titled Woodcraft. 295 illustrations. 580pp. 21951-8 Pa. $4.00

AN INTRODUCTION TO CHESS MOVES AND TACTICS SIMPLY EXPLAINED, Leonard Barden. Informal intermediate introduction: reasons for moves, tactics, openings, traps, positional play, endgame. Isolates patterns. 102pp. USO 21210-6 Pa. $1.35

LASKER'S MANUAL OF CHESS, Dr. Emanuel Lasker. Great world champion offers very thorough coverage of all aspects of chess. Combinations, position play, openings, endgame, aesthetics of chess, philosophy of struggle, much more. Filled with analyzed games. 390pp. 20640-8 Pa. $4.00

SLEEPING BEAUTY, illustrated by Arthur Rackham. Perhaps the fullest, most delightful version ever, told by C.S. Evans. Rackham's best work. 49 illustrations. 110pp. 7⅞ x 10¾. 22756-1 Pa. $2.00

THE WONDERFUL WIZARD OF OZ, L. Frank Baum. Facsimile in full color of America's finest children's classic. Introduction by Martin Gardner. 143 illustrations by W.W. Denslow. 267pp. 20691-2 Pa. $3.50

GOOPS AND HOW TO BE THEM, Gelett Burgess. Classic tongue-in-cheek masquerading as etiquette book. 87 verses, 170 cartoons as Goops demonstrate virtues of table manners, neatness, courtesy, more. 88pp. 6½ x 9¼. 22233-0 Pa. $2.00

THE BROWNIES, THEIR BOOK, Palmer Cox. Small as mice, cunning as foxes, exuberant, mischievous, Brownies go to zoo, toy shop, seashore, circus, more. 24 verse adventures. 266 illustrations. 144pp. 6⅝ x 9¼. 21265-3 Pa. $2.50

BILLY WHISKERS: THE AUTOBIOGRAPHY OF A GOAT, Frances Trego Montgomery. Escapades of that rambunctious goat. Favorite from turn of the century America. 24 illustrations. 259pp. 22345-0 Pa. $2.75

THE ROCKET BOOK, Peter Newell. Fritz, janitor's kid, sets off rocket in basement of apartment house; an ingenious hole punched through every page traces course of rocket. 22 duotone drawings, verses. 48pp. 6⅞ x 8⅜. 22044-3 Pa. $1.50

CUT AND COLOR PAPER MASKS, Michael Grater. Clowns, animals, funny faces... simply color them in, cut them out, and put them together, and you have 9 paper masks to play with and enjoy. Complete instructions. Assembled masks shown in full color on the covers. 32pp. 8¼ x 11. 23171-2 Pa. $1.50

THE TALE OF PETER RABBIT, Beatrix Potter. The inimitable Peter's terrifying adventure in Mr. McGregor's garden, with all 27 wonderful, full-color Potter illustrations. 55pp. 4¼ x 5½. USO 22827-4 Pa. $1.00

THE TALE OF MRS. TIGGY-WINKLE, Beatrix Potter. Your child will love this story about a very special hedgehog and all 27 wonderful, full-color Potter illustrations. 57pp. 4¼ x 5½. USO 20546-0 Pa. $1.00

THE TALE OF BENJAMIN BUNNY, Beatrix Potter. Peter Rabbit's cousin coaxes him back into Mr. McGregor's garden for a whole new set of adventures. A favorite with children. All 27 full-color illustrations. 59pp. 4¼ x 5½ USO 21102-9 Pa. $1.00

THE MERRY ADVENTURES OF ROBIN HOOD, Howard Pyle. Facsimile of original (1883) edition, finest modern version of English outlaw's adventures. 23 illustrations by Pyle. 296pp. 6½ x 9¼. 22043-5 Pa. $4.00

TWO LITTLE SAVAGES, Ernest Thompson Seton. Adventures of two boys who lived as Indians; explaining Indian ways, woodlore, pioneer methods. 293 illustrations. 286pp. 20985-7 Pa. $3.50

HOUDINI ON MAGIC, Harold Houdini. Edited by Walter Gibson, Morris N. Young. How he escaped; exposés of fake spiritualists; instructions for eye-catching tricks; other fascinating material by and about greatest magician. 155 illustrations. 280pp. 20384-0 Pa. $2.75

HANDBOOK OF THE NUTRITIONAL CONTENTS OF FOOD, U.S. Dept. of Agriculture. Largest, most detailed source of food nutrition information ever prepared. Two mammoth tables: one measuring nutrients in 100 grams of edible portion; the other, in edible portion of 1 pound as purchased. Originally titled Composition of Foods. 190pp. 9 x 12. 21342-0 Pa. $4.00

COMPLETE GUIDE TO HOME CANNING, PRESERVING AND FREEZING, U.S. Dept. of Agriculture. Seven basic manuals with full instructions for jams and jellies; pickles and relishes; canning fruits, vegetables, meat; freezing anything. Really good recipes, exact instructions for optimal results. Save a fortune in food. 156 illustrations. 214pp. 6¹/₈ x 9¼. 22911-4 Pa. $2.50

THE BREAD TRAY, Louis P. De Gouy. Nearly every bread the cook could buy or make: bread sticks of Italy, fruit breads of Greece, glazed rolls of Vienna, everything from corn pone to croissants. Over 500 recipes altogether. including buns, rolls, muffins, scones, and more. 463pp. 23000-7 Pa. $4.00

CREATIVE HAMBURGER COOKERY, Louis P. De Gouy. 182 unusual recipes for casseroles, meat loaves and hamburgers that turn inexpensive ground meat into memorable main dishes: Arizona chili burgers, burger tamale pie, burger stew, burger corn loaf, burger wine loaf, and more. 120pp. 23001-5 Pa. $1.75

LONG ISLAND SEAFOOD COOKBOOK, J. George Frederick and Jean Joyce. Probably the best American seafood cookbook. Hundreds of recipes. 40 gourmet sauces, 123 recipes using oysters alone! All varieties of fish and seafood amply represented. 324pp. 22677-8 Pa. $3.50

THE EPICUREAN: A COMPLETE TREATISE OF ANALYTICAL AND PRACTICAL STUDIES IN THE CULINARY ART, Charles Ranhofer. Great modern classic. 3,500 recipes from master chef of Delmonico's, turn-of-the-century America's best restaurant. Also explained, many techniques known only to professional chefs. 775 illustrations. 1183pp. 6⁵/₈ x 10. 22680-8 Clothbd. $22.50

THE AMERICAN WINE COOK BOOK, Ted Hatch. Over 700 recipes: old favorites livened up with wine plus many more: Czech fish soup, quince soup, sauce Perigueux, shrimp shortcake, filets Stroganoff, cordon bleu goulash, jambonneau, wine fruit cake, more. 314pp. 22796-0 Pa. $2.50

DELICIOUS VEGETARIAN COOKING, Ivan Baker. Close to 500 delicious and varied recipes: soups, main course dishes (pea, bean, lentil, cheese, vegetable, pasta, and egg dishes), savories, stews, whole-wheat breads and cakes, more. 168pp. USO 22834-7 Pa. $2.00

COOKIES FROM MANY LANDS, Josephine Perry. Crullers, oatmeal cookies, chaux au chocolate, English tea cakes, mandel kuchen, Sacher torte, Danish puff pastry, Swedish cookies — a mouth-watering collection of 223 recipes. 157pp.
22832-0 Pa. $2.25

ROSE RECIPES, Eleanour S. Rohde. How to make sauces, jellies, tarts, salads, potpourris, sweet bags, pomanders, perfumes from garden roses; all exact recipes. Century old favorites. 95pp.
22957-2 Pa. $1.75

"OSCAR" OF THE WALDORF'S COOKBOOK, Oscar Tschirky. Famous American chef reveals 3455 recipes that made Waldorf great; cream of French, German, American cooking, in all categories. Full instructions, easy home use. 1896 edition. 907pp. 6⅝ x 9⅜.
20790-0 Clothbd. $15.00

JAMS AND JELLIES, May Byron. Over 500 old-time recipes for delicious jams, jellies, marmalades, preserves, and many other items. Probably the largest jam and jelly book in print. Originally titled May Byron's Jam Book. 276pp.
USO 23130-5 Pa. $3.50

MUSHROOM RECIPES, André L. Simon. 110 recipes for everyday and special cooking. Champignons à la grecque, sole bonne femme, chicken liver croustades, more; 9 basic sauces, 13 ways of cooking mushrooms. 54pp.
USO 20913-X Pa. $1.25

THE BUCKEYE COOKBOOK, Buckeye Publishing Company. Over 1,000 easy-to-follow, traditional recipes from the American Midwest: bread (100 recipes alone), meat, game, jam, candy, cake, ice cream, and many other categories of cooking. 64 illustrations. From 1883 enlarged edition. 416pp.
23218-2 Pa. $4.00

TWENTY-TWO AUTHENTIC BANQUETS FROM INDIA, Robert H. Christie. Complete, easy-to-do recipes for almost 200 authentic Indian dishes assembled in 22 banquets. Arranged by region. Selected from Banquets of the Nations. 192pp.
23200-X Pa. $2.50

*Prices subject to change without notice.*
Available at your book dealer or write for free catalogue to Dept. GI, Dover Publications, Inc., 180 Varick St., N.Y., N.Y. 10014. Dover publishes more than 150 books each year on science, elementary and advanced mathematics, biology, music, art, literary history, social sciences and other areas.